Teaching Assistants
The Complete Handbook

Teaching Assistants
The Complete Handbook

Liz Hryniewicz

Second edition

Adamson Publishing

Copyright © 2004, 2007 Liz Hryniewicz

Published by Adamson Publishing Ltd
8 The Moorings
Norwich NR3 3AX
01603 623336, fax 01603 624767
info@adamsonbooks.com
www.adamsonbooks.com

First published 2004, this edition 2007
Reprinted 2008

ISBN 9780-948543-02-9

British Library Cataloguing in Publication Data
A catalogue record for this book is available from the British Library

Cover design by Geoff Shirley
Edited by Stephen Adamson

Printed and bound in Great Britain by Biddles Limited, King's Lynn, Norfolk

Contents

Foreword   7

Acknowledgements   8

How to use this book   9

Introduction: The historical perspective   11

1   Teaching assistants and professional relationships   19

2   Working responsibilities and relationships   33

3   All about your school   49

4   The school and its support system   71

5   The National Curriculum   83

6   The nature of learning   95

7   Learning and teaching   117

8   Assessment   139

9   Approaches to teaching:
The role of the teaching assistant   163

10   Teaching literacy   189

11   Teaching numeracy   225

12   Inclusive education   255

13   Individual needs and inclusion   281

14   Behaviour for learning
– Emotional and social development   299

15   Professional development and training   323

16   Practicalities   339

Glossary   351

Index   360

Foreword

Those who have worked in them for any length of time will know how much, and how rapidly, schools have changed – for example, in the things children are taught, the methods of teaching and the ways classrooms are organised. We expect more of our schools than ever before. Moreover, our pursuit of ever-higher standards of work and behaviour has set a breathtaking pace of change to which the vast majority of schools have responded heroically.

Another notable feature of change for the good, of course, is the increased amount and wider range of human and material resources schools now have at their command. The promise of information technology for enriching and transforming many aspects of education is being fulfilled. Nevertheless, school education is, and is likely to remain, a person-to-person service in which support for the learner and support for the teacher are inter-dependent, crucially important ingredients of success. The high value of well trained and well managed teaching assistants in providing such support is indisputable.

Because they have become such a vital part of the school workforce, there is a great deal that teaching assistants need to know, understand and be able to do in order to work successfully, not only with children and teachers but also with parents and other adults who are engaged with schools. We hope that this book will be a ready source of useful information and guidance to help teaching assistants develop their increasingly demanding and important roles.

Jim Rose

Former HMI Director of Inspection

Acknowledgements

This book is the result of many years of collaborative working. I would like to thank my past and present colleagues in school, at the Kent LEA and Medway Council, at Mid Kent College and Canterbury Christchurch University who have willingly shared their knowledge and understanding. Special thanks go to Gwen Copping.

I am very grateful to my friends and family for their expert advice and encouragement and to my editor for his guidance. My husband has been a constant source of help.

Thanks to Pam Deverill and Stephen Adamson for their input on the Numeracy chapter, and to Stephen Adamson for his patient editing.

Finally, to the many teaching assistants I have worked with or tutored over the years, thank you. I have learned so much from your skill, expertise and professionalism.

How to use this book

This book is intended as a practical guide and reference. You can dip into it to find out more about a particular area or subject, or use it to give you the background knowledge for your work in the classroom. Educational jargon can be particularly difficult to understand, so there is a glossary at the end of the book, which explains all the educational terminology. For those of you who are following a Teaching Assistant qualification there are lists of references for each chapter. Suggestions for further reading are also listed at the end of each chapter and there are separate pages at the end of the book containing lists of useful websites and addresses. Chapter 16 contains photocopiable sheets that you can use to gather information in your own school or class to produce a practical guide for classroom practice.

Introduction:
The historical perspective

Teaching assistants have been the fastest growing section of school staff. Over the past ten years the full-time equivalent number employed in schools has tripled from 50,000 to 150,000, and the figure is still increasing. Teaching assistants can be found in all types of school and at all Key Stages, in a great variety of roles. The value of teaching assistants in all aspects of teaching and learning is well recognised by many researchers and official organisations. They have a vital role to play in supporting the school, the teachers and pupils in all areas of learning and in all parts of the curriculum.

The development of the role of a teaching assistant is a relatively recent phenomenon. A brief examination of the way the role has developed over the years gives us some insight into the diversity and complexity of the modern role of a teaching assistant.

In the 1960s and '70s, it was rare to find adults other than teachers in the mainstream classroom. At that time, most children with Special Needs were educated in Special Schools, some of which were the responsibility of the Health Department. Welfare Assistants were employed to look after their physical and social welfare. Although effectively considered to be non-teaching staff, the Welfare Assistants were often successfully involved in supporting teaching and learning activities across the curriculum. Later, these Welfare Assistants would provide a valuable role model for mainstream education.

In 1978, the Warnock Report recommended that children with Special Educational Needs (SEN) should be educated wherever possible in mainstream schools. This was followed by the Education Act of 1988, which gave Local Education Authorities responsibility for identifying and providing extra help for these children. Those learners with the highest level of need were identified through a formal process of making a statement of Special Educational Need, which defined the amount and type of help required and enabled funding to be available to pay for that support.

Using the role model of non-teaching assistants like the Welfare Assistants, LEAs and schools began to employ extra adults to provide support for children. Often these were helping mums, who were available at short notice to take on the limited number of hours allocated to a child with a statement of SEN, and were prepared to put up with the short-term nature of many of the contracts. Although mostly untrained, they proved to be a valuable resource and came to be known by a variety of names, including Special Needs Assistants or Learning Support Assistants. They often worked outside the classroom with children following individual learning and support programmes and many were employed directly by the LEA, who held the funding for SEN, rather than the school.

The introduction of the National Curriculum in 1988, which gave all children an entitlement to a broad and balanced curriculum, was a further impetus to this development. Assistants were employed increasingly to work with groups of children who did not have formal statements, but who still needed extra support and help in the classroom. At the same time, many nurseries employed Nursery Nurses, who had been trained as specialists in Early Years Education. Infant schools began to take in 'rising fives' and started to employ Nursery Nurses and other 'non-teaching' staff to assist generally in the classroom, particularly in reception classes. The focus of their role at first was care and pastoral duties and they often had a Nursery Nurse or childcare qualification.

In 1993, in a National Training Initiative, the Department for Education set up and funded a new training programme for teaching assistants working at Key Stage (KS) 1, to be known as the Specialist Teacher Assistant Certificate (STAC). Although not intended as a course for assistants supporting learners with SEN, graduates of the course became known as Specialist Teacher Assistants (STA) and were able to fully support the curriculum at KS1. The STA qualification was usually delivered at Higher Education (HE) level, so for the first time a standardised high-level qualification was available for assistants.

The 1993 Education Act moved responsibility for meeting the special needs of children without statements to schools. Again, the focus of the role of assistant began to change as they became increasingly involved in all aspects of teaching and learning. In 1994, the DfEE issued a Code of Practice, which laid down guidance and procedures to be followed for *all* children with SEN. This set up a 5-stage approach to meeting the needs of these learners in school. Schools began to develop their own special needs policies and make detailed provision for learners with SEN. Many schools continued to expand their use of teaching assistants to support individual children, or to provide general support in the classroom.

As a result, although they had little formal training, assistants found themselves working with children who had complex learning and behavioural needs. Education authorities began to develop local training opportunities, sometimes in partnership with colleges and universities. Schools and teaching assistants themselves often took full responsibility for searching out and undertaking relevant courses and qualifications offered by the awarding bodies, like the OCR CLANSA

Qualification and the City and Guilds Certificate in Learning Support. Some Higher Education establishments designed their own certificated courses specifically for Learning Support Assistants in conjunction with their Local Education Authority and local schools.

The 1996 Education Act strengthened the right of children with SEN to be included in mainstream schools and, in 1997, the Government Green Paper, *Excellence for All*, called for a coordinated response to the support of learners with SEN and a training initiative for all teaching assistants. The following year, the Government set out its intention to substantially increase the number of teaching assistants in schools, allocating £350m to recruit 20,000. Two reports were also commissioned, which looked at the national pattern of teaching assistant training and progression routes to qualified teacher status (QTS). The Manchester and Southampton reports both made recommendations for a standardised national qualification system and career structure (Farrell, *et al.* 1999, Smith, *et al.* 1999).

The introduction of the National Literacy Strategy in 1998, followed by the National Numeracy Strategy in 1999, and the catch-up programmes of Early Learning Support (ELS), Additional Literacy Support (ALS), Springboard and Literacy Progress Units (LPU), extended and confirmed the use of teaching assistants. All the programmes had designated roles for teaching assistants and their positive implementation was a boost for the successful deployment of teaching assistants in teaching and learning, rather than in a merely pastoral, welfare and support role.

By the end of the '90s, schools were employing teaching assistants in a great variety of ways: to support individual learners with various additional needs; to provide support in class for literacy and numeracy programmes; as full-time class assistants in Special Schools or at Key Stage 1 and 2; and, increasingly at Key Stage 3/4 to support curriculum areas, or as specialists in particular fields like ICT.

Some LEAs already had their own training schemes but, in September 2000, the DfES issued standardised induction training materials to all LEAs to use with teaching assistants new to their posts (DfES, 2000). The same year, the Local Government National Training Organisation (LGNTO) put forward proposals for a set of national occupational standards for teaching assistants. These then formed the basis of the National Vocational Qualifications (NVQ) now available for teaching assistants. In a clear recognition of the value of their role, DfES announced in 2001 that a further £200m per year would be allocated for teaching assistant recruitment and training. By 2005 this had been increased to £279 million.

More recently, concern about the recruitment and retention of teachers raised the profile of teaching assistants as a valuable and effective part of the workforce. In November 2001, the Secretary of State for Education, Estelle Morris, put forward her view of a re-modelled school staff where teaching assistants could help with the teaching of reading and take over tasks like the invigilation of exams. They could also supervise classes if the work had been set by a teacher. Teaching assistants would not replace teachers but would allow more time for teachers to teach. In January 2002, Estelle Morris paid tribute to the tremendous contribution that teaching assistants have already made, and said:

> "I want to create an environment where greater use is made of all resources and pupils are given the chance to learn at their own speed. Teaching assistants will be crucial in meeting this challenge and I call on all schools and local authorities to recognise this."
>
> (DfES, 2002)

Of course, in some schools, teaching assistants had already been given more responsibility and successfully supported all areas of teaching and learning as a vital part of the school workforce. Sometimes they were even taking classes as unqualified teachers. However, this was still an important recognition of the changing perspective on their role. An Ofsted evaluation of the role of teaching assistants in primary schools in April 2002 found that "Section 10 inspections show that the presence of teaching assistants improves the quality of teaching" (Ofsted, 2002).

This provoked widespread debate on both the role of teaching assistants and their relatively low pay and lack of career structure (Slater and Dean, 2001; Adams, 2002; Brown, 2002). Government emphasis that it was up to local employers (schools and local authorities) to set appropriate pay scales and career pathway, led to many local authorities developing grading systems to reward experienced and qualified TAs.

Recent developments

In 2003, under the banner of raising standards and tackling workload, and in response to teacher shortages, a National Workforce Agreement was signed which introduced workforce remodelling in schools. This agreement was designed to improve teacher workload, freeing them from unnecessary paperwork and administrative tasks and activities such as exam invigilation or cover for absent colleagues. From 2005, teachers have been entitled to use 10 percent of their weekly timetable for Planning, Preparation and Assessment (PPA) time.

This new initiative provided opportunities for teaching assistants to have an expanded role within schools, leading classes and managing children's learning in the classroom, although still under teacher supervision. Teaching assistants now take over whole-class teaching during PPA time, provide cover supervision when work is pre-set by the teacher, take responsibility for the display and presentation of children's work and invigilate exams.

In response to these expanded roles, the new status of Higher Level Teaching Assistant (HLTA) was introduced in 2004 to provide training and a career pathway for experienced TAs. However, in 2005 the National Foundation for Educational Research (NFER) found that there was still no widespread coherent career development for TAs (Whitby, 2005). In 2005 a new school support staff Vocational Qualification (NVQ) based on professional standards for support staff was introduced, emphasising the importance of a whole-school staff approach to training and development.

Teaching assistants have traditionally been seen as a pool of experienced and effective people, some of whom who can make a very successful transition to Qualified Teacher Status (QTS). The introduction of Foundation Degrees for TAs has meant that many have now achieved QTS through this route. Teaching assistants have also played a major role in meeting the needs of children with SEN in mainstream and special schools. With the continuing emphasis on inclusion, the new collaborative approach of Every Child Matters (DfES, 2004) and government recognition of the importance of Early Years provision, the role of an expert and skilled teaching assistant will become even more crucial.

We have come a long way since the first Welfare Assistants. Teaching assistants are now an integral part of 21st century schools and a key factor in not only supporting learners with additional needs, but also in raising standards for all pupils across the curriculum. They are now ideally placed to play a major role in the new school structure and workforce required to meet the needs of our inclusive, modern, diverse and changing society.

Terminology

Over the years, assistants have been referred to by various names: welfare assistants, learning support assistants, special needs assistants, non-teaching assistants, classroom assistants and others. It is now generally accepted that the term 'Teaching Assistant' should be used, so that is the terminology used in the remainder of this book.

Key reading

Key references are given in bold.

National Association of Special Educational Needs (NASEN) (2002), *Policy on Learning Support Assistants*. Available on www.nasen.org.uk/policy/15 *[Statement issued by NASEN underlining the successful role played by Learning Support Assistants with SEN children.]*

Office for Standards in Education (2002), *Teaching Assistants in Primary Schools, An Evaluation of the Quality and Impact of Their Work* (HMI Report 434), London: Ofsted

Available on www.ofsted.gov.uk *[Ofsted evaluation of the work of teaching assistants in primary schools and their impact on the effectiveness of the National Literacy and Numeracy Strategies. Covers all aspects of teaching assistants' working practice, including training.]*

Kay, J. (2002) *Teaching Assistants Handbook,* London and New York: Continuum *[Written for teaching assistants supporting at Key Stage 1.]*

Fox, G. A (2003) *Handbook for Learning Support Assistants,* 2nd edn, London: David Fulton *[A particular focus on supporting learners with special educational needs.]*

Burnham, L. and Jones, H. (2002) *The TA Handbook,* Oxford: Heinemann *[Based on NVQ in Childcare in Early Years.]*

References

Key references are given in bold.

Adams, C. (2002) 'Don't Be Afraid of Help', *TES* 18 January 2002 *[Chief Executive of the General Teaching Council for England argues that the presence of teaching assistants in the classroom will improve the quality of education.*

Brown, M. (2002) 'Fruitful Partnership', *Teachers,* July 2002 *[Analysis of the difference between the teacher and teaching assistant role.]*

DfEE (2004) *Teaching Assistant File – Induction Training for Teaching Assistants,* revised edn, London: DfEE 0131/2000 *[These are the training manuals used for induction training. You may have difficulty obtaining these yourself but your LA/school should have a copy for you to look at. Contains comprehensive information on all aspects of teaching assistant practice.]*

DfEE (2000) *Working with Teaching Assistants: A Good Practice Guide,* London: DfEE *[A complete guide for schools and teachers on the management and use of teaching assistants.]*

DfES (2002) *Professionalism and Trust/ The Future of Teachers and Teaching,* DfES Press Release, London, 16 January 2002. Available from www.dfes.gov.uk or info@smf.co.uk *[Estelle Morris' call for teaching assistants to help forge a world-class education service.]*

DfES (2002) *Teaching Assistant File – Induction Training for Teaching Assistants in Secondary Schools,* London: DfES/0627/2002; revised edn 2004 *[Updated information relating to teaching assistants working in secondary schools.]*

DfES (2004) *Every Child Matters: Change For Children,* London: DfES/1081/2004

Farrell, P., Balshaw, M. and Polat, F. (1999) *The Management, Role and Training of Learning Support Assistants,* DfEE Research Report 161, London: DfEE *[A review of the working practice, management and training of learning support assistants.]*

Griffiths, S. (2003) 'Plugging Gaps in the Classroom', *Sunday Times*, 30 March 2003 *[TTA Chief, Clive Booth's view on how new super teaching assistants can take lessons alone.*

Henderson, S., Martin, S. and Hutchinson, G. (2000) *Medway Induction Programme for Learning Support Assistants*, Chatham: Medway Council *[A published example of an LA induction programme.]*

Lee, B. (2002) *Teaching Assistants in Schools: The Current State of Play,* LGA Research Report 34, Slough: National Foundation for Educational Research *[Local Government Association-sponsored research paper; includes a review of literature on the impact of teaching assistants in schools. Covers the roles, deployment, effective working, conditions of employment and training and development of* *teaching assistants. Has a very useful bibliography.]*

Local Government National Training Organisation (2001) *National Occupational Standards for Teaching Assistants,* **London: DfEE** *[National Standards for Teaching Assistants]*

Morris, E. (2001) '"Para-teachers" to the rescue', *TES*, 23 November 2001 *[Report by Estelle Morris outlining her vision for teaching assistants.]*

Moyles, J. (1997) *Jills of All Trades,* Leicester: ATL *[Review of classroom assistant practice in schools at Key Stage 1.]*

Slater, J. and Dean, C. (2001) 'Proper Jobs that Need Proper Staff', *Times Educational Supplement*, 16 November 2001 *[A critical examination of the use of teaching assistants to solve teacher recruitment shortages.]*

Smith, K., Kenner, C., Barton-Hide, D. and Bourne, J. (1999) *Career Ladder for Classroom Assistants,* Southampton: University of Southampton Research and Graduate School of Education *[Report to the Teacher Training Agency on the career pathways available for classroom assistants.]*

Teacher Training Agency (2000) *Progression to Initial Teacher Training for Teaching Assistants,* **London: TTA** *[A survey of providers of courses that can lead to QTS.]*

Whitby, K (2005) *The Employment and Deployment of TAs*, Slough: NFER

www.teaching-assistants.co.uk

www.remodelling.org.uk

www.everychildmatters.gov.uk

1 Teaching assistants and professional relationships

Inclusion

The greatest influence on the growing use of teaching assistants has been the move to include and successfully educate learners with special needs in mainstream schools. This is part of the wider concept of 'inclusion', which is now firmly embedded as a key part of our educational and social system, and stems from a world-wide focus on the rights of the child. Although some pupils with complex or severe learning difficulties or disabilities are still best placed in Special Schools or units where they can receive specialist help and support, the new 'whole school' approach to inclusion means creating school communities that include all learners, have a flexible approach to teaching and learning, and strive to maintain high standards for all.

However, inclusion is not only an educational issue, and is not just about SEN. It is a much wider concept. Jenny Corbett defines inclusion as "a school culture which welcomes and celebrates differences and recognises individual needs" (Corbett, 2001, p.11). These can be:

- gender differences (between boys and girls)
- cultural differences between ethnic groups
- family backgrounds
- age groups
- differences in the way children learn.

Individual needs might result from:

- gifts and talents
- learning needs like dyslexia or moderate learning difficulties
- emotional and behavioural difficulties
- physical or medical problems or disability
- a sensory loss (hearing or vision)
- a communication or language disorder (e.g. autism)
- interrupted schooling through illness, family difficulties, parental illness or teenage pregnancy (children missing education – CME)
- learning English as an additional or second language
- lack of continuity in schooling (e.g. military service families who have to move frequently, or travellers)
- social or economic deprivation
- being an economic migrant or refugee.

The inclusive school works hard to achieve:

- an inclusive ethos
- a broad and balanced curriculum for all pupils
- systems for early identification of barriers to learning and participation; and
- high expectations and suitable targets for all children.

(DfES, 2001, p.3)

This approach was re-emphasised in *Removing Barriers to Achievement* (DfES, 2004). There the government set out its strategy for SEN and promoted a whole-school approach to inclusion, saying all teaching staff should develop the confidence to support learners with SEN and be able to access specialist information and help as required. It encouraged a more personalised and responsive approach to the individual needs of learners and recognised that more effective inclusion would come about if all staff had positive attitudes to the difficulties that some learners face and a real commitment to removing barriers to achievement. At the same time, the Every Child Matters initiative (DfES, 2004) confirmed a more holistic approach to supporting children's achievement and success. As much a philosophy as a policy, Every Child Matters recognises that children need to feel safe and be happy and healthy to learn. It places a greater emphasis on collaborative working between the agencies and institutions involved in health, childcare and education. Schools are also now developing an 'extended' profile, where they are open for much longer hours and offer a wider range of activities and services, such as breakfast and after-school clubs, childcare and learning opportunities for parents and families.

As you will see from the rest of this book and in particular Chapter 12 (which deals with inclusion in more detail), teaching assistants have a vital role to play in extended schools and in a whole school approach to inclusion. An important part of this is to ensure that all children can reach their full potential and work together. Teaching assistants often work with pupils with SEN or English as an additional language (EAL), or children who just need more time, care or practice to be able to achieve. They have a key role in giving such children access to the curriculum, helping them to feel safe and secure in the classroom, and making them independent and successful learners. They can form a strong partnership with teaching staff to share the workload in the class and provide more opportunities for all learners to achieve. Through their role in the classroom, teaching assistants can:

- look for barriers to learning
- reflect and feed back on methods of teaching and learning
- observe and assess
- deliver individual, tailored support if required
- accept and consider individual differences and cultures
- help all learners to take part in the full life of the school

- make learning interesting, enjoyable, worthwhile and fun!

The way schools implement inclusion, and the role of the teaching assistant in this, is dealt with throughout the book as well as specifically in Chapter 12.

Different roles and working patterns

Teaching assistants have many different roles. You will have your own working pattern and responsibilities. Here are some case studies of teaching assistants and the different ways in which they work:

- Jane is a full-time assistant working in a Year 1 class in a large village school. She is involved in all aspects of the day-to-day work in the classroom and takes the class while the teacher has planning, preparation and assessment time. She has completed STAC.
- Zoe is a voluntary parent helper in a large primary school. She helps individual children with their reading and has an expertise in art, so she helps to design and make many of the displays in the classroom. She is aiming to take a TA qualification to enable her to get a full-time job.
- James is a full-time teaching assistant working in a Special School at Key Stage 3 and 4. He works in several different classes supporting learners with behavioural difficulties and assists in each PE lesson. He has a football coaching qualification and runs the school football team.
- Nita worked for the local authority (LA) Bilingual Support Service with children who have English as an additional language and is now employed directly by schools. She covers four different Key Stage 1 and 2 schools in the local area, spending a day in each. She has a teaching qualification from outside the UK and has attended several courses on language development run by her LA advisory service.
- Kate is employed in a large Key Stage 2 school to give support in the Literacy Hour. She covers all the classes in Year 4 and implements the 'catch up' programmes, too. She has designed and made lots of materials and resources to reinforce the teaching of literacy. She has a particular interest in the teaching of reading and runs the school library. She has an OCR CLANSA (see page 352) and is just finishing a foundation degree.
- Carla works in a Key Stage 4 school supporting a 17-year-old learner with Asperger's Syndrome, who is taking A/AS Levels in Physics, Chemistry and Maths. She has a degree in Chemical Engineering and works for 22 hours per week, liaising with teachers, adapting the curriculum to make it accessible to her student, and providing a secure and ordered emotional environment for him.
- Laura has joint responsibility for a reception class in a Key Stage 1 school in an area that has an entrenched teacher recruitment

problem. She has just finished a Foundation degree in Teaching and Learning and is now pursuing her goal to achieve Qualified Teacher Status (QTS).

- Angela is one of 16 teaching assistants who work in a large, urban primary school with a high proportion of learners with additional needs. She delivers Additional Literacy Support (ALS) and Early Literacy Support (ELS). She supervises the work of the other assistants and is directly responsible to the Special Educational Needs Coordinator for monitoring all teaching assistant involvement in additional learning support. She has completed the NVQ 3 and has Higher Level Teaching Assistant (HLTA) status.
- Mark works in the Hearing Impaired Unit attached to a mainstream Key Stage 2 school. He supports individual children in class, takes part in in-service training for other staff, and takes some individual groups when the children return to the unit for lessons.
- Alyssia works full-time in a large Key Stage 3 and 4 school. She is attached to the Humanities Department and supports learners in those classes. She has used her expertise in desktop publishing to produce differentiated materials for history and geography. There are several learners with dyslexia in the school and she has attended a course for teaching assistants on dyslexia.

Nowadays, it is recognised that it is usually more effective for teaching assistants to be a resource for all the children, rather than for individual learners. Despite the differences in their working practice, all teaching assistants provide support:

- for the pupil
- for the school
- for the teacher
- with the curriculum.

The focus of this book is to look at how you can provide this support effectively.

The teacher–teaching assistant partnership

Why are teaching assistants so valuable? The DfES *Good Practice Guide* says "good teaching assistant practice

- fosters the participation of pupils in the social and academic processes of a school
- seeks to enable pupils to become more independent learners
- helps to raise standards of achievement for all pupils."

(DfES, 2000)

But what do teachers value most about teaching assistants? Here are some very general and informal comments that teachers have made about their assistants:

"She brings another perspective to the classroom – often things I haven't thought about. Sometimes I get a bit stuck in a rut and she'll just suggest something different. It's great having someone to bounce ideas off."

"It's really nice to have someone to share the workload in the classroom – the good and the bad! After a busy day we are exhausted, but we can still laugh, which must say something!"

"It never ceases to amaze me, the skills she has. She's brilliant at art and craftwork, so she does all the displays and suggests creative activities. She has made some beautiful story sacks and she is really good on the computer, so she does a lot with children and IT."

"It's really useful to have someone to feed back on how things are going. Sometimes the kids look at you blankly and she says – 'You didn't explain that clearly because I don't understand it either'!"

"He has worked in industry so he knows all about the practical applications of science, which is really helpful when we're teaching."

"He is invaluable for giving that extra bit of individual help to the children who need it."

"She is so experienced with learners who have English as an additional language. I have learned a lot from her."

Clearly, teaching assistants can bring so much to the classroom: their own skills and talents, their lifetime experiences and knowledge, another perspective and a shared sense of purpose.

Professional teaching practice: The roles of teacher and teaching assistant

The rapid development of the teaching assistants' role and the variety of ways in which they are employed in schools has traditionally led to some blurring of the distinction between them and teachers. The national agreement "Raising Standards and Tackling Workload" (DfES, 2003) introduced a process of remodelling the school workforce to help reduce the amount teachers had to do, at the same time creating an expanded and enhanced role for teaching assistants. The definition of teaching assistant frequently includes learning mentors, staff supporting children's transition between Key Stages and nursery nurses. When they have a clearly defined role within their school to support teaching and learning, IT and science technicians, resource supervisors and library staff can also now be categorised as teaching assistants (DfES/Teachernet, 2004). The DfES has since calculated that there are 500,000 support staff in schools.

Support staff now carry out many tasks that were traditionally undertaken by teachers. These include:

- photocopying
- record keeping and filing
- collecting money
- cataloguing and maintaining equipment
- letter writing
- ordering supplies and equipment
- ICT troubleshooting
- exam invigilation
- cover supervision
- ICT teaching.

Teaching assistants are now able to manage whole-class learning so that teachers have time to plan and prepare (PPA time), or, if the teaching/learning has been pre-planned by a teacher, they can provide short-term cover for teachers who are absent. This is because it is felt that that well-trained (and well paid!) teaching assistants can provide more continuity and stability than using supply teachers. However, their role remains a controversial one and is not accepted by all teachers. Nevertheless, although teaching assistants may plan and prepare work and supervise other members of staff, it is still the teacher (with Qualified Teacher Status) who has ultimate responsibility for the learning outcomes of all the children.

HLTA

In 2004 the government piloted enhanced recognition for those teaching assistants who were fulfilling some of the more demanding and complex roles in schools, or who were working in a more autonomous way. This Higher Level Teaching Assistant (HLTA) status is now available as a career progression route for those who can meet the standards required. Although it is up to individual schools and LAs to deploy staff in the way that they see fit, they are encouraged to use HLTAs to complement the professional work of teachers by taking responsibility for the management and development of specialist areas. For example, an ICT technician with HLTA may be responsible for working with different age groups across the school to deliver the curriculum.

A teaching assistant should always be working under the direction of a teacher, whether working on catch-up programmes like ELS, supporting children with additional needs through individually designed programmes, providing cover supervision or giving general assistance in the classroom. Qualified teachers should always supervise and monitor the practice of teaching assistants. Naturally, the level of monitoring required will depend on individual circumstances, including the qualifications and experience of the teaching assistant. Many teaching assistants are excellent practitioners who work with very limited supervision. However, their role is to support and assist qualified teaching staff in a productive working partnership.

Working with teachers

The close working relationship between teachers and teaching assistants has been at the heart of the drive to raise standards in schools. It is clear that teachers "value highly the support provided by teaching assistants and the benefits of having another skilled adult in the classroom" (Ofsted, 2002). However, as in any workplace, it takes a high level of expertise, skill, time and commitment on both sides to establish a successful partnership. Most of the advice on working collaboratively is relevant here, but there are some specific issues relating to working with teaching staff that you will need to consider. These issues will be relevant whether you are working with only one teacher, or working with several.

Although all teachers work within school policies, they have their own individual styles of working, with their own interests, strengths and ways they like to do things. This is a positive plus for children because it means they will experience a variety of approaches within the structure of a common framework, thus helping them to become more adaptable and ready for adult life. However, it can make your working life difficult if you have to move between teachers, classes and subject areas, and you are not sure what is expected of you. From the start, you will find it easier if you accept that you will need to adapt your working practice to the requirements of each classroom environment and can keep a flexible approach to working together.

It is easier to work in a given situation when you know exactly what you are required to do in advance. It is important to check with the teacher at all times to make sure that you understand the learning outcomes required for the children and that you have the correct resources and materials. More detail on this will be given in later chapters. In any teaching and learning situation, you must be prepared to constantly change and adapt in response to the feedback you receive. You cannot prepare in advance for every eventuality, so your working methods need to be flexible and adaptable. You should confirm the arrangements at the outset, then arrange to review and update with teaching staff as you go along. You might want to arrange a weekly meeting or have a liaison/feedback sheet that you can both fill in, but remember, time is often in short supply in a busy school.

Some teachers and teaching assistants communicate regularly by e-mail, as they find this more time-effective. Don't just limit your discussions to the nuts and bolts of daily classroom practice. Talk to them about their ideals and philosophies, and share your own thoughts and beliefs. To be a good team you need to understand each other. You will find a pro-forma called 'A Passport to Work' in Chapter 16, which will help you decide what to discuss.

Follow the example of journalists who interview celebrities and politicians: Give teachers your list of queries in advance of the meeting – it gives them time to think about their response and make the best use of the meeting.

Planning

Planning is an absolutely vital element of any kind of teaching. Teachers spend a great deal of time planning and preparing for all their teaching and learning activities to make sure they are as successful as possible, and since 2005 all teachers have been entitled to planning, preparation and assessment (PPA) time as part of their normal working week.

All the major reviews and evaluations of the role of the teaching assistant have emphasised the key importance of their involvement with teachers in joint planning activities (Fox, 1997; Lorenz, 1998; DfES, 2000; Ofsted, 2002). Joint planning is often easier to achieve logistically when teaching assistants work in the same class everyday, as often happens at Key Stage 1. The introduction of the Primary and Key Stage 3 Strategies has also helped to formalise the process of planning for teaching assistant involvement, particularly at Key Stage 2. It can be more difficult at Key Stage 3 and 4 when teaching assistants frequently move between subject classes. In some schools, teaching assistants attend departmental or curriculum area planning meetings. Some larger schools hold specific teaching assistant planning meetings. Any involvement that the teaching assistant has with children with additional needs should ideally be planned through the channels of the appropriate school SEN or inclusion policies.

Schools have access to many types of planning systems and documents, which you need to become familiar with. Some teaching assistants have used their expertise to design their own planning documentation, in conjunction with the teacher. You should also be aware that teachers occasionally find planning for another adult in the classroom to be an extra burden (Ofsted, 2002). Any helpful ideas that you may want to suggest will probably be gratefully received! Lesson plans and planning are dealt with in detail in Chapter 8.

> **Key Stage 3 Teacher:** "My teaching assistant designed her own feedback documentation for a course she was doing, and I have found it so helpful that I have added it to my lesson planning. It makes it really easy for me to plan her role and she feels that she has more ownership of it too."

Providing supply cover

The Headteacher will use their professional judgement to decide whether to use a teaching assistant to provide short-term supply cover for an absent teacher. You do not need to have HLTA status to be a cover supervisor, but you should have some appropriate and relevant training (at least NVQ level 3). In general, if you are providing supply cover, you should be prepared to:

• give out work and resources
• manage the behaviour of the pupils
• answer questions from the pupils

- deal with any problems
- collect work
- report back to the teacher

Guidance on the regulations for providing supply cover is available at: www.teachernet.gov.uk/supportstaff

Invigilating exams

A checklist is given in Chapter16.

Working with supply staff

Teaching assistants frequently find themselves working with cover or supply staff. A supply teacher's job can often be difficult if they are not familiar with the class or school. A confident and expert teaching assistant, who knows the children and classroom routines, is a real asset in such a situation. It is important to remember that when you are working with a supply teacher, your role as an assistant should not change. It is easy to take on too much responsibility and then feel resentful because the supply teacher is earning so much more.

Schools sometimes produce a helpful guide for supply teachers that gives detailed information about classroom routines and practices. You may also want to give the supply teacher some of the information in your own 'Passport to Work'. Of course, there may be supply cover to replace you when you are absent, in which case it is equally important to pass on all the relevant information to enable your replacement to operate to your own standards, where possible.

In the best working relationships between teachers and teaching assistants, their different roles fit together seamlessly and there is mutual respect and support.

Collaborative working

Now that teaching assistants have become an essential part of so many schools, the importance of collaborative approaches to working has become even more apparent. This is particularly important in the context of Every Child Matters with its emphasis on multi-agency cooperation and information sharing. Good practice depends on creating effective working partnerships with the pupils, other teaching assistants, teachers, professionals from other agencies and parents. It has always been vital for educators to work as a team and to have common goals and standards. This is even more crucial as we move towards a model of inclusive schools, with their diversity of staff and emphasis on multi-agency working.

Teaching assistants can find themselves working with a wide variety of fellow professionals and volunteers: teachers, technicians, therapists, administrators, advisers, voluntary helpers, parents and other teaching assistants. Flexibility, adaptability and a high level of professionalism are required. You may be lucky enough to work in a school where there is a strong tradition of collaborative working, or you may be a new member of staff and need to understand or establish some procedures and practices. Whatever the case, good teamwork should be an essential part of your role. Successful teamwork depends on the commitment of everyone in the team. You have to work at it. As a teaching assistant, you can make a vital difference to the way your team operates by understanding and following the principles and practices for effective team working. You may find the following ideas useful.

Respect and value each team member

Collis and Lacey, who write about interactive approaches to teaching, say "It is not necessary for everyone in the team to be equal, it is desirable that everyone should be equally valued" (Collis and Lacey, 1996, p.77). In a team, everyone contributes something different, regardless of his or her status, and it is important to value that difference and to respect everyone's individual role. You may have been on a course or have established expertise in a particular area. You can bring that knowledge and expertise to your job as long as you realise that other people too have their own expertise. A good team manager will encourage and use the abilities and skills of all team members.

Rely on each other

This can only be achieved where there is open and honest communication between team members. In a busy school it is easy to become too focused on your day-to-day practice and end up working in isolation. It is important to make an effort to keep lines of communication open, whether by following formal procedures or by a few hurried words during a busy day. It is an essential skill for a teaching assistant to know when and who to ask for help and advice. Listen to your colleagues because the best teams are in places where everyone feels free to contribute. Don't hide your mistakes. Everyone makes them. Allow other people to make mistakes without making it into a big deal and try to use constructive problem-solving rather than blame allocation. If you can use successful conflict resolution yourself, it provides a good role model for the children you support. Remember, you are working collaboratively, not in competition.

Be goal focused

Good teamwork means working towards common goals and objectives, so make sure that you know what these are – and if in doubt, ask! Consistency of approach is always important when working with children and it is hard to be consistent if you are not sure of the outcome required. This is even more vital whenever you are implementing any specialist programme for a learner with additional needs. Being part of that planning and goal-setting process is also a valuable part of your role. (DfEE, 2000)

Communicate clearly and effectively

Develop your own communication skills so that you can be clear and unambiguous in your dealings with your team members. Think about quick and easy ways of communicating, too.

Key Stage 2: "There are two of us working with the same child on different days, so we rarely see each other. It takes too long to write everything down, so now we use a small Dictaphone. I leave her a short written record and then I talk about the details on the tape and leave them both for her. She does the same for me. It works really well."

Be clear about your own role and the role of others

When a team or collaborative approach is set up, it is usually made clear who does what. When you join an already established team it is sometimes difficult to be sure of everyone's roles and responsibilities. These can be unwritten or unsaid, but may not be clearly communicated to you, so it is easy for misunderstandings to occur. Make sure you find out. It is easy to step on someone's toes or leave something undone when you are not sure. You can use phrases like:

- Would you like me to do this?
- Will that be my responsibility?
- Is anyone else involved in this?
- Do I need to pass this information on to anyone else?
- Do I need help and advice from anyone?

Recognise the limitations of your role

Make sure you are clear about the parameters of your job so that you do not step outside your own job role too often. This is particularly important when you are supporting learners with SEN. It was a concern of the 2002 Ofsted evaluation of teaching assistants in primary schools that such children were often spending too much time with teaching assistants and too little time with teachers (Ofsted, 2002). If this is the case in your workplace, make sure you express your concern professionally and tactfully remind the relevant staff of the limitations of your role.

In any school environment it is easy to take on too much and get stressed out! Schools tend to attract dedicated and conscientious professionals who work extremely hard to make sure that children have the best possible learning experience. Make sure you know where your responsibilities end. On the other hand, be prepared to do the boring repetitive jobs that nobody likes – it makes for good morale in the team if such jobs are shared. Teaching assistants have moved a long way from washing paint pots – but the paint pots still have to be washed!

To help clarify the situation you could classify tasks under one of the following headings:

As schools are busy places and subject to constant change, teaching assistants have to be prepared to work flexibly at all times.

Make time for planning

Planning together is not only essential to make sure that things run smoothly and are organised effectively, but it is also a way of using everyone's expertise and giving each person a stake in the outcome. In the busy school environment it is often difficult to find time to plan, and teams can become reactive rather that proactive. Schools can now fund planning time for teaching assistants, so ensure you understand the importance of planning and make yourself available. There is more detailed information about planning in Chapter 8.

Share expertise – sensitively

The saying that "knowledge is power" is relevant here. Don't keep information to yourself – share it! This is particularly relevant when the allocation of funding means that not all staff will be able to attend courses or training. It is then vital that you pass on any information to other members of the team, particularly other teaching assistants. You will be learning all the time, but it is also important to remember that the field of education is so vast that no one can be an expert in everything. Most teachers work extremely hard to keep up-to-date with all the latest information about teaching and learning and will be grateful for any information you can pass on to them. However, be aware that you should do so sensitively. You do not become an expert overnight!

Don't develop cliques

In any situation, you will always gravitate towards people that you instinctively feel comfortable with. However, try not to be involved in developing or maintaining cliques, as they can exclude those around them and may have their own rules and practices, which are not apparent to people outside.

Take part in team building activities

Team building activities play an important part in forming and maintaining effective teams. These can range from daily or weekly meetings, to staff development activities, away days and social events. Teaching assistants should be included in these regular meetings and training sessions. Headteachers can have very creative approaches to their team building programmes. Some recent examples have included all-day craft workshops and short activity breaks for staff. School trips and residential holidays can also serve the same purpose. Make time to be involved wherever possible – they can be fun too!

A good team is a very powerful and effective force in any educational setting. However, setting up a team and maintaining successful team-work is not easy when you are dealing with different personalities, pro-cedures and issues of status, funding and resources – or when teams are implementing change. Working in a school means working as part of a professional team, whether you are in a team of two, or part of a large group of teaching assistants or cross-agency professionals. Make it your responsibility to maintain positive and productive working relationships with your team.

In the United States, teaching assistants have a long established role working alongside teachers and are referred to as 'para-educators' or 'para-professionals'. They have a well-defined responsibility for imple-menting individual learning programmes for children with special needs, because inclusion is a major part of government policy. The multicultural nature of society has also meant that they are often employed to provide a vital bridge between the culture of the school and the culture of individual learners. Para-professionals can be high-ly qualified. They may be experts in a variety of areas, including English as an additional language (EAL), therapy for learners with physical or medical problems, assisted learning technology, sign lan-guage, behaviourism, or other specialities (Doyle, 1997; Skelton, 1997).

Key reading

Fox, G. A (1998) *Handbook for Learning Support Assistants*, London: David Fulton [*A particular focus on supporting learners with special educational needs.*]

Lorenz, S.(1998) *Effective In-Class Support. The Management of Support Staff in Mainstream Schools*, London: David Fulton [*Comprehensive look at supporting learners in a classroom situation.*]

Macgilchrist, B, Myers, K, Reed, J (2004) *The Intelligent School*, London, Sage

National Association of Special Educational Needs (2002) *Policy On Learning Support Assistants* [*Statement issued by NASEN underlining the successful role played by learning support assistants with SEN children.*]

Available on www.nasen.org.uk/policy/15

Ritchie, C and Thomas, P. (2004) *Successful Study Skills for Teaching Assistants*, London: David Fulton

Rose, R. (2005) *Becoming a Primary Higher Level Teaching Assistant: Meeting the HLTA Standards*, Exeter, Learning Matters

Watkinson, A. (2002) *Assisting Learning and Supporting Teaching*, London: David Fulton [*Practical basic guide for teaching assistants.*]

References

Key references are given in bold.

Collis, M. and Lacey, P. (1996) *Interactive Approaches to Teaching*, London: David Fulton *[Examines role of interaction in the education of children with learning difficulties.]*

Corbett, J. (2001) *Supporting Inclusive Education: A Connective Pedagogy*, London: RoutledgeFalmer *[Practical guidance for teachers, based on a real-life inner city school, on how to work with pupils with different learning styles. It includes a chapter on the effective use of teaching assistants.]*

DfEE (2000) *Teaching Assistant File – Induction training for teaching assistants*, London: DfEE 0131/2000 *[These are the training manuals used for induction training. Your LA/school should have a copy for you to look at. Contains comprehensive information on all aspects of teaching assistant practice.]*

DfEE (2000) *Working With Teaching Assistants: A Good Practice Guide*, London: DfEE *[A complete guide for schools and teachers on the management and use of teaching assistants.]*

DfES (2001) *Inclusive Schooling: Children with SEN*, London: DfES/07742001

DfES (2002) *Teaching Assistant File – Induction training for teaching assistants in secondary schools*, London: DfES/0627/2002, revised edn 2004 *[Updated information relating to teaching assistants working in secondary schools.]*

DFES (2003) *Raising Standards and Tackling Workload; A National Agreement*, London: DfES/TDA

DfES (2004) *Every Child Matters: Change For Children*, London: DfES/1081/2004

DfES (2004) *Removing Barriers to Achievement – The Government's Strategy for SEN*, DfES/0117/2004

Doyle, M. B. (1997) *The Paraprofessional's Guide to the Inclusive Classroom*, Baltimore: Paul Brooks *[Provides introductory information for a para-professional working in a team with teachers in an inclusive classroom. Includes photocopiable sheets and can be used as an INSET resource.]*

Fox. G. (1998) *A Handbook for Learning Support Assistants*, London: David Fulton *[Provides a particular focus on supporting learners with special educational needs.]*

Lorenz, S. (1998) *Effective In-Class Support. The Management of Support Staff in Mainstream Schools*, London: David Fulton *[Comprehensive look at supporting learners in a classroom situation.]*

Office for Standards in Education (2002) *Teaching Assistants in Primary Schools, An Evaluation of the Quality and Impact of Their Work*, HMI Report 434. Available on www.ofsted.gov.uk *[Ofsted evaluation of the work of teaching assistants in primary schools and their impact on the effectiveness of the National Literacy and Numeracy strategies. Covers all aspects of teaching assistants' working practice, including training.]*

Skelton, K. (1997) *Paraprofessionals in Education*, Delmar *[Comprehensive American manual for para-professionals.]*

2 Working responsibilities and relationships

The rapid pace of change in the structure and make-up of the school workforce, introduced by workforce remodelling, has meant that the role of teaching assistant is constantly developing and changing. In particular, extended schools bring new opportunities for teaching assistants to contribute to the success and well-being of pupils. In addition, *Every Child Matters: Change for Children in Schools* has identified five key outcomes that should apply to all children during and at the end of their formal education (DfES 2004). Teaching assistants can play a valuable role in helping all children to meet these outcomes in the following ways:

Outcome	What TAs can do
Be healthy	Help children to learn about:
	• positive effects of exercise • good nutrition and healthy eating • negative effects of drugs and smoking • sexual health issues.
	Supervise exercise sessions and after school clubs.
	Promote healthy lifestyle and choices.
	Work effectively with healthcare professionals.
	Help learners and staff to de-stress.
Stay safe	Follow guidelines for safeguarding children.
	Take part in risk assessments on school premises or for school trips and outings.
	Recognise effects of neglect, violence or abuse and follow the correct procedure for reporting.
	Prevent bullying or discrimination.
	Help children to develop concern for others.
	Manage behaviour.
	Provide and promote security and safety in the workplace.

Enjoy and achieve	Promote a positive attitude to learning.
	Listen to children's views.
	Promote equal opportunities and inclusive practice.
	Notice and help to remove barriers to learning.
	Help to personalise learning for all children so that they can reach their potential.
	Implement individual education plans.
	Encourage school attendance and manage behaviour.
	Provide care and support so that children enjoy learning.
Make a positive contribution to the community	Encourage: • independent learning • self-regulation • self-advocacy.
	Help all children to develop a sense of social responsibility and to understand the difference between their rights and their responsibilities.
	Promote anti-discrimination and anti-bullying.
	Promote collaborative working between pupils.
	Work collaboratively with colleagues and agencies.
	Promote opportunities for out-of-school activities.
Achieve economic and social well-being	Provide support for pupils to make transition between settings/schools/Key Stages.
	Provide support for parent partnerships and family learning.
	Update your own literacy, numeracy, ICT and skills for learning.
	Be a good role model for lifelong learning, continuing professional development and training.
	Assist learners to take part in projects.
	Help build all pupils' confidence and skills.

Schools often vary in the way they are structured and organised, and teaching assistants too will work in a variety of ways. This means that, as a teaching assistant, your responsibilities and the members of staff you work with will vary depending on your specific role. However you work, you will be giving support in four ways:

- **Support for the school:** Helping with the organisation and effective running of the school; following professional practice and correct procedures; maintaining discipline.
- **Support for teaching staff:** Helping with teaching and learning in lessons; providing extra resources; professional teamwork.
- **Support for pupils:** Giving emotional and pastoral support; helping with individual needs; personalised learning and curriculum access.
- Helping teaching staff with **subject areas**; giving individual learners access to the curriculum; adding your own expertise.

Management of teaching assistants

The successful use of teaching assistants is clearly dependent on the way they are managed and deployed in school. A great deal of guidance has been issued to schools to help them make the most effective use of their teaching assistants. Much of this is contained in *Working with Teaching Assistants: A Good Practice Guide* (DfEE, 2000), which includes a very useful checklist for schools to audit their practice. In common with the *Good Practice Guide*, Barbara Lee has reviewed the literature on teaching assistants for the Local Government Association and National Foundation for Educational Research (NFER). She also identifies the following common threads that make it easier for teaching assistants to be used effectively.

- Clarity of role.
- Accurate and updated job description.
- Thorough induction and support procedures.
- Clear line management.
- Consideration of the most appropriate deployment of teaching assistants.
- Time for teaching assistants and teaching staff to collaborate.
- Guidance and support for teaching assistants on strategies to use with pupils.
- Support and, where required, training for teaching staff on the most effective ways of managing and working with teaching assistants.
- Communications strategies which ensure that teaching assistants are fully informed, both on aspects of school life directly relevant to their work and more broadly.
- Paid time for teaching assistants to participate in meetings and whole-school activities.
- Paid time for teaching assistants to participate in relevant training and development opportunities.
- Appropriate accreditation and career structures for teaching assistants.
- Salary levels and structures that recognise teaching assistants' skills and expertise and reward them appropriately for their contribution.

(Lee, 2002, p.vii)

Kerry provides further detailed guidance on support staff and their roles, which emphasises that teaching assistants should be involved not only in the whole life of the classroom but also in the planning process and feedback from all teaching and learning (Kerry, 2001). Schools can access training and funding to make sure that they follow best practice in their use of teaching assistants in the school. Teachers are also now subject to monitoring and inspection on their use of teaching assistants and other adults in the classroom, so it is important for you to be able to develop a mutual understanding by listening carefully to their expectations and contributing ideas of your own. You might want to talk through some of the items on this list with your mentor or manager.

Job description

When you are appointed to a post in school or to a LA support service, you should be given a formal job description, which sets out your role and responsibilities and gives you the parameters for your work. Sometimes you may find that this does not happen, in which case you can write your own job description in partnership with the school. Remember that it should be a working document, which reflects your day-to-day practice. It should also be reviewed with you regularly. Job descriptions will vary, depending on the type of role you fulfil, but you should look for these common headings:

- Job Title
- Grade
- School
- Responsible to/Line manager *
- Liaison with
- Main purpose of job
- Duties and responsibilities **
- Support for school
- Support for pupils
- Support for teaching staff
- Support for curriculum
- Arrangements for appraisal.

(DfES, 2000, p.18)

Contract

Following the Workforce Agreement implemented in September 2003, many local authorities have introduced new grading systems, which tie in job roles and responsibilities to pay and conditions of work. You should therefore be clear about your hours of work, what you are required to do and your pay and conditions. For example, will you be paid during term time only? Check whether you will be paid to take part in meetings or staff development days, and whether there will be other more general duties that you will need to fulfil outside the class-

* Make sure you know who your line manager is. You may be working day-to-day with a different teacher so you need to be clear on this.
** Should include any extras like attending parents evenings or off-site trips.

room. Other things to look at include your holiday entitlement; the procedure for phoning in sick; whether it is possible to have time off in lieu; and your entitlement to sick pay and maternity leave. You may have a probationary period, too.

Induction training

If you are new to the job you should be entitled to some form of induction and you will be allocated a 'mentor' to help you. This could be a teacher or an experienced teaching assistant. Local authorities are responsible for providing induction training for teaching assistants, based on a national model There are separate induction sessions for TAs in primary and secondary schools. Details should come to your school, so you will need to ask your line manager about the arrangements. If your LA delivers the induction training centrally, rather than in your school, then your mentor should go with you to an introductory session. The full induction programme takes a minimum of four days (or eight half-days) and covers:

- behaviour management
- literacy and numeracy (Maths at Key Stage 3/4)
- your role within a school environment
- supporting SEN and EAL
- how children learn.

Your LA may offer other optional units or modules, such as one on displaying children's work or on learning through play. During your induction training time you will be asked to undertake some observations and simple activities. Induction training is a valuable place to start your professional life as a teaching assistant.

Professional practice

Once you are employed as a member of a school staff, even if it is just for a few hours a week, you become an educational professional and are bound by the same professional, ethical and legal responsibilities as all other educational professionals. This is particularly important to remember if you have moved from being a voluntary helper to a paid position, or if you are employed in the school that your own children attend. You must be able to demonstrate a high level of professionalism and show that you support the common practices and values within education.

Ethical issues

Confidentiality

As a professional educator, you are required to follow certain ethical codes of practice. Schools retain a great deal of personal information about their pupils, parents and staff. Like doctors, education professionals need to be careful to keep information confidential and they have a responsibility to always be professional in their relationship with parents, outside agencies and other staff. There are four main areas that you need to consider:

Information about the family background of pupils

There is often a fine line between using knowledge of such information to help a child and getting too involved in personal and private matters. It is easy to jump to the wrong conclusions if you are not careful and do not have the relevant specialised knowledge. Be particularly careful where children with SEN are concerned, as there may be legal issues involved. You should always operate on a need-to-know basis.

If you think information really needs to be passed on, then make sure that it goes to the right person and that you have obtained the permission of the parents first. Use your common sense – if you are a parent, you will know yourself what you would like to keep private. No one likes to be the subject of staffroom gossip!

Information about the internal politics and workings of the school

The above relates to staff qualifications, programmes to support individual learners, working methods of teachers, behaviour management issues, staff sickness and absences. It is certainly considered unprofessional to talk about these matters outside the school in a negative way, particularly with parents. If you have concerns, share them with your colleagues. Parents can also be very adept at getting information from you, particularly if you meet them outside school in the supermarket, or at a social event. Unless it is related directly to your own work with a child, always refer them to the relevant teacher. It is particularly difficult if you are a parent and teaching assistant in the same school. In that situation you must always ask yourself: Would I know this as a parent or do I know it as a teaching assistant? The answer will guide you in any decision to discuss sensitive information.

Personal Information about staff and names and addresses

The Data Protection Act should be followed here. Most people do not want their personal information given to a third party without their permission.

Photocopying school documents for your assignments

You should not photocopy any school documents that include children's names, or photocopy children's work, take photos of pupils, or write about their progress for any assignment you are doing for a course, without first checking with the school. Most schools will require parental permission for such material to be used. In all cases follow the guidelines given by your headteacher.

Sensitive problems

There may be times when you are concerned about your working relationship with a teacher. All partnerships have their difficult moments and it is important that you try to resolve any issues by talking to the colleague concerned first, and not by making negative comments about him or her in school. Only if you are unable to resolve the problem in this way should you ask advice from your mentor, or refer the problem (in complete confidence) to your line manager.

There have been very rare instances where teaching assistants have worked with a colleague (either a teacher or a teaching assistant) who has a serious problem with their personal conduct and fitness for their job (for example, drug or alcohol problems, or bullying children). In working closely with that person, the teaching assistant may be the first to recognise the seriousness of the problem. This is always an extremely difficult and sensitive issue, but if this ever happens to you then you owe it to the children you support to voice your concerns. Again, always try to address the problem with the staff member concerned first. Only if there is a continuing problem should you discuss it in confidence with your line manager.

If you are a school governor, you may also learn sensitive information about school matters and will also need to keep this confidential.

Best practice

High expectations for all

Good teaching assistant practice in school helps to raise standards of achievement for all pupils (Farrell, Balshaw, Polat, 1999 in DfEE, 2000, p.9). One of the best ways to do this is to maintain high expectations for all children and to always consider their potential, rather than their difficulties or their achievement. Always remember, too, that you are not dealing with an 'ideal child' but with the child you see in front of you. There are many things in their lives that you can do nothing about, but at all times, you *can* give them your best.

Role model for learning

Really good teachers communicate a love of learning and an enthusiasm for their subject and this is also where teaching assistants can be so effective. Because they have often rediscovered formal education later in life, they have experience and expertise from outside education, and can bring a wonderfully positive, enthusiastic and inspiring approach to learning.

All good teachers and teaching assistants have learned to think about their own daily practice when trying to provide the best and most effective teaching and learning for children. There are some things that may not be in your control, like the use of resources, teaching approaches or

learning programmes, but what you can do is become a 'reflective practitioner' – someone who thinks about what they are doing and works to
improve their practice. To do this, you need to take a step back and
observe what is happening, analyse what went well and why, and think
about what you should change to make improvements for next time.
There is more about this in chapter 15.

It is important to keep yourself as up-to-date as possible with the latest trends in education and work to improve your knowledge in all the
areas of the curriculum that you support. However, keep an open mind
and don't get enmeshed in all the detail to begin with. You will find
that through teaching a subject or concept, you will also develop your
own understanding to a higher level. Don't confuse knowledge and
authority either. As a teaching assistant you should have authority
but you don't have to know everything. A good role model is someone
who communicates the idea that learning is positive, by showing that
they are always learning too!

Personal code of practice

A basic personal code of practice for employees is common in any
workplace. However, in schools it is particularly important to maintain certain standards and follow codes of behaviour because you are
trying to model good practice and values to the pupils. Attendance and
punctuality are both vital issues. It is essential to be dependable.
Being late for lessons all the time will give the impression that learning is not important or valuable. You might also miss the most important part of the lesson! Make sure you have everything you need
before any activity – always be prepared.

Key Stage 1: "Constantly getting up and down to fetch things can be very disruptive in a busy classroom. Organise in advance to make your life easier and the
activity run more smoothly."

Your school may have an informal policy on staff dress/clothing, but if
not, make sure that you follow a sensible dress code. Clothing should
be practical, comfortable and smart. In Key Stage 3 or 4 schools particularly, very short skirts or shorts and revealing tops are not a good
idea, neither is competing with the pupils to wear the latest fashion.
You need to be an object of respect, rather than amusement! Many
schools now have uniforms and these are seen as giving children a
sense of pride and ownership in their school. You may like to settle on
your own uniform as it makes it easier to decide what to wear every
day. Make sure that you follow school rules and policies too.

Working with the children

Any classroom job is tough. It can be very difficult if you've just had a
row with your partner, or are feeling unwell or worried about something. You can't hide away in the corner of an office somewhere until
you feel better; you still have to interact professionally with the children

you support. Just like a showbiz star, the show must go on! No matter how you feel, you must remember to maintain your composure at all times and not inflict your own moods on the children. They need consistency so if you are angry or upset, mistakenly they may conclude that they have done something wrong and be unable to understand why.

Make sure you always encourage the children's independence and do not allow them to become dependent on you or your help. When you are employed to support one child, it means that you may work yourself out of a job when they no longer need your help. In fact, that will be a sign of your success! Move on to help others. This is discussed in more detail in later chapters.

You are often working so closely with children and their families that it is easy to become too emotionally involved. To do so means you can lose the objectivity that you should have as an educational professional.

Tackling discrimination

All staff in school have a duty to give the same respect, understanding and opportunities to all learners, and to ensure that the learning environment is free from discriminatory practice. In an inclusive school you will meet learners of all abilities, cultures and beliefs. These issues are dealt with in the next chapter but you can begin by considering the following points as part of your daily practice.

- Avoid having favourites. We all have people that we get on better with for some reason, just as there are others we clash with. It is just the same with children in school. Although it is often an instinctive feeling, you should never show favouritism. Other children find it difficult to deal with, as does the favourite – it may even invite bullying.
- Beware of making a scapegoat out of any child, or of making up your mind about a child before you have worked with them. Remember – every child deserves a fresh start and an open mind.

Creating a safe and secure environment

Health and safety issues

All members of the school staff have a duty of care towards the children. This is expressed by the phrase *in loco parentis*, which means literally 'in the place of a parent'.

Governing bodies and headteachers are bound by the requirements of the Health and Safety Act (1974) and the Children Act (2004). They also work within guidelines published by the DfES (DfES, 2004) to make sure that children are safe and secure during school time by minimising risk in the school environment. Of course, it is impossible to protect children completely. Accidents can and do happen. However, a great deal can be done to ensure that children and staff are as safe and secure as possible. Children too, need to develop some responsibility for their own safety and be aware of the need to protect themselves from harm. Make sure that you share information and decision-making with them, without frightening them unnecessarily. This can be a difficult balance to achieve in modern society!

As an employee you will need to make sure that you meet the requirements of your school's Health and Safety policy, which may include some of the following:

Criminal Records Bureau (CRB) check

The school has a responsibility to arrange for screening by the Criminal Records Bureau to ensure that employees do not have criminal convictions that might affect the safety of the children or staff that they work with.

Supervision

In some schools teaching assistants are left in charge of classes, and in others they work under the constant supervision of a teacher. There is no fixed legal requirement, although the government has issued guidelines which recommend that 'well trained' support staff should lead classes under the direction and supervision of a teacher. Ultimately, it is the headteacher's responsibility to make sure children are supervised by adequately trained staff. Headteachers will make decisions and judgements according to the circumstances of their school and the profile of their staff. You must follow the accepted practice in your school. If you are unhappy that you are given either too much responsibility or too little responsibility, then you should talk to your line manager. Your Union should also be able to give you appropriate advice.

When you are responsible for running breakfast clubs and after-school clubs it is important that you follow Health and Safety guidelines and complete the required paperwork-

Safeguarding children

During the last few years, following the Soham murders in 2002 and the Victoria Climbie enquiry (2003), there has been a comprehensive review of the issue of children's safety. The government initiative Every Child Matters (2004) emphasises that everyone in school should take responsibility for the safety and well being of all children.

In 2004 schools were issued with updated guidance on safeguarding children in education (DFES 2004). This lists the recent government documents relating to child safety. All staff and volunteer helpers must be familiar with their school or workplace policy and procedures. In addition, all staff working with children should have basic child protection training that enables them to recognise and deal with any concerns about the welfare of children. This training should be updated every three years.

Child protection is a complex, sensitive and serious issue. Each school should have a Child Protection policy, a liaison officer at the Local Authority, and a designated person in school who is responsible for dealing with all child protection issues. Make sure that you know who the named person is in your school.

Schools also educate children themselves about child protection, through the Personal, Social, Health and Citizenship Curriculum. This provides opportunities for pupils to take part in discussions about personal safety and to explore ways in which they can recognise and manage risks or resist pressure from any of their peers or adults who may pose a threat. This is particularly important for children with learning difficulties or disabilities, as they may be at greater risk.

It is extremely important that all staff should provide a secure, safe and caring environment, so that children feel safe to share their difficulties and worries. It is particularly relevant for teaching assistants to be absolutely clear on the legal aspects of child protection, as children often have a closer personal relationship with them and may confide in them. Here are some essential points to remember about child protection:

- If a child discloses something to you that gives you cause for concern, reassure them but *do not* ask them to tell you any more or question them any further. Your evidence could be used in later proceedings so it is important that you do not ask leading questions or jump to conclusions.
- *Do not* promise to keep the information in confidence. You must pass it on to the designated person immediately.
- *Do* take great care to make sure the information you pass on is absolutely accurate. Write it down straight away and ensure you sign it. It is important to distinguish between allegations and facts when you do this.
- *Do* make sure you only pass on information directly to the designated/ named child protection staff member in your school.
- *Do* make sure you ask for training on child protection issues at school, or discuss the procedures you should follow with your line manager.

For legal reasons, it is extremely important to follow the correct procedures in these cases.

Always go to your named Child Protection colleague if you have any worries or queries. Schools should provide regular training for all their staff on child protection issues, so ask. Remember, abuse may be physical, verbal, sexual, or by neglect. Children sometimes live in very difficult circumstances and need help from outside the family, so you should be vigilant with children to check for unusual patterns of bruising, unexplained cuts or burns, and unusual patterns of behaviour. In some older children, these can be a symptom of self-harm too, which makes the issues even more sensitive and complex. Make sure you pass on any concerns to your teacher promptly. But remember, thankfully, cases of child abuse are still relatively rare so do not automatically jump to conclusions. Children get bumps and bruises from normal play.

It is also important to keep an eye on children's social interaction in school. Bullying is a real problem in some schools and may be verbal rather than physical. Again, you may be in a good position to monitor such things, or to support a child who is having a difficult time with peer relationships.

Equipment and resources

- Make sure you know how to use equipment, check that it is in good working order and store it safely after use.
- Check on the condition of electrical equipment and make sure you know who is responsible in school for its maintenance and where you take it if it breaks. If you are supporting in science classes at Key Stage 3/4, this is particularly important.
- Fill in relevant documentation for using equipment.
- Check on trailing flexes and other obstacles around the classroom.
- Make sure bags and coats aren't left on the floor for people to trip over and monitor the temperature of hot water in the hand basins.
- Make sure that both you and the children wear the correct safety clothing and equipment.

Safety rules

Many schools have safety rules and procedures, like age-segregated playtimes, one-way systems in corridors, a ban on running in the school premises and restrictions on the sort of games to be played in certain areas. Find out what these are in your school and enforce them strictly.

Playground/Break duty

Sadly, in spite of safety rules, playtime can sometimes be the most dangerous time in school. Teaching assistants are often asked to do playground duty, so if you are on duty check that you are aware of any danger zones in the play area and make sure you can see all the children. In winter, it is particularly tempting to huddle in a corner or to chat with other staff! Keep moving and keep watching. Be careful with very hot cups of tea or coffee and keep them away from children. You might also suggest some safe games for them to play (think back to your own schooldays!), or some activities related to whatever they are studying in class (e.g. looking for mini-beasts).

Site security

The rise in cases of theft from school premises and tragic events like the school shooting at Dunblane have meant that all schools need to ensure that their premises are open only to authorised visitors. Many schools now have keypad entry and visitor identification systems. Make sure you always follow the site security procedures for visitors and keep a check on people who you see on the school premises. It is also very important to make sure that you know exactly who is authorised to collect the children that you work with.

Fire drill
Make sure you know the location of fire alarms and the exit route and meeting point for each area you are in.

Risk assessment
Some larger schools have a Health and Safety Officer, employed specifically for risk assessment. The Health and Safety Officer will try to keep the school environment safe by looking for potential hazards and risks. However, it is always good practice for teaching assistants to carry out informal risk assessments in their work area from time to time. You often have the opportunity to move around the school from class to class and can notice safety and security issues that might otherwise be overlooked.

Accident reporting
All accidents should be reported and accurately recorded using the school reporting procedure. This is particularly important if any head injury is suspected, no matter how slight, as children can occasionally experience serious complications some time later.

First Aid
You will need to know who the First Aiders on your staff are, and where they can be found. Make sure that you are aware of the location of the First Aid box and check to see whether you can treat minor injuries yourself and how you should do so. It will also be useful to have a First Aid qualification yourself.

Medical information
Whenever you are supervising children, it is vital to know whether they suffer from any allergy or medical condition that could develop very quickly into a potentially serious and life-threatening situation. Make sure you know if any children you work with have nut or insect bite allergies, epilepsy, asthma or heart conditions. Check that you know the correct course of action to take and the staff to contact, by asking your teacher or line manager.

Administering medication
Your school will have a policy on giving medicine to children. This can vary from school to school, so you need to find out the procedure in your workplace. In some schools, parents sign a release slip so that medication can be administered by any member of staff. In others, specially trained welfare/teaching assistants or a school nurse fulfil that role. Where there are children who require medicine to be administered rectally (e.g. for epilepsy), or who need catheterisation, there should always be trained, expert staff in place. You may, however, need to become familiar with the use of an epipen™ in case of severe

allergic reaction. If you are concerned about being asked to do something that you are uncomfortable with, or are not trained for, then make sure that you discuss it with your line manager.

Personal safety and contact with children

Your physical contact with individual children will depend on their age and your school policy. Comforting a small child who has fallen over by giving them a cuddle is one thing, but it is only sensible to be more careful as children get older. Make sure you check with your school on the type of physical contact encouraged or allowed. You may be working with a child with behavioural difficulties, who could be a danger to themselves and others when angry or upset. Many schools now have positive handling policies and train staff in their use (DfES, 2001), because they recognise the value of personal contact, such as a light touch on the arm. It is important to take advice from your line manager and follow the school's guidance. Make sure you ask yourself – what if? It may be too late once the situation occurs.

Educational visits and school trips

Activities outside the classroom, trips and visits are a key part of the learning experience for all children. They may take place in the school grounds or farther afield. You may be asked to take groups of children into the playground or to the local activity centre, or you may find yourself accompanying a school ski trip. All of these activities will have health and safety implications. Schools have to ensure that all staff involved are technically competent to do so, have taken part in a risk assessment and are aware of policies and procedures. There is more information on this at http://www.teachernet.gov.uk/docbank/index.cfm?id=9212.

Key reading

Kay, J. (2002) *Teaching Assistants Handbook,* Continuum, London and New York, *[Contains a great deal of information for teaching assistants supporting at Key Stage 1.]*

Watkinson, A. (2002) *Assisting Learning and Supporting Teaching: A Practical Guide for the Teaching Assistant in the Classroom*, London: David Fulton *[Aims to give an insight into teaching and learning for teaching assistants. Contains a very useful section on child protection.]*

References

Key references are given in bold.

DfEE (2000) *Teaching Assistant File – Induction training for teaching assistants*, DfEE 0131/2000, London *[These are the training manuals used for induction training. Your LA/school should have a copy for you to look at. Contains comprehensive information on all aspects of teaching assistant practice.]*

DfEE (2000) *Working with Teaching Assistants: A Good Practice Guide,* London: DfEE 0148/2000 *[A complete guide for schools and teachers on the management and use of teaching assistants.]*

DfES (2002) *Teaching Assistant File – Induction Training for Teaching Assistants in Secondary Schools,* London: DfES/0627/2002 *[Updated information relating to teaching assistants working in secondary schools.]*

DfES(2004) *Safeguarding Children in Education,* London: DfES/0027/2004

DfES (2004) *Every Child Matters: Change for Children,* London: DfES/1081/2004

Fox, G. (1998) *A Handbook for Learning Support Assistants,* **London: David Fulton** *[A particular focus on supporting learners with special educational needs.]*

Kerry, T. (2001) *Working with Support Staff: Their Roles and Their Management,* London: Pearson *[Guidance for school managers. Includes two chapters on the use and management of teaching assistants.]*

Lee, B. (2002) *Teaching Assistants in Schools: the Current State of Play,* **LGA Research Report 34, National Foundation For Educational Research** *[Local Government Association-sponsored research paper; includes a review of literature on the impact of teaching assistants in schools. Covers the roles, deployment, effective working, conditions of employment and training and development of teaching assistants. Has a very useful bibliography.]*

Lorenz, S. (1998) *Effective In-Class Support. The Management of Support Staff in Mainstream Schools,* **London: David Fulton** *[Comprehensive look at supporting learners in a classroom situation.]*

Office for Standards in Education (2002), *Teaching Assistants in Primary Schools, An Evaluation of the Quality and Impact of Their Work,* HMI Report 434, 2002. Available on www.ofsted.gov.uk *[Ofsted evaluation of the work of teaching assistants in primary schools and their impact on the effectiveness of the National Literacy and Numeracy strategies. Covers all aspects of teaching assistants' working practice, including training.]*

DfEE Circular 10/98 and guidance issued to Chief Education Officers on Positive Handling Strategies in the letter from DfES dated April 24th 2001

The Victoria Climbie enquiry available at http://www.victoria-climbie-inquiry.org.uk

http://www.safeguardingchildren.org.uk/

www.teachernet.gov.uk/childprotection/guidance.htm *[Directions on physical restraint and the use of force. What to do if you suspect a child is being abused.]*

3 All about your school

There are thousands of schools in the United Kingdom and they all operate within a common framework and follow a standard basic curriculum. They are, however, all different. The DfES strategy for primary schools, *Excellence and Enjoyment,* encourages schools to build on and develop their identity (DfES, 2003). As a teaching assistant you may not have moved between schools as frequently as teachers have and your understanding of education may be based on your experience in a single school. For that reason, undertaking a short exchange in another school was an essential part of some STA courses, and it would be a great advantage to look beyond the confines of your own school when you are thinking about practice in education.

However, getting to know the individual character of your school is an important factor in doing your job effectively. Think about the ethos and culture in your school: What is the school's general atmosphere? Start by looking at your school's prospectus and see how it promotes itself to prospective pupils. You may find that it has a mission statement that sums up its philosophy and aims. Here are some example mission statements:

From a secondary school:

> "valuing and developing the individual"

From a Key Stage 2 school:

> "Success for all"

Another useful place to start is to look at the school entrance hall. Is it welcoming? Does it display children's work? What type of notices are there? As you get to know your school, you will become aware of the culture within it and the ethos or belief system that sustains it.

School ethos

The 'ethos' or culture of your school is a complex reflection of several factors. The personality, management style and beliefs of the headteacher are a key element. Although national policies implemented in the school will be the same, local differences will influence its character. All schools are distinct communities with their own strengths and weaknesses. Think about your own school and ask yourself these questions:

- What is the nature of the local community? Is the school in an affluent or impoverished area? What links are there with the local community?
- What types of jobs are available in the local community? Are parents working, or is it an area of high unemployment?
- What is the cultural mix of the pupils and staff?
- What is the profile of exam results? Is there a strong academic tradition?
- Is it recognised as a centre of excellence? Does it have some special status, like a technology college?
- Is sporting achievement or participation an important part of the culture? Does it have a tradition of producing music, art or drama?
- How large is the school? Are the buildings new or old – spread out or compact?
- Is there a big staff turnover? What is the staff profile? Is it young or are most staff nearing retirement? What individual interests and skills do the staff have?
- Does the school aim to be inclusive, welcoming all learners regardless of ability or culture?
- Is there a faith-based element to the school?
- Is there selection at entry on any ground (religious, academic, etc.)?
- Is there a school uniform?
- What are the expectations for behaviour and how are these enforced?
- Does the school run lunchtime or after school clubs?
- Are parents welcome in the school?

As manager, the headteacher is in a very powerful position and usually sets the overall tone of the school. When appointing a new head, the school's governors will be concerned to appoint a person whose aims and style are in keeping with their view of the school's ethos. Heads can have very different styles of leadership. Their vision of how teaching assistants should be used varies too, which will have an impact on your role.

The hidden curriculum

Sometimes we refer to a school's 'hidden curriculum'. This represents what is taught or learned unofficially, based on the assumptions, customs and protocol of each individual school. So, for example, a culture of respect towards teaching staff could be engendered by the fact that children stand up when a teacher enters the room. In another school, teachers may be referred to by their first name, indicating a more casual approach.

Here is a pupil in a Year 9 class talking about the ethos in their new school:

Pupil: "The teachers are friendly and they expect you to do a lot on your own. At first I found it difficult because I'm used to being told exactly what to do all the time, so it was hard. Then I realised it was more of a partnership with us and the teachers – you take more responsibility for your work."

Here are some teaching assistants talking about their schools:

Key Stage 2: "We pride ourselves on the way we deal with our children with SEN. They all get the chance to do well at something and achieve something. All the teachers spend a lot of time with us working out how we can help them – you don't feel it's just your problem. "

Key Stage 3/4: "Children get bussed in from all over the place. We have a working farm on the site so that children can learn to look after the animals and understand about farming. We have a lot of contact with the local community. There aren't many after school clubs because of the buses home, but we run some at lunchtime."

Key Stage 1: "Our school is on the _____ estate. It's a really deprived area so we have a nurture group in the school. It's for the ones that need help with social skills. They are not ready to learn really. We have a breakfast club, too, because lots of them come in the morning without eating anything. You can't learn if you are hungry, can you? We didn't see a lot of the parents but [the Head] has started a coffee club for parents when they drop the kids off in the morning, so some are coming in now. "

Key Stage 2: "Ours is a Green school – we have got special status as an environmentally-friendly school. One of the staff started it a few years ago. The children learn all about recycling and we collect materials from the community. They have a garden on the site and all the children are involved in growing things. We do loads of projects on the environment in History, Geography and Science and we do green literacy! Everyone is involved."

Key Stage 1/2: "It's just a really happy school. Parents are always coming in to help and the kids stay after school doing various clubs and activities. Everyone on the staff just mucks in, including the Head! There is so much going on. Every day is different – it's never dull!"

Key Stage 2/3/4 Special School: "We all work together – parents and the staff. The children have such difficult problems but the staff are a real team. There is no division between assistants and teachers. We all contribute and everyone has their own expertise."

It is important to work in a school where you are happy and comfortable with the environment and feel that you can add something positive to the school experience.

Staff structure

Employed staff

Check that you are familiar with your school's management structure and that you know who does what – your school may already have a printed copy of this. If not, it is worthwhile making a quick organisational diagram of everyone's roles and locations. You can often find photos of the staff in the entrance hall so that you can match faces to names.

Larger schools will of course have much more complex 'family trees', but in smaller schools you may find one person doing several jobs. In one memorable small village school, the Head was also the Special Educational Needs Coordinator, Key Stage 2 Coordinator, caretaker and secretary!

Management team

The Senior Management Team (SMT) is responsible for the day-to-day management of the school. SMT membership will vary from school to school, but might include:

- Headteacher – responsible for all aspects of the day-to-day running of the school, including budget management, staffing, teaching and learning.
- Deputy Head(s) who deputise for the headteacher but also have specific responsibility areas, e.g. assessment, arranging supply staff, etc.
- SENCO (Special Educational Needs Coordinator) or INCO (Inclusion Coordinator) – responsible for managing the day-to-day operation of the school's SEN policy and for coordinating provision for learners with SEN (DfES Code of Practice, 2001). Detailed information on the SENCO's role is given in Chapter 12.
- Heads of each Key Stage/Key Stage Coordinators* – may also be referred to as Head of Upper/Lower/Middle School; Early Years Coordinator/Foundation Stage Leader.
- Head of Sixth Form*.
- Heads of Year*.

Others responsible for management include:

- Curriculum/Subject Coordinators or Managers, Department Heads, or Faculty Managers. In secondary schools, this might be an area (e.g. Head of Modern Languages, or a subject, e.g. Head of French). In primary schools, it is usually a curriculum area, e.g. Literacy Coordinator or Science Coordinator. The coordinator is

*All of these will manage an age group or range of pupils.

usually responsible for ordering resources, chairing planning meetings and arranging training for other members of staff.

- Advanced Skills teachers – high-quality teachers who want to remain as classroom teachers but are given time to share their expertise in *pedagogy* (the art and science of teaching children) with other members of staff.
- Excellent Teachers – since September 2006 teachers with extensive experience, expertise and high-quality teaching skills have been able to apply to their headteachers for Excellent Teacher status. This role gives them the opportunity to gain career enhancement by helping colleagues to improve their teaching (DfES, 2006)
- Learning Managers – responsible for leading and managing effective student learning across the curriculum.
  Under new arrangements teaching staff can be awarded Teaching and Learning Responsibility points (TLR) for leading and managing other members of staff or curriculum areas.
- Policy Coordinators. This could be a coordinator for a school policy like behaviour or equal opportunities, or someone who manages a process like assessment. In some large secondary schools there will also be an Examinations Officer to administer external exams. There should always be a Health and Safety coordinator.

Teaching and support staff

- Teachers:
  - At Key Stage 1 and 2, teachers usually take a class, but you may find various other members of staff (often part-time) supporting different areas of the curriculum. These could include staff that support children with SEN or teach subjects like Music or Art. Flexible working hours mean that more and more staff are working part-time.
  - At Key Stage 3 and 4, most teachers have responsibility for a subject. They will teach many different classes and age groups.
- Nursery Nurses – work in the Foundation Stage to support teaching and learning and provide care and support.
- Teaching Assistants – including HLTAs or cover supervisors.
- Pastoral staff – they may look after a particular age group, or be school counsellors.
- Home-school liaison worker, or Family Liaison officer.
- Learning mentors: employed to support learners who are at risk of underachievement but do not necessarily have SEN. They work to remove barriers to learning and give individual, focused support. They often provide support for pupils in transition through Key Stages.
- Staff Development Officer. Some larger schools have a designated member of staff to deal with staff training issues.
- Educational visits coordinator – responsible for planning and administration of school visits
- Careers staff – responsible for giving pupils careers advice. At Key Stage 4 they often help with university applications.

- Facilities Manager/Site Manager – responsible for the management of the buildings and facilities and any commercial use of the school buildings (some larger schools derive a considerable income from this).
- Finance Officers – responsible for the day-to-day administration of the budget.
- Bursar – responsible for management of finance and the school's facilities.
- Librarian/Library assistants.
- Admin Staff/Secretaries and Personal Assistants – may have individual responsibilities for pupil data, examination entries or SEN paperwork. The Headteacher usually has a Personal Assistant.
- Technicians – responsible for maintaining equipment and setting up apparatus.
- Breakfast club supervisors.
- Sports coaches.
- Caretakers.
- Lunchtime supervisors.
- Cleaning staff.
- Kitchen staff.

Check that you know what everyone does and where to find them in the school. Don't forget that the Secretary and the Caretaker are also essential people to get to know.

You will see how you fit in to this structure and should be able to confirm your line management too. Schools have such different organisational arrangements that you could be managed in any area, depending on your job. Familiarise yourself with the special requirements of your management area in terms of communications and meetings.

Extended schools

The concept of extended schools is part of the agenda of Every Child Matters (DfES, 2004). Extended schools are open between 8am and 6pm and provide one, some or all of:

- childcare
- parenting and family support
- a variety of after school activities, including sport and music clubs
- swift and easy referral to specialist services like speech therapy.

In these schools school facilities may be available for use by adult and community groups and may offer opportunities to take qualifications or follow courses. All schools are to provide some extended services by 2010, but they do not have to provide all of them, or offer them on school premises. They may form partnerships with other schools, in which each specialises in providing some of the activities, or may come to arrangements with private providers, who may offer the services either on or off school premises.

Full-service extended schools

Full-service extended schools offer a comprehensive range of services in health, social care and education, all located on the school site. Basing all these professional services in the same place means that they are more readily available for children and families, and professionals can work closely together to achieve the best outcome for all children.

These schools are often sited in areas of social and economic deprivation and may have a separate coordinator to enable the headteacher to concentrate on teaching and learning. There is more information on this at www.teachernet.gov.uk/wholeschool/extended.

Communications

Every school has its own communication system to ensure that information is circulated around the school structure. Don't forget that this should always be a multi-way process. Your information management system will depend on the size of your school. It is a great deal easier when everyone uses the same staff room daily, but in some larger schools there can be several buildings, each with a separate staff room. E-mail has certainly made communication more accessible, but you still need to have the time and resources to access a computer!

Most schools communicate and make decisions through a series of meetings. These can be within year groups, departments, or whole school meetings. You may also have regular meetings with the SENCO/Inclusion Coordinator if you are supporting children with SEN. Some other examples of school communication systems are illustrated below.

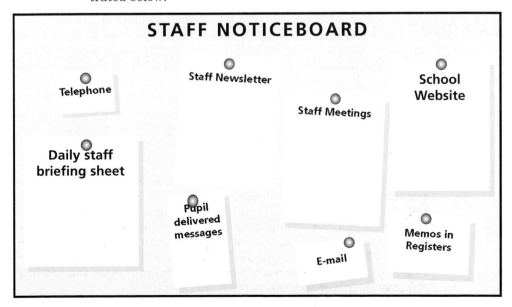

STAFF NOTICEBOARD

Telephone

Staff Newsletter

Staff Meetings

School Website

Daily staff briefing sheet

Pupil delivered messages

E-mail

Memos in Registers

Whatever the system in your school, make sure you use it effectively. We live in an age of information overload, whether it is paperwork, via computer, or through the media, and sometimes it can seem overwhelming just to keep up with it. It is a skill to identify and prioritise what is relevant and essential. It is no use flooding a system with inessential information, but it is crucial that the right people get the information they need. This will be particularly true for your manager. Finding out an important piece of information from someone external, which staff are already aware of, is guaranteed to upset most managers.

Key Stage 2: "There are 15 teaching assistants in our school and we were not getting information because we didn't have time to go through everything to find it. I asked the Head if I could produce a teaching assistant information sheet and she was happy for me to try. Now I read all the weekly information in school and produce a weekly teaching assistant newsletter. I start by looking at the school documents and then go through some of the paperwork she passes on to me from the LA and DfES. Recently, I've also gone through the TES and highlighted articles too. Some of the teaching assistants are on courses and said it has been really helpful. They bring lots of information in too. Now I'm thinking of starting a small teaching assistant library – it seems to have grown and grown!"

Profile of your school

School layout

Most schools have a site plan that shows all the building and room locations. School design varies enormously, depending on when they were built. In Victorian times it was felt that children should not be distracted by goings-on outside the school, so many of the buildings have high windows. In the '50s and '60s, schools were built with big expanses of glass, so even though they are bright and airy, they can sometimes be adversely affected by sunlight. Open plan classroom space has also influenced the design of many schools and a rapid growth in the numbers of pupils in the '70s and '80s meant that many schools used huts and temporary accommodation, and some still do. However, the opposite problem of a declining birth rate since then means that many primary schools are now amalgamating.

Your school will have its own profile. Obviously, modern facilities and a pleasant, ordered learning environment are important, but remember that many excellent schools make the very best of poor facilities. Check on the individual facilities available in your school. Note whether there is a learning support base room or area. Check whether the school uses facilities like swimming pools in the local area. Keep an eye out in your locality for useful places to visit too. Suggestions for school trips or places where children can go to research information are gratefully received, especially if they are free!

Key Stage 3/4: "When I first started as a teaching assistant I made my own map of the school, with all the buildings' room numbers and resource areas. I found it really helpful. Year 7 children often have difficulty finding their way around the school – it's daunting after primary school. Now we get new Year 7 children to make a school map as a settling in activity in September. They get into pairs and make a map of the school. They practise seeing how long it takes to get to the different subject areas. It helps them to make friends too."

The number of children on roll will generally influence what the school can offer in the way of staff expertise and educational experiences, as the main element of schools' funding is determined by the number of children who attend. Schools may also attract extra money through other government initiatives, or may be lucky enough to have a PTA that raises considerable amounts of money. Many teaching assistants are actively involved in fundraising initiatives in their schools.

Regular routines

Schools have an annual calendar, which will include term dates, holidays and staff development days. Each school will have its daily hours of work and lesson times, including the timings of breaks. They will also have individual rules and regulations for where pupils are allowed to go and to play during the day, particularly at lunchtime.

Resources

Schools are full of all kinds of equipment and resources. There will be procedures or guidelines for their use, including booking schedules and repair and maintenance systems. Ensure that you know how to use the library or resources areas. Schools often have to make the most of limited budgets for equipment and resources, so it is important to encourage pupils to value and look after anything they use. All teachers are used to being on the lookout for extra resources to bring to their teaching and teaching assistants play a very valuable role in organising, making and adapting resources for the classroom.

Be careful about photocopying – there may be copyright or confidentiality issues – and it can be expensive! If you are copying from books then a copyright fee needs to be paid. Make sure you ask your line manager or mentor for guidance.

School Development Plan

Schools are always looking at their performance and achievements and planning improvements for the future. They use a five-stage cycle to help them consider how to set targets, as shown overleaf (DfEE, 2001).

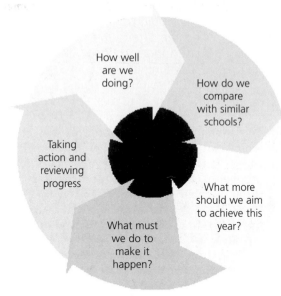

Setting targets using a 5-stage cycle

Every school has its own long-term plan, referred to as the 'School Development Plan' (SDP), or the 'School Improvement Plan' (SIP), which lists its strengths and weaknesses, and sets out its long-term strategic aims and medium-term goals. These are developed by the management staff and governing body, using feedback from inspections and information from consultation with LA advisers, staff and parents. National initiatives are also taken into consideration. The plan will cover all aspects of teaching and learning in school, including:

- raising pupil achievement
- management of resources
- promoting social inclusion and equal opportunity
- promoting staff performance
- ensuring effective leadership.

Within the plan, the school will set targets to be completed within timescales and will also identify the source of funding to pay for improvements. The plans also identify who is responsible for the targets and include monitoring procedures and success criteria. You should consult your school's plan so that you can be fully aware of the direction it is hoping to take and make sure you are involved. You also need to know if there is anything in the plan that refers to any part of your job role. You can make really helpful contributions to school development by thinking about your practice and passing on suggestions and ideas to help your school in its quest for improvement.

Example of Targets from a School Development Plan

ICT:

Focus	Action	Monitoring
Raise pupil standards in ICT	• Keep samples of work • Update ICT policy • Resource QCA scheme of work	Coordinator
ICT & Internet structure	• Extend Internet access • Establish class e-mail accounts	Coordinator

Partnerships with parents

The value of a close, working partnership between schools and parents is well recognised, and extended schools offer more opportunities to develop it. A parent is a child's first teacher and, as such, has a great deal of expertise to share with schools (Webster-Stratton, 1999; Whalley, 2000). It is clear that education is most successful when parents and teachers work together. Establishing and maintaining that relationship has become an essential part of the drive to raise standards in schools, particularly where children with SEN or additional needs are concerned. All schools are required to have a 'home–school agreement' which reflects the commitment of the pupil, school and parents. An example is shown below.

The **pupil** agrees to be polite and work hard

The **parents** agree to ensure that the pupil attends regularly

The **school** agrees to provide a safe and secure learning environment

A home–school agreement

You can find examples of home–school agreements on the DfES standards website: www.standards.dfes.gov.uk/parentalinvolvement

Of course, not all children are looked after by a parent. Some live with other relatives, foster families, or in local authority care, and their carers have an equally valuable part to play in their education. Information about a child's progress needs to be shared with parents and their views and wishes should always be taken into consideration.

It is essential to follow your school's guidelines on communicating with parents. Some schools are very happy for teaching assistants to play an active role. Others prefer any communication with parents to be through teaching staff. Make sure that you find out the procedure in your school.

Each school has its own method of communicating with parents. In some Key Stage 1 schools, it may be done informally at drop off and pick up times. Others operate a strict appointment-only system, as talking to parents at length in the morning can disrupt the organisation of the start of the day.

Key Stage 1: "Every morning my teaching assistant greets the children and takes any messages from parents. She also deals with any reading books or items that come into school. She will refer anything important or urgent straight to me and I will either talk to the parents then or later. Because she deals with all the routine information in the morning, I can concentrate on giving the children a calm and ordered start to the day. In the evening, we swap roles. My teaching assistant organises the children and then starts the clearing up while I talk to parents. It works really well."

Informal progress meetings, open evenings, newsletters, discussion groups, and parent information evenings are all valuable methods of general communication about pupil progress and curriculum issues. Each school will also have its own method that parents can use to contact staff if they have a query. Many primary schools use parent volunteers and keep a list of parent skills and talents so they can call on them for assistance.

You may be working one-to-one with a child and have very close contact with the parents. A sympathetic and professional teaching assistant can be a wonderful support for a parent or carer, and can provide a very effective bridge between teaching staff and the home. Teaching assistants can often be more approachable for parents. In some areas of the country, schools are now employing home liaison staff (often ex-teaching assistants) to fulfil this role full-time.

Sometimes relationships with parents can be difficult and challenging, which is why it is so important to maintain a positive approach and follow professional, confidential practice under the supervision of teaching staff. In all your dealings with parents you should always strive to be respectful and non-judgemental. More on working with the parents of children with SEN is included in Chapter 12.

School policies and procedures

All schools must comply with relevant requirements as set down in law. However, when in the case of guidance issued by government, schools have the choice whether to follow it or not. For example, schools are legally required to deliver the National Curriculum. However, they do not have to follow government guidance in the Primary Strategy (Literacy and daily Mathematics lesson) if they can show that they have a system that is equally successful. Schools use the legal framework and the guidance available to develop and implement their own policies and practices, summarising these in school policy documents.

It is important that everyone in the school has a clear understanding of these. School policies are public documents, which you can have access to. Some of them can be very lengthy but look through them and check on their general principles and note any aspects that will be relevant to you in your job. Much of this is discussed in further detail elsewhere in the book, but as a general guide here are some examples of the policies you should find:

Health and Safety

This policy is dealt with in detail in Chapter 2. Under the 1974 Health and Safety at Work Act you have a duty to take reasonable care of yourself and others by:

- using correct equipment safely
- using personal protective equipment, where required
- reporting all accidents
- complying with safety arrangements given by line managers
- reporting any defects in equipment.

Data Protection and Freedom of Information

Schools must comply with the Data Protection Act (1998) and the Freedom of Information Act (2000), keeping a minimum of personal information and making sure that it is secure. Staff, parents and pupils may ask to see any personal information relating to them, and other people may have rights to see certain information. If you are involved in record-keeping, you need to keep this in mind. There is guidance from Becta which explains this and also covers safe Internet use (Becta, 2000).

Behaviour

Schools are also required to have a behaviour support plan or behaviour policy, which describes the whole-school approach to maintaining positive behaviour in the school. Often this is combined with elements of the home school policy. Where behaviour management is concerned, it is really important that everyone in school has a consistent approach, so make sure you consult your school policy and find out:

- the strategy behind the policy
- the standards required
- any particular issues relevant to the school
- rewards and sanctions to be used
- your own role in managing behaviour.

Behaviour management issues and policies are discussed in more depth in Chapter 14.

Curriculum policies

Schools interpret the requirements of the National Curriculum in their own way, bringing their own particular strengths and skills. Schools will have written policies for each of the curriculum areas, which summarise their aims and objectives and set out their teaching and learning strategies. However, these policies will vary from school to school. Some may have separate reading, spelling, writing, hand-writing, speaking and listening policies, while others include all these subjects in an overall English policy. Policies can be very long and detailed, but schools often produce a more user-friendly version in the form of a quick summary for parents, which you may find a useful starting point.

Each curriculum area policy should contain:

- aims and objectives
- the way the subject is taught throughout the school
- support strategies for pupils experiencing difficulties
- monitoring and assessment methods.

Information and Communications Technology (ICT)

ICT policy is particularly important, as the use of ICT varies widely in schools. The best examples have ICT fully integrated across all areas of the curriculum and use it as a tool in all areas of learning. You need to make sure you are aware of all the uses of ICT within your school. There is more on ICT in Chapter 15.

Other policy areas

You will also find whole-school policies on:

- Teaching and Learning
- Assessment.

Besides those mentioned above, schools must have a number of other policies relating to, for example, admissions, careers, school lettings, nutritional standards and sex education. Although many of these will not impinge directly on your role, two that will are complaints (main-ly from parents) and staff discipline. It is worth familiarising yourself with your own school policies on these matters. There may also be poli-cies for homework, staff development, and the use of resources. Some schools will have a policy on the use of teaching assistants.

Special Education Needs (SEN)/Inclusion

Schools are given very clear national guidelines on making provision for children with SEN. Each school should have its own SEN policy that sets out the management of provision for learners with SEN, including information on monitoring and evaluation. If you are sup-porting learners with SEN you will find this policy particularly rele-vant to your job role and it will give you a good overview of the over-all provision in your school. This may be part of an Inclusion Policy too. More details on this are included in Chapter 12.

Equal opportunities

We live in a diverse, multi-cultural and multi-racial society. Each school has its own unique mix of children and staff and it is vital that we treat everyone fairly and equally, regardless of their social background, gender, race, culture, religion or ability. It is really important that we do not deny children opportunities or disadvantage them in any way. However, this doesn't mean that we should treat everyone exactly the same. Children will have different needs and these should be met in different ways.

Now that inclusion is a central part of our approach to achievement for all, every school will include children with learning difficulties and disabilities. Many of these learners will require extra support, and teaching assistants have a vital role to play in providing that support in a sensitive and effective way. However, the very presence of a teaching assistant may sometimes be a disadvantage, by making the learner appear different and isolating them from their class and peer group. You need to be aware of this and make sure that your daily working practice helps the child to be included. Teaching assistants can do so much to help all children be a real part of their school community.

Your school policy will set out its procedures and practice to allow all children to be treated fairly and with respect. You need to:

- follow the principles in your own practice
- ensure that all pupils are given guidance on all the issues involved
- monitor the learning environment to make sure that all the principles are upheld.

Practising fairness and equality

Since May 2002, all schools must have a written race equality policy that sets out their commitment to promoting racial equality and tackling discrimination (CRE, 2002). The Special Educational Needs and Disability Act (SENDA, 2001) brought in new legislation to ensure that children with SEN are treated fairly and equably. Some basic principles of good practice are given below.

High expectations for all

All children should have the opportunity to reach their potential. Sometimes it is difficult, especially when a child comes from a disadvantaged background or has a disability. Even though you may find yourself thinking negatively about what they could achieve, they certainly deserve every opportunity to try.

Welcoming and appreciating diversity

Cultural diversity has always been a feature of British society, and should be celebrated.

Key Stage 2: "One teaching assistant reported that her class undertook a project on family trees and found that many of the children had ancestors who came from different countries. That led to discussions about the way they had been accepted and how they were now a valuable part of British society. It enabled the teacher and teaching assistant to focus on the reality of a multi-cultural society."

Tackling discrimination

Throughout the ages, different groups have faced discrimination in society. By discrimination we mean treating someone badly or denying a person an opportunity just because of who they are, rather than because of their behaviour. Discrimination usually begins with stereotyping and prejudice.

Stereotyping

This is a way of categorising people by commonly-held assumptions. We often identify people by their membership of a recognisable group. For example, over the years there have been Mods, Rockers, hippies, Essex girls, 'ladies who lunch', Goths, computer geeks, skaters and emos. Such groups have recognisable behaviour patterns and styles of dress, etc. We judge people by how they appear. The problem arises when we then stereotype them into a category and no longer see them as individuals. Here are some examples that you may have come across in school.

"All dyslexic children are good at art."
"Asian children are so hard-working and good at Maths."
"Boys are more interested in science than girls."
"Girls are much better at language work than boys."

There is a big difference between recognising and accepting cultural characteristics and developing a stereotypical view of a child. This can lead to prejudices that are then reinforced in a self-fulfilling cycle of discrimination.

Prejudice

This is often a negative attitude to someone or something, based on a pre-formed opinion. It is possible to be prejudiced against a child, a class, an ethnic group, or a whole culture. Here is an example: Two children from a family with social difficulties attend your school. They both have behavioural problems. A younger sibling starts in the reception class. What do you expect from him/her?

You will be able to think of examples from your own experience. You may find that some members of staff have negative viewpoints or prejudices about teaching assistants, based on their own assumptions!

Today, the following groups may still be marginalised or discriminated against:

• people from ethnic minorities
• people from other cultures

- asylum seekers or refugees
- people who do not look the same as their peer group, or who behave differently to them.

The way you interact with all children and the language that you use will send a powerful message to the other children, who learn attitudes and viewpoints from adults around them. This is particularly important if your school is in an area where there are negative perceptions about some people in the local community, e.g. asylum seekers in Kent.

Girls or Boys

A great deal of progress has been made in giving equal opportunity to girls and boys, but there are still occasions when children can be discriminated against because of their gender. There is considerable research to show that boys and girls do learn differently, but schools still need to work hard to ensure both have equality of opportunity.

Many of the staff in Key Stage 1 and 2 schools are women, and there has been concern that the 'female culture' engendered in schools is now disadvantaging boys. Boys are often seen as noisy or disruptive. This is made worse by the fact that boys have few male role models to follow in school and, when they are identified as having difficulties, the teaching assistants allocated to support them are usually women. Some educationalists feel there should be some positive work on anti-discrimination where boys are concerned. There has been particular concern about the low achievement of boys from Afro-Caribbean backgrounds. This has been the subject of much research, both in the UK and USA (Griffin and Tyrell, 2003).

Gays/Lesbians

This can be an issue among teenagers. Some may even go through stages of insecurity about their own sexuality. Sometimes they will project this onto anyone who doesn't fit their perceived norm.

Disabled people

Disabled people can be denied opportunities simply because appropriate facilities are not made available. Some people do not see past the disability to the person. Some staff may find children with disabilities to be a challenge but the important point to remember is that such pupils have every right to be in school. The Special Educational Needs and Disabilities Act (SENDA, 2001) and the Disability Discrimination Act (DDA, 2005) have done much to redress the balance for children with learning difficulties and disabilities in school.

What Can I Do?

As a teaching assistant, you have an opportunity to contribute to anti-discriminatory practice and equality of opportunity in school. For example, you can:

- Maintain high expectations for all learners.

- Have a real commitment to making realistic inclusion work.
- Familiarise yourself with the particular equal opportunity issues in your school.
- Help children to value and develop their own cultural identity. Ask them about their culture or religious beliefs, but remember that some children do not like talking about these in class. Be sensitive and check with them first, or wait for them to initiate discussion. There are many books and TV programmes available that give us information about different cultures.
- Celebrate diversity; modern society is such a varied and fascinating place. You need to welcome and use that in the classroom. Let pupils share their beliefs and customs with other children. Use that information to inform and extend your teaching, without focusing only on festivals and food, which are the outward manifestations of a culture.
- Develop an interest in the interaction of culture/gender on educational achievement. Observe what is happening in the classroom and discuss this with your teacher.
- Watch your practice! Be careful that you do not make unfounded assumptions about pupils.
- Be aware that children with English as a second language often have good receptive language. They can usually understand what is said to them before they are able to answer confidently, so do not assume they cannot understand and exclude them from conversation or talk about them in their hearing.
- Do not patronise disabled children by calling them 'love', 'sweetheart', 'dear' or 'darling', when you would not use that terminology with other children in the class.
- Try not to label children as 'my statement/PH child/dyslexic', etc. Use their names whenever possible.
- Check that you are giving equal amounts of attention to girls and boys and allocate classroom jobs fairly.
- Make sure you are a role model in the way you talk to and treat all learners.
- Monitor the learning environment. Are the materials you use (books, etc.) representative of all cultures and social groupings?
- Monitor the way pupils talk to each other. Do you see any evidence of racist or discriminatory behaviour, even if said as a joke? If so, it should be made clear that this is unacceptable. Issues like these need to be talked through with the children concerned at a suitable time.

Key Stage 3/4: "I was supporting a learner in a small Year 8 class where there were only two girls. Whenever the teacher moved to the front of the class, several of the boys constantly made offensive comments to the girls and called them 'slags'. The girls seemed resigned to it. Although I told the boys to stop, I noticed that when I was out of earshot it carried on. I referred it to the teacher and we dealt with these issues as part of PSHE. The behaviour stopped."

- Make sure you are sensitive to the individual circumstances of children. If you are aware of these you will avoid upsetting a child unintentionally.

> **Key Stage 2:** "I knew that the father of one of the children in our class had recently died. We were going to be making Father's day cards that afternoon. I chatted to him alone at lunchtime and gently asked him what he wanted to do. We agreed that he would make one for his mum instead."

- Be aware of the culture in the school. An anti-'boffin' culture can be a threat to equal opportunities and make the able and academic children unpopular and unhappy and discourage achievement. Keep these issues as subjects for discussion, so that they do not become part of the hidden curriculum.
- Be careful when you are using information about a child in data handling examples. The only child in the class with red hair may get fed up with being picked as the only one in their category, whilst the child that doesn't have a pet may be unhappy too! Use different information – perhaps what the children would like to have, instead!

Bullying

All schools have a commitment to prevent bullying and most will have a policy that sets out their procedures. Bullying is defined as someone using their power to threaten, insult, physically attack or exclude another. Although physical violence is deeply unpleasant, verbal, social and emotional bullying can be even more damaging.

Girls who are experiencing friendship difficulties can often be particularly nasty to each other, by excluding or ignoring each other. Any child can become the target of bullies, although children with disabilities and those who look or behave in a different way to their peer group are particularly vulnerable.

Your school policy will set out how it intends to prevent and stop bullying, and will tell you what your own responsibilities are. There is more about bullying in Chapter 14.

What makes an effective school?

A great deal of research has been carried out on why schools are effective. You have seen that all the following factors contribute:

- strong, professional leadership
- a disciplined, calm and ordered learning environment
- friendly, caring staff
- a culture of equality with no dominant group
- shared vision and goals
- high expectations for all learners
- an explicit approach to behaviour management

- clear learning outcomes for all learners
- fair and helpful feedback on learning
- a plan for continuous improvement
- a willingness to seek and share best practice
- partnership with parents
- effective staff recruitment, training and motivation
- a culture of welcoming diversity
- a culture of learning for staff and pupils
- collaboration with the community
- staff teamwork.

As a teaching assistant you are in a position to make a real difference in your school!

You will find a proforma in Chapter 16 to help you fill out your school details. It will help you by recording a lot of important information about the school all in one place.

Key reading

ASE (2001) *Be Safe: Health and Safety in Primary School Science and Technology,* 3rd edn, Hatfield: Association for Science Education

Cheminais, R. (2006) *Every Child Matters – A Practical Guide for Teachers,* London: David Fulton

DfES (2005) *Guidance on the Duty to Safeguard and Promote the Welfare of Children,* London: DfES

MacGilchrist, B., Myers, K., Reed, J. (2004) *The Intelligent School,* London: Sage *[Describes the characteristics of effective schools and learning environments.]*

References

Key references are given in bold.

Becta (2000) *Data Protection and Security: A Summary for LEAs and schools,* Coventry: Becta Bec1-15110

Commission for Racial Equality (CRE) (2001) *Statutory Code of Practice on the Duty to Promote Racial Equality – A Guide for Schools,* London: CRE. Available on CRE website www.cre.gov.uk *[Practical guidance to school governing bodies.]*

DfEE (2002) *Supporting the Target Setting Process,* London: DfEE/0065/2001 *[Guidance for schools on target-setting.]*

DfES (2001) *Special Educational Needs Code of Practice,* London: DfES/581/2001 *[Practical guidance for schools, LAs and early years settings for supporting pupils with SEN.]*

DfES (2003) *Excellence and Enjoyment – A Strategy for Primary Schools,* London: DfES/0377/2003 *[DfES vision for primary schools for the future – to combine excellence in teaching with enjoyment of learning. Schools are encouraged to be creative and innovative.]*

DFES (2006) *Excellent Teachers,* London: DfES 0164-2006DBW-END

Disability Discrimination Act 2005 (2005) Chapter 13, London: The Stationery Office

Griffin, J. and Tyrell, I. (2003) *Human Givens – A New Approach to Emotional Health and Clear Thinking,* East Sussex: Human Givens Publishing *[A wide-ranging book covering human emotional and psychological development. Specific chapter on gender differences.]*

Special Educational Needs and Disability Act (SENDA) 2001, London: HMSO

Webster-Stratton, C. (1999) *How to Promote Children's Social and Emotional Competence,* **London: PCP** *[Very practical hands-on manual for teachers and teaching assistants that looks at strategies for helping children develop their social and emotional competence. Includes lots of suggestions for positive behaviour management. Also has a useful chapter on the importance of parents in a child's education.]*

Whalley, M. (2000) *Involving Parents in their Children's Learning*, London: PCP *[Focuses on the importance of parent partnerships in early years settings]*

DCSF Standards website:www.standards.dcsf.gov.uk

4 The school and its support system

The provision of State education is a Government responsibility managed by the Department for Education and Skills (DfES). Authority and funding are delegated to local authorities (LAs) and to schools themselves. Several other organisations and agencies also have roles to play, and their roles are shown later in this chapter. In the private sector, schools are still subject to regulation by the Government, but they have more freedom in terms of what they teach and the way that they teach.

The school governing body

Every school has its own governing body, responsible for the effective overall management of the school. It is made up of volunteers from the local community, parents and staff, and has responsibility for the staffing, finances and policies in the school. Day-to-day running of the school is delegated to the headteacher, but the governing body will set the aims of the school and have a strategic view on issues like discipline, admissions, the curriculum, staff pay, school effectiveness and improvement. Although the governing body determines the school's general policy and approach to *all* learners, they also have a particular responsibility for setting up and maintaining the school's general approach to meeting the needs of learners with SEN. They will naturally be closely involved in any inspection process.

The make-up of governing bodies will vary slightly, but will include:

- an elected Chair and Vice Chair
- elected parent governors
- elected staff governors
- co-opted governors
- LA-appointed governors
- Governors from religious or charitable bodies (only some schools)
- a paid clerk to the governors.

One of the governors will take special responsibility for SEN. The involvement of the governors in finance, staffing and all school policies (including how SEN children are supported effectively) means that they will have an interest in how teaching assistants are employed and used in the school. You need to get to know who the governors are and what they do. Find out how often they meet, how they can be contacted and whether there are subcommittees of governors who deal with specific issues, like SEN or the curriculum. Check to see whether there is a governor from the support staff – most governing bodies have to have one, who can be a teaching assistant or from the administration. Each governing body produces a yearly report for parents that you will be able to read. You may yourself be a member of the governing body of a school, either as a parent governor or co-opted governor.

School councils

Schools are encouraged to set up schools councils to which pupils elect representatives to take part in discussion and decision-making about school activities and policies. School councils can be a very effective way of encouraging a partnership between pupils and teachers that benefits the school community as a whole. Pupils often have valuable contributions and suggestions to make, and councils encourage taking part in active citizenship

Education organisations

The Government monitors and directs what happens in schools. It does this through various organisations and agencies. Nationally, the Department for Children, Schools and Families (DCSF) is responsible for state-funded education and training. It controls the education budget and passes resources to LAs and schools. LAs are local government-based and are responsible to the Secretary of State and local electorates. Under the Government policy of local management of schools (LMS), their priority is to give most of the money to schools and keep central funds to a minimum.

The Training and Development Agency for Schools (TDA) is an executive non-departmental public body, whose main purpose is to raise school standards by attracting able and committed people to teaching and by improving the quality of teacher training. The Qualifications and Curriculum Authority (QCA) is also an executive non-departmental public body, which was established to develop and maintain the curriculum and accredit examinations and qualifications, including NVQs, GCSEs and A/AS Levels.

Finally, the Office for Standards in Education, Children's Services and Skills (Ofsted) has been established to provide an 'independent external evaluation of the effectiveness of a school'.

Department for Children, Schools and Families (DCSF)

Government Department of State, responsible for State-funded education and training. Previously known as DfES and before that DfEE, it controls the education budget and aims to coordinate all the services provided for children. Its objectives are to secure the five outcomes of the Every Child Matters agenda, i.e. to ensure that all children and young people:

- stay healthy and safe
- secure an excellent education and the highest possible standards of achievement
- enjoy their childhood
- make a positive contribution to society and the economy
- have lives full of opportunity, free from the effects of poverty.

DCSF publishes regulations and guidance for schools. It has a useful website: www.dcsf.gov.uk (which includes all publications from its predecessors the DfES and DfEE). Includes information on recent news items and press releases. Links to the online DCSF magazine for teachers: http://www.teachernet.gov.uk/.

DCSF publications centre: dscf@prolog.uk.com (tel: 0845 602 2260) has copies of all Government consultation papers. Has special section for teaching assistants.

Local Authority (LA)

Local government-based and responsible to the Secretary of State and local electorates. Under the Government policy of local management of schools (LMS), their priority under 'Fair Funding' is to give most of the money to schools and keep central funds to a minimum. Their role is largely to coordinate and advise, but they retain a strategic responsibility for:

- providing a school place for every child of school age within their area
- monitoring, challenging and supporting schools.

Their priority is to promote high standards in education and to support self-improvement in schools. LAs:

- provide local strategic leadership
- can step in to help failing schools, or to identify best practice. LAs have responsibility for SEN but many delegate funding directly to schools and provide advice and support
- provide curriculum advisers to schools for areas such as literacy and numeracy
- may provide induction training for teaching assistants
- set pay scales for support staff
- provide pupil services.

Local Authority Children's Trusts

By 2008 all LAs will be expected to have set up a Children's Trust. These are partnerships, which bring together all the organisations involved in commissioning and delivering services for children under the leadership of a Director for Children's Services or Children's Champion. They are intended to make it easier for all professionals working with children to collaborate effectively, supported by common procedures and processes and using pooled budgets to buy services more efficiently.

Children's Trusts have representatives from education, health, social services and the voluntary sector and employ a range of professionals, including family support workers, health visitors, social workers, school nurses, educational psychologists, speech and language therapists, and child and adolescent mental health professionals. They have a strong role to play in supporting schools, particularly extended and full service schools.

Training and Development Agency for Schools (TDA)

The TDA is an executive, non-departmental public body, which was formally known as the Teacher Training Agency (TTA). The change of name in 2005 signifies that it now has a role and relationship with all the different staff in schools, not just teachers. The TDA has three main goals:

- to attract able and committed people to teaching

- to provide schools and staff with good information on training, development and workforce remodelling

- to create a training and development environment that enables the whole school workforce to develop its effectiveness.

The TDA is involved in setting up a framework for professional and career development for school support staff and administering HLTA standards.

Tel: 020 7295 3700

www.tda.gov.uk

Qualifications and Curriculum Authority (QCA)

An executive, non-departmental public body established in 1997 as the 'guardian of standards'. The QCA:

- develops and maintains the curriculum

- is responsible for accrediting teaching assistant qualifications, including NVQs

- accredits and monitors qualifications such as GCSEs and A/AS Levels

- is developing a national framework of qualifications

- maintains assessment

- administers SATs

- takes part in development projects, e.g. *Arts Alive*, to enrich the curriculum with music and art.

Tel: 020 7509 5555

www.qca.org,uk

Ofsted
School self-evaluation
Self-evaluation is now at the heart of the Ofsted process.

Schools are encouraged to undertake a constant process of reflection and self-evaluation in which they analyse their strengths and weaknesses by looking at evidence from their results, monitoring their procedures and practices and consulting with staff, pupils, parents and outside agencies. This is intended to be an open and transparent process, which encourages a culture of self-reflection. As part of it at least annually schools complete a Self-Evaluation Form (SEF), which is verified by Ofsted inspectors when they visit the school to make an inspection. You can see examples of the SEF at www.ofsted.gov.uk.

The evaluation schedule
The framework used by Ofsted for its inspections is published on its website. Inspection is now tied in closely to the five outcomes of Every Child Matters (see pages 33–4). The framework applies to all nursery, primary, secondary and special schools. Independent schools buy in the services of the Independent Schools Inspectorate to provide external evaluation. When they inspect a school, having studied the SEF, Ofsted will consider the following key questions:

- How effective and efficient are the provision and related services in meeting the full range of learners' needs and why?
- How well do learners achieve?
- How good are the overall personal development and well-being of the learners?
- How well are learners cared for, guided and supported?
- How effective are leadership and management in raising achievement and supporting all learners?
- How effective are teaching and learning?
- How well do the curriculum and other activities meet the range of needs and interests of learners?

They will give the school or setting a rating for each of these areas as follows: outstanding, good, satisfactory, inadequate.

What happens during an Ofsted inspection?
Schools and settings receive only three or four days notice of a visit by Ofsted. The team of inspectors, led by an HMI, spends two days in the school watching lessons, looking at resources, examining pupil records and *(cont. overleaf)*

achievement, talking to the staff and parents and listening to the pupils' view-points. They use this information to check against the school's own self-evaluation information in the SEF. Schools receive a short written report which focuses on good practice and gives clear recommendations for improvement. A school can expect to be inspected once every three years, unless the inspectors are concerned by what they see, in which case they will come back after a few months.

The inspection process should be seen as a positive one, which highlights strengths rather than focusing only on weaknesses. It is intended to build upon the school's own evaluation process. It is not intended that teachers should be involved in a lot of extra work. The feedback process should be clear and helpful. As a result of the inspection, schools will decide what to do about the areas identified as needing attention. Any school that has serious weaknesses will be placed in Special Measures and will have up to two years with re-inspections to make the necessary improvements. Schools that have been placed in Special Measures can become excellent examples of practice, through a supportive re-inspection process. Her Majesty's Inspectorate (HMI) – the core of Ofsted – gives general reports to Parliament, based on their inspections of individual schools.

www.ofsted.gov.uk/publications

Outside agencies

Schools work collaboratively with many different groups, organisations and agencies. Under the remit of Every Child Matters inter-agency and collaborative working is a crucial part of meeting the needs of all children (DfES, 2004). With the advent of full service and extended schools this will become an even greater feature of school practice. You may find any of the following working in your school.

LA support services

- Learning Support Service. A team of specially qualified staff who support the learning and development of children with SEN. The Learning Support Service may be known by various names in different parts of the country and can have special sections like Specific Learning Difficulties Support.
- Language Support Service. Again, can be known by various names in different parts of the country but supports learners with EAL. These are children who have learned their family language as a first language and English as their second or subsequent language because they originate from another country or culture.
- Behaviour Support Service/Behaviour and Education Support Teams (BEST). Supports learners with emotional and behavioural difficulties.
- Educational Welfare Officer. Sometimes referred to as the School Liaison Officer. He or she will deal with attendance and home difficulties.
- Educational Psychologist. Provides specialist advice and help for

pupils with SEN and their teachers. He or she will also be involved in testing and statutory assessment procedures. Some have specialist responsibility for particular areas of SEN, e.g. dyslexia or social and communication disorders. They plan and monitor intervention programmes.

- Hospital School Service. Provides tuition for children with long-term medical problems.
- Physical/Sensory Service. Provides structured support, help and advice for pupils with sensory loss like visual or hearing difficulties and advice for their teachers.
- Library Service. Provides librarians and resources to support both literacy and the whole curriculum.
- Sure Start. A government programme which aims to improve outcomes for all children, parents and communities in the Early Years sector.

Health authority services

Your local health authority will also provide a number of services:

- Child and Adolescent Mental Health Services (CAMHS). Provisions and support for learners with mental health issues, and their families.
- Occupational Therapist. Provides advice for teachers and works with pupils' physical disabilities.
- Physiotherapist. Provides advice for teachers and works with pupils' physical disabilities.
- Speech Therapist. Provides support for learners with speech and language difficulties, and advice for their teachers.
- School Nurse. Responsible for providing vaccinations as well as health advice and education.
- School Dentist. Provides dental care and information on preventing dental problems.

Other local services

- Connexions. A locally delivered, combined career, education and welfare service for young people aged 14+ years. www.connexions.gov.uk
- Social workers. Involved in the welfare of children who are looked after by someone other than their parent or guardian, e.g. children in local authority care, or who live with foster parents.
- Peripatetic Music Teachers. These are music teachers who work with a number of schools to provide children with individual tuition on musical instruments.

Feeder schools

Your school will have links both with the schools that send pupils to you and the schools that you send pupils on to, as illustrated overleaf.

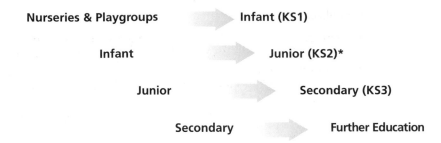

Nurseries & Playgroups	**Infant (KS1)**
Infant	**Junior (KS2)***
Junior	**Secondary (KS3)**
Secondary	**Further Education**

During the transitions between Key Stages and schools, pupils, parents and relevant staff will often make familiarisation visits.

Other links

Your school will probably have links with:

- Community groups and church organisations.
- Police/Fire and other emergency services for information on drug awareness, road safety, fire safety, etc.
- Voluntary organisations and charities.

Business partnerships

In addition, most schools have partnership arrangements with local businesses, which may include work experience arrangements, talks, information sessions and staff exchanges. Some businesses provide mentors for pupils.

Excellence in Cities

Excellence in Cities (EiC) is a programme specifically targeted at pupils in urban areas which focuses on their needs and aspirations. It encourages schools to cooperate to raise standards and to look for new sources of funding. Excellence in Cities has seven key strands: Learning Mentors; Learning Support Units; City Learning Centres; more Beacon and Specialist Schools; EiC Action Zones; and extended opportunities for gifted and talented pupils.

Different types of school

The school system is based on pupil age ranges:

Primary:	Ages 5 > 7	Infant Schools
	Ages 7 > 11	Junior
Secondary:	Ages 11 > 16+	

Or, a 3-tier system of:

First School	Ages 5 > 8
Middle School	Ages 8 > 14 [age ranges vary; some are 9 to 13, some 8 to 13]
Upper School	Ages 14 > 16+

* More often than not, infant and junior will be within the same school (primary).

Schools can be:

- Community schools. These are the largest category and are run by the LA. They make strong links with the local community.
- Voluntary Controlled. Owned by a charitable foundation (usually the Church of England or the Catholic Church) but run by the LA, who sets the admissions policy.
- Voluntary Aided. Run by charitable foundations, e.g. churches. They are mainly funded by the LA but usually set their own admissions policy.
- Foundation School. Although funded by LAs, these schools have a greater degree of autonomy than community schools, for example, they are the employer of their staff, rather than the LA. They can be selective.

Special schools

Special schools have an expertise in areas of learning and SEN, for example, autism, MLD, SLD, emotional and behavioural difficulties, or physical disabilities and other categories of need. Some may be residential and have boarding facilities. You may be working in a Special School, or be part of a link or collaborative scheme between mainstream and Special Schools. The focus on inclusion views Special School staff as a resource for helping teachers in all schools to meet the needs of learners with SEN. Special schools should not be confused with 'specialist schools', which are mainstream schools with a curriculum area speciality.

Special units

Many schools have specialist units attached to them. These could be for learners with visual or hearing impairments, behavioural difficulties, physical disabilities, speech and language difficulties, or specific learning difficulties.

Pupil Referral Units (PRUs)

These are specialist referral units for pupils with emotional and behavioural difficulties. They are staffed by teachers and teaching assistants with specialist training. Pupils often spend short periods of time in PRUs before returning to mainstream schools with support from PRU staff.

Schools with a difference

These include:

- Academy. A school sponsored by a business community or voluntary organisation and run jointly with the LA.
- City Technology College (CTC). State funded but privately run with an emphasis on teaching technology.
- Grammar schools. Schools which select on the basis of academic ability.
- Faith schools. They incorporate more spiritual or religious elements

into the curriculum than other schools, and have a strong link with a church or other religious body.

- Networked Learning Communities. A group of schools that work together to pursue a common interest.
- Federation of schools. A group of schools that work together and are jointly governed.
- Leading Edge schools. Their practice is deemed to be excellent and a model for other schools. They are funded to share their skills with other schools.
- Specialist schools. Have a special focus on one of ten areas of expertise:business and enterprise, languages, sports, science, arts, technology, engineering, music, humanities, or maths and computing. They receive extra funds.
- Training school. A school where teachers receive Qualified Teacher Status (QTS) through on-the-job training.
- Full service school. This type of school aims for social inclusion and offers:
  - child care
  - study support
  - family and lifelong learning
  - health and social care
  - parenting support
  - sports and art facilities
  - ICT access.
- Extended school. Provides a variety of extra services all year round, including access to childcare from 8am-6pm, parenting and family support, referral to services such as speech and language therapy, or physiotherapy, community use of facilities such as sports or ICT, and varied activities such as music, sports or study support clubs.
- Trust school. A foundation school which sets itself up as a self-governing trust, enabling it to have the freedom to work with outside partners such as businesses, employ its own staff and set its own admission requirements. Has to have a parents council, where parents can express their views on the running of the school.
- Children's Centres. These provide a multi-agency service to meet the needs of children under five and their families. They offer integrated early learning, care, family support and health services, on the same site, where the focus is on the needs of the child and their family. They also offer outreach services to children and families who do not attend the Centre, as well as access to training and employment advice. They provide full day care from birth. An early years expert, who undertakes to complete the National Professional Qualification for Integrated Children's Centre Leaders (NPQICL), leads each Children's Centre.

More information on types of school is at www.direct.gov.uk.

Key reading

All of the following documents should be available in school:

- National Curriculum documents
- DfES Circulars
- Ofsted Evaluation Schedule.

You might also find the following websites useful:

- Teachers' site set up by the DfES: www.teachernet.gov.uk
- The main DfES site: www.dfes.gov.uk
- Ofsted: www.ofsted.gov.uk
- Qualifications and Curriculum Authority: www.qca.org.uk
- Training and Development Agency for Schools: www.tda.gov.uk

5 The National Curriculum

The National Curriculum was first introduced in 1988 by the Education Reform Act, in response to concern about the variation of teaching and learning in schools across the country. It was thought that a standard curriculum, which applied to the whole country, would give all children better access to a high level of education. It would also make it easier to ensure that what is taught in schools is appropriate for the needs of modern-day society.

Since then, the National Curriculum has been subject to several changes and is constantly evolving to ensure it is appropriate to our ever-changing society. In September 2000, a revised National Curriculum came into force and further changes continue to be made. The National Curriculum applies to all pupils aged 5–16 in State schools in England and Wales, and sets out their legal statutory entitlement to learning. It states what will be taught, sets out the required standards and indicates how these will be assessed and reported. Although independent schools do not have to follow the National Curriculum, in practice most of them are guided by its content. As a teaching assistant you will be working within the National Curriculum framework.

Aims and principles of the National Curriculum

The aims of the National Curriculum are:

- To provide opportunities for all pupils to learn and to achieve.
- To promote pupils' spiritual, moral, social and cultural development and prepare all pupils for the opportunities, responsibilities and experiences of life.

The key principles of the National Curriculum are the entitlement of all pupils and the inclusion of all pupils. When teachers are planning and teaching, they must take into account the following factors:

- To set suitable learning challenges.
- To provide for the diversity of pupils' needs.
- To overcome potential barriers to learning and assessment for individuals and groups of pupils, for example, to provide support for pupils with SEN, English as an additional language, or disabilities.

As we have seen in Chapter 1 under Inclusion, teaching assistants can play a vital role in all these areas to ensure all learners have equality of access to the curriculum. More detailed information on how you can do this is given throughout the remainder of this book.

National Curriculum terminology

The National Curriculum has its own terminology. It is arranged in Key Stages that relate to the age of the pupil, as shown below.

	Key stage 1	Key stage 2	Key stage 3	Key stage 4	
Age	5–7	7–11	11–14	14–16	
Year groups	1–2	3–6	7–9	10–11	
English	■	■	■	■	National Curriculum core subjects
Mathematics	■	■	■	■	
Science	■	■	■	■	
Design and technology	■	■	■		National Curriculum non-core foundation subjects
ICT	■	■	■	■	
History	■	■	■		
Geography	■	■	■		
Modern foreign languages			■	■	
Art and design	■	■	■		
Music	■	■	■		
Physical education	■	■	■	■	
Citizenship			■	■	

In Wales Welsh is also a core subject.

Each subject has its own colour-coded National Curriculum booklet, published by DfES and QCA, which sets out the legal and teaching requirements (DfEE/QCA, 1999).

Schools are also required to teach Personal, Social and Health Education (PSHE) and have a sex education policy. Sex Education is compulsory at Key Stages 3 and 4 and Careers Education and Work-based Learning at Key Stage 4, but are not part of the National Curriculum. Similarly, although Religious Education is not a National Curriculum subject, schools have a legal requirement to teach it at all Key Stages. Religious Education is therefore taught through a locally-agreed syllabus to cater for the individual nature of faith-based schools. All schools must have a daily act of collective worship. Most schools do this in an assembly, which is also an important part of the school communication system. Schools at Key Stage 2 are also encouraged to offer modern foreign languages. Your school will have copies of the National Curriculum documents, or you can obtain your own from QCA (www.qca.org.uk) or via the National Curriculum Online website (www.nc.uk.net).

Each subject and Key Stage has its own programme of study that sets out:

- Knowledge, skills and understanding – what has to be taught in the subject during the Key Stage.
- Breadth of study – the context, activities, areas of study and range of experiences through which the knowledge, skills and understanding should be taught.

From the programme of study, teachers develop their own schemes of work, often combining with their colleagues to produce a school scheme of work for a year or Key Stage. This is translated into practical teaching plans and lessons.

All National Curriculum subjects have attainment targets, which set out the "knowledge, skills and understanding that pupils of different abilities and maturities are expected to have by the end of each Key Stage" (Education Act, 1996). For example, the Mathematics curriculum includes MA3: Shape, Space, and Measures, and MA4: Handling Data, and the Science curriculum includes SC1: Scientific Enquiry, and SC4: Physical Processes.

Each attainment target consists of eight level descriptions of increasing difficulty, with an extra level for exceptional performance. Level descriptions provide the basis for teachers to make judgements about pupil performance at the end of Key Stages 1, 2 and 3. Pupils sit Standard Assessment Tests (SATs) at the end of each Key Stage. At the end of Key Stage 4, national examinations (GCSE) are taken. Children working below Level 1 are now assessed against eight 'P' levels in each curriculum area, which break attainment down even further. P levels are used in both special and mainstream schools (QCA, 2003).

Range of levels within which the great majority of pupils are expected to work		Expected attainment for the majority of pupils at the end of the Key Stage	
Key stage 1	1–3	at age 7	2
Key stage 1	2–5	at age 11	4
Key stage 1	3–7	at age 14	5/6

(Source: www.nc.uk.net)

It takes a long time to get to know the National Curriculum in detail. As a teaching assistant you could be working with learners in many different areas of the curriculum and at a variety of levels. Becoming confident in every aspect of the curriculum will take a while, so use the National Curriculum booklets as reference books and look up what you need to know. You will become more familiar with the documents as you work with them. However, you should always make an effort to know how the teaching and learning activity you are involved in fits into the overall framework of the curriculum and which level the children you support are working towards. You will increase your subject knowledge as you work with learners.

Working across curriculum areas is also a very effective strategy. If you reinforce literacy during history and teach mathematics during science, it is a valuable and interesting way to allow children to apply their learning and to practise skills and concepts. The key areas shown below should also be promoted by working across the curriculum:

- spiritual, moral, social and cultural development
- personal, social and health education (PSHE)
- skills development
- financial capability, enterprise education and education for sustainable development.

(DfEE/QCA, 1999)

Remember that the National Curriculum sets out the *minimum* entitlement for learners. Most schools will not restrict themselves just to the National Curriculum content and will have a focus on other areas of interest too, depending on the local community and the culture and ethos of the school.

Primary Strategy

Although the National Curriculum initially played an important part in raising standards in schools, there were still concerns about the ability of pupils leaving school to read, write and use mathematics effectively. In response to this, in 1998 the government introduced the National Literacy Strategy into Primary schools. This set out a novel and detailed approach to the teaching of literacy, and included a framework of teaching objectives and the provision of a highly structured daily lesson, known as the Literacy Hour. This was followed a year later by the National Numeracy Strategy, which had a similar structure and focused on Mathematics. Although schools did not have to follow these if they already had successful strategies of their own, in practice, most did so. An approximate breakdown of how the Literacy and Numeracy Hours were structured is shown overleaf.

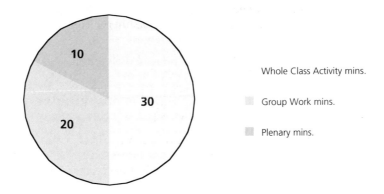

Whole Class Activity mins.

Group Work mins.

Plenary mins.

Breakdown of the original structure of the Primary Strategy: Literacy Hour and Daily Mathematics lesson

The National Literacy Strategy and National Numeracy Strategy are now subsumed into a single Primary National Strategy (NPS), and this is the term that you will encounter.

Following concerns about the prescriptive nature of these strategies and the heavy emphasis on literacy and numeracy lessons, the DfES updated the Primary Framework in autumn 2006 (DfES, 2006). Schools are now encouraged to be more flexible and adaptable than before in their approach to the teaching of literacy and numeracy, building on the following government initiatives:

- Excellence and Enjoyment. This government strategy for Primary Schools (DfES, 2003) stresses pupils' need for a 'rich and exciting' experience of learning. It calls on schools to be creative and innovative, using their own characteristics to take ownership of the curriculum and to design an individual approach to the use of the Primary Strategy materials.
- *ARTS Alive!* A website which is the outcome of a QCA project to identify ways in which the contribution of the arts to pupils' education can be extended. Designed for use by headteachers, arts subject leaders, school governing bodies and arts practitioners, the site invites schools to contribute their own work so that other schools can benefit (QCA, 2003, http://www.qca.org.uk/artsalive/).
- *All Our Futures* (September 2000). Guidance to schools on developing creative and cultural education across the curriculum. (http://www.artscampaign.org.uk/campaigns/education/futures.pdf).
- *Speaking and Listening Initiative at Key Stage 1 and 2* (November 2003).

Catch-up programmes

A range of intervention programmes for primary schools have been introduced because some children require extra support and help to catch up with their peer group in literacy and numeracy. These programmes are designed for teaching assistants to deliver to small groups of children. For literacy they are:

- Additional Literacy Support (ALS) for children in Year 3 and 4.
- Early Literacy Support (ELS) for children in Year 1.
- Further Literacy Support (FLS) for children in Year 5.

Each of the above programmes are highly structured and are based on the framework for the Literacy Strategy. The programmes include:

- all the practical support materials
- teachers' guidebooks
- teaching assistants' guidebooks
- audio visual material.

There are similar intervention programmes for numeracy, Springboards 3–6. These are intended for children in Years 3 to 6 (hence the numbers in the title) who have not reached the expected level in mathematics, but who might be able to do so with extra support. Springboard is carefully structured, and is based closely on the framework for the Mathematics Strategy.

If you are working with these programmes, you will be familiar with the content. If you are asked to implement them, make sure you request training so that you are confident about their content and underlying concepts. You will then be able to teach effectively rather than just read a script. Teaching assistants have made a major contribution to helping children to improve their literacy and numeracy skills by professional and imaginative implementation of these initiatives.

Curriculum enhancement

Recent DfES policy has been to emphasise that schools do have a tremendous amount of freedom in how they deliver the curriculum and to encourage them to use their own expertise and individual character to develop their own interpretation. Guidance to primary schools has encouraged them to allow teachers flexibility in deciding:

- how much depth they should go into
- how long to spend on each subject
- how to arrange their day, grouping subjects and working across the curriculum if necessary
- how to use programmes of study from other Key Stages as required, and using a remodelled workforce to deliver the curriculum.

(DfES, 2003)

Key Stage 3 Strategy

In 2001, the concept embedded in the National Literacy and Numeracy Strategies of a structured programme with a formal taught lesson procedure and associated catch-up programmes was extended to Key Stage 3. The objective of this is to raise the standard of achievement of 11–14-year-olds (http://www.standards.dfes.gov.uk/keystage3/).

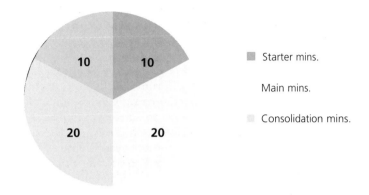

Starter mins.

Main mins.

Consolidation mins.

Breakdown of the structure of Key Stage 3 Strategy lesson

Although initially introduced with English and Maths in 2001, the scheme was extended the following year to science, ICT and the foundation subjects. The strategy also has a focus on supporting pupils with SEN. Working within the National Curriculum framework for each subject, it has an emphasis on whole class interactive teaching. Once again teaching assistants have a huge role to play in the implementation of this strategy.

Catch-up programmes for use with small groups

The catch-up programmes listed below should be available in school, or can be accessed through the DfES website (www.dfes.gov.uk):

- Springboard for Mathematics, Years 7–9
- Literacy Progress Units (LPU)
- Science Booster Kit, Years 7–9

The Foundation Stage

Children between the ages of 3 and 5 are said to be at the Foundation Stage of learning and have a separate programme that gives them the building blocks for successful transition to Year 1 and the National Curriculum. The Foundation Stage curriculum is laid down by QCA, and gives guidance to teachers in planning and delivering lessons. It applies to Early Years settings, Nurseries and Reception classes.

Principles of the Foundation Stage include learning through play, an emphasis on early recognition of special needs and early intervention programmes, supporting children with English as an additional language, and partnership with parents/carers.

Six areas of learning and development are identified:

- Personal, social and emotional development
- Communication, language and literacy
- Mathematical development
- Knowledge and understanding of the world
- Physical development
- Creative development.

Each area of learning has a set of related Early Learning Goals (ELGs), which children work towards. There is clear recognition that children will develop at different speeds and reach the goals at different times, so each Early Learning Goal is underpinned by Stepping Stones. These give guidance to Early Years practitioners on a child's progress towards the ELG. Children in Nursery education and Reception classes are working towards ELGs. At the end of this stage, a First Profile assessment, or Foundation Stage Profile, is completed for each child. This gives a profile or baseline assessment of the child's attainment and progress.

The 14-19 curriculum (Key Stage 4 and transition to post-compulsory education)

Major changes that have taken place in recent years in the 14–19 Curriculum mean that students at Key Stage 4 are offered a more flexible and personalised approach to learning. The education of students in schools and colleges used to be funded by separate bodies, but in 2001 all funding for 16–19 year olds was transferred to the Learning and Skills Council (LSC). Further Education colleges and other providers are also involved in delivering successful vocational qualifications for students below the age of 16 who find work-related study or a college environment more relevant and motivating.

At this level, most students are following a curriculum of their choice, using individual qualifications like AS levels, vocational qualifications, or a mixture of both. There is now an emphasis in the 14-19 curriculum on:

- work-related learning
- a smaller science curriculum, including scientific literacy (learning about scientific concepts and issues in the context of everyday modern life)
- entitlement to study in one area of arts, design and technology, humanities, or a modern foreign language, leading to a recognised qualification.

This new curriculum is intended to provide a more flexible approach to learning, which is still broad and balanced, but offers students more choice by collaboration and partnership with other organisations. The government objectives for 14-19 are to:

- secure the basics – literacy and numeracy

- stretch every pupil to their full potential
- offer a high-quality vocational route
- re-motivate the disengaged
- prepare all young people for the world of work.

(DfES, 2005)

By 2008 students should be able to study for specialist vocational diplomas. There is more information on this at www.teachernet.co.uk or www.DfES.gov.uk/14-19gateway.

At this level, most students are following a curriculum of their choice, using individual qualifications like AS levels, vocational qualifications, or a mixture of both. There are proposals to make further changes in this area to give a more flexible approach for 14–16-year-olds. It is proposed that the statutory requirements will be:

- a small core of compulsory subjects: English, Mathematics, Science and ICT
- compulsory areas of learning: Physical Education, Citizenship, Religious Education, work-related learning, careers education and sex education
- entitlement areas: modern foreign languages, Design and Technology, the arts and the humanities.

(DfES, 2002)

Key Skills

The core skills that run throughout both the National Curriculum and the 14–19 curriculum are referred to as Key Skills. These are:

- Communication, including speaking, listening, reading and writing.
- Application of Number – the use of mathematics.
- Information Technology – using ICT, decision-making and creative thinking.
- Working with others – collaboration and cooperation.
- Improving own learning and performance – self-improvement and reflection.
- Problem solving – thinking skills.

Students can show evidence of these from their work in any area of the curriculum. You will probably have to do so yourself if you are studying for a qualification.

Parents and the curriculum

It is well recognised that parental interest and involvement in their children's education can have a big impact on their progress in school. The DfES has a website at www.parentcentre.gov.uk which provides information on parenting and education, including the curriculum.

Curriculum changes for the future

In keeping with the pace of change in society the curriculum is constantly reviewed and updated, always following consultation. During 2006 the Foundation Stage curriculum, Key Stage 3 Strategy and Primary Strategy were all subject to consultation. As a result, proposals were tabled for changing KS3 that include:

- a history curriculum that emphasises the place of the British Empire in world history

- swimming to be dropped from the PE curriculum and replaced by an emphasis on personal fitness and exercise

- the inclusion of the history and purpose of mathematical study and thinking

- a new emphasis on inclusion and diversity in modern society as part of citizenship.

The ten-year childcare strategy (DfES, 2004) sets out to ensure that every child has the best start in life, and as part of this a new Early Years Foundation Stage curriculum for all children in early years settings will be launched in 2008, covering care, learning and development from birth to age five.

Examples of National Curriculum work

The government website, National Curriculum in Action, includes examples of pupils' work deriving from the programmes of study. You can browse these online at www.ncinaction.org.uk.

Personalised learning

The move away from a very structured and prescriptive curriculum and the increased flexibility and choice offered to pupils are all part of a drive towards schools providing more personalised learning. According to this philosophy, schools and other educational settings need to tailor learning to the needs, aptitudes and interests of all pupils to enable them to reach their potential. Teaching assistants and other support staff have a vital role to play in helping to remove barriers to achievement and ensuring that all learners have a relevant and supportive learning environment to meet their needs.

Key reading

Cable, C. & Eyres, I. (eds.) (2006) *Primary TAs Curriculum in Context*, London: David Fulton

Moon, B. (2001) *A Guide to the National Curriculum*, Oxford: Oxford University Press

Riley, J. (2003) *Learning in the Early Years*, London: PCP *[Review of Early Years curriculum.]*

All of the following documents should be available in school.

* National Curriculum documents
* DfES Circulars
* Ofsted Evaluation Schedule

You might also find the following websites useful:

* Teachers' site set up by the DfES: www.teachernet.gov.uk
* The main DfES site: www.dfes.gov.uk
* Ofsted: www.ofsted.gov.uk
* Qualifications and Curriculum Authority: www.qca.org.uk
* Teaching Training Agency: www.tta.gov.uk
* Standards: www.standards.dfes.gov.uk
* National Curriculum: www.nc.uk.net

There are numerous resources for supporting the curriculum. Virtually every schools publisher produces lesson plans and materials that can be used or adapted by teachers and teaching assistants. There are also many websites that have downloadable lesson plans and work schemes.

References

Key references are given in bold.

DfEE (1998) *The National Curriculum: Handbook for Primary Teachers in England, Key Stages 1 and 2*, London: DfEE/QCA

DfEE (1998) *The National Curriculum: Handbook for Secondary Teachers in England, Key Stages 3 and 4*, London: DfEE/QCA

National Curriculum Documents (1999) London

DfES (2002) *14–19 Extending Opportunities, Raising Standards*, London: DfES/0744/2002

DfES (2002) *Designing and Timetabling the Primary Curriculum. A Practical Guide for Key Stages 1 and 2*, London: DfES

DfES (2003) *Excellence and Enjoyment: A Strategy for Primary Schools*, London: DfES/0377/2003 *[DfES vision for primary schools – to combine excellence in teaching with enjoyment of learning. Schools are encouraged to be creative and innovative.]*

DfES (2003) *Speaking, Listening, Learning: Working with Children in KS 1 and 2*, London: DfES 0627-2003 *[Learning objectives and teaching activities to support the development of speaking, listening and learning at Key Stages 1 and 2.]*

DfES (2004) *Choice for Parents, the Best Start for Children*, London: DfES

DfES (2005), *14-19 Education and Skills*, White Paper, London: DfES 1268-2005DCL-EN. Available at http://www.DfES.gov.uk/14-19 gateway

NERF (2006) *Involving Parents in Their Children's Learning*, Bulletin 5, available at www.nerf-uk.org

QCA (2001) *Planning, Teaching and Assessing the Curriculum for Pupils with Learning Difficulties*, London: QCA

QCA (2003) *Foundation Stage Profile Handbook,* London: QCA/03/1006

www.connexions.gov.uk
http://www.artscampaign.org.uk/campaigns/education/futures.pdf
http://www.qca.org.uk/artsalive
http://www.standards.dfes.gov.uk/keystage3/

6 The nature of learning

Whenever you work with children in school you will be concentrating on their ability to learn. But what do we mean by learning? The normal definition of learning is that there is some permanent, recognisable change in a person's behaviour: either they can do something that they couldn't do before, or they understand a concept or make a connection that they didn't before. We often say of someone "they never learn" when we mean that "they never change or move on".

The whole concept of children and learning is a very complex one. Over the centuries people have studied, experimented and written a great deal about how we learn. Theories have been put forward that have influenced the way schools were run and children were taught. These theories have then been challenged or amended by further research. Today, medical technology makes it possible to scan a person's brain whilst they are completing an activity or task, providing us with further exciting insights into the way children and adults learn.

As a classroom practitioner, you will be working in a stimulating and dynamic environment that is constantly changing because of our ability to adapt and improve our teaching methods and styles to take into account new knowledge.

Working in school with children and watching them learn, together with trying out new ideas and observing and evaluating their success, is what makes teaching such a stimulating and interesting profession. As a teaching assistant, you have a wonderful opportunity to be at the forefront of educational research in the classroom and can add to our knowledge of how children learn by your own observation and practice.

This chapter reviews some of the major theories about learning. Keep them in mind when you are working in the classroom and use them as a starting point for your own thinking. Look for examples in school practice that support them and also for evidence that argues against them. Remember, your opinions and viewpoints are just as valid as anyone else's – provided they are based on real evidence!

Individual differences/differentiation/ personalised learning

Although there are similarities in the ways that human beings develop and learn, there are also subtle differences. Consider this analogy: we all have a nose and eyes, yet everyone looks different because of their inherited characteristics and, perhaps, the way they use jewellery and make up (and plastic surgery!). We are beginning to realise that there are also subtle differences in the way people learn and, to make teaching more effective, we need to take these differences into account and plan teaching programmes accordingly. It is no longer effective to just teach the same thing in the same way and hope for the best!

In an inclusive school there will be learners who have considerable differences in the way they learn, because of learning difficulties and disabilities, social problems, gaps in their knowledge or because English is not their first language. It is then even more important that the way they learn is taken into account and used to make teaching and learning effective. Because of this, the concept of *differentiation* is built into the National Curriculum, and is a key part of the way we meet the needs of every learner in the classroom. This concept of individual differences needs to be at the heart of your practice in the classroom. It is part of personalised learning, using effective teaching and learning to meet the needs of all pupils.

How children develop and learn

Physical, Social, Emotional and Cognitive Development

Throughout childhood, children develop physically, socially, emotionally and cognitively. Although the full details of these are outside the scope of this book, you can use any book on child development or psychology to look up the general expectations of development for the age group you are working with.

- Physical development – motor skills, perceptual development, maturation.
- Social development – relationships with parents, peer group and adults.
- Emotional development – ability to understand and regulate emotions.
- Cognitive development – the development of mental processing.

Although rapid physical development takes place in childhood and teenage years, it is now recognised that all development is a life-long process and childhood, adolescence and adulthood are all important stages for the development of learning, thinking and behaviour.

Children follow a similar timetable for development, which roughly approximates to age ranges, but this is rarely a smooth, continuous process. It varies from child to child. Just as some children go from sitting to walking comparatively quickly and others spend a long time in the crawling phase, children will have differing patterns of development. Sometimes they may appear to be 'stuck' at a certain stage of development and other times they will make more rapid progress.

> **Key Stage 4 Observation:** "Sometimes the boys seem to go through a rapid physical growth spurt and become gangly and uncoordinated. They are always crashing into things – almost as if their body is bigger than their brain thinks it is! Then, when they come back in the sixth form, they seem to have matured and their brain has caught up with their body."

What influences the way children follow this pattern of development? Is it their genetic makeup, inherited through their biological family, or is it due to their experiences in their environment? Opinion has changed over the years. In Victorian times it was thought that children were 'blank slates' whose characters developed in response to their environment. The thinking then changed to the idea that everyone has an unchangeable genetic inheritance, and finally to our present understanding, which sees development as a complex interaction between genetics and experience, or *nature* and *nurture*. A review of some of the theories of learning and approaches to learning gives an idea of the complexity of the issues involved.

Some theories of how children learn

Behaviourism

The behaviourist approach is based on the study of observable learning. Much of the original research was conducted on animals by researchers such as Thorndike (1898), Pavlov (1927) and Skinner (1953).

E L Thorndike

Thorndike, an American psychologist working at the end of the 19th and beginning of the 20th century, put forward the idea that learning (a change in behaviour) is the result of a person's response to events that take place. His studies of hungry cats and the way that they learned to escape from a box and find food were the basis for his theory that actions which are followed by a reward are more likely to recur. Once the cats had learned how to escape and get the reward of food they were able to repeat the behaviour again and again.

I Pavlov

Pavlov was a Russian physiologist who studied the digestive system of dogs in the early years of the twentieth century. As a by-product of his research, he made some discoveries about the way animals learn which became the basis for theories of *Conditioned Learning*. He noticed that when dogs saw food they salivated in readiness for eating. He conducted experiments where he rang a bell before he presented the food. He then rang the bell without showing the food. He found that even though the dogs couldn't see food, they salivated in anticipation. He reasoned that the dogs' initial response to the food was a reflex, but the dogs had learned to associate the bell with the food and their response to the bell was learned behaviour, conditioned by the actions he had taken. His ideas are very relevant in school today. Children have learned behaviour, based on what has happened to them in their lives so far.

B F Skinner

Skinner extended and refined Thorndike and Pavlov's theories through his studies of rats. He looked at how rats were able to learn to press a lever in their cage to produce a food pellet. He found that there were three crucial factors that affected the way the rats learned to press the lever:

- Positive reinforcement – the use of rewards.
- Punishment – the use of an unpleasant consequence.
- Negative reinforcement – the removal of an unpleasant consequence.

Skinner applied his findings to the concept of human learning and developed the theory of *Operant Conditioning* – that behaviour is influenced by its consequences. It is called 'operant' because the rat produced a consequence by operating on its environment. You will be able to identify many of his ideas still being used in the classroom today in the way children are motivated and taught. There are several key features of operant conditioning:

- Behaviour/learning that is positively reinforced will recur. It is even more effective when the behaviour is only reinforced now and again. There are many ways in which learning/behaviour is reinforced in school, from a quiet word of praise to the award of stickers, marks for work, merit points, badges, golden time, names on the 'proud cloud', special mention in assembly and many others. You will be able to think of many examples from your own school. Some Key Stage 3/4 schools have complex reward programmes in conjunction with business partnerships, which involve earning tokens for CDs or fast food meals. Skinner's research also showed that reinforcement was most successful when it was intermittent. You will find that if you praise or reward children indiscriminately the effectiveness decreases, so it is important to be realistic and appropriate when you do offer praise and rewards.
- The use of punishment leads to a decrease in the behaviour. At one time, schools used draconian forms of punishment like caning. Nowadays, we use the word 'sanctions' to refer to the punishments that a school will have. These can range from a quiet look or word of disapproval to names on the board, withdrawal of privileges like going out to play or to football club, time out, letters home to parents, or suspension and expulsion.
- Negative reinforcement is when an unpleasant stimulus is removed – this leads to an increase in the behaviour. A child who finds the classroom environment noisy or threatening may well learn better in a quiet corridor with a teaching assistant. They may therefore unconsciously continue to behave in a way that means they have to receive extra help.

> **Key Stage 2:** "I was working with a Year 5 child on a structured language pro-
> gramme. Every week we used to go into a quiet room by the library to work. He
> made really good progress and I praised him and kept telling him that soon he would
> be good enough to go back into class. It was really frustrating because he would do
> well and then slip back again. We thought he had a real problem with his memory.
> We tried changing the programmes but nothing seemed to work. Then I suddenly
> realised that he didn't want to go back into class. His reward was being outside one-
> to-one! Subconsciously it stopped him making that final progress."

- Shaping can be used to encourage the learning/behaviour that is desired. This is one of the key elements of teaching to targets or small steps approaches. If information is presented in small chunks the response is reinforced each time, then eventually the desired result will be reached. You can see this in the way children learn to write. When they first enter school their mark making and copying is rewarded and by the end of Key Stage 4 we are rewarding them for writing a well-argued essay. During that time a constant process of shaping has taken place. It is also apparent in many of the programmed learning schemes that are found in school, like the 'Attack' spelling/writing programme, where skills are broken down into chunks, taught and then reinforced.
- Reinforcements can be generalised to encourage similar types of learning/ behaviour. An example of this is that once you learn to stand still when a whistle blows, you will be likely to do so whenever you hear one. So, for example, if pupils are encouraged to learn study skills and these are reinforced, they should be able to use them in other situations, not just in a study skills class.

Behaviourism has had a huge influence on teaching and learning. You will be looking at behaviourism again, as part of behaviour management, in Chapter 14.

Skinner attempted to explain many human behaviours and cognitive processes only through the idea of conditioned learning. He did not look at the development of any higher order thinking skills and did not consider the developmental approach to learning. For example, he thought that children acquired spoken language through conditioned learning. However, in the years since he did his research it has become clear that the process by which children learn to speak is far more complex than that. However, Skinner himself did not consider operant conditioning to be a theory of learning but more of an approach to learning. The focus was on how the child and the environment interacted and the history of learning reinforcement that had taken place. Behaviourists argued that if behaviour is learned, then it can be unlearned in the same way.

Cognitive learning

The study of cognitive development looks at how children learn to gather, process and use information in order to know and understand.

The most significant researcher in this field was Jean Piaget, a Swiss biologist and psychologist, who formulated a theory of cognitive development from infancy to adulthood.

Piaget began by studying his own children's development and then moved to looking at other children's development in laboratory studies. The most important features of his theory are:

- Children do not just learn more facts as they get older. They move cognitively through a developmental timetable that relates to appropriate age ranges.
- Children have qualitatively different ways of thinking and reasoning at each different stage of this timetable.
- Children's thinking becomes increasingly more complex as they move through this ordered sequence of stages.
- Learning is a result of a child's *active* role in constructing meanings as they interact with their environment.
- Teachers and adults can help children to construct these meanings by guiding, helping them, offering learning experiences and using language to explain.

Schemas

Piaget described the way children organise, construct and develop their thinking through schemas. These are mental constructs or patterns of thought that become increasingly sophisticated as they develop. Piaget thought that children changed their mental constructs or schemas to make sense of experience after a process of cognitive conflict or disequilibrium. Teachers use disequilibrium to challenge children's thinking. Children use assimilation and accommodation to adapt their thinking and to restore equilibrium.

- Assimilation is incorporating new ideas and experiences into an already existing schema or pattern of thought.
- Accommodation is adapting or changing a pattern of thought to be able to accommodate new information.

Assimilation and accommodation can be thought of in these very simple terms: You have a filing cabinet with separate folders for your bank statements, car insurance, credit cards and so on. When a new bank statement arrives, you simply make room for it in the appropriate folder. This is assimilation. However, if you have a new experience, like making a holiday booking, you will need to open (or create) a brand new folder to put that information into. This is accommodation.

Piaget's stages of cognitive development

Piaget thought that children went through stages as they developed their thinking (cognitive) processes.

Stage	Approx age	Title	Stage of learning
1	0–2	Sensory Motor	1. Babies use their senses (sight, hearing, touch, smell, taste, physical movement) to explore their environment. They are focused on sensory and motor experiences, like sucking objects. 2. They learn from trying out and repeating actions. 3. They are egocentric and see the world as revolving around them. At 8 months old, they develop object permanence – the idea that even if they can't see something or someone, it still exists.
2	2–7	Pre-operational	1. Children can use language to express their thinking. 2. They can use symbols to stand for something (e.g. a cardboard box as a play boat). 3. They believe that non-living things and animals have human feelings – animism (e.g. toys might come alive at night). 4. They remain egocentric and unable to take account of another point of view. 5. They focus on the appearance and look of items.
3	7–11	Concrete operational	1. Children can see things from someone else's point of view. 2. They can deal with several different things at the same time – can classify and order material. 3. They can use some abstract symbols (e.g. + and – signs). 4. They still need 'concrete' items like counters or blocks to help them solve problems. 5. They can conserve numbers or amounts and understand that amounts stay the same when arranged differently.
4	11–18	Formal operational	1. Children can use formal problem-solving methods such as hypotheses and deduction, rather than trial and error. 2. They can think in an abstract way (e.g. manipulate ideas or understand concepts like democracy). 3. They can understand morality from a realistic point of view and understand the difference between intention and action. 4. Their thinking becomes more flexible.

Piaget's tasks

Piaget and his researchers used several tasks to examine the way children think and behave:

Object Permanence Show babies a bright attractive object then hide it behind a cushion. Before 7 months they will lose interest in it. After that, they will expect to see it return and look for it eagerly.

Centration If children are given 18 brown beads and two white beads, all of which are wooden, and asked if there are more brown beads than wooden beads, they say 'more brown beads'.

Conservation The experimenter shows two equal sized balls of clay. The balls are rolled out so that one is longer than the other. The child thinks that the longer ball has more clay.

You can try these out for yourself with children in school or at home.

Criticisms of Piaget's theory

Margaret Donaldson suggested that Piaget had not considered the context that the children were asked to do the tasks in. She thought that the setting for the testing was too formal and that the children were trying to answer the questions within the adult's frame of reference, rather than their own. When children were given tasks in a more 'meaningful' context, they could complete them perfectly well.

James McGarrigle suggested that Piaget understated the importance of language in the experiments. He found that when the questions were phrased differently, children could complete the tasks without any problem (Donaldson, 1979).

Piaget thought that some children might never reach the Formal Operational stage of thinking, but he did not fully explore the idea that children would move through the ages at different speeds. Some educationalists have interpreted his work by suggesting there are stages of 'readiness' for learning and teachers should wait for this readiness before they move children on. This has led to a rigid approach to age-related learning that may have underestimated children's abilities and not been beneficial to all learners.

You may want to look in more detail at Piaget's theory and the criticisms of it by looking at books on child development or *Wood's Review of How Children Think and Learn* (Oates, 1999; Wood, 1998). Piaget is known as a 'constructivist' because of his ideas about the way children construct their thinking. We try to make learning an active process for children because of his ideas.

Vygotsky

Vygotsky was a Russian scientist who died in 1934 but whose work was translated into English in the '60s and '70s. It was at this time that he became influential in our understanding of the way children think and learn.

Vygotsky had similar ideas to Piaget about the way children move through cognitive development stages. The difference was that

Vygotsky placed far more emphasis on the role of the child's social environment and the importance of adult interaction and help in learning. He saw learning as a social process rather than an individual one.

Several basic themes emerged in Vygotsky's research:

- Social interaction and communication within cultures play a big part in the way children develop and extend their cognitive processes. Family, peers, teachers and friends give help, guidance and instruction to children, within their own cultural framework.
- All learners have a *Zone of Proximal Development* (ZPD), which is the difference or gap between what they can do alone and unaided and what they are able to achieve with the help of an adult or capable peer. A sensitive and knowledgeable adult or peer can guide and support a child by giving them the right help so that they can eventually complete the learning task alone. In this way, the child does not just have a cognitive readiness to learn, but a potential, based on the assistance available at the time.
- Learners use language to explore, extend and confirm their thinking about concepts and ideas. Unlike Piaget, Vygotsky saw the role of language as central in the way children construct meaning. As they grow, children's external speech becomes an inner train of thought, which enables them to extend their conceptual thinking and understanding.
- Children's development is influenced by the cultural and social norms of their families and society.

(Adapted from Vygotsky, 1978)

Vygotsky's research has placed more focus and emphasis on the learner as an apprentice and on the role of the helping adult or peer in the classroom. As an informed and expert adult, the teaching assistant has a vital role in the cultural transmission of knowledge, skills and concepts. The ability to check where a child is in their thinking and learning and move them on to the next stage is a key part of this. Helping them also requires a high level of skill. Giving them too much help may stop them deepening their own understanding; not giving them enough help means they may become demotivated and confused.

Some of Vygotsky's ideas are used extensively in the support of children with SEN, through individualised intervention programmes. For example, *Reading Recovery* uses a highly structured system delivered with intensive adult support. Vygotsky is known as a 'social constructivist' because of his belief in the importance of social interaction in the way children construct meaning.

Bruner

Jerome Bruner is an American psychologist whose research has built on the ideas of Piaget and Vygotsky. However, Bruner had some fundamental disagreements with Piaget's concept of age-related critical periods for learning. Bruner accepted that learning is an active process and agreed with Vygotsky that the role of both language and interaction with others is crucial, but argued that the way that new information is presented to learners is a vital factor in how children learn. He thought that anything could be taught to a child at any stage of development, providing it was structured and presented at the right level and in the right way.

Scaffolding and learning

Bruner emphasised the importance of scaffolding in learning. Building on Vygotsky's ideas of the importance of expert help, he envisaged the idea of adults making a 'scaffold' or support system for children to help them develop their thinking and reasoning. The teacher or peer helps the learner with tasks that are just beyond their current capability, while allowing them to do as much as possible on their own. The scaffold, or help, can then be gradually removed to help the child complete a task unaided.

As you work with children in the classroom, consider the scaffolding you are helping to make for them and how you can move them on to the next level of thinking by your support.

Modes of representation

Bruner described three ways that people show their understanding:

- Enactive – through doing and through movement.
- Iconic – through the use of images and pictures.
- Symbolic – through the use of symbolic representation.

The above modes of representation can be illustrated by the example of a child learning to add.

- In the *Enactive* phase, a child would use apples to count.
- In the *Iconic* phase, a child would be able to use a picture of apples.
- In the *Symbolic* phase, a child would be able to use numbers and the addition symbol or algebra.

Bruner's ideas have been reflected in the way we try to give children hands-on active experience of learning when they are introduced to new concepts. Adults will still use the enactive phase when they are learning something new. Anyone who has tried to master a computer will understand that practical experience is the only way to learn. When you are working with learners in the classroom, you need to use every opportunity to support them with concrete examples and apparatus. This is particularly important when they are in the early stages of learning, or when they are having difficulty understanding and retaining a concept.

Spiral curriculum

Bruner investigated the idea that learners revisit topics and concepts at different times in their school life, developing a greater depth of learning and understanding each time. He called this the *spiral curriculum*. For example, at Key Stage 1 children may study the Gunpowder Plot as a commemorative day, focusing on fireworks and bonfires. At Key Stage 4 they may study it again as a part of the political and religious complexities of the early 17th century. However, critics of this method say it is more effective for learners to study a concept or subject in a real depth to begin with, using a project approach.

It is important to help learners to focus on the opportunities for learning and the learning outcomes desired in each lesson, rather than just the subject matter. Bruner is referred to as a 'social constructivist' because of his belief that learning is an active process that needs structure and support from adults or peers. Both Bruner and Vygotsky's ideas are represented in the catch-up programmes used at Key Stages 1–3 to support children's learning.

Bandura – social and cognitive learning

Albert Bandura's theory of social learning has its roots in behaviourism but because he considered the effect of a learner's perceptions on their behaviour, he is also seen as an important figure in the cognitive psychology movement. He undertook some key research into aggression that enabled him to suggest how adults and children learn.

Bandura's experiment – the Bobo doll

Bandura used a Bobo doll – a toy with a weighted bottom that meant it would bob back up again when it was hit. He filmed one of his students hitting the doll repeatedly and shouting aggressively and then showed the film to children. He then left the children in the room with the Bobo doll. He found that the children copied the researcher's behaviour by hitting the doll and shouting. He carried out other experiments in which the researcher was also rewarded for hitting the doll.

From these and further experiments, Bandura formulated his theory of Social or Observational Learning – that children learn by imitating and modelling the behaviour of others. Later he refined his theory to show that:

- Children learn through a combination of imitation and reinforcement.
- Children are more likely to copy the behaviour of someone they admire.
- Children are more likely to copy a behaviour if it has an outcome they value.
- Children are motivated by:
  - past reinforcement
  - promised reinforcement at some time in the future
  - vicarious reinforcement – seeing someone else rewarded for the required behaviour.

These ideas have become a powerful part of our classroom practice. Some examples of the use of observational/social learning in the classroom are given below.

- The Primary Strategy includes many opportunities for teachers and teaching assistants to model learning and learning behaviours when children are learning literacy and numeracy.

- Classroom management strategies that include praise for pupils who are working well rather than those who are not, and a focus on examples of successfully completed work.
- Peer tutoring and assessment, where pupils work together to learn and assess each other's work, is being used more and more, particularly at Key Stages 2–4.

Bandura's theories can help to explain why some children who have been very good at learning socially from adults in early childhood, become more difficult as they get older. As a natural consequence of adolescence, the influence of their friends and peer group becomes more important and they transfer their social learning compliance to them. Sometimes they can become too reliant on approval from a peer group with negative attributes, or who think learning is irrelevant or 'uncool'.

Reciprocal interaction

Bandura argued that a person and their environment affect each other in a continuous loop. So, as the environment affects a child, so the behaviour of the child will in turn affect the environment. This is a key finding for anyone involved in classroom practice and contributes to our understanding of the classroom as a social learning environment.

> "My teacher is very much into creative writing and she is really inspirational. We have a writer's corner, a writing chair, and the classroom is full resources and materials. The children write plays, stories and book reviews. We are always reading and imagining. Everything they do is on the wall or read out. The children love to write, even the ones with difficulties."

The importance of play

Both Piaget and Vygotsky believed that play was an important part of the cognitive development of young children, an opportunity to learn new skills and explore and model behaviour patterns. This is well recognised in the Foundation Stage curriculum, where learning through play has a key role.

Whether it is structured or free, play isn't just relevant in the development of young children. It is an essential part of the activities of older children and adults. Anyone who observes break time in a Key Stage 3 and 4 school can witness the complexities of play time behaviour from impromptu football games to card games or complicated rule-based activities, made up by individual groups of children. What changes as children grow is the type of play they are involved with.

Many researchers have noted the importance of symbolic play in early childhood, from pretending a stick is a sword to dressing up and playing shops. Schools develop this by having stimulating role-play corners that offer a variety of imaginative experiences to children at Key Stage 1. Sara Smilansky (1968) emphasised the importance of the role of a sensitive adult in this socio-dramatic play, to extend the thinking and development of children while they are playing by suggesting activities and ideas, without taking over or dominating. This is referred to as play tutoring and can be an important role for a teaching assistant to take. As children grow, their ability to use rule-based play activities, card games and equipment like board games indicates development in their cognitive and social abilities. They also learn to be competitive and enjoy quizzes, sports and competitions.

Play is also the way children develop and extend their social skills. From the earliest years when children first learn to collaborate with others, to the complex world of adult society, play performs an important function in teaching children how to get on with others. As children move into teenage years, you will notice that more and more of their free play involves socialising. However, some children whom you will encounter in an inclusive school may have difficulties with social interaction because they have autistic spectrum disorders. A programme should be in place to enable everyone to understand and deal with their difficulties and they will need skilled intervention to support their development. There is more on this in Chapters 12 and 13.

Other children will have difficulty with social skills because they do not have enough experience of learning to socialise. In days gone by, children often played out together, largely unsupervised by adults. They learned to socialise by trial and error. In our modern world increased media reporting of dangers and heavier traffic has meant many children are kept at home, often watching TV or playing computer games. They lack the learned social behaviour to enable them to play effectively with others and need to be taught this in school.

Play has another important function. It enables children to practise and generalise learned skills. Many teaching assistants can provide extremely valuable and enjoyable reinforcement for learning by playing appropriate games with small groups of children or one to one, while at the same time encouraging social skills. There are some excellent games available in schools.

Key Stage 2: "I spend a lot of time playing games with children to reinforce basic concepts like sound or number patterns or spelling. I'm quite artistic so I really enjoy making my own games because I can be really imaginative and make them as colourful and multi-sensory as I can. My teacher says I should start my own business because the kids love playing them and the other teachers are always borrowing them!"

Although there is evidence that play is affected by the cultural environment that children come from, and that there are gender differences in the way children choose to play, it is important to:

- maintain equal opportunities in play and offer the same experiences to all children
- monitor any play environment to make sure that the same children do not always dominate
- allow children to learn by trial and error
- join in, but don't take over!

For more information on play, see Moyles (2005), Barnes (1995), or Kay (2002).

Biological development – how the brain works and the mind thinks

Our knowledge of the neurological structure of the brain and the way it functions is expanding at a very rapid rate. This is due to the use of techniques such as Magnetic Resonance Imaging (MRI) and Computer Axial Tomography (CAT) to study the brain while it is working. We are now able to use this information to give us greater insight into the way children learn.

The brain is made up of nerve cells or neurons, which look a bit like spindly trees. An adult brain has about 200 billion neurons. Each neuron talks to others by receiving messages at one end and sending information from the other end. The message is an electrical impulse that jumps across to the next neuron through a synapse – or connection. Chemicals or neurotransmitters help this process to be completed effectively.

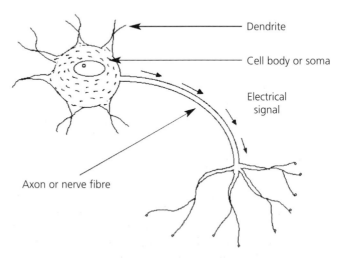

Dendrite

Cell body or soma

Electrical signal

Axon or nerve fibre

A neuron

In an adult brain, each neuron has made connections with about 10,000 other neurons. This means that there are literally trillions of pathways or connections that have been made during the transition from child to adult. The more frequently these connections are made, the more permanent the learning will be. So, each individual brain will have memories and experiences that will be represented by different patterns. As Helen Neville, a leading American neuroscientist says, "A functional brain system is a pattern of connections" (Neville, 2003).

However, it is not a simple process. Very young children develop far more synaptic connections in the brain than adults (so the child you are working with at Key Stage 1 will have far more than you!). As they grow, many connections are made and reinforced while others are discarded because they are unused. During teenage years, there is a particular time period of rapid growth in the part of the brain that governs planning, self-regulation and emotion. Researchers have speculated that this may be the reason for the anti-social nature of some teenagers – their brains are literally changing to be effective for the demands of adult life (Giedd, 2003).

Recent research by neuroscientists has shown that the structure of the brain is not mature until around the age of 20 and there are sensitive time periods, or windows of opportunity, when experience can shape that pattern of connections. In simple terms, the brain has 'plasticity' and it can be moulded by experience at certain times. The best-known of these critical time periods is the one that affects the acquisition of spoken language (which will be discussed more fully in Chapter 10).

It is clear that the years 0–8 are the crucial time period when spoken language can be acquired more easily and effectively. Trying to learn a spoken language later is never as easy as it is in early childhood. Neuroscientific research is taking place now to identify the sensitive periods of development when experience can shape the mechanisms involved in other areas of development. Helen Neville believes that this will make "a significant contribution to the design of educational programmes and intervention programmes in the future" (Neville, 2003). As a teaching assistant you can play a vital role in helping children to develop their own individual pattern of connections and to maximise their development at every stage.

Further research about the brain tells us that there are different areas that deal with the different functions.

- Brain stem – oldest evolutionary part – this deals with the primitive or automatic body functions like breathing, etc.
- Limbic system (hippocampus, amygdala, hypothalamus) – this deals with motivation, emotion and memory.
- Cerebral cortex – the outer layer that deals with thinking, generalising, meaning and patterns.

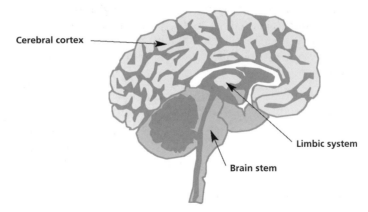

Cerebral cortex

Limbic system

Brain stem

The large scale structure of the brain

The way the brain is structured means that emotion or stress can have a major effect on brain function. When a learner is stressed or feels threatened the brain stem and limbic system go into survival mode and override the cerebral cortex. In simple terms it is hard to think straight when you are very frightened or very worried.

Left and right hemispheres

The brain also has two distinct sides, left and right. It is split into two halves connected by a tough band of fibres called the *corpus callosum*. We call these the Left and Right Hemispheres (from the Greek meaning *half-circle*). Although all of the brain is involved in most activities through the neural connections, research has shown that each side of the brain has primary responsibility for dealing with certain kinds of information. These are listed below:

LEFT	RIGHT
Reasoning	Intuition
Logic	Artistic ability
Analysis	Imagination
Memory of words and numbers as symbols	Dreams/daydreams
Processes	Dealing with several things at once
Use of language	Tone of voice/ body language/ facial expression
Sequences and procedures	Higher level maths
Calculations and formulae	Visual recognition
Facts	Rhythm – music

The left side deals with information logically, step-by-step, and the right side deals with information as a whole, or holistically. There is also a connection between the preferred side of the brain and left/right handedness. In left-handed people information coming into the brain through the left hand or left visual field reaches the *right* side of the brain first, then crosses the *corpus callosum* to the left side. In right-handed people information coming into the brain through the right hand or right visual field reaches the *left* side of the brain first before crossing to the right side. This has implications for the way we teach children. There is some evidence that left-handed children are more highly represented among children who have difficulties acquiring literacy. This may be because our teaching methods favour a more left-brained approach to learning (Chasty, 1990).

It is therefore important to integrate both sides of the brain in any teaching and learning activity by using colour, music, visual stimuli and imaginative activities in addition to the more logical step-by-step analytical left brain activities. Alistair Smith calls this 'whole brain learning' and it is a vital part of the system of Accelerated Learning (Smith, 1996). There are some very specific applications of this in teaching children to spell and read as the ability to read fluently involves both side of the brain (see Chapter 10).

"When the children have understood the patterns involved, we use music, rhythm and raps to reinforce times tables."

"We use pictures and music to stimulate children's imaginations when they are writing."

What can affect brain functioning?
Nutrients

As with any part of the body, the brain relies on nutrients to keep it healthy and functioning properly. Several studies have been made over the years about the effects of vitamin supplements on brain development and although some results have been inconclusive, it is clear that a healthy diet is important for all brain functions. Fish oils are often called 'brain-building' and essential fatty acids (EFAs) are thought to play a complex role in some areas of mental functioning. Protein is an essential building block for neurotransmitters too. Many schools now have a policy on healthy eating for learning.

Too many additives and fizzy drinks are thought by many to have a detrimental effect on concentration and behaviour in certain children. You may be asked by a parent to monitor a child's diet and behaviour, or you may yourself notice that this is a problem and pass the information on to your teacher.

Oxygen

The brain needs plenty of oxygen to function well. A good walk will often clear your head and enable you to think better! Some schools have exercise breaks to re-oxygenate the brain after periods of physical inactivity.

Diet

Anyone on a strict dietary regime that cuts out red meat and green vegetables can become anaemic. Some medical conditions also have anaemia as a side effect. Because the brain needs a plentiful supply of oxygen, one of the symptoms of anaemia is an inability to concentrate or think clearly. Teenage girls seem to be particularly prone to dieting so it is often relevant at Key Stage 3/4.

Water

Dehydration can interfere with brain function. Children need a plentiful supply of water. Some schools allow children to have water bottles on their desks to drink from while working, although they will need regular toilet breaks!

Recreational drugs

Any use of 'recreational' drugs will affect the way the brain operates in both the short- and possibly long-term.

Medicinal drugs

Many medicinal drugs have side effects, e.g. hay fever medicine can make a child sleepy and unable to concentrate.

Brain damage

Brain damage as a result of birth damage or an accident can affect specific areas of brain function.

The future

What will our brains be like in the future? Richard Restak, an American neuropsychiatrist, suggests that through the use of new technology like computers and mobile phones, we are literally 're-wiring our brains' (Restak, 2003). So, as our society becomes technologically more advanced, our brain structure is changing to adapt to the needs of our new world. Perhaps this is an example of Bandura's interactionism.

Theories of intelligence

We are all aware of people who are considered to be clever or intelligent. However, the study of human intelligence remains controversial. In the early years of the 20th century, Alfred Binet, a French psychologist, developed a standard test to measure intelligence, or the mental abilities of reasoning and remembering. The test gave an age-related score, translated into an IQ or Intelligence Quotient. Later, other psychologists extended this concept to develop a more complex test that measured the ability to think and reason in a more detailed way (Weschler Intelligence Scale (WISC)). For many years, IQ scores were used to allocate children to grammar or secondary modern schools, based on the idea that everyone is born with a fixed IQ that does not radically change as they develop.

Our understanding of the nature of intelligence has moved on since then. We are now more aware that experience moulds and develops intelligence, in other words, the idea of 'learnable intelligence'. There has also been a great deal of discussion about the whole concept of intelligence. One of the more influential researchers in this field is Howard Gardner, whose theory of multiple intelligences has been widely reported and used. He studied some of the more successful people in society and found that they were not necessarily the ones considered academically intelligent. In fact he thought that having good interpersonal skills ('people skills') was a better predictor of happiness and achievement. Gardner believed that we need different intelligences to enable us to solve problems in our modern changing world. He thought that:

Intelligence is defined by the culture of society, i.e. intelligence is considered to be what is valued at any one time by a society.

Traditional intelligence testing identifies those with verbal and mathematical abilities, but that concept is too narrow a definition of intelligence.

We should encourage different intelligences to prevent children from considering themselves 'dumb'.

Gardner describes eight types of intelligence:

Verbal / Linguistic	Reading, writing, linguistic skills. Vocabulary, crossword puzzles
Logical / Mathematical	Cause and effect, numbers, patterns, problem-solving, computers, chess, calculations
Musical / Rhythmical	Rhythm, music, singing, background music, tone
Interpersonal	Managing relationships with others, friends, socialisation, working collaboratively, empathy
Intrapersonal	Managing yourself, objectivity, analysis, independence, hobbies and interests, metacognition
Kinaesthetic	Movement, sport, practical activities
Visual / Spatial	Patterns, images, 3-D, puzzles, films, machines, mazes, art
Naturalist	Outdoor activities, sorting, classifying

There is more information on this at http:/pss.uvm.edu.

He thinks that everyone has a different profile of skills and ability and that academic intelligence is only one of them (there has been criticism of these ideas). He is also uneasy about the use of formal tests of intelligence as he thinks that these favour students with linguistic and mathematical strengths (Gardner, 1983 & 1993).

Concerns have been raised that the narrowness of the curriculum and the emphasis on literacy and numeracy has squeezed out time for the more creative subjects that allow children a chance to shine. It is a very useful role for a teaching assistant to help the teacher to plan and deliver varied learning experiences so that every child can demonstrate their ability in the way that suits them best.

How are Gardner's ideas used in the classroom?

- By an acceptance and recognition that all learners have different individual strengths.
- By designing and offering learning experiences that play to the strengths of all learners.
- By valuing other 'intelligences'.
- By raising the profile of those who are good at traditionally non-academic areas in order to motivate them to learn.

Here is an example of using all intelligences in activities to encourage writing skills:

- Verbal – write a poem.
- Logical – describe a sequence.
- Musical – listen to music, write a review.
- Interpersonal – survey others, write up results.
- Intrapersonal – write about a personal experience.
- Kinaesthetic – role play with an analysis.
- Visual spatial – design a poster with writing.
- Naturalist – playground search and write up.

Example: David Beckham The former England football captain, David Beckham, has often been the subject of negative media comment about his academic intelligence. However, he evidently has an extremely high intelligence quotient in visuo-spatial skills (his passing ability) and kinaesthetic skills (movement), which make him a world-class footballer. He is valued highly in our society and a role model for many children. The narrow definition of academic intelligence does not reflect the scope of his different intelligences.

Profiling learners' intelligences

The most effective way to discover the different profile of strengths and abilities of all children is to:

- talk to them about their interests and hobbies
- notice the way they learn

- watch the activities they choose and enjoy
- observe the way they interact with others.

There are also many examples of published checklists you can use (Gregory and Chapman, p.28, Smith; 1996, pp.60–61).

Emotional intelligence

Several researchers have picked up on Gardner's ideas of interpersonal and intrapersonal skills to investigate how we can encourage people to be more emotionally intelligent and manage their own and other's emotions more effectively. Daniel Goleman (1996) has written several books on emotional intelligence that are used across the whole spectrum of society, from the family to the workplace, but which have a really useful application in school. These will be explored in detail in the next chapter.

This review of some of the relevant theories of learning has given us some key insights into how children learn, and shows:

- the importance of critical time periods in development
- learning needs to be an active process
- the value of skilled and sensitive adult and peer support in learning
- the importance of active learning or learning by doing
- the interaction between language and thought
- the varied and changeable nature of intelligence
- the importance of observational or modelled learning
- the importance of play.

Key reading

Key references are given in bold.

Armstrong, T. (2000) *In Their Own Way, Discovering and Encouraging Your Child's Multiple Intelligences*, New York: Tarcher/Putnam *[Practical and straightforward advice.]*

Carter, R. (1998) *Mapping the Mind*, London: Weidenfeld and Nicholson *[Illustrated book of how the mind works.]*

Claxton, G. (1999) *Wise Up: The Challenge of Lifelong Learning*, London: Bloomsbury *[Concept of learning to learn.]*

Davenport, G. C. (2001) *An Introduction to Child Development*, London: Collins *[Useful for all aspects of psychology and learning and child development.]*

Greenfield, S. (2000) *Brain Story*, London: BBC Publications *[Lavishly illustrated simple guide to the workings of the brain.]*

Kay, J. (2002) *Teaching Assistants Handbook*, London: Continuum *[Comprehensive reference book for teaching assistants supporting at Key Stage 1.]*

Moorey, C.G. (2002) *Theories of Childhood*, Minnesota: Red Leaf

Moyles, J. (2005) *The Excellence of Play*, Buckingham: Open University Press, 2nd edn *[Looks at the importance of play in learning.]*

Moyles, J. (Ed.) (2002) *Beginning Teaching, Beginning Learning*, Buckingham: Open University Press, 2nd edn *[Review of teaching and learning*

strategies in the classroom.]

Oates, J. (Ed.) (1994) *The Foundations of Child Development,* **Milton Keynes: Open University/Blackwell** [A very useful review of early childhood development, including discussion of Skinner, Piaget, Vygotsky and Bruner.]

Wood, C. (1997) *Yardsticks: Children in the Classroom Ages 4-14: A Resource for Parents and Teachers* Turners Fall, Ma.: Northeast Foundation for Children [Easy reference book for general expectation about children's growth and development.]

References

Key references are given in bold.

Bandura, A. (1997) *Social Learning Theory,* New York: General Learning Press [Discussion of social and cognitive learning theory.]

Bandura, A. (2003) *Lecture at Smithsonian Institute,* Washington DC, 15 November 2003

Barnes, P. (1995) *Personal, Social and Emotional Development of Children,* Buckingham: Open University Press/Blackwell [Discussion of social development.]

Chasty, H. (1990) *Lecture at Christchurch College Dyslexia Institute*, Canterbury, 1990 [Discussion of learning requirements of pupils with dyslexia.]

DfES (2004) *Every Child Matters: Change for Children*, London: DfES/1081/2004

Donaldson, M. (1979) *Children's Minds,* London: Fontana Press [Critique of Piaget's theories.]

Gardner, H. (1983) *Frames of Mind,* **London: Heinemann** [Gardner's original Multiple Intelligence ideas.]

Gardner, H. (1993) *Multiple Intelligences; The Theory in Practice,* New York: Basic Books [Practical application and expansion of Multiple Intelligence theory.]

Giedd, Dr J. (2003) *Your Child's Developing Brain: New Insights into Young Minds,* Parents Council of Washington, 6 November 2003 [Lecture.]

Goleman, D. (1996) *Emotional Intelligence: Why It Can Matter More Than IQ,* **London: Bloomsbury** [A review of how emotional intelligence can be nurtured and strengthened.]

Gregory, G. and Chapman, C. (2002) *Differentiated Instructional Strategies,* **California: Corwin Press** [Practical manual on flexible teaching and learning in the classroom.]

Neville, H. (2003) *Lecture on Cognition and Neuroscience,* Georgetown University, Washington DC, 23 April 2003 [Discussion of critical time periods in learning and development.]

Piaget, J. (1971) *Biology and Knowledge,* Edinburgh: Edinburgh University Press

Restak, R. *The New Brain: How the Modern Age Is Rewiring Your Mind,* Philadelphia: Rodale Books [Looks at the effects of fast-moving images on concentration and attention. Sets out the idea that the modern world encourages visual rather than verbal intelligence.]

Sara Smilansky (1968), cited in Barnes (1995)

Skinner, B. F. (1953) *Science and Human Behaviour,* New York: Macmillan

Smith, A. (1996) *Accelerated Learning in the Classroom,* **Stafford: Network Educational Press** [Practical manual describing the principles of accelerated learning.]

Vygotsky, L. S. (1978) *Mind and Society. The Development of Higher Psychological Processes,* M. Cole, V. John-Steiner, S. Scribner and E. Souberman (eds.), Cambridge, Mass.: Harvard University Press

Wood, D. (1998) *How Children Think and Learn – The Social Contexts of Cognitive Development,* **Oxford: Blackwell** [Fairly complex discussion and update of Piaget, Vygotsky and Bruner's' theories of learning.]

7 Learning and teaching

Everyone has their own preference for the way that they work. An informal survey of teaching assistants taking a college course revealed a wide variation in the way they dealt with their assignments. Some liked to shut themselves away upstairs in total silence. Others were quite happy to work at the kitchen table, surrounded by family noise and distraction. Some couldn't settle until they had finished jobs around the house; others used academic work as a welcome distraction from the gardening or ironing. Some liked to complete assignments bit by bit, well before the deadline. Others were happy to stay up all night the night before it was due in and do it at one sitting. Some liked to talk it over with colleagues, while others preferred to read and work alone. All of these can be referred to as 'learning preferences'.

Most adults have developed their learning preferences over a long period of time and they are the result of both learned behaviour and reflections of individual psychological, social, cognitive and emotional characteristics. As adults, we can often choose the way we work and learn, but we usually tell children how to work, often echoing the way that we like to work ourselves.

Although your work as a teaching assistant requires you to develop detailed curriculum knowledge in the areas you support in, it is also vital to have expertise in all aspects of *learning* so that you can make the best possible use of any teaching and learning opportunity. In the previous chapter you looked at some theories of how children learn, but there are other factors that influence the way we teach and support teaching in school. All these factors need to be taken into consideration in order to create an effective, inclusive and positive classroom climate for learning.

Each child will develop their own profile of learning preferences based on a combination of factors. All children are a complex interaction of behaviour learned through experience and a biological blueprint from their genetic make up. When you look around each classroom, you will see children who not only have different biological profiles, but who have also had very different experiences in their lives. All of these will impact on the way children learn. Perhaps their home background means they have different cultural ways of learning. In some cultures, for example Afro-Caribbean, there is much more emphasis on collaborative learning and so these children may learn better in social groups (Karabenick, 1998, p.53). Other societies have a tradition of valuing certain curriculum areas, like science, more than other subjects. In other societies most people are bilingual. Some cultures have very different approaches to learning. For example, travelling communities have a particular social structure and conventions that make some of the learning in school less obviously relevant to their lives.

Although many children benefit from a supportive home environment, some children have difficult home lives, disrupted by family illness, unemployment, or relationship difficulties. They may receive little support for their school activities because basic survival is more important. For some, poverty means they do not have a healthy diet or access to resources like computers, or they may not have the same opportunities for enriching and interesting activities outside the classroom. Such children will have received different messages about the value of learning and will come to school without the strong foundations for learning that others have. Of course, some children may have the pressure of a high level of parental expectation to deal with too! It is important that we take all of these factors into consideration when we are planning teaching and learning.

Each child's approach to learning may also depend on their position in their family. A first-born child may be under more pressure to succeed, while a younger child may be more passive, used to older siblings meeting their needs. Middle children can sometimes have to fight for attention, which affects the way they learn. An only child may be used to learning through undivided adult attention. This is not because they are spoiled. It is their learned behaviour, based on their experience in life. They need sensitive guidance to enable them to fit into a classroom learning situation. By looking at the factors below, you can begin to understand each child's learning profile, thus helping you to make learning experiences more relevant and effective.

- physical
- environmental
- social
- emotional
- psychological/cognitive.

The physical environment

The classroom

Schools have very different buildings and facilities. Some are lucky enough to be in up-to-date purpose-built buildings with every facility available. Others cope with poor facilities and out-of-date, overcrowded accommodation. The important point is to recognise the effects that these physical factors will have on learning and make the most of what is there. Having an attractive, stimulating, well-ordered and well-organised learning environment makes it easier to learn. It is a very useful role for teaching assistants to be able to monitor the physical environment – they may have more opportunity to notice the effects of the classroom environment on individual learners. Although they do not have unlimited resources, teachers can use this feedback when they are planning their classroom layout and organisation.

Light

Very bright sunlight can be distracting, especially if it is falling on the face of a child. Make a point of watching for this and moving a child or closing a blind if you can. Autistic children can become totally involved in a pattern of light or movement. On the other hand, make sure there is enough light available, particularly for close work. It is hard to concentrate when there is a flickering fluorescent light in the classroom yet it is surprising how many classrooms have these! Report flickering lights to the relevant person in your school, as children who suffer from epilepsy or migraine may find that this will trigger an attack. More use is now being made of overhead projectors (OHPs) and interactive whiteboards. Check that sunlight is not making the projection unreadable. If you are at the front of the class it is often difficult to see how the children view the projection. If there are any children with visual impairment, a careful analysis of the classroom environment should be carried out in conjunction with a specialist teacher of the visually impaired.

Noise

Classrooms can be noisy places, particularly if the room is open plan and there are other classrooms nearby. Sometimes classrooms have to be used as corridors to other rooms, or they are next to a hall where lunch is served and pots and pans are clanged noisily. This is a particularly important factor when children are being asked to listen to sounds in words, for example, in the Catch Up literacy programmes or specialist language programmes. Most teachers have protocols for certain types of work – sometimes they will tolerate higher levels of noise and other times they will make children aware of the need for quiet working. When you are used to a high level of background noise it is sometimes difficult to fully understand the effect of this on children trying to learn.

Research has shown that different kinds of classical music can have a calming effect on pupils and can facilitate certain types of working (Campbell, 1978). More controversially, researchers at Strathclyde University have claimed that listening to pop music while working can improve pupil performance. Many pupils working at Key Stage 3/4 listen to music while they are doing homework. There is no doubt that music can be stimulating and enjoyable to listen to, but again it depends on the type of activity taking place and the preference of learners involved. One teaching assistant noticed that listening to music containing words interfered with the learning of some pupils when they were trying to write, whereas instrumental music did not. Many teachers use music to signal the beginning or end of an activity. Some use a gradually decreasing volume of music to settle down the class at the beginning of a lesson.

Temperature

It is difficult to concentrate if you are too hot or too cold. School classrooms can get overheated in winter or when there is strong sunlight through glass in the summer, and children who sit right next to a radiator may struggle to stay awake at times! Some temporary buildings can be cold and draughty too. Having warm up activities or keeping fresh air circulating are both important.

Furniture

Schools have limited budgets so cannot always choose the ideal furniture for children's age range. However, if constant fidgeting is a problem check to make sure chairs are comfortable, support the back and do not have wobbly legs. Even small adjustments like sticking round pieces of felt on the base of chair legs can make a difference by preventing wobbling and loud scraping noises whenever a child moves their chair. Sometimes laboratory stools can be uncomfortable for extended periods of time too. Making sure that all children can sit and work comfortably is important.

With the advent of the Primary Strategy, most children at Key Stage 1/2 spend time sitting on a carpet on the floor. This can be uncomfortable for them, so it is worth monitoring the conditions.

Key Stage 1: "The children sit on a carpeted area of the classroom for literacy hour. I was supporting a learner with attention difficulties and the teacher asked if I would sit with him on the floor to keep him on task. It was a real eye opener! There was a freezing draught coming from under the door, the carpet was so thin that I was really uncomfortable, and it was hard for me to stop myself squirming about! I talked to the teacher and we made some changes – moved the carpet area to the other side of the classroom and put some padding under the carpet. All the children's concentration has improved now!"

Resources

A well-organised classroom environment is clearly conducive to learning. Teaching assistants are often heavily involved in the administration and organisation of resources and this is an excellent way to share the teacher's classroom workload and contribute your own expertise. Each teacher will have their own way of organising the classroom, but it is always useful to have another viewpoint so that the best use can be made of the space available. Some classrooms have individual workstations, e.g. a writing corner, computer corner, etc. Others have a mix of resources for children to find and use at their desk. The best resource organisation systems mean that all learners can access them without constantly asking teaching staff and without disrupting other learners. A useful role for a teaching assistant is to monitor the level of disruption caused by learners getting resources of various kinds. It can lead to a change round in furniture! Children should always be encouraged to look after any equipment, under the supervision of a teaching assistant or teacher. It should not be part of your role to constantly clear up after them.

Whatever system is used, the following procedures should be in place.

- All resources used regularly are stored in an accessible place and labelled.
- Every child knows where everything is and how and where to return it.

Resources can include:

- consumables, like stationery
- writing implements, coloured pens, calculators, scissors, scientific equipment, rulers
- dictionaries and reference books, word banks
- art and craft materials
- ICT-based resources like tape recorders, TV and video, computers, interactive whiteboards and OHPs and associated programmes and tapes
- blackboards, whiteboards and flip charts
- games and workbooks
- construction and play equipment
- specialist intervention equipment for learners with SEN.

In some classrooms children manage the use of the resources, including helping the teacher to prepare overheads and presentations. It is a very useful way for them to learn. As a teaching assistant you need to be fully aware of how all the classroom resources can be used effectively. You can monitor the use of resources, be involved in adapting and making them, and make suggestions, particularly for individual learners.

A variety of easily accessible, well organised and looked after resources can provide a stimulating and varied learning experience and can make it easier for all children to achieve. A child with dyslexia who can communicate better through word processing needs to have that facility available whenever possible.

Key Stage 2: "We have an open plan school with sliding doors to each classroom. I take a small group of learners for a maths reinforcement activity. We sit outside the classroom, in the corridor where it is quieter, and the children face away from the classroom. Although the area is a bit of a dumping ground for old resources, I put covers over the equipment so that the children are not distracted. Each child has a visual checklist and collects and brings all their equipment. When the plenary starts we pull back the sliding doors and turn and face the classroom so that my group is included with the class."

Display

Teachers work hard to make their classroom a stimulating, welcoming and enjoyable environment, and classroom display is part of this process. Display isn't just about decoration, although it should always be finished to a good standard. It should be an extension of the teaching and learning outcomes and it should reflect the talent and achievement of the children rather than just the expertise of the teaching staff.

Although most teachers are good at display, they will often welcome support and help in this area, particularly from a teaching assistant who has an artistic flair. Teaching assistants have been responsible for designing and putting up some wonderfully inventive displays and arrangements that support work that the class is doing. Children are motivated by seeing their own work displayed around the classroom to reflect a learning community. It is important that every child is valued in this way and not just the ones with neat writing or the most creative storytelling. A sensitive teaching assistant will help the teacher to make sure every child has the chance to display something.

Displays of information should be clear and prominent, e.g. class rules, lists of correct spellings, word banks for different curriculum areas, procedures for the use of resources, diagrams of scientific or geographic processes, history timelines and photographs, etc. Some classrooms include living material like plants or even animals. Making sure these are well cared for sends a powerful message to the children about valuing things.

Displays need to be kept up-to-date. Research shows that the brain very quickly gets used to information seen in the same place every day and skims over it. Moving displays around regularly, particularly of things that you want the children to see and remember, is a very useful idea. Note that sometimes classrooms can have too much on display; their environment is too 'busy' and overstimulates the children. Some teaching assistants may also be involved in whole-school displays as part of their job responsibilities.

Emotional and social learning

Making the classroom welcoming, inclusive and safe

You have already seen the importance of social learning and begun to look at some of the effects of emotion on the way we learn. There is such a strong interrelationship between the brain and the body that it can be hard to untangle physical and emotional issues. Research has shown that children learn best when they feel safe and valued, and when they take responsibility for their own learning rather than just following instruction. This is now recognised in the government strategy Every Child Matters (2004), in which being safe is one of the desired five outcomes (see pages 33–4).

What motivates children to learn?

Psychologist Abraham Maslow's research in the 1950s identified a hierarchy of needs. Although he did not intend his findings to relate specifically to children, his ideas have been used in education for some time. He argued that all humans have a range of needs, ranked in order from the most basic (food, shelter, safety) to the highest (self-actualisation). Maslow thought that people are not motivated by higher level needs until their basic needs have been met. There is some reflection of his ideas in the world today, where people may not be interested in self-rule or democracy when they do not have enough water, food and electricity for their families.

There is no doubt that basic physiological needs like water, food and safety are key elements in the ability to learn effectively. We have already looked at things that can affect brain function. Food intake can have a short- and long-term effect on children's learning and behaviour. A child that has no breakfast will find it hard to concentrate beyond mid-morning, by which time their blood sugar level will have dropped, and a child that eats a large starchy meal at lunchtime may feel sleepy during the afternoon.

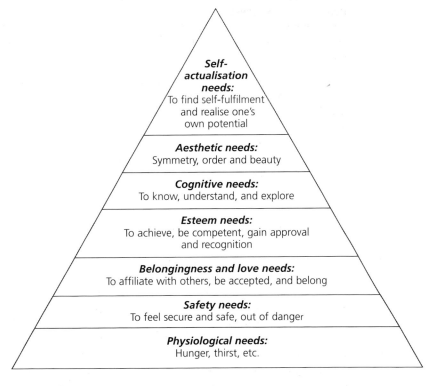

Self-actualisation needs:
To find self-fulfilment and realise one's own potential

Aesthetic needs:
Symmetry, order and beauty

Cognitive needs:
To know, understand, and explore

Esteem needs:
To achieve, be competent, gain approval and recognition

Belongingness and love needs:
To affiliate with others, be accepted, and belong

Safety needs:
To feel secure and safe, out of danger

Physiological needs:
Hunger, thirst, etc.

Maslow's Hierarchy of Needs (Maslow, 1968)

Schools are working hard to provide nutritious, healthy meals for children, and the provision of these, together with vending machines on site, is now one of the subjects of Ofsted inspection (Ofsted, 2003). The government has issued a Healthy Schools Initiative, which aims to provide education and resources for children and their families about nutrition, health and learning and to encourage the provision of fruit and healthy snacks in school (www.dh/gov.uk/ and www.wired-forhealth.gov.uk). Some schools provide breakfast clubs to ensure children have a healthy start to the day. Schools may also try to adapt their curriculum to the physiological profile of the children – for example, moving literacy to after lunch when children are happy to sit quietly, and moving the very active and creative subjects to the morning. You will find yourself that there are times of the day when you work better and others when you have difficulty concentrating. If you have any concerns about these issues with children that you work with, always discuss them with the teacher.

Safety

Maslow's argument that people need to feel safe to learn was not just about physical safety. He was also referring to the need for *emotional safety*. The classroom climate created by teaching staff can be hugely influential in the way children consider themselves emotionally safe. If the classroom is disorganised, or there is poor discipline and control, it can feel a frightening place. Children also need intellectual safety – the freedom to suggest and try without fear. Here are some examples of ways to encourage a safe environment.

- Have regular routines in the class. A well-structured and predictable environment feels safe.
- Do not use sarcasm with young children (Key Stage 1/2). They cannot understand the difference between what you say and what you mean (your body language) and are confused. Older children, who are cognitively able to understand sarcasm can quite enjoy it, but you should use it sparingly.
- Encourage the idea that trial and error is fine and it is acceptable to make mistakes. Let them see that your mistakes are part of learning. Welcome originality.
- Accept all answers from children positively, even if they are not right.
- Do not have favourites or scapegoats in the classroom.
- Listen to children's worries and fears and don't dismiss them as babyish or silly. Reassure them. Give them practical help.
- Monitor the whole school environment for any element of bullying. Give children skills to cope if they are bullied.
- Do not tolerate unkind behaviour in the classroom.

Maslow also emphasised the importance of being accepted and belonging. Inclusive schools will contain learners with all kinds of differences. It is a real skill to make every child feel they are welcome and belong, and are not just tolerated because they have to be there. Children need to feel part of their peer group too, and a teaching assistant has the extremely important role of helping every child to be an accepted part of their class and group. This requires positive strategies rather than vague ideas, focusing on the needs of the learner at all times. It can involve specific social and friendship coaching; what makes a good friend; how you talk to people; what you talk about; friendship behaviours; listening skills and sharing, etc., rather than vague suggestions like "Be nice" (Thompson and O'Neill, 2001).

It will also involve helping other learners to understand and empathise with any difficulties or problems a child may have (Besag, 2006). Children with learning difficulties may find it is even more difficult to be an easily accepted part of their peer group, and it takes a sensitive and skilled teaching assistant to support them in this. In adolescence the acceptance and approval of their peer group becomes even more important to pupils, sometimes more important than the approval of an adult. For example, in some cases it is not 'cool' to answer questions correctly and praising a child in front of their peers may be embarrassing to them. Teachers work hard to create the right learning environment for each age group, while encouraging a positive approach. You need to be sensitive to this.

Working with others

Group or paired work plays an important role in children's learning. Social learning preferences relate to whether children prefer to work alone, with other learners or with adults. Children vary in their ability to work effectively with others and it is helpful to observe the way children work so that you can keep a check on this. Some enjoy the stimulation of sharing ideas; others find it extremely frustrating to rely on other children. Gifted children sometimes prefer to get on with their work alone as they can work at a faster pace. Children may need specific coaching to enable them to make the best of the collaborative learning opportunities they have so that they can:

- take turns
- share ideas
- share expertise
- negotiate.

Motivation and self-esteem

Some researchers have looked at motivation in more detail and considered the relationship between motivation and self-esteem (Gurney, 1988). Self-esteem is the way we view ourselves and our abilities and compare ourselves to others. It influences the way we respond to any aspect of life. However, our self-esteem is not fixed. It will vary depending on what we do and whom we are involved with in our lives. The messages that other people give us about ourselves will have a big effect on how we view ourselves and our abilities.

The whole area of self-esteem is a controversial one. Thousands of books have been written about the importance of self-esteem – the so-called self-help revolution! It is clear that it has a major impact on how we learn, but a review of research by Nicolas Emler has questioned the whole scientific basis of self-esteem and argues that we may have overestimated its importance in some ways. Other researchers have argued that it is important to have self-respect and respect for others rather than self-esteem. However, Emler does make clear that the successes and failures we have in life will affect the way we see ourselves, so being able to achieve in school will play an important part in the development of our self-esteem (Emler, 2001) (Baumeister *et al.*, 1996).

Children with low self-esteem can be frightened to try new things and constantly put themselves down. It can be hard for them to work independently as they are worried about getting things wrong. They can also be boastful and overconfident in an attempt to boost their own self-esteem or may try to make others feel bad as a strategy to raise their own self-esteem. It is easy for them to get stuck into a self-fulfilling prophecy of failure that becomes harder to break as it goes on. This is why it is so important to recognise all the different skills and abilities and intelligences that children have, rather than constantly focusing on what they can't do.

As a teaching assistant you are often working with children who have the most persistent difficulties or who find learning really hard. Your role should be to build self-esteem and encourage confidence by:

- focusing on what they can do and are good at
- helping them to learn in the way that is best for them
- breaking learning down into achievable parts
- giving them skilled structured help for the things they find difficult
- using stimulating and motivating methods and resources that will help them to enjoy learning
- encouraging them to value and respect each other's diverse skills and abilities
- treating each child decently and fairly
- explaining that learning is not always easy or fun.

A learner with positive self-esteem will be confident and more likely to try. They will learn from their failures, persevere, work independently and believe in themselves. Most schools will have a whole school strategy for self-esteem that may be based on their PSHE provision or could be through Circle Time or a similar approach.

"Getting to know children you work with regularly is very important. The best way is to let them talk. You need to know what the 'key' is for every child – I try to find out what they are good at, even if it is something not connected directly with school."

Intrinsic and extrinsic motivation

People can be motivated by factors outside themselves (extrinsic motivation) or within themselves (intrinsic motivation). For example, praising a child or giving them a sticker or a prize would be considered an extrinsic reward or reinforcement. The child's own feelings that they want to do well for a personal feeling of satisfaction would be considered an intrinsic reinforcement. There is a complex interaction between these systems. For example, an extrinsic reward system can be very successful to start with but there is a tendency for motivation to drop away after a while, whereas a personal sense of achievement tends to be a more persistent feeling. You should therefore try to encourage this in all learners, rather than making them dependent on praise from an adult or the promise of a sticker or prize. However, using extrinsic rewards is valuable to get children used to the feelings of achievement and motivation and many schools have extensive extrinsic reward systems in place.

Attribution theory – success and failure in the classroom

Children will attribute their successes and failures to different causes. It may be that they see the problem as outside their control ("that exam was too difficult") or as something within themselves that is unchangeable ("I'm hopeless at writing"). They also vary in the way that they view their ability to improve their performance, but the first step is to help them understand that they can. The way you feedback to a child can be crucial in developing their belief in themselves. If you praise them too much for doing easy tasks, give them too much help or show surprise at their achievement, it can give them the message that they are not expected to do well or give them unrealistically high expectations. You should:

- Help pupils believe in themselves by commenting on what they do well, not just giving them a reward.
- Give an honest and detailed response to their work, e.g. "You have some really good ideas and you have started the story well, but you need to give more detail in the middle and perhaps consider another ending," rather than simply saying, "That's not very good" or "You tried really hard".

(Adapted from Leadbetter *et al,* 1999)

Emotional intelligence

Daniel Goleman built on the original research by Salovey and Mayer (1990) to identify the whole concept of emotional intelligence. He said "people who are emotionally adept, who know and manage their own feelings well and who read and deal effectively with other people's feelings, are at an advantage in any domain of life" (Goleman, 1996, p.36). His ideas have been widely discussed as being particularly relevant to the school environment and to have major implications for the way children learn. They affect the way children respond to teachers, how they motivate themselves to learn and how they get on with others. You may see this referred to in school as Emotional Literacy and it forms part of the concept of Circle Time and other whole school approaches to social development. As a teaching assistant you have an important role in children's emotional and social development and in helping them to develop emotional literacy. Goleman also tells us about a self-science curriculum that includes:

- self-awareness
- personal decision making
- self-acceptance
- managing feelings
- handling stress
- personal responsibility
- conflict resolution
- empathy
- insight
- communicating with others
- group dynamics.

Children need to be encouraged to understand feelings by identifying and labelling a feeling, assessing its intensity, and being able to manage and express it appropriately. For example, it is useful to know that often the feeling of fear is expressed by anger and aggression or that you can 'catch' moods from the people around you.

Sometimes children can be overwhelmed by feelings of inadequacy, fear or even excitement. Helping them to understand the 'emotional hijacking' that takes place, when these intense feelings cause them to act impulsively, will enable them to manage their feelings better. They should be given the opportunity to develop and use techniques to manage and reduce their own stress levels.

It is also important to understand the difference between a feeling and an action. Children need to understand that although you can feel what you like, you should not necessarily act on that feeling. For example, it's okay to feel jealous, but not to scribble all over someone's work because you do so. Empathy involves being able to recognise emotions in others and understand their perspective, and this is another key element in handling relationships that children may need help with, although it will remain a persistent problem for some children with autistic spectrum disorders. Such children may need specialist intervention.

Goleman also looked at the concepts of gratification and motivation. According to research, children who at the age of four were able to delay eating a marshmallow when promised two instead if they waited were more successful in later years in school. They could delay gratification or reward instead of behaving impulsively and were able to use this concept to motivate themselves in the classroom.

Persistence is also an important attribute for children to develop, and is related both to their emotional response to learning and to their motivation. For some children the idea that all learning is broken into short chunks of time because "children can't concentrate for long" leads to constant frustration because nothing is ever finished to their satisfaction. They lose interest in the outcome and become demotivated. Others may need constant breaks to be able to persist to the end of an activity and need you to help them by setting smaller, achievable goals. The ability to adapt the curriculum to cater for the needs of individual pupils is part of the concept of personalised learning. Like anything else, children are more likely to persevere with a task if they see a reason for the activity, they feel able to achieve it and they have some ownership of the outcome.

Habits of mind

Persistence is also identified by Arthur Costa, an American educationalist, as one of several effective 'Habits of Mind' which pupils use to respond to problems or dilemmas. Other habits of mind include:

- Thinking about thinking (metacognition).
- Listening with empathy to others' points of view.
- Thinking flexibly and creatively.
- Thinking interdependently by working with and learning from others.
- Applying past knowledge to new situations.
- Striving for accuracy and precision (being careful and precise in work or language and taking care not to generalise or make assumptions).
- Managing impulsivity.
- Questioning and problem solving.
- Remaining open to continuous learning.

These are integrated into the curriculum in some American schools by encouraging pupils to use these habits in each activity and by helping them to reflect on which habits were used after the activity is finished (Costa, 2000).

Psychological and cognitive learning

Memory

All teaching assistants will be familiar with the child who appears to have learned something, yet by the next day or week has forgotten it all. For learning to really take place the change must be permanent, so to learn we need to remember. An understanding of how memory works and a good grasp of techniques available to enhance memory skills of all children are important for anyone working in school.

We take in information constantly through all our senses: touch, vision, hearing, smell and movement. Much of this passes us by without leaving a memory trace but if our attention is caught by something, it goes into a short-term memory store where it stays for several seconds. Further processing of this information moves it into long-term memory store. Later, we should be able to recall or retrieve that information when we need it.

Memory types

There are different kinds of memory:

- Procedural memory is the memory of sensory information including auditory, visual and kinaesthetic memory. Some of this may be automatic or involuntary.
- Declarative memory includes:
  - Episodic – the memory of events and the order in which they occurred.
  - Semantic – the memory for meanings.

So, if we use the example of driving a car, *procedural memory* helps you to remember physically how to drive, using motor, auditory and visual skills. *Episodic memory* helps you to remember what happened on previous occasions when you drove a car. *Semantic memory* helps you to remember what a car is and how it works.

What can affect the way we process, store and retrieve information?

- **Using selective attention** to focus on and process what we want to remember.
- **Understanding**. If you understand something it makes sense and is easier to recall.
- **Making connections**. The brain likes to make patterns and connections, so helping a child to see where something fits in or connects will help them to remember it. You can then use association to help them recall by cueing them in.
- **Organisation**. If information coming in is sorted, matched and associated with other information it forms a network. It is then easier to store and find. You can compare this to throwing things into a cupboard in a jumbled mass and having to rummage through later to find them. Organising items into categories and stacking them neatly makes them so much easier to find!
- **Using all the senses**. Information that comes in through more than one sense leaves a stronger memory trace. We often refer to this as multi-sensory because hearing, vision, motor movement, touch, smell, etc. can all be used together. Multi-sensory learning is important for all children, but it is used particularly in intervention for children with SEN. It is, for example, an important part of the way we teach children to spell.
- **Amount of information received**. Keep it in manageable amounts, and chunk together into groups. Between three and seven items for short-term memory is an appropriate amount.
- **Pace of information presented**. Some children can take in, process and remember huge amounts of information, particularly

if it is relevant to their individual strengths. Others need more time and practice.

- **Time to think**. Procedural memory can often be retrieved quickly but it may take a few seconds to bring back complex information. Give children time to think.
- **Rehearsal and review**. In order to move information into long-term store and to keep it there we use rehearsal or practice. This could be revision for exams or summing up at the end of a learning activity; drawing a child's attention to a fact or concept that they know by giving an example; or using different kinds of learning activity to reinforce a concept. Make sure children know that all these techniques will improve their memory.
- **Emotion**. Emotion can heighten or block memory. If you think back to your early childhood, your first memories will probably be ones associated with a strong emotion. Some people remember the weather was much better when they were children because all they remember are sunny happy days! A child that is frightened by a school bully or worried about a difficult situation at home will find that this interferes with their ability to remember and to learn, because their brain is constantly processing the fear or anxiety rather than the new learning. Pressure to 'perform' in front of a class can also cause stress. Remember that not all children are the same. Some children respond very positively to the pressure of exams and find that it stimulates their memory!

"I had to do a presentation as part of my CLANSA course at college. There were three presentations before mine but I couldn't tell you what they were about. I was so nervous about mine I couldn't concentrate. It's a shame because everyone said they were really good! It made me realise how important it is to have a stress-free environment to learn and now I go out of my way to tune into children's worries and make sure I help them."

- **Choice**. If you have a choice in what you remember and how you remember it then it gives you more ownership and makes it more individual. Children need to be aware of how their memories work best and how they can improve. Don't enforce ideas, just suggest them and give them a chance to practise them and see how well they work – it will be an individual thing.
- **State-dependent memory**. When you try to remember something it is often easier to do so when you are in a similar situation to when you first stored the experience in memory. A familiar piece of music or smell can bring memories rushing back! The police use this technique when they re-enact crimes. You can use it in the classroom by providing 'memory joggers' for children, reminding them of sensory information that was there when they learned or by replaying information. For example, "Remember when we learned this last week? You were sitting next to Kim and it was a hot day and we'd just seen that video about dolphins?"

You need a good memory yourself for this technique! Some teachers use music to cue in similar learning activities, just like the theme for *Match of the Day*. Auditory memory often leaves a strong trace, which is why an annoying tune you heard on the radio in the morning pops into your head all day long!

- **Strong images and sensations, including humour**.

Individual memory skills

All children will have an individual profile of memory skills. Some of this will depend on their learning preferences or intelligences. Some children experiencing difficulties in learning to read or spell have a poor memory for sound (auditory memory) but may have an excellent episodic memory. Other children may have a very good visual memory; such children are often very successful at revising for exams. Some learners with autism have unusual memory profiles and are able to recall huge amounts of information without necessarily showing a deep level of understanding. The important thing to remember is that you should help all learners to improve their memory skills, while making sure that you use the pathways that they find easy too.

"I am supporting a learner with dyslexia who has real problems with auditory memory so can't remember tables or number bonds. He told me he remembers telephone numbers by the way his hand moves on the telephone dialling keyboard, so we have used that system to help him with tables by making a number square and physically pointing out the numbers."

Memory changes with age. Young children working at Key Stage 1 do not have the same conscious ability to rehearse and review and need help to learn to use these techniques. They are very reliant on visual memory. As people get older they often lose the ability to recall information in the recent past, while remembering everything that happened 40 years ago in great detail. This is thought to be because the strength of the memory trace when it was laid down makes it easier to recall.

In summary, memory skills are extremely important. Ways in which you can provide skilled help are given below.

- Keep learning as stress-free as possible – don't use sarcasm or undue pressure.
- Draw children's attention to the relevant information that needs to be processed to be remembered, e.g. "Listen very carefully to this. It's important."
- Make connections, then remind learners of these connections by relating new information to previous learning.
- Minimise distractions.
- Help children to organise information to store.
- Present information at the right pace. Chunk information. Give plenty of opportunity to rehearse and review.

- Use cues (association, state-dependent memory, mind pictures) to help learners store, recognise and recall.
- Use language to help children understand and explain, by asking them questions.
- Give children time to retrieve the information from memory.
- Help a child to profile their own memory skills and to learn the skills to enhance them.
- Use all types of memory, particularly with pupils who have difficulties in certain areas.
- Use multi-sensory learning.
- Use music, colour and strong visual images.

For more information on memory skills look at Bristow, Cowley and Davies (1999).

The effective teaching of writing and spelling should use all types and aspects of memory and this is covered in more detail in Chapter 10.

Cognitive preferences and learning styles

We have already seen that the way the brain processes information may affect the way people prefer to learn. A great deal of research has taken place to investigate the whole concept of psychological and cognitive learning preferences and there are many theories about how children learn best. The important point to remember is that this is a complex area. The best way to really understand a child and the way they learn is to work with them and observe them over a period of time and to remember that most children are a mix of several preferences.

Visual, auditory and kinaesthetic preferences

One common method of classifying learners is by using their preference for taking in and processing sensory information. An understanding of these can help the teacher to plan their approach to teaching and learning in the classroom. This is because they are able to offer learning experiences that allow all learners a chance to use their preferred mode if they want and to improve their ability to use other modes. According to Dunn and Dunn (1992), learners have three different ways of taking in and processing information:

Auditory learners

These children prefer information that is heard, i.e. spoken language, music, etc. They like to listen to a teacher, tapes or the radio, or to discuss things with others. They like to read so they can hear the sound in their own head. Traditionally many teachers have been auditory learners and therefore assume that everyone else learns through 'chalk and talk'. Phrases related to auditory learners:

"It sounds good to me."

"I hear what you are saying."

Application in the classroom: Auditory learners will usually enjoy whole class teaching, listening to someone explain something, or hearing a tape. They may like to read out loud, talk constantly to others, or find they blurt out answers without waiting their turn. You can help by teaching them to verbalise in their head rather than out loud; giving them plenty of opportunities to talk and discuss; and letting them know when it is important to keep silent.

Visual learners

These children learn best from seeing information. They also like to read, look at diagrams, pictures and videos. Colour is usually a particularly effective way for them to learn. They often like to see a demonstration of something. Phrases related to visual learners:

"Let me show you."

"Just imagine."

Application in the classroom: Visual learners get bored without a visual stimulus. They need something to focus on while they are listening, so they may need to draw, colour or look at a diagram. As they enjoy using colour they may like brightly coloured pens and inks. They can learn to use mind maps while they are listening too. Videos, pictures and diagrams are successful ways for them to learn.

Kinaesthetic learners

These children learn best by moving and being physically involved in every activity. They enjoy visits, activities, role-play, construction, making things, etc. Phrases related to kinaesthetic learners:

"Let's try to grasp this."

"Run that past me again."

Application in the classroom: Kinaesthetic learners need practical activities while they are working. They like to be involved in 'doing' while they work. They are often thought of as fidgets, or even misdiagnosed as having Attention Deficit (Hyperactive) Disorder, but they may just need the constant stimulation of movement. Some teachers allow them to have worry beads or squeezy foam balls to manipulate in the classroom. They may need to draw a diagram or doodle while they work. It is sometimes useful to let them have times when they can move around freely, provided that they also know when they should keep still.

Multi-sensory learning

The reason multi-sensory learning is so effective in the classroom is that it utilises all the senses at the same time. No child will just be one or the other type of learner, but they may have a preference that helps them to learn.

Cognitive styles

Categorising learners by analysing their thinking styles may also be relevant to your practice. Children can be global thinkers, who like to see things as a whole, or analytical thinkers, who prefer to break everything down into its component parts to deal with it. Understanding how a child likes to work can be an important part of helping them. They may be reflective thinkers, who take their time to think through everything first (and may need a little help in getting moving), or impulsive thinkers, who rush into things without waiting to see what is really required (and may need help in slowing down and thinking through). You may like to relate these to your own style of working to give you an insight into the way children learn. Don't forget that as teachers we tend to assume that everyone learns like we do!

It you want more information about these learning and cognitive styles, you could look at Kolb (1976), who categorised people as *Accommodators, Assimilators, Convergers* and *Divergers*, by the way they perceived or processed information.

Honey and Mumford (1992) saw people as:

- Activists – enthusiastic about new activities, thrive on challenge, enjoy working with others.
- Reflectors – like to step back and think things through, are naturally cautious, like observing others.
- Theorists – love to adapt and integrate all ideas into a theory or viewpoint. Enjoy synthesising and analysing.
- Pragmatists – love to try out new ideas and see problems as a challenge.

There are many more of these learning theorists. If you are interested in learning more you may like to look at Gregorc (1982), Grasha and Reichmann (1975) or Myers Briggs. People tend not to fit exclusively in any one category. Many pupils are a mixture of several. Also, learning styles can change, and research has cast doubts on the use of questionnaires in determining learning styles (LSDA, 2002). Nevertheless, it may help you to understand the way children (and you yourself) learn if you keep these in mind. Obviously no adult is able to always teach each child differently, according to their learning style, although you may have the opportunity if you are working one to one. However, teachers can take these learning preferences into account when they are planning teaching and learning.

The effect of gender on learning

The National Curriculum (1999) requires teachers to make sure that boys and girls are able to participate in the same curriculum and to ensure that they avoid gender stereotyping when offering interests for curriculum work (e.g. offering food technology for girls and go-kart design for boys).

At one time, there was concern in the educational world that girls were not achieving as highly as boys. Now the situation has been reversed and it is boys who seem to be falling behind, particularly at Key Stages 3/4 and particularly in literacy. A great deal of research has been undertaken to help us to understand the differences in the way boys and girls learn so this can be taken into account when designing teaching and learning programmes.

Michael Gurian (2003) has investigated the influence of gender in learning, based on the biological, neurological, chemical and hormonal differences between boys and girls. Basically, boys mature later than girls (which has an implication for teaching at Key Stages 3/4); are prone to different hormonal influences; are stronger in spatial skills and weaker in language skills; have different cultural group learning behaviours; and enjoy competition rather than collaboration.

Of course, these are generalisations and we should be careful not to stereotype all boys in this way. Research findings have warned against gender stereotyping (NERF, 2006). Plenty of boys enjoy collaborative activities and there are many articulate boys who use language very effectively. Use your observations of boys and girls learning to see whether you can support this viewpoint.

Ofsted produced a report in July 2003 that identified strategies for raising boys' achievement. These include:

- Whole school organisational approaches:
  - emphasis on a disciplined environment
  - encouraging a culture of achievement for all.
- Social/cultural approaches:
  - making learning 'cool' and acceptable
  - modifying the macho 'laddish' culture in school.
- Classroom management/teaching:
  - seating girls and boys in pairs so that they share their strengths
  - using short, focused activities or competitive activities to motivate boys
  - using texts and literature that interest and appeal to boys
  - using support strategies to improve boys' literacy skills
  - encouraging collaborative behaviour
  - using IT, which is seen as effective in motivating boys.

As a teaching assistant you need to be aware of these initiatives and think about the influence of gender on learning in your school. For example, a useful report on gender and achievement can be found in 'Raising Boys' Achievement' at: http://www-rba.educ.cam.ac.uk/report.html.

Gary Wilson has also produced a checklist for good practice that you can access at:

http://www.Standards.dfes.gov.uk/genderandachievement/goodpractice.

Key reading

Key references are given in bold.

Cooper, V. (2005) *Support Staff in Schools: Their Role in Promoting Children and Young People's Emotional and Social Development,* London: National Children's Bureau Enterprises

Dowling, M. (2000) *Young Children's Personal Social and Emotional Development,* London: Paul Chapman [Comprehensive discussion including information on moral and spiritual development.].

Hughes, M. (1997) *Lessons are for Learning,* Stafford: Network Educational Press [Good explanation of the learning process in the classroom.]

May, P. Ashford, A. Bottle, G. (2005) *Sound Beginnings – Learning and Development in the Early Years*, London: David Fulton

Moorey, C.G. (2002) *Theories of Childhood*, Minnesota: Red Leaf

Pritchard, A. (2005) *Ways of Learning: Learning Theories and Learning Styles in the Classroom*, London: David Fulton

Smith, A. and Call, N. (2001) *ALPS Resource Book: Accelerated Learning in the Primary School*, Stafford: Network Educational Press [The accelerated learning approach.]

Webster-Stratton, C. (1999) *How to Promote Children's Social and Emotional Competence,* London: Paul Chapman

References

Key references are given in bold.

Baumeister, R. Smart, L. Boden, J. (1996) 'Relation of Threatened Egotism to Violence and Aggression: The Dark Side of High Self-Esteem', *Psychological Review*, 1996 Vol 103, No. 1, 5-33

Besag, V. (2006) *Understanding Girls' Friendships, Fights and Feuds: A Practical Approach to Girls' Bullying*, Maidenhead: Open University Press/McGraw Hill

Bristow, J., Cowley, P. and Davies, B. (1999) *Memory and Learning: A Practical Guide for Teachers,* London: David Fulton [Lots of information on how memory works.]

Campbell, D. (1978) *The Mozart Effect,* New York: Avon Publishing [How to tap the power of music to strengthen the mind and unlock creativity.]

Costa, A. and Kallick, B. (2000) *Describing 16 Habits of Mind,* Adapted from: *Activating and Engaging Habits of Mind* (2000), Alexandria VA: ASCD [Used at Wolf Trap Elementary School, Virginia, USA.]

Critique of Systematic Review *British Journal of Sociology of Education* 26, 3 July2006, pp. 415–28.

DfES (2004) *Every Child Matters: Change for Children*, London: DfES/1081/2004

Dunn, R. and Dunn, K. (1992) *Teaching Elementary Students Through Their Individual Learning Styles: Practical Approaches for Grades 3–6*. Boston, MA, Allyn & Bacon [Description of basic learning styles and teaching approaches.]

Emler, N. (2001) *Self-Esteem: The costs and causes of low self-esteem*, London: Joseph Rowntree Foundation

Goleman, D. (1996) *Emotional Intelligence: Why It Can Matter More Than IQ,* London: Bloomsbury

Gregorc, www.gregorc.com (date of research: 1976)

Grasha, A. and Richlin, L. (1996) *Teaching with Style: A Practical Guide to Enhancing Learning*, Pittsburgh: Alliance [Updated account of Grasha and Reichmann's research]

Gurian, M. and Ballew, A. (2003) *The Boys and Girls Learn Differently Action Guide for Teachers,* New Jersey: Jossey Bass Wiley, *[Practical teachers' guide based on Gurian's research.]*

Gurney, P. W. (1988) *Self-Esteem in Children with Special Educational Needs,* London: Routledge

Karabenick, S. (Ed.) (1998) *Strategic Help Seeking: Implications for Learning and Teaching,* New Jersey: Lawrence Erlbaum Associates

Lawrence, D. (1988) *Enhancing Self-Esteem in the Classroom,* London: Paul Chapman

Lawrence, G. (1993) *People Types and Tiger Stripes*, Centre of Applications of Psychological Types, 1993 *[Describes Myers Briggs' research and gives a useful checklist.]*

Leadbetter, J., Morris, S., Timmins, P., Knight, G. and Traxson, D. (1999) *Applying Psychology in the Classroom,* London: David Fulton *[Written by educational psychologists. Focuses on using psychology to improve teaching and learning in the classroom.]*

Learning & Skills Development Agency (LSDA) (2002) *Learning Style Taxonomies for Post-16 Learners: An Evaluation.*

Maslow, A. (1968) *Towards a Psychology of Being*, New York: Van Nostrand

NERF (2006) *The Gender Gap: Tackling Boys' Underachievement*, Bulletin 6, May 2006

Ofsted (2003) *Boys' Achievement in Secondary Schools [Gender differences in achievement.]*

Strathclyde University at www.strath.ac.uk/press/news *[Press release about research.]*

Thompson, N. and O'Neill, C. (2001) *Best Friends, Worst Enemies: Understanding the Social Lives of Children*, New York: Ballantine Books *[Interesting discussion about children's social lives at different stages of development.]*

8 Assessment

What does assessment mean?

The word *assess* originally meant to weigh something and find out its value (like gold, for example). Now we use it to mean the way we judge whether a learner can do (or know) something and how well they do it.

It is always necessary to find out what learners already know or can do, so that the right support and help can be given to enable them to move on. Assessment is the process used to find out about a learner's achievements and progress. It is not, however, some completely separate procedure. It should be a continuous process, forming an integral part of all teaching and learning in the classroom. Teachers use information about learners' achievements to help them plan the next stages of learning and to see whether their teaching strategies are successful. They work hard to make accurate and helpful assessment a consistent part of their practice. This can be a time consuming process, so an informed teaching assistant working closely with them can provide excellent support and help.

The role of a teaching assistant is absolutely vital, as your feedback to the teacher will be used in all aspects of planning for teaching and learning. If you are an HLTA you will probably work in partnership with teachers to plan for assess children's learning. However, even though you may not be involved in designing assessment processes, you will be making judgements about children's achievements as you work with them every day, watching how they learn and thinking about their successes, or the difficulties they encounter. You will be looking at their social and emotional development too, not just the subject-based curriculum. All this is part of assessment. A good basic understanding of assessment and related issues is essential for you in your working practice. Giving accurate and informed feedback to the teacher is a skill you can practise.

The National Curriculum has its own assessment framework and it is a statutory requirement for schools to administer this assessment and then report the outcome. Schools are required to have an assessment policy in place and teachers must show that they use assessment effectively with all learners. This information will form a central part of the planning in school. Make sure you are familiar with your school assessment policy. You will also need to make sure you are aware of the assessment used at your particular key stage or year group. This will vary considerably, as will your own part. At the Foundation stage you may be fully involved in assessing for the Foundation Stage Profile, whereas at Key Stage 4 you may have less direct input into formal assessment, as this is normally the responsibility of subject specialists. If you are working in a Special School or Unit, you will find assessment is always very closely linked with all aspects of teaching and learning, so you will be using a wide variety of assessment methods at all times. You may be involved in the multi-disciplinary Common Assessment Framework (CAF) that was introduced as part of Every Child Matters (DfES, 2004) Whatever Key Stage you work at, you have a vital role to play in assisting teachers with all aspects of the assessment process.

Why do we need to assess?

Teachers need to find out what learners already know and can do, so that they can plan new learning objectives and set new outcomes for learning. Your knowledge of the major learning theorists such as Piaget, Bruner and Vygotsky, will help you to understand that it is important to find out what learners already know so that you can give them the right help to move on to the next stage. Teachers use this assessment information to help them to set new learning objectives and plan new teaching and learning opportunities. This is part of the planning, teaching and assessing cycle, which should form a continuous loop:

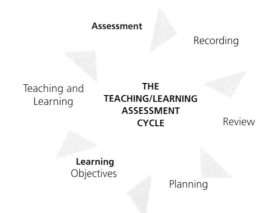

The teaching/learning assessment cycle

Teachers also use this information to measure the success and value of their teaching methods, strategies, use of resources and ability to make the curriculum accessible for all learners. This is a very important reason for assessing and one that you should keep constantly to the forefront of your practice. If you are working one-to-one with a child and they experience difficulty understanding something, you might assume that it's a problem related to their ability to learn. If you are working with a group and the same situation occurs, you are more likely to think that it might be because you have not explained it well, or used unhelpful resources or materials. If a child does not learn, look at the teaching methods and strategies used and the way you have implemented them first, before you consider the failure to be within the child. Of course, teachers also need to identify those pupils who are experiencing persistent difficulties, or any areas of the curriculum that cause problems for them, so that effective help can be given as soon as possible.

There are other reasons for assessing. We need to make sure that pupils have information about their own progress so that they can improve their performance. Encouraging learners to take control of their own learning is an important part of educational thinking. This is known as self-regulation and is part of personalised learning. Parents also want reliable and accurate information about pupil progress so that they know how their child is doing. Involving parents in a partnership with schools has been shown to be an effective way of improving standards. There is more information on this at www.standards.dfes.gov.uk.

Other people need to know about pupil performance too: national government and local authorities require information that tells them how learners' achievements compare across the country or across different age groups. Information from National Curriculum testing (SATs and Teacher Assessment and from other qualifications like GCSEs and A/AS Levels) can be used to compare the performance of schools or the relevance and popularity of certain subjects in the curriculum. A/AS Level results are used as entry qualifications to universities.

Employers rely on the results of assessment information (from GCSE to higher level degrees) as a way of finding out whether candidates are qualified to do the job required.

The reasons why we assess, therefore, are to:

- allow teachers to plan and meet teaching objectives
- give pupils information about their progress
- help teachers and teaching assistants to evaluate their teaching and learning strategies
- help teachers to judge the progress of the class and individual learners within the class
- provide information for parents about their child's progress
- provide information to schools, authorities, employers and national bodies on learner progress and achievement
- diagnose learner strengths and weaknesses
- see whether the school curriculum is accessible for all learners.

Types of Assessment

Norm-referenced assessment

This is assessment that measures the relative achievement of pupils against their peer group. It could be informally, within a class, or more formally as a result of standardisation. Standardisation means that trialling has been carried out to agree a level of achievement or a 'norm' for learners of a particular age or a similar profile. Pupils are then tested against the 'norm' and the results show whether they are above, at, or below the norm. Sometimes they will be given a ranking or a percentage score. Here are some examples of norm-referenced tests:

- Reading or spelling tests that give a reading or spelling age. These are often used to see which pupils are falling behind their peer group. However, they give limited information about the child's difficulty or strategies to improve.
- Cognitive abilities tests that give a score for verbal and non-verbal intelligence. These are sometimes referred to as CAT tests and are often given to Year 7 pupils to help with setting and to 'predict' GCSE results. This makes it easier for schools to make long-term plans.
- GCSEs and A/AS Level. Grade boundaries are moved to make sure that the achievement rates remain fairly stable. The students' achievements are relative to their peer group because the mark required to get a certain grade can change from year to year.

Criterion-referenced assessment

Pupil achievement is measured against pre-set criteria, regardless of how their peer group achieves. This is easier when there is a specific task to do and where there is a minimum standard required. It is assessed on a 'can do' or 'not yet ready to do' model. The principles of criteria referenced testing are often brought into all assessment by providing checklists for learners and markers to follow. Here are some examples of criterion-referenced assessment:

- A swimming badge awarded for being able to swim 10 metres.
- Tick lists used as check-up sheets in Maths.
- Checklists used in Special Schools to track children's developmental progress.
- NVQ for teaching assistants – includes set criteria for knowledge, performance, and scope, which the teaching assistant must show evidence that they have met.
- National Curriculum Standard Assessment Tests (commonly called SATs). These are nationally set, statutory tasks given to learners at the end of Key Stages 1, 2 and 3. Results are published so that comparisons can be made between schools.
- Pre-screening for Early Learning Strategy (ELS) in Year 1.
- Foundation Stage Profile. This is a way of measuring the progress and identifying the learning needs of young children in the

Foundation Stage. It is based on the Early Learning Goals and is used during the final year of the Foundation Stage. Schools have to send results to their LA at the end of the year. They may use their own assessment recording information if they wish, rather than the given profile.

Combined assessment

Some assessment is both norm-referenced and criterion-referenced.

- Level descriptors for National Curriculum subjects are a complicated issue. They give an Attainment Level and are assessed by the teacher. The level descriptors require teachers to make a 'best fit' judgement of the level each learner has achieved by assessing what they can do. The test is marked against set criteria, but the mark levels are moved up or down, according to the 'norm'. The level descriptors themselves are the product of research to discover what a learner should be able to achieve at a certain age – so they are norm-referenced in their set up!

- P Levels are below Level 1. They are used to further break down the assessment framework when a pupil is working towards Level 1. They are used widely in Special Schools.

Ipsative assessment

This type of assessment compares a learner's performance and achievement with their previous performance and achievement. It is used by athletes when they concentrate on improving a personal best. Ipsative assessment is a very useful way of motivating and challenging all learners, particularly those very able pupils who are achieving at a higher level than the rest of their peer group. It is also very successful in Special Schools where children may be working on individual learning programmes, and with children with SEN, who may have persistent individual difficulties to overcome. The use of target setting is an important part of this approach.

Assessment strategies

We often talk about two kinds of assessment, summative and formative. Both have a place within the school assessment framework for different reasons. Summative assessment gives an instant measure of pupils' achievement. Formative assessment helps us to influence and shape the development of learners as they progress. Some types of assessment have both summative and formative elements. For example, the Foundation Stage Profile can be used as a summative guide at the end of the year, or as a running, working document. It is usually easier to compare schools and institutions using summative assessment information.

Summative assessment

This is a snapshot of a learners' performance at any one time, *sum - marising* what has been achieved.

- It provides final judgements about achievements.
- It records attainment at that moment in time.
- It provides comparable information for schools, parents or outside organisations.
- It helps schools to keep organised track of pupil performance.

There are many examples of summative assessments in school, as indicated in the table below.

Summative assessments	
SATs	Nationally set Standard Assessment Tasks given at the end of KS 2 and 3 to measure pupils' achievement in certain areas of the National Curriculum.
Optional Tests Years 3, 4 and 5	Non-statutory voluntary tests taken during KS 2 to allow schools to track pupil progress.
GCSEs	Tests given at the end of KS 4 in place of statutory testing. Administered by awarding bodies/QCA. Gives a final assessment for school leavers. Results enable comparisons between schools (league tables) and act as entry qualifications for FE.
AS/A Levels	Assessment taken in Years 12/13. Used as entrance qualifications for university/higher education.
End-of-year exams	In-school end-of-year tests, set by teachers.
End-of-module exams	Tests given at the end of a taught unit.
Foundation Stage Profile	Establishes a baseline profile of learner's progress at the Foundation Stage. Emphasis on recognition of problems so that early intervention can take place.
Diagnostic tests	Specialist testing for pupils with suspected additional needs.
Weekly tests, e.g. spelling/tables	Set by teachers regularly to monitor progress and help pupils to practise learning.
Teacher assessment Years 2, 6 and 9.	Teachers identify a level of attainment for each learner in the core subjects, based on professional observation and judgement.Work is often moderated (compared to check standard) across year groups or classes.
World Class tests	Optional tests for learners with exceptional ability (top 10%) in Maths, Technology and Science. Given at age 13.
Standardised tests	Commercially produced tests, which examine different areas of learning, e.g. non-verbal/verbal reasoning, spelling ability, etc.
Class or revision tests	Teacher-set practice examinations (e.g. mock SATs and GCSEs) to practise examination techniques.

Summative assessment standards are compared within schools (for example, by all year group teachers meeting together to compare pieces of learners' work at the end of a Key Stage) or externally (for example, at moderation meetings for GCSE coursework examiners). This process is known as standardisation, moderation or agreement trialling.

Formative assessment

Formative assessment monitors progress continuously, day-by-day, using the information gathered to feed back into the teaching cycle. It is called formative assessment because its aim is to form or influence teaching, learning and assessing. The importance of formative assessment in helping children to learn is well recognised (Black and William, 1998).

- It is built into everyday teaching.
- It gives immediate feedback to the teacher and the learner.
- It focuses on positive achievement.
- It encourages pupil involvement.
- It helps teachers to evaluate the success of teaching strategies used and to adapt their teaching quickly.
- It identifies areas of future learning.

Formative assessments

Questioning	Way of establishing what pupils know and extending their learning.
Sampling	Making a representative sample of pupil work. Sometimes kept in portfolio form.
Pupil self-evaluation	Method of encouraging pupils to evaluate their own progress.
Discussion with pupil	Opportunity to talk with pupil about their work and gain insight into their own perception of their progress, including strengths and weaknesses.
Analysis of work	Looking at pupil work in detail to identify problem areas, recognise progress and identify future teaching and learning needs.
Marking and feedback	Verbal or written feedback to the learner on their work/achievement/progress.
Observation	Formal or informal observation of pupils as they learn.
Target setting	Using information from assessment and the curriculum to set targets for pupil achievement.
Talking with colleagues	Discussions with other teachers or teaching assistants, or other professionals to gain an insight into the progress, achievement or difficulties of learners.

Discussion with parents	Use of parents' expertise and perspectives to add to an understanding of learners.
Sharing learning objectives	Making sure that pupils understand what is required and with pupils why it is required.
Half-termly assessments	Set by teachers in core subjects.
Planning	Building information from assessment into future planning: • Short-term • Medium-term • Long-term.

Diagnostic assessment

You may also encounter diagnostic assessment. This is a process that produces a profile of learners' strengths and weaknesses. It is often used with children with SEN to help plan an intervention programme. For example, a commercially produced reading test may be used to find the particular areas of reading that cause difficulty for a learner. A behaviour checklist might be used to identify a child who could have Attention Deficit Disorder or an autistic spectrum disorder. The Aston Index (a commercially available battery of different tests, e.g. visual memory) could be used to give a profile of a learner suspected of having a specific learning difficulty. Some of these diagnostic assessments are computer based, like COPS (computer profiling system), which provides early identification in dyslexia. These can be used to provide evidence for extra help in the classroom or even special concessions for exams.

Recording and review

Teachers record the results of assessment in different ways, depending on the Key Stage they are working in. Some of this will be informal notes and jottings based on their own observations and some will be formal records that include marks and results of tests or tasks. They will often keep examples of pupils' work in portfolios or files and may use these to compare standards across year groups or between schools.

You will be involved in some of this record keeping. For example, there may be a place on your Literacy Hour planning sheet for you to record how each individual child responded to the task, or your teacher may ask you to annotate a learner's work indicating the type of help and prompting you gave. You could be recording the results of a tables test or filling in a Foundation Stage scale. If you are implementing a specialist programme you may need to keep detailed records for your own benefit and to inform any other member of staff who works with the same learners.

Recording information is important in case you are absent or moved to work with another class. However, try to keep a balance and do not spend so long making notes that you do not have time to work with the pupil. Remember, nobody grew just by being measured! As always, make sure you are clear on what you have to record and what format it should be in.

Planning

Teachers use the information gained from assessment to plan their teaching and learning. We have already seen that schools have Development or Improvement Plans. They will also have long-term, medium-term and short-term plans to map out how the curriculum is delivered and taught. Teaching assistants have an essential part to play in this process. Your role should be clearly identified in the plans and your feedback on learning should be used when new plans are made.

Long-term plans

Schools use the syllabus or Programme of Study for each curriculum area to make a long-term plan for the year ahead. Many of these are already in published form and could be:

- the Programme of Study for each National Curriculum subject at each Key Stage
- the relevant syllabus from each awarding body at GCSE/A Level
- a developmental syllabus for some Special Schools
- the Early Learning Goals for the Foundation Stage
- the Primary Strategies
- the Key Stage 3 Strategy.

(The last two include guidance on how to teach each element.)
These are called 'Schemes of Work' and they set out what has to be taught and learned. If you are doing a teaching assistant course, you will have a scheme of work too, based on the requirements of the course.

Medium-term plans

Teachers translate the information from the Schemes of Work into 'learning outcomes' or 'objectives'. These are what the pupil should be able to do, know, understand or be aware of, for example, be able to derive doubles of whole numbers to 100; be able to evaluate a cartoon as a primary source in history. Teachers will then plan the teaching activities and resources needed for the pupils to learn, including the requirement for any specialist resources like books, visits, or any extra teaching assistant help in the classroom. In most cases, teachers will join with others teaching the same year group, or teaching in the same subject area, to collaborate to make a framework for their teaching. It is a complex and skilled job that is now being made easier by the number of published lessons and unit plans that can be bought or downloaded from the Internet. They may also combine with teachers in other subject areas to work in a cross-curricular or topic-based way.

All the strategies and intervention programmes have detailed medium-term plans to follow. You may be delivering the ELS/ALS and FLS and have worked with these. These plans are usually made over a term or half term, which is why they are referred to as medium-term plans. Teachers will adapt and customise them for the needs of individual schools, classes and learners, and use their own interests and skills to make the learning activities as interesting and varied as possible.

Short-term plans

Teachers will make short-term weekly and daily plans, which give a more detailed description of the daily and weekly activities. This is often in the format of a timetable. They will then produce individual lesson plans, many of which are now in published form or can be purchased commercially. You may also be using the very detailed and prescriptive plans for the Springboard, ELS, ALS, and ELS Intervention Strategies, or tightly focused SEN support lessons like Beat Dyslexia or PAT (Phonological Awareness Training). Any of these may include:

- learning objectives/intentions
- whole class activities
- group activities
- activities for each level of ability, including extension and support (differentiation)
- all resources needed
- use of adult help in the classroom (if available)
- language focus
- targets (if applicable)
- plenary or end discussion
- assessment
- evaluation (how it went).

Your own role in the lesson should be planned and you should be able to give the teacher useful feedback and evaluation on how it went, i.e. whether pupils learned; what they found easy/difficult; what resources were useful; what strategies worked, etc.

Teachers adapt and change their plans in the light of information provided from assessing pupils so your feedback is essential. Some teachers use published planning and feedback sheets, others have their own. They do not need to be neat and clean. They should be working documents, annotated and written on as required. Teachers are usually happy for you to consult their planning file if you are unsure. Everybody has a different way of planning and, sometimes, you need to design your own pro-forma just to get your head round the whole concept of planning. Although it is important to focus on the learning objective and not get too sidetracked, never stick rigidly to a plan that isn't working. Teaching is all about adapting, changing and being flexible. This is why it is important to have a good working relationship with your teacher and to be as knowledgeable as possible, so that you can adapt and change your input if it isn't working. Sometimes you will find that the best learning is unplanned – it arises spontaneously during a lesson.

Your role in assessment

Your expertise in working closely with learners and your partnership with teachers enables you to play a very valuable part in assessment and feedback, particularly when pupils experience difficulties. You have a particularly valuable role to play in all types of formative assessment. Here are some of the methods used in assessing children, with an analysis of the role you can play.

Making learning outcomes clear

Teachers use their planning to set up teaching and learning activities for pupils. Each will have a purpose and a learning outcome. You may see these referred to as learning intentions or learning objectives. It is important that you are absolutely clear in your own mind what the outcome of the activity is so that you can give the required support, or manage the lesson effectively when working unsupervised. It will also give you a focus. The Primary National Strategy documents and Additional Support programmes make learning outcomes clear. However, you may need supplementary outcomes for some sessions, or you may be responsible for implementing an SEN programme where you have a good deal of input into the planning.

- There may be several learning outcomes for the same group, particularly as learners become more skilled.
- A learning outcome may last for several sessions.
- Outcomes can be differentiated across groups of learners so your group may have a different one to the rest of the class. Published schemes of work often have differentiated outcomes.
- Learning outcomes need to be clear and unambiguous and should use positive sentences, e.g. from ICT: "At the end of this lesson you will be able to use an icon to start a CD-ROM."
- There may be other learning outcomes that you wish to achieve alongside the main activity, e.g. to sit quietly during reading or to ask for help at a certain time.
- If learners can complete the learning outcome quickly and successfully you should have extension activities available. Make sure you report this to the teacher or have it built into your own planning.
- Make sure you do not have too many outcomes for the age and development of the pupils you work with so that they become confused or demotivated. Learners with SEN often need learning outcomes broken down into small steps.

It is important for everyone that learning outcomes are expressed clearly and unambiguously. Always ask your teacher if you are unsure or need guidance.

Although it is important to focus on learning outcomes, you should also take advantage of opportunities for learning which occur spontaneously in the classroom. Ignoring these can make learning rigid and dull.

Key Stage 2: "Knowing the learning outcome has been important for me. As a TA I sometimes feel under pressure to get the pupils just to finish, so they have at least something to show for their time with me. If I focus on the learning outcome I don't worry about whether they have written a page or finished everything – just what progress they have made towards the learning outcome."

Sharing learning outcomes and intentions with pupils

Research has shown that sharing learning outcomes with children in simple, pupil-friendly language helps them to be more focused and become more involved in their own learning (Clarke, 2001). In many schools the outcome is written on the blackboard or the whiteboard. Shirley Clarke believes that children respond well to the visual impact of seeing the learning outcome rather than just hearing it. It motivates the more able children to keep on task and reminds less able children what they are supposed to be doing. This is then reinforced in the final stage of the session. You may see this referred to in school as the WALT programme – We Are Learning To. Some teachers like children to copy down the learning outcome, although this often uses up time which would be better spent on the actual activity.

Sometimes learning outcomes are put in pictorial form, particularly for children with certain types of SEN like autistic spectrum disorders. You need to make sure you separate the instructions for the activity from the learning outcomes too, so that they know the difference between what they are learning and what they actually have to do. Tell them why they are doing it too – "You need to learn to save your work on the computer so that you will be able to find it again when you need it. We are going to do this by writing a poem and then saving it."

Key Stage 4: "When I went back to college to do a TA course I found it really difficult at first to write assignments. I didn't know what the tutors were looking for. Then they gave us some criteria to match and it became much easier. It has made me realise that, as a TA, *I* know when the children are succeeding, but *they* do not necessarily know what we are looking for!"

Encouraging learners to set success criteria

Teachers are clear on what they want to be achieved at the end of the learning activity, but children are often not aware of the characteristics of a successful learning outcome. You can help them by discussing success criteria with them and letting them set their own success criteria whenever possible. You may see this referred to as WILF – What am I Looking For?

Helping with the target setting process

Target setting seems to be a constant part of everyday practice in school. Everybody has targets, from the Secretary of State for Education to the pupils in the classroom. LAs help school governing bodies use information from pupils' performance to set targets for themselves. These are part of the School Development Plan and relate to improved grades for summative assessment in public examinations like GCSEs or SATs.

Schools use benchmarking to set their projected standard. This measures their performance in relation to other schools in the area and takes into account things like the number of pupils who have free school meals, or the number of learners with SEN, in addition to the performance of the best schools locally. Schools used to have a PANDA (performance and assessment data) report from Ofsted that included all the relevant statistics and data. This has now been merged with the DfES's Pupil Achievement Tracker (PAT) in a single, on-line document, RAISEonline.

Once they have benchmarking data schools set targets for staff, and encourage teachers to target-set for classes and learners. The Primary and Key Stage 3 Strategies for Literacy and Mathematics have their own guidance for target setting and assessment (QCA, 1999). Targets for P Scales link into existing assessment schemes.

Many schools have computer recording systems that enable them to keep track of pupils' progress as they move through the National Curriculum levels. They use this information to focus on the areas that need to be improved. For example, a school may wish to get better SATs results for children's writing. Teachers will focus on setting simple targets for year groups, like improving use of punctuation or spelling. Targets need not necessarily be curriculum subject-based either. Children can have behavioural, social or study skills targets to meet. For example, a learner may have a target to answer one question in class, or to put their hand up before they speak.

It is the teachers and teaching assistants who work everyday with children in the classroom who are at the forefront of raising standards. Teachers rely heavily on a teaching assistant's experience with the children they work with when they are target setting. It is also important to share this process with pupils and let them be fully involved in creating and meeting their targets. Parents can also play a role in this and reinforce some of these targets at home if necessary.

- Targets can be for year groups, classes, groups of learners or individual children.

- Ensure you know the targets of every child you support. Consistency is important and children deserve praise when they meet their target. Some children will have target cards on their desk; others may keep them in a book or tray. In some Key Stage 3/4 schools learners have them on small cards like credit cards in their pockets. Check to see how you should document this.
- It is ideal if you are fully involved in the target setting process in the classroom. You should certainly be involved in any feedback on targets.
- Targets can cover all areas of learning. Teachers use both curriculum information and their knowledge of individual learners to set targets. For example, they may decide a learner needs to be able to use more descriptive words in their writing, so may use that as a target to move them towards the next level. A learner may have a behavioural problem that makes them distract other children so may have a target to work alone for five minutes without interfering with other children learning. Setting targets for individual children is very time-consuming so you may find class targets are used instead.
- Make sure the targets are specific and measurable. For example, "Write more" is too vague; "Include six facts in your writing" is more quantifiable.
- Don't give learners too many targets at once as it can become too much.
- Make sure the targets are achievable. Asking a child with AD(H)D to keep still for an hour is not likely to be successful. Nor is asking a child with dyslexia to always check their spelling in a dictionary. Dictionaries are for checking meanings rather than spellings, as you have to know how to spell the word to look it up in a dictionary. However, asking a learner with dyslexia to check for *b d* reversals (with a prompt) is achievable.
- Make sure targets are challenging enough. This is particularly important if you are working with high-achieving pupils.
- Encourage a learning culture by sharing your own self-set targets with pupils to help them understand the whole concept of target setting. For example, your targets might be: to use a dictionary when you come across a word you don't understand; to use the Internet to book a holiday; to sit down for five minutes at lunchtime!
- Feedback information to the teacher. You will be able to make relevant and helpful suggestions for different targets.

There is some criticism of target setting because it concentrates on the outcome rather than the process of learning and can be difficult to do well. Giving learners a target in one area can make them lose focus on others. It can also lead to an unmanageable workload unless very carefully and sensitively implemented.

Using effective questioning as part of assessment

All teachers ask learners questions to check their understanding and to help them extend and develop their thinking. The type of questions teachers ask, and the way they encourage pupils to answer, has a big impact on the successful development of learner's thinking and understanding. Effective questioning is a skill that you can continue to develop throughout your career as a teaching assistant.

Types of questioning

- Closed question. This requires a one-word answer, for example, "Do you understand that?" or "What letter does this word begin with?"
- Open question. This requires an open-ended answer, for example, "What did you do during the holidays?" "What do you understand by the term 'industrial revolution'?" "How can you show me you are listening?" "Can you explain why the bulb lit up?"

You will need to use both types of questioning, but the use of open questions will give children more opportunity to clarify and extend their thinking through language and discussion.

Directing questions

Make sure you distribute questions evenly around the class or group. It is easy to overlook some children or ask the same children again and again. Be sensitive to shy pupils. A non-threatening atmosphere in your teaching practice and an interactive approach where you encourage learners to talk to you will help. Check your body language too. If you look enthusiastic and interested you will encourage pupils to take part. A simple nod of the head or a smile can be used to encourage a response. Do not always insist on eye contact while you are questioning. Some children find it very threatening. Ask them to demonstrate another way to show you they are listening.

Giving wait time

If you ask an open question, ensure that you give learners time to think by waiting for their response. It is easy to jump in and answer the question for them. Thinking can take time and children will get very frustrated if they are never given an opportunity to answer in a detailed way. Obviously there are occasions when a quick-fire response is required too, as in the Mathematics lesson, and other children may get bored and restless if they have to wait for some children to answer. In many classes whiteboards and number or letter fans are used. These allow individual learners time to respond to a question whilst doing something all the time, either by answering on the board or holding up the correct letter or number on the fan.

Prompting an answer

There are several techniques you can use to prompt answers:

- Ask another simpler question.
- Give part of the answer to break it into steps.

- Give an additional piece of information.
- Repeat the pupil's answer to help them clarify their thinking.
- Ask another pupil to help out.
- Remind the pupil of information from a previous lesson.
- Rephrase, using different vocabulary or context.

Responding to answers

Make sure you respond positively to a pupil's contribution, even if it is not right. For example, you could say "That is an interesting point but..." You should say what is correct and build on the answer; keep in mind that an opinion cannot be wrong.

If questioning in a group or class situation, use the pupil's name when you are responding: "Sally told us that..."

Show an interest in a learner's thinking processes: "How did you think of that?" "What was your strategy?"

Extending or probing pupils' thinking

This is a very important part of the questioning technique. Watch how your teacher uses questioning so that you can copy their techniques. You can ask questions like:

- Can you tell me more about...?
- Why do you think that is the case...?
- Can you give me another example...?
- Can you compare that to...?
- Is there another way we can look at this...?

Bloom's taxonomy

Benjamin Bloom, an educational psychologist, and his colleagues identified three domains or types of learning:

- affective – feelings, attitudes and emotions
- psychomotor – motor skills
- cognitive – thinking and mental processing.

Within the cognitive domain, Bloom categorised different types of thinking in a taxonomy (a hierarchical structure or classification of data). He identified and classified different levels of intellectual behaviour important for cognitive learning, from the simple recall of information to the most complex abstract thinking. Teachers and educationalists have used this information to help them set educational objectives for learners and to help them extend learners' thinking by using appropriate questioning. You can use knowledge of Bloom's taxonomy to ensure that you use effective questioning when working with all learners.

- Evaluation – judging information using personal reflection to justify an approach
- Synthesis – applying previously learned or analysed learning in a new way to create original ideas

- Analysis – breaking down information into component parts and analysing the relationship between each
- Application – applying previous knowledge and understanding in new learning
- Comprehension – showing understanding by explaining
- Knowledge – recalling facts and information.

(Adapted from Bloom,1956)

Bloom's taxonomy was revised in 2001 by Anderson and Krathwohl.

National Literacy Strategy

Shirley Clarke, an adviser on assessment, includes some very useful strategies for questioning, taken from the original National Literacy Strategy. For more information on effective questioning, see Clarke, 2001 or Teachernet (www.teachernet).

Talking to pupils – helping children to evaluate their own learning

Just as learners need to be involved in the whole process of target setting, they should also be encouraged to use self-evaluation techniques, rather than relying on the teacher to always give them feedback. Of course, this will depend on the subject area and the level. Anyone who has spoken to students coming out of an A Level exam will know how difficult it can be to evaluate your performance under exam pressure. Sometimes we spend too much time observing, analysing and assessing children's performance without consulting them. Talk to them about their work; ask them how they did something, what they found easy and what was hard.

This is particularly important with a child who has any kind of additional need. Their own insight into their difficulties is a vital part of any approach to meet their needs. As a teaching assistant you often have the time and opportunity to do this. The Primary and Key Stage 3 Strategies have in-built evaluation sessions, when learners are encouraged to discuss how the activity went and what they have learned. You might want to use this as a model when you are working with learners to round off the activity and review the learning that has taken place. It also gives you an opportunity to check their understanding and skill development, and helps children reflect on how they learn (there is more on this in Chapter 9). You can help children by encouraging them to talk about the following:

- Whether they have achieved the learning outcomes.
- Any problems or difficulties they encountered.
- How they overcame these difficulties.
- Strategies they found helpful.
- What they enjoyed most.
- How they could use this learning elsewhere.
- What materials or resources were most helpful.
- Whether they have improved on a previous performance ("Did you understand more than last time?").

You should always use the recording documentation provided by your school to complete with the pupil, or ask the teacher if you can design your own if none is available.

Evaluating pupils' work

Teachers look at pupils' work to gain an idea of their achievement and progress. This is something that happens every day. For example, at Key Stage 4 a teacher might be marking a History/Politics essay, whereas a Reception Class teacher could be looking at a child's attempt to write a simple sentence. It is not just about writing, though. The work could be a piece of design; something the learner has made or generated on the computer or through digital media such as a video or tape; a musical or sporting performance; or a talk or discussion. Teachers will be assessing against the learning outcomes for the activity. These could be improving skills and abilities, developing understanding or increasing knowledge. They will also be looking at the way the learners have undertaken the activity and the pointers it gives to the next phase of learning. As a teaching assistant, you should work in partnership with your teacher to evaluate pupils' work. Here are some examples:

- An analysis of a piece of free writing can give a very useful blueprint for constructing a spelling programme. The kind of mistakes the pupil makes will give an indication of what they need to learn next.
- A PE teacher will look at a pupil's performance and suggest strategies for improvement, like practising passing or stick control in hockey.
- An analysis of pupils' end of year Physics paper might suggest that the whole class needs to go over a certain topic again.
- Listening to a pupil doing a language oral exam might tell the teacher that the pupil needs more practice in memorising vocabulary.
- Marking a Year 12 student's History essay might tell a teacher that the learner needs to develop the skill of seeing both sides of an argument.
- If a teacher or teaching assistant hears a child read, they can rate their reading performance and gain an excellent insight into the strategies used. A relevant reading intervention could then be set up, rather than just giving the learner more practice.
- An observation of role-play may suggest that a particular learner needs to work through a social use of language programme.
- Of course, a pupil's work may just be extremely good and not present any ideas for improvement!

Feedback to the learner

Assessing pupils' work is a central part of teaching and learning. It is vital that learners are then given feedback, so that they know how they are doing. They also need to be given positive suggestions to show them how they can improve. Sometimes this is referred to as formative feedback. All teachers need the time to use their expertise to guide and develop pupils' learning through detailed assessment and feedback. Some feedback will be informal; some will be formal. At Key Stage 1/2 you may be involved in giving verbal and written feedback. At Key Stage 3/4 your feedback may be more verbal than written. You will develop your own expertise in feeding back to learners but there are some basic guidelines to follow.

- Check on the school policy for feedback and make sure that you are familiar with each individual teacher's and subject area requirements. Always check with the teacher how much feedback they would like you to give.
- Make sure you know any marking scheme method, whether stickers are given, and how ticks or coloured pens are used.
- Take time to look at work properly.
- Make sure you understand the learning outcome and targets so that your feedback is accurate. For example, if pupils are writing under time constraint it is no use feeding back that they should take more time to make their handwriting neater. Your feedback should first tell them the progress they are making towards the learning objectives.
- Be as detailed as you can in your response, if you have the time available.
- Comment on what is good first so that you can be encouraging: "Well done, you have described Lady Macbeth's motivation really well."
- Recognise the effort they have put in, not just the achievement.
- Say what you enjoyed/liked about their work.
- Ask the learner how well they think they have done.
- Give practical suggestions for improvement or development: "You could make a finger space between all your words/use two colours in your diagram to make it clearer/leave more space round your working out."
- Be accurate and realistic. Do not just say it is wonderful when it is not. Most pupils hate blanket praise when they know something is not good.

Sometimes pupils will be given a grade or a mark for their work. Research has shown that some learners do not take much notice of any formative comments once they have seen the grade or mark. Yet it is the formative comments that are most helpful for future development because they tell pupils how they can improve. A very valuable role for a teaching assistant is to work with a learner to help them to interpret what the grade means and reinforce ways in which they can improve. You will need to check with your teacher before you do this, so that you can ask them what the pupil needs to do.

Remember that learners are just that – learners. They need encouragement, praise, positive feedback and the right kind of help to keep them motivated and make them successful. As a society we invest a great deal in providing enjoyable and successful opportunities for adults to learn. Most adults would never take up a new hobby or activity if they were taught the same way that some children are made to learn!

Always check with a teacher if you are unsure about how you feedback to learners. They are experts in assessment and will be able to give you guidance.

Observation

Teachers constantly monitor the way that children learn and how successful their teaching strategies are. They build a profile of learners' individual strengths and weaknesses. Observation is an absolutely vital part of this process. It is an extremely useful role for a teaching assistant to be able to look at what is happening in the classroom and feed that information back to teaching staff. This can be informal observation, as part of general observation of learning, or more formal, structured observation to look at a specific area of a learner's development.

Informal assessment

When you work with pupils you make observations all the time about the way children learn. Perhaps a particular child finds something difficult and you think the work may be set at too high a standard. Maybe you notice that a child is always alone in the playground. You could have an idea for helping a child understand something by watching the strategies they use to learn. You may think that an extra resource could be of use, or notice a group of children racing through an activity that looks too easy for them. You could see that one child has difficulty interacting with others, or that another finds it hard to focus during unstructured activities. You might be checking to see what level of skill a learner has in a particular area.

These are all informal observations and you should develop the habit of always noting what is happening when children are learning. It is easier to do this when you are not directly involved in the teaching activity, which is why a teaching assistant is such a valuable resource in the classroom. A teaching assistant is able to observe things that the teacher may not have the opportunity to see. In a good working relationship teaching assistants and teachers will support each other, observing and using constructive evaluation to improve teaching and learning in the classroom. Keep a notepad or notebook with you so that you can jot down informal observations – it is easy to forget in the hustle and bustle of the classroom! Always let the teacher know what you are doing, though.

Formal observations

In many schools teachers go in to other teachers' classes to see how a subject is taught by other staff. This is referred to as curriculum or subject monitoring. Sometimes a more formal observation of teaching and learning is required. You may be asked to undertake an observation for the teacher if there is some concern over a child's progress or behaviour, or if they would like feedback about the usefulness of a resource or teaching strategy.

First make sure you are very clear on what the teacher requires and why they would like you to do the observation. You could be asked to undertake a 'participant observation', where you are participating in or part of the activity (watching how learners respond during your group work, for example). Alternatively, you may be involved in an observation where you are an outside observer (monitoring the way a child responds to the teacher in a lesson, for example). You could be focusing on physical, cognitive, emotional, social or language development; watching how a child at Key Stage 1 plays; or focusing on a particular curriculum area or teaching strategy (use of problem-solving, for example). There are several ways to do this:

- tracking or following an individual child over a period of time
- using a checklist to record instances of certain learning behaviours
- using a tape recorder to record a learning activity
- making a narrative or running written record
- taking a time sample of learning behaviour at a certain pre-set interval (e.g. every 10 minutes).

Recording observations

Make sure you are clear on how you should record information and the format to be used. Your school may have observation sheets that can be used or you may be able to design your own. Always remember that you must be objective in your observation. It is easy to see the behaviour that you are expecting to see, even if it is not there! You may be asked to provide an evaluation of your own work, or the teacher may want to evaluate themselves. As always, keep the issue of confidentiality in mind.

Discussion with colleagues/parents

Talking with colleagues is an important method of increasing your understanding of learners. Teachers rely very heavily on the expertise of teaching assistants, particularly when they work closely with individual learners. Make sure you benefit from your colleagues' experiences. They may have a successful strategy that you could try, or have used a resource that could be helpful. If you do have contact with parents then their expertise and insight is an essential part of building a whole picture of learners' abilities, strengths and difficulties.

Feedback to teachers

The way you feed back assessment information to teachers will vary depending on the type of assessment used and your working practice. It could be an informal chat over coffee at break time, or a more formal written record. Some teachers like you to annotate children's work with brief comments, but always check before you do this. Many teachers use the formal planning/feedback sheets in published schemes to give teaching assistants directions and to receive appropriate feedback. It is often far more difficult to do this at Key Stage 3/4 when teaching assistants are moving between classes and subject areas. Then you might find a brief summary handed to the teacher as the lesson ends is effective, or you may be able to give verbal feedback at a weekly departmental meeting. Either way, it is up to you to make sure the teacher receives relevant information.

Make sure the information is accurate, useful, short and to the point. No teacher has time to read long rambling descriptions of anything, let alone use that information effectively. See Chapter 15 on Professional Development and Training for more guidance on this.

Recording and reporting

Recording refers to the way we keep a record of assessment. *Reporting* refers to the way that information is given to any relevant and interested parties, children, parents and school management, etc. Schools have a legal responsibility to publish the results of National Curriculum assessment. These results form part of the league tables that are used to compare the relative performance of schools.

How do we report assessment?

Schools report on learners' progress in several ways:

- Information from statutory assessment is published by the school governing body.
- Learners are given a Record of Achievement or Learning Profile.
- Progress cards or reports are produced and sent to parents.
- Consultation evenings are held for parents to have the opportunity to discuss their child's progress with teachers. At Key Stage 3/4, this is normally through subject area specialists.
- Learners with additional needs have individualised assessment records through the relevant process (e.g. Code of Practice).

You may be required to attend a parents' meeting or asked for your opinion by a teacher compiling a report. When you work in a Special School your input is an absolutely essential part of all assessment and reporting.

Issues in assessment

Assessment information is recorded and reported in many different ways. It is important that the purpose of recording information is very clear so that it does not become just an end in itself, but is useful and relevant. Many teaching assistants who have developed extensive recording systems in their work with children with SEN complain that no one ever has time to look at their notes! Make sure you discuss issues of recording with your teacher/teachers so that the best use is made of your time and expertise.

Always keep the key principles of assessment in mind and ask the teacher if you have any concerns. Ask yourself:

- What *exactly* is being assessed here?
- Is this assessment accessible for all pupils? (More on this in Chapter 12.)
- Am I being objective?
- Am I being fair?

Assessment remains a controversial issue in schools across the world. Sometimes it seems difficult to get the right balance between the effective use of assessment to raise standards and over-assessing learners so that they become anxious and demotivated about learning. There have also been concerns about pupils being over-taught the techniques and methods used to pass exams, rather than being able to learn freely. It is a real skill to assess pupils without restricting the curriculum and making them feel anxious. This is another key role for teaching assistants – to tune into the worries and fears of learners, build their confidence and help them to have a fair chance.

> **Key Stage 2 Teacher:** "My teaching assistant has played an absolutely essential part in giving our learners with SEN the opportunity to do well in SATs by giving them the confidence to learn and helping them to practise all the skills they need."

An examination culture usually benefits those pupils with learning styles that enable them to shine in exams; those with good visual and verbal memories who like to work 'in the flow'. Coursework benefits learners who find the time constraint and memory overload of exams difficult and like a more research-based, methodical and analytical approach. You need to be confident about supporting learners in both types of assessment, particularly at Key Stage 3/4. Where coursework is concerned, make sure you understand exactly what is being assessed and how much help you can give so that the work is produced by the pupil and not you.

The timetable for Key Stage 1 SATs was altered so that schools have more freedom to give them when children are ready. There have also been ideas for a diploma to replace A/AS Levels to lessen exam pressure on students. Assessment changes all the time.

Teachers can often feel overburdened with paperwork and find the whole subject of assessment to be anxiety provoking. There are so many ways that you can be of great assistance both to teachers and the pupils you support. Keep your focus on the main purpose of assessment, as a vital part of teaching and learning.

Key reading

Key references are given in bold.

Ayers, H., Clarke, D. and Ross, A. *(1996) Assessing Individual Needs – A Practical Approach,* London: David Fulton *[Includes photocopiable forms for various assessment techniques.]*

Berger, A. (Ed.), Buck, D. and Davis, V. *(2001) Assessing Pupils Performance Using the P Levels,* London: David Fulton *[Guidance on standards for P Levels.]*

Brooks, V. (2002) *Assessment in Secondary Schools: The New Teachers' Guide to Monitoring Assessment, Recording, Reporting and Accountability,* Buckingham: Open University Press

Brown, G. and Wragg, E.C. *(1993) Questioning,* London: Routledge *[Useful explanation of questioning techniques in the classroom.]*

Lawson, H. *(1998) Practical Records Keeping,* London: David Fulton *[Examples of record keeping formats.]*

Sharman, C., Cross, W., Vennis, D. *et al.* (2001) *Observing Children, A Practical Guide,* New York: Continuum International Publishing Group – Academi *[Observation techniques working with under 8s]*

Tilstone, C. (Ed.) *(1988) Observing Teaching and Learning: Principles and Practice,* London: David Fulton

Wragg, E. C. (1994) *An Introduction to Classroom Observation,* London: Routledge *[The basics of classroom observation.]*

References

Key references are given in bold.

Anderson, L. W., & Krathwohl, D. R. (2001) *A Taxonomy for Learning, Teaching, and Assessing: A Revision of Bloom's Taxonomy of Educational Objectives,* New York: Addison-Wesley Longman

Black, P. Wiliam, D. (1998) 'Inside the Black Box: Raising Standards through Classroom Assessment', *Phi Delta Kappa,* Vol. 80, 1998

Clarke, S. (2001) *Unlocking Formative Assessment: Practical Strategies for Enhancing Pupils' Learning in the Primary Classroom,* London: Hodder & Stoughton *[Comprehensive overview of basic assessment processes.]*

DfEE *(2001) Supporting the Target Setting Process,* London: DfEE 0025/2001

DfES (2006), *Primary National Strategy,* London: DfES

QCA *(2001) Planning, Teaching and Assessing the Curriculum for Pupils with Learning Difficulties,* London: QCA

QCA *(2003) Foundation Stage Profile Handbook,* London: QCA/03/1006,

9 Approaches to Teaching: The Role of the Teaching Assistant

Teachers have many different factors to take into account when they are planning lessons. You have already looked at the need to cover the curriculum requirements and the effect of the classroom climate or environment, and have considered the way children learn. You have also looked at the central role of assessment in teaching and learning. The diagram below illustrates the many factors that affect learning. This chapter will focus on some of the teaching approaches that may be used in the classroom, with an analysis of the role of a teaching assistant in helping and supporting learning in each case.

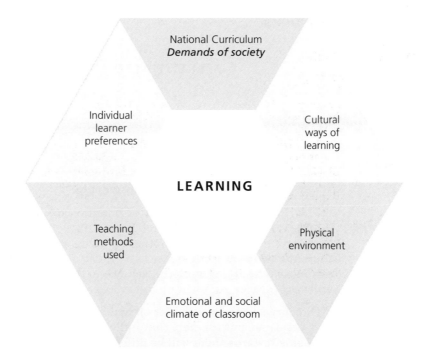

The factors that affect learning

Teachers use a variety of strategies and techniques to manage learning in the classroom. They will set learning objectives for the pupils, choose the best way to reach those objectives by planning all the activities and procedures, help, advise, instruct and guide pupils, and then arrange opportunities to assess their progress.

163

Your school will contain a diversity of learners with unique learning styles and intelligences, different cultural and social backgrounds, different needs and a variety of skills and abilities. Yet all learners are entitled to have access to the same broad, balanced curriculum wherever possible. How can we make sure that this happens? One of the most crucial things to remember is that effective and successful teachers have a strong belief in the potential of all learners and work really hard to find ways for children to learn and achieve. They have high expectations for all learners and this should always be a key part of your thinking and practice. The concept of 'differentiation' is also an important part of this and it has a key role in the personalisation of learning.

	Evaluation	Observation & Assessment	
Teaching Strategies			What the learner can already do
Pace	**DIFFERENTIATED LEARNING**		Curriculum
Grouping			Classroom Environment
	Resources	Learning Activities	

The teaching cycle

Differentiation

Differentiation is a process used to adjust and adapt teaching and learning so that all learners can achieve to their maximum potential. Baroness Warnock summed up the process when she said:

> "The purpose of education for all children is the same, the goals are the same, but the help that individual children need in progressing towards them will be different."

(Warnock, 1978)

The term 'differentiation' was originally used in relation to children with SEN, but it is now a key part of the process of inclusion for *all* learners and is judged as such by Ofsted. It means that all teachers are required to:

• Set suitable learning challenges for individual pupils

- Respond to pupils' diverse learning needs
- Overcome potential barriers to learning and assessment for individuals and groups of pupils.

Although this whole book reflects the concept of differentiation, there are some basic principles that can be summarised here. A confident and expert teaching assistant is a wonderful resource to help teachers to differentiate teaching and learning.

Planning for differentiation

Teachers will take the following elements into account when they are planning for all learners.

Learner profile
- Attainment level (what the learner can do)
- Individual abilities/intelligences/strengths
- Learning style
- Individual learning needs (SEN, EAL, etc.)
- Individual problem areas in the curriculum (maybe a child has missed teaching time because of absence or just struggles with one particular concept)
- Interests
- Cultural ways of learning
- Personal targets
- Disability.

Curriculum
- Learning outcome required
- Cross-curricular learning
- Group targets for class
- Assessment required.

How to differentiate

Teachers will consider different factors, adapt the content and pace of teaching and use a variety of different methods and resources:

- Learning environment
  - Time of day
  - Classroom resources
  - Room or learning space.
- Adult help
  - Staffing available (teaching assistant or voluntary helper, etc.).

Teachers will differentiate in the *content, process* or *outcome* of teaching and learning, as follows overleaf.

Content

Content is concerned with what is taught and learned.

- The content of lessons can be varied to meet the needs of individual learners.

- Some learners may need:

    - reinforcement of previous learning, while others may be ready to move on to a different level immediately (use of practice activities and extension activities)
    - an activity broken into steps, whereas others can cope with the activity as a whole (small steps)
    - specific teaching in areas like vocabulary or spelling, while others are confident about all the language used
    - direct teaching in sub-skills for the activity, while others already have mastery.

- Some learners may be:

    - working at a different level in the same subject area. For example, if we look at the concept of adding, some will be adding up numbers below 10, while some will add numbers above 100.
    - still working to understand a concept while others can use their understanding of that concept to apply to other areas of knowledge, e.g. using the ability to add up and take away to solve a word problem in Maths.

Process

Process refers to the methods used to enable the children to reach the learning outcomes. This means a teacher may choose *how* the children learn by varying the:

- teaching methods (e.g. whole class, group, paired working, one-to-one working, investigation, problem solving, and role-play)

- learning activities used (e.g. project work, collaborative game, brainstorm, visitor talk, trip, practical activity)

- materials used (written, taped, picture format (e.g. visual prompt) concrete apparatus, simplified texts, multimedia, ICT

- staff resource (use of a teaching assistant or voluntary helper, or peer support, or ICT)

- pace of learning (taking some activities more slowly for some groups, faster for others).

The teacher may also:

- provide keep-on-task strategies for some learners

- choose different types of ongoing assessment (discussion, questioning observation, videoing, tests, etc.).

> **Outcome**
> Outcome refers to what is produced by the learner to show they have met the learning outcome. Learners could:
>
> - use a different task, for example, draw a picture, write a story, produce a quiz, produce a tape, make a poster, give an oral presentation, draw a diagram, or make a game
>
> - use a different resource, for example, word processor with a spellchecker, use of a teaching assistant to scribe, whiteboard
>
> - use a group response or a response partner.

You will be able to think of many occasions when the teacher has used you as a resource to differentiate the teaching and learning process!

Teaching methods and the teaching assistant's role

The old image of the teacher as a fount of all knowledge, standing at the front of the class instructing pupils (didactic teaching) is not so relevant in modern schools, although there are still many occasions when teachers do need to instruct. Teachers are now managers or facilitators of learning – guiding, supporting and directing pupils to enable them to learn. As a teaching assistant your role will always be a varied one, because the support needed by both the teacher and the pupils will depend on the teaching and learning activities being used at a particular time in the classroom.

Here are some examples of teaching and learning activities that you may come across in the classroom:

- collaborative working
- practical activity
- computer program
- structured intensive programme
- research
- brainstorming
- question and answer
- exposition
- exploration
- games
- projects
- investigation
- role-play
- demonstration
- use of multimedia
- problem solving
- modelling
- one-to-one tutorial
- quiz
- debate.

Teachers will choose the methods of learning and the appropriate activities based on the requirements of the curriculum or subject matter; the individual preferences of the learners; the resources and staff available; and their knowledge of how children learn best. They will be trying to help children to increase their:

- Knowledge – e.g. the ecology of the rainforest, letters in the alphabet, how to learn
- Skills – e.g. ability to write, ability to kick a football accurately, use of mind maps
- Understanding – e.g. the causes of the First World War, why we should work together, how ions are formed.

Most learning activities will be a combination of knowledge, skills and understanding.

Whole-class teaching

Whole class teaching refers to sessions when the teacher or teaching assistant teaches the whole class together. This may also be known as discursive teaching, exposition or the plenary. Whole class teaching plays an important part in the way the curriculum is delivered. It is directed by the teacher who will use the opportunity to inform, model, describe, guide and explain. It is a technique used extensively at the beginning and end of the Primary and Key Stage 3 strategy lessons. It can be used to:

- introduce a topic or idea
- explain a concept or a series of events
- model a skill
- make comparisons
- give information which the pupils have to think about and then draw their own conclusions from
- introduce a problem solving activity
- give instructions for a following activity.

Teachers also use whole class discussion as an opportunity to create a dialogue with all the learners by talking and questioning. It provides a useful opportunity to explore and evaluate ideas and involves skilled use of questioning techniques. You may already be whole-class teaching as part of PPA time. However, if you are working in partnership with the teacher it is important to play a full part in whole-class work. Don't view it as an opportunity to pop out and get some photocopying done! You should always know how a lesson is introduced, as it sets the scene for learning, and how it finishes, as this should bring it all together. It's often the time that homework is set too. There are a number of opportunities for you to participate in whole-class discussion, as indicated below:

- Check your own understanding of the learning outcomes and the subject matter.
- Increase your own understanding of the subject area.

- Observe the way children are responding and interacting. You can:
  - monitor who is taking part
  - check on the understanding that learners show
  - check on any children who are having problems with specific areas of a topic
  - check on children's learning preferences – some may find auditory learning difficult and will need a visual prompt, etc.
- Encourage participation. You can:
  - use supportive body language (smiling, nodding) to encourage children to contribute
  - encourage children who do not normally contribute.
- Support behaviour management. You can:
  - monitor individual pupils and keep them focused with a look or quiet word
  - sit near learners to keep them on task
  - model listening behaviour
  - draw the teacher's attention to learners who may be overlooked.
- Extend your own teaching skill by watching and copying the teacher's skills and techniques.
- Support individual pupils with specific needs, e.g. learners with hearing impairment or English as an additional language, who may need specialist help or resources.
- Support the teaching. You can:
  - join in
  - add comments or ideas
  - provide a double act with the teacher by demonstrating or modelling or questioning.
- Help with resources:
  - distribute resources at the appropriate time
  - monitor the usefulness and level of resources used.

This information should not only be fed back to the teacher but should also be used by you in forming your own approach to teaching and supporting children in the class.

Active learning

In Chapter 6 you looked at the ways in which children learn. It is widely recognised that learning through doing or active learning is more successful, so teachers will plan plenty of opportunities for children to learn through practical activities. This will also appeal to those children who prefer a kinaesthetic approach to learning. The important point to remember is that leaving children to get on with a practical activity on their own won't necessarily result in much learning. Active learning often needs a high level of planning, direction and guidance to be effective.

Discovery/experiential/investigational learning

Pupils learn through being given structured opportunities to discover or find out information through their own experience. This could range from finding out what will sink and float by using the water play area at Key Stage 1, or becoming "detectives" to investigate a historical mystery, to discovering the principles of Pythagoras' theorem through trial and error in GCSE Maths coursework at Key Stage 4. Teachers will try to build in active learning to many of their teaching sessions. They may begin a lesson with a whole class discussion and then move on to a period of active learning. This may require a change in the room layout or grouping, and a change in the focus of your role. Every day you will be involved in helping children to learn in this way. If you are an experienced teaching assistant you will have developed the ability to give just the right amount of help in these situations. It is a real skill to be able to prompt and guide without leaving a pupil floundering or giving too much help.

Problem solving

Children are often presented with problems to solve that may be open ended. This is quite a challenging activity to support, as there may be no single right answer. Some ways in which you can be involved in this type of problem solving are given below.

- Check learners are clear on the learning outcomes required.
- Help them to identify and clarify the problem.
- Make sure they have the correct resources and materials they need. Remember that these may vary depending on the needs of the learners.
- Help them to formulate hypotheses or suggestions.
- Help them to formulate a plan.
- Monitor the activity, encouraging them to think through each idea.
- Prompt them to move to the next phase of the activity.
- Use questioning to help them consolidate and extend their learning.
- Step in to help if required. A starting point may often help a less confident pupil to get going. Sometimes, the problem itself may need to be restructured.
- Accept lateral thinking.
- Encourage different approaches to problem solving.
- Help them to recognise when a possible solution is reached.
- Help them to evaluate the activity.
- Feed back information to the teacher.

Project work

Learners may be asked to complete project work or individual studies, following the direction of the teacher. The emphasis for your role will be much the same as for any active learning. However, you may need to give more help with selection, access and understanding of resources, e.g. using the library, using the Internet, questioning other people, approaching outside organisations. Obviously, this will be in consultation with the teacher.

Group work

Learners frequently work collaboratively. It is not only an important part of learning to socialise and cooperate together, but also an excellent way to develop and build skills and understanding. Some children enjoy working together and thrive on the interaction with their peers. But others, particularly learners with high levels of intrapersonal intelligence, often get frustrated at working with other children and having to slow the pace or consider the viewpoints of others. Some children lack the social skills to be effective members of group-learning situations. The more experience all children have of this type of learning the more they develop these essential skills. It also enables teachers and teaching assistants to give targeted support to individual learners within the group.

Research has shown that in-class grouping is effective in raising standards by personalising learning for pupils (NERF, 2006).

There are many ways that teachers organise group work. If learners are undertaking a problem solving, investigational or project-based activity together, the dynamics of the group set-up are absolutely vital. Teachers will choose and form groups according to the profile of the learners, resources available and the intended learning outcomes. Or there may be tightly controlled teacher- or teaching assistant-led activities, where the set-up of the group is not so vital.

Group size

Teachers may decide on small group work, large group work or paired working. Choosing the right size of group is essential to success. Too large (more than around five children) and some children may be left without much to do; too small and children may get stuck without the stimulation of different skills and viewpoints, or have too much to achieve. The availability of resources (only having a certain quantity of bits of equipment, for example) may mean that groups are bigger than necessary. Paired working is useful to enable children to begin to work together cooperatively in a controlled setting. Younger children (at Key Stage 1) often find it difficult to work in larger groups and may need to work in twos or threes.

Type of grouping

Teachers may choose to group learners in different ways, as follow.

Grouping by ability

Pupils work in groups with learners of similar ability. They can work with information or material that is challenging and interesting for their level of ability. This is often easier for a teacher to plan for because the way learning outcomes are reached is fairly similar. In some classrooms children will work in the same groups all the time. In this case, you may find that you are always working with the same group of learners because you are allocated to the ones who need the most support. It is important for you to occasionally work with the high ability groups so that you get an accurate picture of what can be achieved and keep high expectations for all learners.

Flexible or mixed ability grouping

Students can be grouped according to their experience, skills or knowledge. For example, some pupils may have a particular interest in a certain area of history or science, and may know more about it than other learners. They can be used in each group to provide knowledge for others. Some children may be better at certain skills (like reading or ball skills). They can be used within each group to model and improve the skills of others. These are referred to as expert-to-beginner groups. Sometimes the teacher will form each group as a complete profile from high achieving to low achieving children. This mix of ability gives children a chance to learn from each other. All of these grouping methods are valuable, and are of particular importance when considering how children with SEN can be successfully included. Their particular skills and talents can be recognised and used. For example, a learner who has dyslexia and finds reading difficult, but has good Maths skills, can be grouped with learners who are good readers but find Maths difficult.

Friendship groups

This can often work successfully because, if children get along well together everyday, they already have the ground rules of friendship and cooperation that enable them to work productively together. However, sometimes they need to be focused on the task otherwise they tend to chat about what they did in the playground or what they are going to do at the weekend! In a secondary school it can be less valuable to work in friendship groups, as peer social groups are stronger at that age and learners are more likely to argue or be distracted from the work in hand.

Multi-age or vertical grouping

This involves putting together groups of children of different ages. It is often used in small schools where there are a limited number of children from different age groups, but it is an effective strategy for all. Children can learn through being mentored by an older pupil and the older pupils can extend their understanding by having to explain to a younger one. Socially it works well too. Children who struggle with attainment in their own peer group can be seen as experts by younger children, and receive a boost to their self-esteem. However, there can be differences in the way each age group understands language so it needs careful planning.

Some of these groupings are more formal and long term. Some Key Stage 3/4 schools have literacy and numeracy mentoring schemes where Year 11 and above students help Year 7 students with basic skills. One Key Stage 1/2 school used vertical grouping during a science week; Year 5 children set up and implemented various activities for Year 2 children, e.g. feeling and identifying different materials.

Key Stage 1/2: "We have a reading club at school. The Year 4 pupils help the Year 1 children to practise their reading every week. This year we encouraged them to make pop-up books for the Year 1 children to read. They have made some really colourful and interesting ones. It has given all the Year 4 children a chance to make something. Some of the best, most creative books, have been made by children who had trouble with their own reading. They are really keen to help the younger children and it's really nice to see.

Interest groups

Putting children who have the same interests together, whether it is computer games, dinosaurs or *Harry Potter*, can often be a really effective way to learn.

Random grouping

Learners can pick names out of a hat to find their group. This is useful if there are entrenched friendship groups who don't like working with others.

Ground rules for investigational group work

Group work has to be well organised to be successful. Here are some of the procedures and practices that should be followed to make this kind of group work effective.

Teach cooperative skills first. Children often need a high level of coaching to enable them to operate successfully in a group situation because they need to use the competencies identified by Goleman (1995) of managing emotions:

- self-motivation
- social skills
- self-awareness
- empathy.

It is important to give children specific help to be able to:

- take turns
- listen carefully to others
- respect the opinions of others
- deal with conflicting ideas and personalities
- follow procedures
- ask for help
- accept responsibility for group decisions.

As a teaching assistant you will be involved in modelling such behaviour and providing guidance and help for pupils. These types of behaviour are something that they need to practise.

Improving the quality of group work – scaffolding discussion with learners

Research has shown that teaching learners explicitly to listen carefully to others and to express themselves clearly helps them to organise and clarify their own and others' thinking and understanding. "Children trained to work in cooperative groups were good at giving explanations that their peers understood"' (NERF, 2006, p.8).

You can challenge pupils' thinking and help them to use effective collaborative problem solving and investigational strategies by scaffolding their discussions. For example, you could:

- Challenge students to identify problem issues – *what is the main problem here?*
- Reflect meaning – *it sounds as though you have found that….*
- Consider alternative perspectives – *have you thought about…?*
- Probe and clarify to extend pupils' thinking – *what makes you think this?*
- Acknowledge and validate their ideas and efforts – *you have worked that out after a lot of hard thinking.*
- Make their thinking explicit – *are you thinking that…?*
- Offering tentative suggestions – *you could try….*

This can help learners to justify and defend their own viewpoints and accept the validity of other pupils' ideas to develop a shared approach. (Adapted from NERF, 2006)

Below are some other factors that must be observed if group work is to succeed:

- Learning outcomes and end products are made absolutely clear in everyone's mind. It is important for each group to have a way of checking this without constantly asking the teacher. Information may be written up on the board or each group can be given their own whiteboard with instructions.
- Roles are allocated. Groups work effectively when everyone has an allocated role. The teacher may choose to do this or, as children become more skilled at group work, they may allocate roles in the group themselves. Although this approach may give opportunities for children to opt out, Gayle Gregory and Carolyn Chapman give some useful guidance on allocating roles according to industrial type jobs:
  - Production manager – oversees production of the project.
  - Information manager – makes sure work is accurate and reported back effectively.
  - Resource manager – makes sure everyone has the right materials and resources.
  - Personnel manager – makes sure morale is high and the right people do the right jobs.
  - Technology manager – uses computer and associated technology.
  - Time manager – keeps everyone on schedule by liaising with the rest of the team.

(Adapted from Gregory and Chapman, 2002, p.98)

Teachers will use other methods, too, to make sure that everyone collaborates together and plays an equal part. They may structure the activity in sequence with each person being responsible for one part of the sequence, or they may ask pupils to share resources. For this method to succeed, resources should be clearly available and accessible, and the method of reporting back must be clear.

As a teaching assistant supporting this kind of group work, you will need to:

- check that you are aware how and why the group is structured
- make sure you are familiar with the individual needs of every learner
- check you are fully aware of *all* the learning outcomes, including social skills or any individual targets for specific learners
- reinforce and monitor the message that everyone has to work cooperatively
- encourage learners to think about and reflect on their own role in any group work
- ensure all resources are used effectively.

Directed teaching with groups

All the above good practice relates to supervising a group of learners who are involved in a self-directed group activity. However, teaching assistants are frequently asked to teach and direct a small group of learners in a more formal and structured way. This may be in any part of the curriculum or as part of a structured programme like the Primary or Key Stage 3 Strategies, or the Catch Up programmes. You could be explaining the concept of weathering in Geography, taking children through a structured language or spelling programme, taking a social use of language (SULP) group, teaching the concept of adding fractions, or showing a group of learners how to paint or draw. Whatever the content, there are some basic guidelines that you can start to follow to help you make the maximum use of these opportunities.

Before you start:

- Check on the learning environment to make sure it is conducive to learning.
- Make sure you have all the relevant material and equipment.
- Check the time available to complete the activity.
- Make sure you are confident that you know what is required.

You should know:

- The learning outcomes for the activity.
- The individual needs of every child in the group, relevant to the activity.
- Any individual targets learners may be working towards.
- How the activity will be assessed.

When you start:

- Share the learning outcomes with the children.

175

- Cue them in to the activity using any relevant memory techniques.
- Set the activity in the context of their previous learning so that it is relevant to them.

During the activity:

- Try to give an equal amount of time and attention to all the learners in the group. Teachers learn this skill over a period of time, so it is something that you should work on, although it can be a difficult balancing act. Sometimes one particular learner can dominate a group because they have behavioural or learning difficulties, or they just like the attention! Boys can dominate some mixed gender groups too. Monitor how well you respond to the quieter children. It may mean that you don't sit in one place in the group but move round the table.
- Try not to dominate the group too much yourself, though, or you will limit opportunities for children to learn and develop confidence in themselves.
- Have a mini whiteboard with you to explain any words, concepts and ideas in visual form.
- Have reinforcement activities available for the learners who need more practice and keep extension activities available for learners who finish quickly. These should always be agreed with the teacher first.
- Note down any key teaching/learning points to tell the teacher or use in your planning later (how children have responded, any difficulties they faced, any techniques or ideas that were successful, etc.)
- Remember that you are modelling good learning behaviour.

At the end of the activity:

- Make sure any completed work is put in the correct place.
- Review what has been learned. This is also important for filing the information away in memory.
- Make sure learners know when they will have an opportunity to complete any unfinished work.
- Make sure the ending of the activity is ordered. Don't allow everyone to get up and walk away without structuring the ending.

After the activity:

- Feedback to the teacher or teaching assistant colleagues.

One-to-one working

Teaching assistants are often involved in working one-to-one with learners. This is particularly relevant if you are supporting a child with EAL or SEN. You may be working outside the classroom, or delivering a structured speech and language, spelling or reading programme. There are some extremely skilled and well-qualified teaching assistants who are experts in the delivery of such programmes.

In some secondary schools and further education colleges, specialist teaching assistants provide lunchtime tutorial support for pupils in every curriculum area, reinforcing and explaining key ideas and concepts and helping them with coursework. This can be a very rewarding way of working, but it can also have its drawbacks. Learners can become reliant on individual help. The boundaries between what is the work of the teaching assistant and what is the work of the learner can sometimes become blurred too.

General principles for one-to-one (tutorial) working

One of the strengths of working one-to-one is that you can work at the learner's own pace; it is also easier to tune in to their needs. Lessons can be tailor-made for the learner. For example, you could use a tape recorder to help a child with reading fluency problems, which might be more difficult to do in a large group. Learners' interests and strengths can also be used to choose appropriate resources to make learning even more relevant.

> "While working with some children from travelling communities I found that they could understand numeracy much better if I related it to using money, as they worked on stalls with their parents outside school."

Working on a one-to-one basis may present you with opportunities to investigate children's learning styles and preferences, so that you can present information in the most appropriate way.

- You could provide more visual material for a visual learner, or use imagination and imagery to help with memory.
- You can also use each curriculum area to provide material to reinforce all the basic skills like reading and spelling, e.g. use words from the Biology syllabus to teach spelling/reading to a GCSE student.
- Try using a whiteboard or notepad to explain vocabulary or show spelling patterns or number concepts. When working one-to-one you often have more opportunity to move away from the main teaching point.
- One-to-one can become a little overpowering at times, so check the seating arrangements to make sure you both have enough personal space and you are not dominating the situation too much. Give the learner frequent changes of pace and activity.
- Give learners time to think and respond. Don't feel you have to be talking all the time just because there are only two of you!
- Learners may be more confident about talking without their peer group present, so take every opportunity to encourage the use and understanding of language.
- Try not to be too controlling – listen to your learner and occasionally let them direct the way the lesson goes.

- Take an activity with you to occupy yourself while your learner is completing work.
- Monitor constantly to make sure your learner is developing independent learning skills and is not becoming too reliant on you.

Helping pupils to become independent learners

In your role as a teaching assistant you should always strive to make sure that the children you support are developing independence. After all, it is the target for everyone to become an autonomous learner. Some children are happier than others to accept help. It is important that learners understand that asking for help isn't an admission of their own failure, but an effective strategy to be used to give them control over their learning. As a teaching assistant you need to encourage this approach but it is a real skill to be able to intervene and give just the right amount of help to move a learner on to the next stage without making them dependent on you. To be a good teaching assistant you need to be an effective help-giver (Karabenick, 1998).

> **Key Stage 3** "I support a child who lacked confidence in herself and was terrified of giving the wrong answer. When the maths teacher was taking a whole class activity and asked a question, my learner whispered the answer to me and if it was right I told her to put her hand up. Gradually she has become more confident and now she will answer without telling me, even if she is wrong."

Using rote learning

We use the term 'rote learning' to describe memorising something by repeating it over and over again, until it is fixed in memory. There has been some controversy over the use of rote learning in education. Some educationalists feel that it is always far more valuable to understand something and work it out rather than learn something 'parrot-fashion'. However, there is an important place for rote learning in the classroom, particularly when the information to be learned is fixed or unchanging and needs quick recall. Some examples of this include:

- Number bonds – 4+4=8, 3+5=8, etc.
- The alphabet – crucial for using an index, dictionary or telephone directory
- Multiplication tables – the basis for calculation
- Calendar – days of the week, months of the year
- Dates – useful for history and other humanities subjects
- Quotations – from literature, or poetry learnt by heart
- Specialised curriculum area information – e.g. the periodic table in chemistry, classifications in biology, and names of bones for beauty therapy.

Helping a child to learn by rote is an important part of your role in these cases. You can use the following techniques:

Multi-sensory rote learning

- Colour – learners can write the information down in a different colour to help them memorise visually, e.g. all dates in purple, all quotes in green.
- Movement – some teachers use PE to learn by rote through movement – the same way that actors pace up and down when they are learning their lines!
- Chanting – learners can repeat the information over and over again to help them remember. Using a strong rhythm also helps, which is why there are commercially produced rap tables tapes and adverts have jingles!
- Mnemonics (from the name of the Greek goddess of memory). This is a memory cue system that uses the first letter of each word to bring back the information needed. It is a system used by many professionals, for example pilots, to remember fixed information. It is important that mnemonics are memorable and individual, so encourage learners to make up their own. Here is a useful one to remember directions of the compass:

  - N Never
  - E Eat
  - S Shredded
  - W Worms.

- Practise and recall – tables tests, vocabulary tests, etc.
- Use of ICT – for example, a screen saver with times tables.

Supporting scientific thinking

Although Science is taught as a separate curriculum subject, you need to be aware of the place and importance of science and scientific thinking in everyday life and to encourage scientific literacy. Science is a major part of our modern world. Although some teaching assistants may have industrial scientific experience, traditional stereotypes about gender and science mean that many teaching assistants are a little nervous about supporting in this area because they feel they do not have the right background knowledge. Pupils may experience the same anxieties about science and this may be made worse by its rather stuffy image, or by a heavy emphasis on the written recording of science. You can do a great deal to encourage learners to be interested in and enjoy science, and to be scientifically literate, by helping them to look for the science in:

- everyday experiences like eating, playing with toys, PE, the playground or hobbies
- other areas of the curriculum like Art or Geography.

You can do this for yourself if you feel a little underconfident.

You can also encourage learners to:

- be curious

- experiment by trying out ideas and reflecting on the results (safely!)
- respect and observe the environment
- understand the great tradition of scientific enquiry and discovery by talking about famous scientists and their discoveries
- talk about current scientific issues in society (GM food, global warming, cosmetic surgery, for example).

Key Stage 1: "My TA was worried about supporting in Science. She felt that she didn't know enough. I told her to forget the complicated stuff and concentrate on everyday science. She has proved to be a real asset. She can find an application for science in any activity we do. Last week she suggested a role-play activity, where each child represented a planet to show how the solar system works."

Scientific concepts

Children tend to base their understanding of concepts on their previous knowledge. However, sometimes in science, they may already have misconceptions or mistaken ideas, which can prove difficult to change. For example, they may think that the sun disappears at night, or that plants feed, or that objects sink if they are heavier than water. There are several ways to help them to overcome this:

- Start by talking about their understanding of concepts using everyday language.
- Present evidence that challenges their conceptions.
- Use everyday objects to explain and illustrate scientific ideas.
- Introduce appropriate scientific language when talking about scientific ideas.
- Use concept cartoons to help pupils to use discussion. You can find out more about concept cartoons at www.azteachscience.co.uk.

Although Science is practical, it is taught formally through language. This means that you should help learners to understand and use precise scientific language. This can be categorised in several ways:

- Labels – water, Bunsen burner, mercury
- Processes – cooling, evaporation, combustion
- Concepts – temperature, pressure, field.

Knowing the difference between the categories of scientific language can help you support learners effectively. As concepts are more difficult for learners to understand, it helps if you can explain them clearly. You should also help them to:

- learn the rules of scientific enquiry and experiment by testing and analysis. You will need to use the techniques of effective questioning described in Chapter 8 to extend the thinking of pupils and encourage them to use scientific enquiry.
- record their findings accurately and appropriately.

There is more information on supporting science at www.ase.org.uk.

Encouraging thinking skills

The National Curriculum states that opportunities should be taken in all curriculum areas for learners to develop their thinking skills. Facts and information are important but if children learn to think effectively then they can apply this ability across all aspects of the curriculum and life in general. In our modern, fast changing, technological world, the ability to think effectively and flexibly is becoming more and more important. By thinking skills we mean the ability to use higher order thinking to analyse, investigate, reason, problem solve and construct arguments.

Many specialist thinking skills programmes are used in schools, but what is really important is providing an environment in which children are encouraged to develop and use thinking skills in all aspects of their work. Teaching assistants can play a really significant part in this by creating an atmosphere in which learners are allowed and encouraged to reflect, predict, contradict, question and talk about their thinking processes. You need to be confident as a teaching assistant to enable learners to have the freedom to develop their own thinking skills and strategies. The kind of environment that encourages this development is where the supporting adult:

- allows time for the child to think things through
- actively listens
- shows a real interest in their thinking processes
- sees learning in mistakes
- uses open-ended questions
- is always available for help
- values a child's idea
- has a positive attitude
- is non-judgemental
- learns with the child
- shows curiosity
- encourages discussion and collaboration with others.

(Adapted from Fisher, 1990, p.38)

Many of the techniques and strategies involved in developing thinking skills and strategies can be taught, and there are several commercially produced programmes and specialist resources that schools use. You may be supporting in a classroom where one of the following methods is being used.

Feuerstein's Instrumental Enrichment (IE)

This is one of the older thinking skills programmes first used in Israel after the Second World War with slow-learning adolescents. Feuerstein believed that everyone could be a fully effective learner given the right learning experience. His system uses mediated learning (human interaction) to develop thinking processes. The mediator (or teacher) intervenes between the learner and his environment so that learning can take place. The materials used are content free and require no background knowledge, so that learners can concentrate on the process rather than the outcome. One of the 'instruments' used involves joining up dots. Evaluations have shown that Instrumental Enrichment has positive effects on non-verbal reasoning skills (McGuiness, 1999). It has been used very effectively with dyslexic learners, too.

Somerset thinking skills course

A similar programme to IE, produced in the UK, but using materials more relevant to everyday life.

Robert Fisher

Fisher has written extensively on thinking and learning. He has also produced books of poems and stories to encourage thinking, which include lists of questions and discussion points to use with learners. These encourage children to use inference, deduction, analysis and evaluation.

Edward De Bono (Cognitive Research Trust, 1992)

De Bono is an exponent of the importance of lateral thinking. Teachers understand the relevance of this when they are expecting the one 'right' answer; they may have a tendency to dismiss anything that does not fit their expectations, rather than using these suggestions as an opportunity to explore a child's thinking processes. De Bono has also put forward the idea of having different coloured thinking hats for different types of thinking (emotional, creative, cautious, factual, etc.).

Philosophy for children (Lipman, 1980 and Fisher, 1998)

This approach is used across the whole curriculum to develop philo-sophical thinking using discussion and questioning. It is particularly important in the area of moral and social education. Children are encouraged to engage in *Socratic* style discussion by posing questions like:

- Is there such a thing as truth? (logical)
- Is it right to steal? (ethical)
- How do we know something? (epistemological)
- What is time? (metaphysical)
- Is beauty in the eye of the beholder? (aesthetic)

This system has been used extensively in the USA and has been shown to develop children's ability to formulate and respond to argument.

Subject linked cognitive acceleration

This system, targeted at 11–14-year-olds, is particularly relevant for Science and Maths. Its aim is to promote scientific and mathematical thinking skills to enable learners to sequence, analyse and plan. It has now been extended to some humanities subjects, namely History and Geography. An example of this system is CASE: Cognitive Acceleration through Science Education. Research has shown that cognitive acceleration in Science also improved attainment in Maths and English (NERF, 2006).

You can find out more about cognitive acceleration at www.kcl.ac.uk/depsta/education/caseprogrammes.

Using ICT to develop thinking skills

The huge growth in the application and use of technology in the classroom has made it an ideal environment for encouraging and developing thinking skills. The use of networks can help learners to think collaboratively, and the use of multimedia, digital and video technology enables learners to use different media to design, model and conceptualise their ideas. The Internet has become a vital research tool and, more than ever, learners need to develop skills to sort, classify and evaluate information.

Encouraging metacognition

Metacognition is the conscious understanding and control of one's own thinking processes – the ability to think about thinking! It follows on from the whole concept of self-evaluation, which you looked at in the previous chapter. As an adult you have developed an understanding of the way that you mentally process information and the way that you learn. This is an important skill for children too. Children need to be helped to understand, monitor and evaluate their own thinking processes so that they can become more effective, active learners. Even young children at Key Stage 1 can be encouraged to think about the things they find easy or difficult to learn and the way they learn best. Older learners at Key Stage 3/4 can be encouraged to develop a more sophisticated understanding of their own cognitive processes.

Many of these metacognitive approaches to learning can be taught, so as a teaching assistant you have an excellent opportunity to help pupils to reflect on and improve the way they think and learn. Any type of learning activity in any curriculum area can be used to help pupils explore the questions below. You may then be able to discuss options with them and make helpful suggestions, for example, ideas for collaborating with others, support available, ways to plan, or ideas for techniques, strategies and resources. The structure of the Primary Science and DT units of work encourage this type of approach, known as the 'investigation train'. Some teachers use prompt cards with these questions on to encourage pupils to think about their metacognitive skills.

Before pupils begin:
- What do I need to do?
- What knowledge do I already have that will help me?
- How will I be able to work best?
- Where should I start?

- How much time have I got?
- Should I work with anyone else?

While pupils are doing the activity/self-monitoring:
- How is it going?
- Do I really understand?
- Do I need any other resources/materials?
- Should I change my approach to be more successful?
- Do I need help from anyone and if so, what?
- How can I keep myself going/motivated?
- Do I have the right amount of time available?
- What can I do if I get stuck?

When pupils have completed the activity:
- How well did it go?
- Were there other strategies that might have worked better?
- How can I improve next time (if necessary)?
- Can I use this experience somewhere else (transferable learning)?

'In the flow'

Research has shown that we learn effectively when we are totally focused and involved in an activity. This is called being 'in the flow' (Czsikszentmihalyi, 1990). This refers to the period of time when someone is completely focused on what they are doing and almost oblivious to outside stimuli. You can help children to understand this concept of learning in the flow. They can look at the examples of athletes or performers in the flow to give them more understanding. You may experience it yourself when writing an assignment, making something, watching a TV programme, playing a musical instrument or playing sport. You also need to be aware of this as a teaching assistant so that you can leave pupils alone when they are in this optimum learning state!

Creativity

Following the emphasis on Literacy and Numeracy, the recent focus in the curriculum has moved onto creativity. This goes beyond the traditional idea of creativity through, for example, painting, writing, drama or music (the creative arts). It has a much broader meaning, being about thinking and working creatively across the whole curriculum, whether as a teacher, teaching assistant or as a pupil.

Caroline Sharp of NFER defines the creative process as:

- imagination
- originality (the ability to come up with ideas and products that are new and unusual)
- productivity (the ability to generate a variety of different ideas through divergent thinking)
- problem solving (application of knowledge and imagination to a given situation)

- the ability to produce an outcome of value and worth.

(NFER, 2004)

Creative thinking in this context can lead to new and innovative ideas and beneficial experiences of benefit. You will be able to think of numerous occasions when you have had to think creatively to solve a problem at work or at home.

In 1999, the National Advisory Committee on Creative and Cultural Education (NACCCE) argued that there should be a national strategy for creative and cultural education. According to NACCCE, creativity is not just restricted to some outstanding individuals (such as Leonardo da Vinci, Picasso, Lennon & McCartney). The report said, "In our view, all people are capable of creative achievement in some area of activity, provided the conditions are right and they have acquired the relevant knowledge and skills" (NACCCE, 1999 p.29).

Czsikszentmihalyi (1996) also emphasises that it is difficult to be creative in any area without already having a competent level of skills and knowledge. For example, James Dyson, the entrepreneur who invented the innovative bagless vacuum cleaner, was a trained engineer who used his knowledge creatively in a novel approach to design.

The Foundation Stage curriculum emphasises the role of creativity through children's curiosity and exploration. The focus of the National Curriculum is more on the idea of creativity as a characteristic in the future workforce. "Pupils should be able to think creatively and critically, to solve problems and to make a difference for the better. It should give them the opportunity to become creative, innovative, enterprising and capable of leadership to equip them for their future lives as workers and citizens." (QCA, 2004)

There is more on creativity at www.ncaction.org.uk/creativity. You might also like to look at an Early Years curriculum in Italy, which emphasises creativity, at http://zerosei.comune.re.it/.

Self-regulation

All of these strategies will help pupils to develop an understanding of their own learning processes and enable them to see the connection between what they do and what they achieve. Helping them to develop their own strategies and skills rather than imposing your own learning style on them is a far better long-term strategy for all learners. This is sometimes referred to as self-regulation and is an important part of allowing pupils to take responsibility for their own learning.

Whole school approaches

You may encounter some of the following approaches in your school. Ask the teacher to let you know when any of these techniques, including the ones listed earlier, are being used.

Brain gym
Looks at the full potential of learners through movement and multi-sensory learning to integrate all parts of the brain. For more information see Dennison and Dennison (1989) or www.braingym.org.

High scope
An educational approach that uses active learning and concentrates on developing pupils' independent learning skills. Children are supported to plan, do and review through a structured regime. Used at Key Stage 1. More information can be found at www.highscope.org.

Accelerated learning
Practical approaches to learning, based on teaching responses to brain diversity (Rose, 1985; Smith, 1996). For more information, go to www.acceleratedlearning.co.uk.

In Chapter 16 you will find a photocopiable learning activity prompt sheet that you can use to gather relevant classroom and whole school information for use with any activity.

Key reading

Key references are given in bold.

Capel, S., Leask, M. and Turner, T. (1995) *Learning to Teach in the Secondary School,* London: Routledge *[Manual for new teachers that gives some useful information.]*

Cockburn, A. (2001) *Teaching Children 3–11,* London: PCP *[A manual for teachers.]*

Costello, P. (2000) *Thinking Skills in Early Childhood,* London: David Fulton *[Theory and practice of thinking skills.]*

Davies, D. and Howe, A. (2003) *Teaching Science and DT in the Early Years,* London: David Fulton

Dickenson, C. (1996) *Effective Learning Activities,* Stafford: Network Educational Press *[Particularly relevant for able learners.]*

Farrow, S. (1999) *The Really Useful Science Book: A Framework of Knowledge for Primary Teachers,* London: RoutledgeFalmer *[Increases knowledge and understanding of science.]*

Kitson. N. and Merry, R. (1997) *Teaching in the Primary School,* London: Routledge

McNamara, S. and Moreton, G. (1997) *Understanding Differentiation,* London: David Fulton *[Comprehensive guide to differentiation.]*

Montague-Smith, A. and Winstone, L. (1998) *Supporting Science and Technology,* London: David Fulton *[Useful for Early Years.]*

Rogers, S. (2003) *Role Play in the Foundation Stage,* London: David Fulton *[Includes advice on the role of adults in play.]*

Shayer, M. and Adey, P. (2002) *Learning Intelligence,* Buckingham: OU Press *[Rationale for the use of thinking skills.]*

Sherrington, R (Ed.) (1998) *ASE Guide to Primary Science,* London: Stanley Thornes

Wallace, B. (Ed.) (2002) *Teaching Thinking Skills Across the Middle Years,* London: David Fulton

http://www.teachingthinking.net/Thinkskills.htm

http://www.teachthinking.com/*[Website for Questions Publishing]*

References

Key references are given in bold.

Czsikszentmihalyi, M.(1990) *Flow: The Psychology of Optimum Experience,* New York: Harper and Row

Csikszentmihalyi, M. (1996) Creativity Flow and the Psychology of Discovery and Invention, New York: Harper Collins

De Bono, E. (1995) *Six Thinking Hats* Boston: Little Brown & Co.

Dennison, P. and Dennison, G. *(1998) Brain Gym (Teachers Edition)* Georgia Bay NLP Centre, Ontario: Edukinesthetics.inc *[Sets out kinaesthetic approach to learning.]*

Department of Education and Science (DES) (1978) *Special Educational Needs* (The Warnock Report), HMSO (ISBN 0 10 172120 X) *[Publication by the Warnock Committee (1978) entitled Special Educational Needs. The report put an end to labels previously used in education, such as 'handicap', and replaced them with the label 'special educational needs'. Recommendations were included in the Education Act, 1981.]*

Fisher, R. (1998) *Teaching Thinking,* London: Cassell

Fisher, R. (1995) *Teaching Children to Learn,* London: Stanley Thornes

Fisher, R. (1990) *Teaching Children to Think,* London: Stanley Thornes

Gregory, G. and Chapman, C. (2002) *Differentiated Instructional Strategies,* California: Corwin Press

Karabenick, S. (Ed.) (1998) *Strategic Help Seeking: Implications for Learning and Teaching,* New Jersey: Lawrence Erlbaum Associates *[Explores the idea that it is important for learners to develop the ability to ask for and accept help.]*

Lipman, M. (1980) *Philosophy for Children,* Oxford: Blackwell

McGuiness, C.(1999) *From Thinking Skills to Thinking Classrooms: a Review and Evaluation of Approaches for Developing Pupils' Thinking,* London: DfEE

NACCCE (National Advisory Committee on Creative and Cultural Education) (1999) All our futures: creativity culture and education, London: DFEE

NERF (National Education Research Forum) (2006), *Bulletin* 6, Summer 2006, available at http://www.Nerf-uk.org

QCA (2004) *Creativity, find it, promote it.*

Rose, C. (1985) *Accelerated Learning Systems*, New York: Dell

Sharp, C. (2004) 'Developing young children's creativity: What can we learn from research?' *NFER Topic*, Autumn 2004, Issue 32

Smith, A. (1996) *Accelerated Learning in the Classroom,* Stafford: Network Educational Press

10 Teaching literacy

Literacy is at the heart of all learning in school. Whether children are learning Geography, English or Science, they are usually working through the medium of print. They have to be able to read and write to learn, so any difficulties they may have with literacy will have a negative impact on their achievement in any subject area. However, literacy is not just reading and writing. The development of spoken language is an important part of the literacy process in every school. All learners need to be able to use language effectively, which is why the development of Speaking and Listening is such an important part of the school curriculum. In a Special School for learners with complex learning difficulties you will be supporting the communication and expressive skills that are the foundation for literacy.

In the modern media-driven world, being literate is an essential skill for everyday adult life. As a teaching assistant you will spend a great deal of time supporting pupils as they develop their speaking and listening, reading and writing skills. You will play an essential role in this most important process, so it is vital that you have a good understanding of the theories behind literacy development, the strategies now used in school to promote that development, and the intervention programmes available for learners who encounter problems. You may have difficulties with your own literacy, perhaps because the strategies used in school when you were a pupil were not effective for you; all the more reason to use your time as a teaching assistant to learn *with* the pupils!

Literacy teaching – a short history

The way literacy has been taught in schools has varied considerably over the years. It has also been the subject of much controversy. At one time, children were taught to write by copying or modelling the teacher's writing, but there was some concern that this method gave them little purpose and was stifling their ability to think and write creatively. In the 1970s, the Whole Language approach concentrated on integrating the teaching of reading and writing and pupils were encouraged to write about their own ideas, thoughts and feelings. It was felt that they would learn the mechanics of writing with practice and experience, guided by the teacher. However, many pupils struggled with the basics of writing like spelling, punctuation and grammar. Some were unable to write confidently and effectively.

Similarly, the way reading is taught has changed. In the early years of the last century, children were taught to read by the Phonic method, learning the names of letters and the sounds they make, then putting these together to make words and sentences. Because the reading books were highly structured and used very limited vocabulary (so that they could repeat the phonic patterns e.g. *go up, up, up. you go up*), some children found this approach boring and repetitive. In fact Dr Seuss developed his own style of rhyming and nonsense words when he was writing these primers and trying to make them more fun. By the 1960s, this had been superseded by 'Look and Say', where children learned to read each word individually by sight. However, that approach was not successful for every child. Some found it hard to remember all the words, particularly as they got older and were exposed to more and more vocabulary. The Apprenticeship and Real Books approaches were introduced, where children learned to read with adults by using books and stories that interested and motivated them, but which did not have a recognised structure. However, some children, including those with dyslexia, failed to become confident readers using this strategy, and there was a move to reintroduce structured phonic teaching.

By the mid-nineties, there was concern that, in spite of the introduction of the National Curriculum, standards of literacy in the population were in decline. In response to this, the National Literacy Strategy was introduced in 1998 to provide a practical way of teaching the English National Curriculum at Key Stage 1/2. The strategy contained a framework of teaching objectives and instructions for teaching a highly structured daily Literacy Hour. It incorporated some of the ideas and strategies from all of these historical approaches within the framework, but its main emphasis was on whole-class interactive teaching, the modelling of literacy skills by adults and the teaching of phonics. The Literacy Strategy was not statutory and schools did not have to follow it if they could show by their assessment results that they already had high literacy standards. However, most schools did follow the Literacy Strategy training and used the daily Literacy Hour as standard practice. Several intervention programmes were also developed that could be used by trained teaching assistants to support children who were not reaching their expected literacy level. The success of this approach led the then DfEE to develop a similar strategy for Key Stage 3, which was introduced in 2000. This programme had the same structured format for lessons and incorporated best practice from the experience of the Key Stage 1/2 strategy.

Most schools became confident about the implementation of the Literacy/Primary Strategy and adapted and extended it to produce their own in-school literacy teaching programme. In October 2006, following the recommendations in the Rose Report (DfES, 2006), the Primary National Strategy was re-launched, incorporating the principles of the government initiatives Excellence and Enjoyment (DfES, 2003) and Every Child Matters (DfES, 2004). This extended the framework for literacy and numeracy to the Foundation Stage. It also created a more flexible approach to teaching and learning, tied in with the assessment used for the Early Learning Goals and the National Curriculum, in order to provide learners with the best chance for progression. One of the key recommendations in the Rose Report was a renewed emphasis on the importance of speaking and listening skills. This was not only because they are fundamental to children's development of knowledge and understanding, but also because they are the foundation for reading and writing skills. The Literacy framework therefore now incorporates materials used in the Speaking, Listening and Learning strategy (DfES, 2003). The Rose Report also emphasised the importance of early systematic phonics teaching: phonics "first and fast". The new framework includes the specific teaching of phonics from the Foundation Stage, including the idea of *encoding* sound symbols to spell and *decoding* sound symbols to read.

The controversy around how we teach children to read and write remains. Although it is widely accepted that the teaching of phonics is essential, experts are still divided as to whether these should be best taught by analysing words to look for common sound patterns (analytic phonics) or by the structured teaching of letter sounds and word patterns, like *c-a-t* and *s-a-t* (synthetic phonics). The controversy will continue because teachers are always reflecting on their practice and trying to find more effective ways for children to learn. When you are working with children to improve and develop their literacy skills think about which methods are most successful, particularly where individual children are concerned. Use your own experience to join in the great debate! Because of the importance of literacy in all aspects of the curriculum, you should take every opportunity to help children to develop their literacy skills at all times.

The Primary Framework for Literacy

1. Format

The renewal of the Primary Framework has provided an opportunity to re-examine the approach to teaching literacy. Although the concept of a daily literacy lesson is still embedded in the new framework, flexibility is now encouraged, which has assessment and planning at its heart.

There are several key areas for schools and settings to consider and develop as they implement the new framework. The framework is available electronically for easier access at http://www.standards.dfes.gov.uk/primaryframeworks/.

2. Outline structure

The framework provides a simplified structure which identifies 12 strands of learning, closely tied to the National Curriculum and Early

Learning Goals, focusing on four key areas; speaking, listening, reading and writing:

- Speaking
- Listening and responding
- Group discussion and interaction
- Drama
- Word recognition: decoding (reading) and encoding (spelling)
- Word structure and spelling
- Understanding and interpreting texts
- Engaging with and responding to texts
- Creating and shaping texts
- Text structure and organisation
- Sentence structure and punctuation
- Presentation.

3. Planning and assessment

Learning objectives are provided by year group and by strand so that teachers can plan for the achievement of all learners. The planning materials are all available on the electronic framework and include:

- Long-term plans (up to four-week blocks of themed work)
- Medium-term planning
- Examples of activities and resources
- Guidance on assessment so that learning can be reviewed and re-planned interactively.

4. Teaching early reading

This incorporates the teaching of high-quality systematic phonic work, including the skills of segmenting and blending and an emphasis on the sound symbol relationship. There is also an emphasis on the two aspects of reading: decoding, which needs to be developed very early in a child's school life, and reading comprehension, which develops over a much longer period. This reinforces the importance of developing phonological awareness in young children.

5. Speaking and listening

The framework emphasises the importance of speaking and listening skills in developing literacy. These are included as two separate strands.

6. Flexibility

Teachers are encouraged to adapt their teaching and learning activities to take more account of the needs of individual learners – for example children with SEN or EAL, or children who are high achievers – rather than stick rigidly to the format of a three-part one hour daily lesson. The emphasis should be on achievement and progression for all learners, particularly in view of the statutory inclusion statement contained in Curriculum 2000.

7. Structuring cross-curricular learning

Opportunities are taken to look at cross-curricular ways to teach and reinforce literacy skills, by planning activities for literacy learning during other subjects. Teachers need to plan for links between learning and find opportunities to practise and apply literacy skills in other areas of learning. It is particularly important to find real experiences to develop these skills.

8. Raising expectations

A key focus for the framework is for teachers to make their planning responsive to the needs of learners so that there are high expectations for all. They are encouraged to track backwards or forwards in their planning and delivery of the objectives so that all learners can achieve their potential. A teaching assistant can have a key role here in helping teachers to individualise learning and support objectives for groups of learners. For example, a pupil who is struggling may revisit an objective, or one who is working above the level of their peer group could complete work of a greater depth or breadth. The concept of pace has also been redefined so that lessons are not just rushed through to provide momentum but are expected to be lively, varied and interesting.

9. Teaching and learning (pedagogy)

One criticism of the NLS was that the structure of the one-hour lesson was rather inflexible. The framework promotes different types of teaching approaches to be used, depending on the learning objective, the activity involved and the group of learners. Teachers can plan for periods of activity longer or shorter than an hour and use any of the following teaching approaches:

- directed
- inductive
- exploratory
- experiential
- enquiry
- problem-solving
- role-play
- simulation.

The use of ICT is actively encouraged for both teaching staff and learners.

10. Role of the teaching assistant in the daily literacy lesson

Teaching assistants are a particularly valuable resource in helping all learners to make maximum use of the daily literacy lesson. Although most of the guidance on whole-class teaching is relevant, there are specific ways you can help.

Role of the teaching assistant in whole-class activity
- Draw in reticent pupils ("Go on James, you know that word...").

- Support individual learners with additional needs, e.g. scribing or re-explaining.
- Use supportive body language (nodding, smiling).
- Draw the teacher's attention to a child wishing to contribute ("I think Sophie wants to say something...").
- Make suggestions (without interrupting the child).
- Focus the attention of inattentive children on the teacher.
- Demonstrate for the teacher (e.g. the use of a word bank or a way of reading).
- Reinforce or re-word what the teacher has said to individuals.
- Act as a partner for children during thinking time (for them to try out an answer on you).
- Model responses.
- Keep a child on task.
- Break a task into smaller steps.
- Draw a child's attention to previous learning/experience.
- Help slower pupils to formulate and try out responses, or check responses first.
- Note points to revisit later.

Helping with props and resources
- Prepare, distribute and collect resources.
- Use specific resources for learners with additional needs.
- Help pupils use resources properly (pen hold, etc.).
- Help with the use of OHPs and Big Books and check that children can see them clearly.
- Make sure everyone has a pen-highlighter, whiteboard or card.
- Partner a teacher in the use of resources, e.g. puppets.

Observing pupils
- Notice how individual pupils are responding (who can and who cannot).
- Notice any behaviour management issues.
- Notice how pupils use resources.
- Assess progress to report to teacher and take part in re-planning.

Manage group work and activities
- Monitor learning activities.
- Supervise individual group work.

Literacy intervention programmes

There are a number of literacy intervention programmes (outlined below) and you may be involved in delivering them. These programmes are specifically designed to give targeted support to learners to help them achieve the required standards. The programmes include training and highly structured and scripted materials and resources. Your school or LA should provide you with appropriate training to be able to use these effectively. Research has shown that trained TAs can deliver very effective phonic intervention programmes (Savage and Carless, 2005).

Many experienced teaching assistants are highly skilled in the delivery of these programmes and are experts at adapting and extending them. In such cases, teaching assistants develop a real expertise in the way individual learning difficulties can affect the acquisition of literacy skills. They can provide appropriate and relevant ways to use the intervention programmes to help as many learners as possible. These teaching assistants already fulfil the role of HLTA in their work with the literacy intervention programmes. The following intervention programmes are used with the Primary and Key Stage 3 Strategies.

Early Learning Support (ELS)

ELS is aimed at children in Year 1 who need extra support. Learners are identified at the end of the first term and the programme is delivered in the second and third terms. It focuses on key literacy objectives from Reception and Year 1. The programme is delivered by teaching assistants to groups of six children in 20-minute sessions outside the literacy hour. The programme includes a screening procedure and 60 structured literacy sessions, which include a balance of reading, writing, spelling and activities to take away and practise.

Additional Literacy Support (ALS)

ALS is for children in Years 3 and 4 who reached Level 1 or 2c by the end of Key Stage 1 (Level 2 is divided into a, b and c). The programme consolidates key literacy skills and is delivered by teaching assistants to groups of six children within the independent or group time of the Literacy Hour. The materials include a video.

Further Literacy Support (FLS)

FLS is targeted at Year 5 children who are working at Level 3. It includes screening procedures and three modules of literacy support materials, focusing on key objectives from Years 4 and 5. The programme is delivered by teaching assistants to groups of six children in 20-minute sessions. The emphasis is on writing and independent tasks.

Year 6 Booster Units

These are examples of units of work that cover key writing objectives to help learners to achieve Level 4. They are delivered by teachers and teaching assistants.

Literacy Progress Units (LPU)

LPU is for learners who are still working at Level 3 in Year 7. The materials include work at word, sentence and text level. There are six units covering: writing organisation; information retrieval; spelling; reading between the lines; phonics; and sentences. Each unit has 18 fast-paced 20-minute sessions and relates to the objectives in Year 7 of the Framework for Teaching English. The programme is based on the teaching principles and practice of the National Literacy approach (highly interactive; linking speaking and listening; reading and writing; building pupil confidence) and is designed to be delivered by teachers, teaching assistants or librarians.

Further details of these programmes can be found on the National Literacy website at http://www.standards.dfes.gov.uk or DfEE publications (e-mail: dfee@prolog.uk.com; tel: 0845 60 222 60).

Speaking and listening

At one time it was common for teachers to do most of the talking. Now we understand the importance of supporting and guiding children in developing their own talking abilities. Some teachers working in the Foundation Stage have reported that children seem to arrive in school with limited use of language, particularly social language skills. There is some speculation that this may be because children nowadays spend more time at home watching TV rather than out playing with friends. Recently there has been concern that children's speaking and listening skills may have been neglected because of the emphasis on written literacy. As a result, there is now a renewed focus on the development of speaking and listening in both the Primary and Key Stage 3 Strategies.

The teaching of speaking and listening should always be fully integrated with that of reading and writing. A curriculum for Speaking and Listening will be part of the Foundation Stage Early Learning Goals, the National Curriculum English Programme or GCSE and A Level syllabuses, depending on the age group you support. Make sure that you familiarise yourself with the requirements for this part of the curriculum.

However, spoken language has a more fundamental role in every pupil's daily life, as a major part of the way they construct and develop their thinking and a key part of the way they socialise with and collaborate with other children and adults. Your school may use Circle Time to develop children's language and social skills. Spoken language is also the foundation for the development of literacy. A learner has to be able to think and say something (even if it is just in their head) before they can write it. A vital part of your role will be to help them extend and consolidate their spoken language skills. You can help every child to develop language skills anytime, anywhere!

How language develops

No matter how technologically advanced, every society in the world has a way of communicating through language. Although these languages vary from country to country, they all have a common feature – the use of spoken sounds to represent objects, ideas and concepts. Of course, there are also sign languages too, which use movement, as in the case of specialist languages for the deaf. People need to be able to communicate at a basic level to:

- have their needs met
- learn/teach
- negotiate
- explain
- tell stories
- express feelings
- discuss
- persuade others
- socialise.

People communicate in two ways: by the way they receive and understand the things that they hear and see (receptive language) and the way they use language to express themselves (expressive language). Language doesn't just refer to actual speech. The physical act of speaking is often referred to as 'articulation' and is a further part of expressive language skills. But how do children learn this complex skill and how can you help them effectively?

Language acquisition

There has been a tremendous amount of research into how children acquire spoken language and because of this our ideas and teaching approaches are changing. There are three main theories that you need to consider:

By imitation and reinforcement (behaviourism)

This is probably the simplest theory. According to this, children watch and hear adults and other children talking and then copy what they do. They are rewarded by further interaction with the adult or children and so learn to develop their own language skills. This explanation is part of the behaviourist theory. There is no doubt that the process plays an important part in the development of language. An environment where adults use language well can produce children who are confident and competent language users, and conversely an impoverished background can explain why some children have very limited language skills.

Cultural and social differences would then explain the variation in some children's language development. Interestingly, the kind of 'baby talk' (known as 'motherese') that most family members engage in with a very small child, such as "goo goo" and "doggy", is an important part of this process because it simplifies and repeats sounds to help the child to learn the early stages of language. According to this theory when you work with children you become an important role model. You can influence their language skills by the way you demonstrate the use of language and the way you encourage their response. However, this is not the only way children learn to speak and to listen.

Language Acquisition Device (LAD)

Research has demonstrated that the way children learn to speak and communicate is part of the biological development of the brain. According to Pinker (1989), Chomsky (1994) and Neville (2003), the development of language is an innate (inborn) instinct that all human beings have, and which is at its most powerful during the early years up to around the age of 8. It is like a window of opportunity when the brain is receptive to learning the sound patterns required for language.

This is based on experiments that show that children learn to speak by trying out words and phrases that could not be copied or imitated from what they hear adults say, but which are attempts to apply the rules of language. For example, at a certain stage a child will say "I goed" or "I holded". It is their way of applying a language rule – that *ed* on the end of a word is the past tense. They could not be copying this from adults because an adult would say "I went" or "I held".

According to this theory, children also learn the sound patterns or accent they speak with at an early age. You may notice yourself that it is difficult to speak a foreign language without an English accent when you are older, but children who grow up bilingual are able to speak both languages with the correct accent. This is one of the reasons why starting the teaching of foreign languages has been moved into Key Stage 2.

The original research is now being extended by a new generation of neuroscientists, who use brain scanning techniques to examine the areas of the brain that deal with language at sensitive age periods. They have suggested that although language is innate or inborn, its nature is developed by a process of self-organisation, influenced by culture and community. Bruner referred to this as a language acquisition support system. Andrew Wedel, an American linguistic researcher, compares this process to the formation of ripples of sand or the pattern of a honeycomb through repeated small-scale interactions that result in a much larger overall structure over time (Wedel, 2005). Through your work with children you will be part of these interactions. Other researchers have noted that older children learn languages best through using methods like language immersion (Ramscar, 2003).

If you work at the Foundation Stage and Key Stage 1, you have an absolutely vital role to play in helping children to develop and use language skills when their 'window of opportunity' is open, by giving them the chance to experiment and practise.

Through cognition

Piaget recognised the importance of the interaction between adult and child in developing the child's cognitive (thinking) processes. Vygotsky (1978) also recognised the importance of language in helping children to construct their thinking: the first words and sounds develop into 'inner speech' in their head. According to this theory, the way you talk with a child helps them to develop their cognitive processes – their knowledge and understanding. So, if you are working at Key Stage 1 supervising a child playing with water, the way you use words like "splash", "full" and "empty", and the way you help them to verbalise and explain what they are doing while they fill up and empty containers, is helping them to develop both their vocabulary and their ideas about the concept of volume. It is the same process at every Key Stage, but the concepts and vocabulary will become more complex as pupils develop. If you are working at Key Stage 3 you may be helping them to understand complex concepts like democracy.

Bruner took this concept further and described how an adult could 'scaffold' conversations with a child to help them make sense of a task and guide them in developing their own understanding. He said this was done by talking through each stage and gradually withdrawing support until the child was confident to act alone (1978 in Mercer, 2000).

These three different theories each have important elements and all reinforce the crucial part that you can play in helping all children to use language effectively.

A timetable for development

The development of language usually follows a recognised pattern throughout childhood. Check that you are aware of the sort of norms of development for any child you are working with. You can use a child development book to give you that information or ask your teacher. There are some key points to remember:

- Receptive language is usually more advanced than expressive language, so a child may understand far more than you think. Do not underestimate their ability to understand and judge their language ability only by how they express themselves.
- The link between language and intelligence is a complex one, in spite of the cognition theory of language development. Some children can use language very well yet do not have a high level of functional intelligence (those with Williams' Syndrome for example, a genetic condition with specific effects on language and cognition (Semel and Rosner, 2003)). There are many children with language difficulties who are very able in other ways. Keep an open mind when you are working with all children. Be careful not to always use their language ability alone to make a judgement about their overall ability.
- Non-verbal (body language) is an important part of communication. There are cultural differences in the way we use our body language too.
- Children's individual personalities and learning preferences will affect the way they listen and speak. Some may be impulsive and

need to learn to wait and listen. Others may be introverted and think things through in great detail and may need encouragement to share their thinking by talking to others. For some shy children the idea of speaking in front of others is absolutely terrifying. They need sensitive support to build their confidence and ensure that other children do not tease them. Observe the way children take part in Speaking and Listening so that you can tailor your support appropriately.

- Keep in mind the differences in the way that boys and girls use language to learn. There is some evidence that girls prefer to use social discussion more effectively than boys, while boys can sometimes dominate group discussion situations (Corden, 2000, p.97).
- Children who have English as an additional language are probably very competent speakers of their first language. You should always take this into account when you are working with them.

Terms you may come across

Phonology

We refer to the way that sounds are combined into words and language as 'phonology' (from the Greek *phonos* meaning sound). You may see the ability to process and use these sounds described as phonological processing ability. It is an essential skill in the development of language, and also in how children learn to read and write. The smallest unit of sound is called a phoneme, so 'cat' has three phonemes, c - a - t. The ability to process sound varies from person to person, but can be developed by activities like rhymes, songs, chants, and stories, etc. This is a very important part of the Pre-school, Foundation and Key Stage 1 Curriculum. Some learners may have problems with phonology, which will cause them difficulties in reading, spelling and sometimes spoken language. These include some learners with specific learning difficulties like dyslexia and dyspraxia.

Syntax

Syntax is the set of rules or conventions that govern the way we combine sounds and words in language. It is like a spoken grammar, which deals with the order we put words in and the parts of speech we use at different times. For example, in English we usually put a describing word (adjective) in front of a noun (e.g. 'a *red* ball'). This is not always the case in other languages where the adjective is often placed after the noun (e.g. 'una bola *vermelha*' in Portuguese). Some children will have difficulties with syntax and structure. They may miss the endings from words, or get the tense wrong. This can be the result of a Specific Language Impairment (SLI).

Semantics

Semantics refers to the meaning of language – so when you are helping children to understand what *floating* means, or what *transpiration* is, you are helping with their semantic knowledge. Some meanings are very subtle. Try to define the difference between a house and a home!

Much of the work you do in school will be to increase a learner's semantic knowledge, which will help them with the development of their conceptual thinking.

Pragmatics

This is the way that we use language, particularly in social interaction. You may ask someone "How are you?" as a politeness rather than actually wanting to know. There are conventions and procedures for the way we communicate with others. Children need to know when we are asking a rhetorical question (i.e. one to which we do not actually require an answer), or phrasing a command as a question ("Would you like to stop talking?"). Keep a look out for these conventions in your society, school and family. Help children to understand and use them well by modelling and explaining them. Some learners who have autistic spectrum disorders have particular problems using language in this way and need skilled support to be able to communicate effectively.

All of these difficulties are dealt with in more detail in Chapter 13.

Helping children to listen

Listening skills are an important part of communication. Children need to listen to identify sounds in words, learn from auditory information and hear what people are saying. You can help children by modelling good listening.

- Be interested in what they say.
- Value their opinions.
- Give them time to respond.
- Give them feedback on what they have said – "Am I right in thinking that you mean...?"
- Paraphrase – "So you are saying that you think...?"
- Use non-verbal communication like a smile or a nod to encourage a response.
- Make relevant responses or comments.
- Stay focused.
- Use eye contact, but remember that not all children have to give you eye contact to be listening. In fact, recent research from Stirling University has shown that children may need to look away to think (Doherty, 2006).

Discuss these points with learners and make sure they understand the importance of listening and how they can show good listening skills.

Types of talk

Mercer (2000) identifies three types of talk that learners engage in:

- disputational talk, where learners disagree and make challenges and counter challenges
- cumulative talk, where learners confirm and build on each other's ideas

- exploratory talk, in which learners engage in reasoning by justifying their own ideas and challenging others' ideas to develop their thoughts.

It is helpful if you can identify and support these different kinds of talk.

Effective questioning

Teachers use questioning to assess learners' knowledge, review their understanding, encourage them to participate, and ask them to explain their thinking. Good teachers always do this very well, so watch them and learn. Make sure that pupils know how to back up what they say and always respect their opinions, even if you do not agree with them. Use phrases like "That's an interesting point but…" rather than reject them out of hand. Similarly, be sensitive if they give an incorrect answer. Children who have plucked up courage to say something will never forget it if you are dismissive. They are unlikely to speak freely again. Here are some strategies you can use to encourage children to speak:

- Ask them to clarify, explain or elaborate ("Why do you think…?").
- Model a response ("I think that… because…").
- Listen and encourage ("That sounds really interesting.").
- Ask a question.
- Give them information ("You are using a metaphor here.").
- Relate it to their previous experience ("Remember you enjoyed reading…").
- Suggest ("It might be an idea if…").
- State a fact or point of view ("This story is about…").
- Ask their opinion ("What do you think…?").
- Use your own experience to comment ("I prefer to…").

In the Foundation Stage, you will be taking part in sustained, shared thinking with young children to help them to develop their conceptual understanding.

Good practice – helping children to develop language

As a teaching assistant you have excellent opportunities to help pupils with language at all times. Ask them about their interests or favourite TV programmes. Ask their opinion on what is happening around them. Remember, every teaching and learning opportunity should be a chance to help with language. From cooking to PE, from the playground to the queue for lunch, from English to Science, it should be a learning outcome for every activity you take part in. Even if learners do not have the opportunity to speak, you can still be developing their receptive language. You will need to use more focused techniques for supporting learning in individual curriculum areas – for example, history debates.

Check the curriculum area you are working in so that you know the

way individual teachers use talk, discussion and role-pl
activities. For example, at Key Stage 4, many teachers u
ed discussions to challenge and extend pupils' thinking a
social and vocabulary skills. At Key Stage 1, you may l
role-playing in a travel agency or shop corner to achieve the same end.

Make sure that you are fully aware of the teaching objectives in Speaking and Listening for each learner or group of learners supported by you. Use the curriculum documents or ask the teacher. As pupils become more mature they will be using language in an increasingly sophisticated way, to argue, persuade, influence, reflect and present. Remember that older learners may have to give an assessed presentation or take an oral exam as part of other curriculum subjects, too.

Check that you are using language appropriate to the child's level of development and, if in doubt, explain what you mean. Model good practice by using language effectively yourself. You should be using Standard English wherever possible. Standard English means the correct use of spoken grammar. It is the commonly accepted dialect, which makes it easier to be understood by everyone. Be clear and direct in your approach and keep things simple if you can. Lengthy explanations can confuse children even more. Make sure you do not use too much controlling, managing or directing talk ("Sit down", "Put that away", "How many times have I told you?", etc.) as it can give a negative view of communication.

Show that you enjoy language. Let children know if you are learning new words or ideas. Language is always a living, growing thing, so explore the way our language is changing and adapting.

Remember each curriculum area has its own language. Maths is a language all on its own! You should be aware of the vocabulary and meanings in the areas you support.

Key Stage 4: "When I began supporting a pupil in Geography GCSE I had trouble with some of the terms they used, so I got my pupil to start a book and put in all the words and what they meant. We got some from the glossary in the textbook and looked up the rest. I asked the teacher if we weren't sure of anything. Learning it together gave us both confidence. He soon got to know the vocabulary and it helped with his spelling as well. The teacher asked us if he could give out the list to the other pupils too, which made us both feel good!"

Be sensitive – for example, if a learner pronounces a word wrongly you can just say it back to them correctly without further comment, rather than drawing attention to their mistake. Also, be sensitive to regional accents. As long as a pupil can be understood, then their home dialect or accent should always be respected.

Children who have English as an additional language already have expertise in their language. Don't assume that because someone is unable to say much in English they do not have a good grasp of language in general and that they are not articulate in their own language.

Check that you are aware of the cultural differences in the way we use body language and communication. For example, some children find standing too close to them an invasion of their personal space; others find giving eye contact a little disrespectful. Others, particularly teenagers, don't like to feel they are being interrogated. Don't forget that there are also cultural differences in the way we enjoy using language at different ages.

Technology and computers can be used to enhance rather than replace communication. If you are working with a child on a computer, it can be a wonderful opportunity to talk while you both focus on the activity. There are some excellent resources to use too, like talking books or taped stories that can stimulate discussion.

Give children time to respond by being patient. Remember that most children can think faster than they speak, so try not to interrupt too soon. Because it is difficult to monitor yourself when you are involved in a Speaking and Listening activity, you may find it useful to ask a colleague to watch you or, with the permission of the teacher, to tape yourself when you are working with children and to listen to it later.

Key Stage 1: "I taped myself helping some learners to retell and discuss the characters in a story. It really surprised me when I listened to the tape because I realised how much talking I did. I didn't really give the children a chance to respond because I was trying to manage the discussion too much. Now I consciously stop myself and let them talk. It helps me to really listen to what they are saying."

Use every opportunity to teach semantic knowledge and meaning. Have a dictionary with you at all times – it will help you increase your word power too!

Key Stage 2: "We divided the class and gave half of them a different word each and the other half the word meanings. We mixed them all up and they had to find their partner, i.e. each word had to find its definition. I moved around the class helping them to ask the right questions and explaining anything they didn't understand. At the end of the time each pair introduced their word and meaning to the rest of the class, then we shuffled the cards and started again. The children really enjoyed it!"

Activities to encourage speaking and listening and literacy skills

You may be asked to help with, or organise any of the following:

Question and answer sessions	Practical activities
Circle time	Hot seating
Cultural activities	Brainstorming
Class discussions	Topic work

Presentations
Games
Role-play
Interest areas
Debates
Dressing up
Social activities
Social Use of Language
  Programme sessions (SULP)
Story telling
Drama
Poetry

Collaborative work
Experiments
Meetings
Reviews of TV programmes
Interviewing visitors
Puppets
Quizzes
Story Sacks
Collaborative art activities
Jokes and word play
Outside guest speakers

Further activities are suggested in Browne (1996).

Reading

Although reading and writing should always be taught together, there are subtle differences between these skills. To read you need to be able to translate written symbols into sounds and meaning. To write you have to hold the sounds and meaning in your head and choose and reproduce the symbols that represent them. Some children may become confident readers but continue to struggle with writing; SATs results consistently show better scores in reading than writing.

Any activities you are involved in should support both reading and writing. Helping children with their writing skills will improve their reading, and vice versa. Always have a small whiteboard or some paper and coloured pens with you when you are supporting learners with literacy so that you can show them word patterns and vocabulary.

Reading is not just about decoding the written word on the page. It is about being able to understand and use that information. You may well spend a great deal of your time helping children to learn to read, either within the Literacy strategies or as part of a support programme. If you are working in a Special School you could be helping with the foundation blocks for reading, or at Key Stage 3/4 you could be assisting learners with the high-level reading skills of scanning, speed reading and evaluating written sources. Whatever Key Stage you work in, you will find children reading many different things – maths problems, computer data, stories and poems, class rules, text books, worksheets, science experiments, and much more. A great deal of what is learned in school is delivered through the written word so your role in helping children learn to read is always absolutely vital as it will give them access to the whole curriculum.

Motivation

- Research has shown that a key predictor of reading success is whether or not a child has been read to regularly, before he or she starts in school. As a teaching assistant you can be a positive role model and show that reading is pleasurable, enjoyable and serves a useful purpose. Make sure children see you reading regularly and know why you read.

- Ensure that learners enjoy their reading time with you and, if you have the opportunity, choose relevant, interesting, age-appropriate materials set at their level. Ask the teacher to check if you are unsure. This is particularly important if you are working with older children. Reading material can be adapted and simplified if necessary, using the pupil's interests or hobbies (sports, fashion, TV, computers, etc.). Harry Potter books have demonstrated that a good story can really motivate children to read, but many learners prefer non-fiction.
- Sometimes it is easy to think that lack of motivation is the cause of reading difficulties, but it is usually the result. It is hard to be motivated when you find something really difficult.
- Remember that we all like familiarity and, in the same way that sports players warm up before they play, learners may wish to read something they are familiar with just to give them confidence. Sometimes there is a temptation to push them on too quickly – parents can be guilty of this with reading books!
- Remind learners that they need to practise to get better.
- Make sure you are familiar with the range of texts that the pupils you support will study.
- Look at ways that your school encourages and motivates pupils to enjoy reading. These may include a well-stocked and easily accessible library, use of TV programmes, book week, storytelling sessions, visits by authors, wall displays, book review competitions, quizzes, varied reading material like comics, magazines and cartoons, role play corners, silent reading sessions, ERIC (Everybody Reads In Class) reading schemes, pupil-made books, taped books, computer software, games and Big Books.

Language experience

We have already seen that a rich experience of language is not just important for spoken language but is also the basis for reading and writing. If you do not know the meaning of a word, then it is harder to read it. To really understand what you read you must be able to relate it to some previous knowledge. You will find this yourself when you read an unfamiliar word in an education textbook. Learners can gain this vital language experience in many ways: talking with peers and adults; role-play; watching TV; listening to the radio; using talking books; using the computer; and, of course, reading. The problem comes when a child has a reading difficulty that cuts them off from fluent reading. It is then even more important that they have these other experiences.

Reading is a very complex skill that involves many different sub-skills and a confident reader will use several different strategies at one time.

Phonic knowledge

Phonological skills

We have already seen the importance of phonology in speaking and listening. This provides the foundation for reading, as words are the representation of sounds and meaning in written form. Being able to hear, use and manipulate these sounds is called 'phonological processing' and has been identified by several researchers as a key skill in learning to read and write (Goswami and Bryant, 1990; Beard, 2000). Words can be broken down by sound in several ways:

Phonemes

These are the smallest unit of sound: *c, a, t*

Onset and rime

Onset refers to the consonant at the beginning of a word and *rime* refers to following vowel(s) and consonants. English words all have at least one rime.

Word	Onset	Rime
ball	b	all
match	m	atch
pair	p	air

The use of onset and rime is important in helping learners to use analogy to read. So, if they can already read 'pair' they can use analogy to work out how to read 'hair'. There are hundreds of families of rhyming words like 'night', 'sight', 'flight', etc. Knowing these will give learners a good basis for reading.

Syllables

We can also divide words into chunks of sound or syllables:

ball	*ball*	one syllable
carpet	*car/pet*	two syllables
individual	*in/div/id/u/al*	five syllables

It is a really helpful strategy to show a pupil how to break down and sound out longer words, particularly in curriculum areas like Science or Geography. It will also give them a useful basis for spelling.

Segmentation

This refers to the learner's ability to hear and identify sounds in a word. For example, if they hear 'hop' they should be able to tell you that the *h* sound is at the beginning, that the *p* is at the end, and that there is an *o* sound in between.

Blending

This is the ability to combine the sounds together. So, in the word 'splash' there is a blend of three consonants, *s, p* and *l*.

Activities to encourage phonological skills

You may be involved in using any of the following as a supplement to the Literacy Strategy: games; rhyming pairs; word wheels; dominoes; wall displays of sound families; skipping games; playground jingles; advertising jingles; nursery rhymes; poetry; songs; raps; chants; computer programs; jigsaws; nonsense words; and popular music. Using alliteration (where the words all begin with the same sound, e.g. 'soft silent snow') helps learners to develop sound awareness too.

You could also be involved in delivering Phonological Awareness Training (PAT) to identified learners. Whatever the case, make sure that you produce the sounds accurately yourself as a model for learners. For example, do not be tempted to tack a vowel sound on to the end of a consonant as it makes it hard to blend; the sound is *f* not *fuh* and *b* not *buh*. You should be familiar with these sound patterns so that you can draw learner's attention to them whenever necessary, whether it is in the Literacy Hour or a Key Stage 4 Chemistry lesson. Phonological skills are a vital part of learning to read.

Learners with phonological processing difficulties may need a tremendous amount of support to help them. In some cases, where children have persistent phonological processing difficulties, it is easier to use a visual approach to reading, like 'look and say'.

Sound symbol relationship/phonics

To be able to read a learner has to know the relationship between the sound and the symbol that represents it. This is a combination of graphic and phonic knowledge (sometimes called 'graphophonic' knowledge). The unit of sound is referred to as a 'phoneme' while the symbol that represents it is referred to as a 'grapheme' (from the Greek *graph* meaning writing or pictorial representation).

There are only 26 letters in the alphabet but 44 different sounds and over 140 different letter combinations to make those sounds. The sound symbol relationship is therefore not always straightforward! For example, the grapheme *ch* can make the sound *ch* as in chip, *sh* as in machine, or *k* as in Christmas, depending on the language it comes from. The sound *ue* can be made in many different ways: canoe, flu, blue, through, you, too, to, flew. The letter *y* can be considered as a vowel or a consonant.

The Primary framework emphasises the need for children to be taught phonic knowledge systematically from an early age. As a teaching assistant you should be familiar with basic phonic patterns. Here is a simplified list:

Vowel sounds

/ a /	acorn	/ a /	cat
/ e /	even	/ e /	peg

/ i /	find	/ i /	tip
/ o /	open	/ o /	log
/ u /	unicorn	/ u /	up

Vowel digraphs – two vowels together which make one sound, e.g.:

/ ae /	pain	day	gate	
/ ee /	sweet	heat	thief	these
/ ie /	tried	shine		
/ oe /	road	bone		
/ ue /	moon	blue	tune	
/ oo /	look	would		
/ au /	haul			
/ ow /	shout			
/ oi /	coin			

Vowel and R consonant sounds:

/ air /	stairs	bear	hare		
/ ear /	fear	beer	here		
/ ar /	cart	fast (regional)			
/ ur /	burn	first	term	heard	work
/ or /	torn	door	warn (regional)		
/ er /	circus	sister			

Consonants:

/ b /	big	/ j /	jam	/ p /	pop	/ v /	van
/ d /	dog	/ k /	king	/ q /	quarrel	/ w /	win
/ f /	fox	/ l /	let	/ r /	rice	/ x /	x-ray
/ g /	gate	/ m /	mouse	/ s /	set	/ y /	yacht
/ h /	hill	/ n /	net	/ t /	toast	/ z /	zebra

Consonant blends, e.g.:

pl

br

st str

Consonant digraphs (two consonants together that make one sound) **e.g.:**

wh	ch
sh	th

Knowing what a word begins with (the initial sound) can help learners read the word.

There are many structured programmes that teach the sound symbol relationship, and you may come across any of the following:

- *Progression in Phonics* (PIPS) – structured activities and resources from the Primary Strategy programme.
- *Jolly Phonics* – A phonic programme that includes a multi-sensory approach.
- *THRASS* – a multi-sensory structured phonic programme to introduce the sound/symbol relationship.
- *Beat Dyslexia* – a commercially produced highly structured programme to reinforce spelling and reading.
- *Alpha to Omega* (1999) – a handbook for teachers to use that includes common spelling, grammatical and reading patterns.
- *Reading Reflex* – a structured programme that teaches the sub-skills for reading, including phonemic awareness, moving from the sound to the letter (McGuinness and McGuinness, 1998).
- *Spelling Made Easy* – a spelling programme with associated workbooks.

You may also be using core and other texts to learn sound patterns.

Word recognition and graphic knowledge

Visual recognition – look and say

Although the emphasis is now on the systematic teaching of phonics from an early age, many learners still use whole-word recognition to read, recognising the difference between the shapes and patterns of words. The ability to look at a picture or a word and put a name to it is called 'rapid automatic naming'. It is a key skill in learning to read and one that is particularly useful when words are not phonetically regular, like 'tongue' or 'yacht'. Pre-school and Foundation Stage learners can be given lots of experience in this by naming items in picture books. Learners need to see the words frequently to remember them. You may have wall displays in the classroom, or word lists taped to desks. Classroom items are often labelled, although after a short time learners may become used to them and ignore them. One teacher in a Year 1 class used to move them around overnight so that the first activity the children had to do in the morning was to put them back in the right place!

> **Key Stage 1:** "The teacher and I choose a different high-frequency word every day and pin them to our clothes just at the children's eye level!"

You may be involved in activities like bingo or other games, which help to reinforce children's memory of commonly used words. You can also help them with words in all subject areas by concentrating on curriculum-specific vocabulary. It is much easier for pupils to remember a word when it is associated with a strong visual image, for example, 'fire' or 'elephant'. The smaller words like *this* or *then* are much more difficult as there is no easy visual or semantic image to help them, so those small words may seem easy but are actually harder to remember and will need more reinforcement. You can help a learner to remember words by drawing their attention to any common patterns or unusual shapes or talking through a helpful visual image.

Key Stage 3: "I used a football game to help some Year 7 learners with the words they need for Science. We drew a football pitch and players on the board. They had flashcards with the words to read. They could pass or shoot if they could read the word. If they couldn't they were tackled by the opposition. They adapted the rules themselves as they went on and then brought their own words along that were even more difficult! It really motivated them."

Alphabet knowledge

Learners need to know the name of a letter, not just the sound it makes. If you pronounce *a* like the *a* in cat, it is then hard for them to read it as 'acorn' or 'path' or 'about'. They should know that each letter has a name, but can make different sounds.

Learners also need to know the order of letters so that they can use an index, a dictionary and reference books. There are many ways to learn this. You can use plastic or wooden letters for a multi-sensory approach, or there are some excellent computer programs which teach and reinforce letter order. You may have used *Letterland*, which has a strong visual image to go along with each letter. Some classrooms will have alphabet lines on the wall or on learners' desks as an added resource, or you can help learners make up their own letter line using an interest or hobby (A–Z of music, or dinosaurs, for example).

Grammatical knowledge

Using syntax

Learners use their knowledge of *syntax* – how words are put together in sentences and how punctuation is used – to help them decide what kind of word will come next. So, if they see 'the boy __ down the road', they might guess it would be a verb like *runs*. They may also use their knowledge of grammar to help them to read, for example understanding that *ous* is an adjective ending.

Narrative conventions

Learners need to become familiar with the format and shape of written material or texts. They need to know that the print carries the meaning and that in English, unlike some other languages, we read from left to right. They need to understand that there are different styles of book (e.g. fiction, non-fiction) and be familiar with their structure (beginning, middle, end). They should also understand about authors and title pages and how to use an index.

Knowledge of context

Using context

Learners use their knowledge of the text to guess or predict what will come next. So, for example, if the book is about a girl making a kite they might assume that a small word beginning with a 'k' could be kite, or if there is a picture of a kite being blown around on a page, they might assume a word beginning with 'w' could be windy. You can help children to use contextual understanding by drawing their attention to the storyline or the pictures, talking through the subject matter or story. However, although the use of context is important in building fluency, it should not replace accurate decoding of the words. After all, you would not want a chemist to give you the wrong dosage of drugs because they were taking a guess at what was on the prescription!

Fluent reading skills

Even if a learner can decode the text well they may still need some help with fluency and comprehension. You can model fluency to learners, using the correct intonation. This is an important part of guided and shared reading too. Sometimes getting learners to tape and listen to themselves can also help.

Comprehension – reading for meaning

Learners need to understand what they read, so helping them with comprehension is an important part of your role. You can talk through the content with them, explaining any new word meanings and drawing attention to the structure of the text. You can also encourage learners to use any knowledge of the subject matter they may already have, to help them or discuss the ideas and concepts in further detail. However, helping them to accurately decode the text is the most important starting point.

If learners have to complete a comprehension exercise it is often helpful to show them how to mark photocopied text with highlighter pens to draw attention to key facts, or to read the questions before they read the text to give them a reference framework. The ability to understand and respond to different texts is a key part of English at all levels, but becomes particularly important at Key Stage 3 and 4. Then learners must use inference confidently, and analyse how different styles, structures and types of writing can influence and affect meaning.

Information retrieval

This refers to the ability to skim and scan for information, use images and print, be selective in using information and use notes to summarise. These are particularly important skills to be able to use when obtaining information from the Internet and form one of the teaching units of the LPU at Key Stage 3.

Reading genres

Learners should be familiar with a broad range of fiction texts, such as modern and classic fiction, poetry, traditional stories and plays, and a range of non-fiction like reference materials, magazines, information books, biographies and diaries.

Reading difficulties

From this analysis of the skills and strategies required to read, you will see that reading difficulties can be complex both to diagnose and give appropriate support for. A child who has problems with finding words may lack language experience or may have a word retrieval problem associated with a speech and language difficulty or dyslexia. A child who cannot read well because he or she doesn't know the sound/symbol relationships may have a phonological processing difficulty or may just have had limited experience with phonic programmes. The type of support helpful for one child may not be appropriate for another, so it is important to be careful when you observe them reading. Report their difficulties accurately to the teacher, if necessary, who can then discuss appropriate alternative support strategies.

Mears Irlen Syndrome (Scotopic Sensitivity Syndrome)

Some learners have difficulty reading black print against a white background. This is referred to as *Mears Irlen Syndrome* after Helen Irlen, the American psychologist who first discovered it. Learners find it uncomfortable to read because of glare and fluctuating movement in the text. They are helped by coloured lenses or overlays, which need to be individually prescribed. This is a rare syndrome, but is occasionally associated with a specific learning difficulty like dyslexia. If you observe any child reading and think that they may have this difficulty, tell your teacher, who will refer them to an optician for screening. It is important not to ask a child whether the letters jump about, as they will almost certainly say "yes"; instead, ask them to tell you how it feels when they read.

Key Stage 1: "One of the Year 1 children I was working with in literacy told me the writing in her book seemed to be jumping about. I remembered a session I had had at college about children who benefit from wearing spectacles with coloured lenses. I mentioned this to the teacher at the end of the lesson. We found some coloured acetate sheets and let the child try reading her book through different coloured overlays and she found some colours seemed much better than others. After that the teacher discussed the matter with the child's parents and now she has pink lenses prescribed by a specialist. In the meantime, instead of photocopying onto white paper for her, we used a pastel colour which seemed to decrease the jumping effect."

Supported Reading Checklist

Do you have a dictionary, a small whiteboard and pens?

Beginning:
Remind learners of learning objectives and previous experience ("We are continuing with the story that we started last week", etc.). Talk about characters, motive and storyline in fiction, and information or subject in non-fiction.

Suggested Strategies and Cues to Help Learners:

Sound/symbol patterns (phonics)	Shape of words
Sight vocabulary	Initial sounds
Pictures	Sentence structure (syntax)
Subject matter	Splitting words into syllables
Leaving words and then re-reading using context of sentence	

Encourage Use of:
Prediction
Inference

Draw Attention to:
Phonic patterns
Analogy
Patterns of sound, e.g. alliteration, rhyme
Words in the classroom
Words used in games
Curriculum words (subject vocabulary)
Word derivation
Conventions of print

Discuss the Text:
Format of the story or text
Ideas and Concepts
Style of writing; language; mood; setting
Characters; motivation
New vocabulary; concepts

Interaction:
Do not intervene too much as it impedes fluency
Use focused praise and feedback ("I like the way you...")
Ask learners how they read; what strategies are successful?
Check comprehension by discussion and questioning.

Observe:
Strategies learners use to read.

Feedback to Teacher:
Information on materials, learner achievement, and strategies.

Writing

Writing is closely connected to reading and is taught at the same time, but the writing process has separate strands: the *transcription* part – spelling, punctuation and handwriting – and the *compositional* part that deals with what we write and how we write it. Both are inextricably linked. It is hard to write creatively and interestingly, or to use exactly the right word in the right context, if your vocabulary is limited by what you can spell or if no one can read your handwriting. Using oral language means you can explain what you mean, but with written language you have to make your meaning clear on the page without a second chance to explain.

Children's writing development takes them from simple mark-making in the Foundation Stage to the ability to construct a sophisticated written argument by age 16. As with all aspects of literacy, it is important to use every opportunity in the classroom to improve pupils' writing skills and to give them the confidence to express themselves freely. Writing is a complex skill and needs expert support. However, the use of ICT and word processing has made writing even more accessible for many learners.

Motivation

Some learners are articulate when they use spoken language but find it hard to get their thoughts down on paper. They need to learn the sub-skills for writing in a structured and organised way. It is important to motivate them by providing interesting and varied writing tasks, which have a purpose. Some classrooms have a writing corner, full of different writing materials like pens; coloured pencils and paper; forms; diaries; highlighters; stencils; card; folders; book cover materials; computers; dictionaries and whiteboards. Wall displays can include examples of different kinds of writing, prompts for writing, alphabet friezes and common spellings. There are some excellent computer programs available which deal with spelling or the structuring of written work too.

If you are working in more than one classroom you can carry writing materials around with you like coloured gel pens, pens with different shapes and sizes of grip (if allowed), and various kinds of paper and encourage learners to try them out. Show learners that you enjoy writing too!

Writing genres

You will be encouraged to make sure learners are aware of the audience they are writing for and the different styles and formats for writing. These are referred to as 'writing genres' and can include simple labelling at the Foundation Stage, instructions and messages at Key Stage 1, narrative at Key Stage 2, and complex exposition and argument at Key Stage 4. Pupils need to imagine and explore feeling, inform and explain, persuade others, and review and comment through their writing. You should be helping them to explore the different forms and styles of writing.

Opportunities for writing

You may be involved in any of the following types of writing activities in the classroom:

Poetry; role-play corner; stories; descriptions; letters; e-mail; play-writing; games; diaries; reports; research summaries; magazine articles; reviews; slogans; songs; competitions; nonsense rhymes; essays; and experiment write-ups.

Teaching assistants can often give pupils real confidence in writing by giving them individualised support in a small group setting. This is particularly important in creative writing, when pupils may find it difficult to be imaginative. You can make suggestions, give them a structure to follow, or help them brainstorm ideas.

Writing processes

For each writing task, pupils need to learn to:

Plan → Structure → Draft → Redraft → Complete

Good practice in supporting writing
- Check you have paper or a whiteboard and a dictionary.
- Make sure learners understand why they are writing and whom their audience is.
- Help them to plan their writing.
- Encourage them to talk through writing with other pupils.
- Learners are now encouraged to draft and improve their writing with the teacher acting as a guide and facilitator, so make sure you are following the class guidelines on drafting and marking.
- Check they understand the style and length of writing required.
- Help them with the structure of their work, using writing frames if necessary.
- Use visualisation (talk through a visual image) to help them add depth to their description.
- Draw attention to patterns, rules, conventions and meaning to help with spelling. Suggest strategies for words.
- If they have a real spelling difficulty, encourage them to write and worry about the spelling later.
- Use scribing if necessary, where you write for them to help them clarify their ideas.
- Draw attention to grammatical structures, punctuation and paragraphing. It is better to do this in context as you go along.
- Talk through facts, concepts and ideas.
- Talk about the vocabulary and words they have chosen, using the correct terms like verb, etc.

Handwriting

Children are usually encouraged to print when they first begin to make marks and write, but it is now believed that learning to join up handwriting right from the start helps them to achieve a more fluent style of writing. Research based on approaches used in schools in France has shown the importance of combining the teaching of art, PE and handwriting to develop the fine and gross motor skills necessary to automate the hand (Thomas, 1997). Some Key Stage 1 schools use the Write Dance© programme that involves whole body development of handwriting using art, music, games and stories. Using cursive or joined-up handwriting also helps learners to spell words correctly, because the brain remembers the motor sequence used to write a word. This is sometimes referred to as 'kinaesthetic spelling' and is a fundamental part of the multi-sensory approach to remembering the spelling of words:

- Say the word.
- Write it in joined-up handwriting saying each letter as you do so.
- Say the word again.

Sue Cowley, who writes about teaching English at Key Stage 3/4 suggests using warm up exercises for the fingers before pupils begin to write (Cowley, 2002). It is always useful to remember that writing is a physical exercise, and needs to be treated as such. Most schools will have their own handwriting policy that you should follow. It should have guidelines on starting points and correct movement for forming letters and suggestions for materials and resources to use.

Supporting handwriting

- Make sure you know if a learner is left-handed so that they can then be seated to the left of their partner (otherwise they will clash arms!).
- Check they have the correct position at the table, sitting upright with the paper at the right angle.
- Check they have a pencil or pen that is easy to use.
- Check they are using the right grip and are not holding the pen too tightly as this can cause cramps.
- Check they are not pressing down too hard either – writing should flow across the page. An effective strategy in this case is to get them to close their eyes while writing – it takes away the visual input and enables them to feel the movement.
- Model the correct formation of letters and words.

Spelling

Supporting spelling

Check with your teacher to make sure you follow the class approach to spelling and writing. Depending on the Key Stage at which you work, children may be encouraged to have a go at spellings, use word books and dictionaries. Spelling is often a problem-solving activity, when the learner has to choose the correct strategy to use to spell a word. The following diagram gives an idea of the kinds of strategies that all learners should use to spell. It explains why multi-sensory techniques are so important in the teaching of spelling.

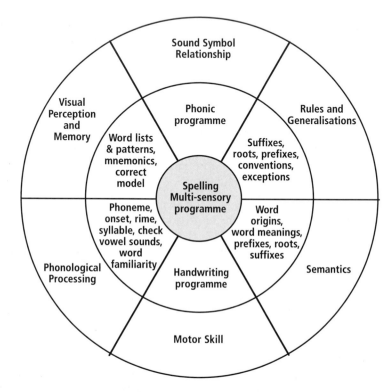

Spelling multi-sensory programme

Visual memory

Most good spellers use their visual memory to check if a word is right, but some pupils, particularly those with dyslexia, really struggle with this. You can help by:

- teaching lists of words emphasising the visual pattern rather than the sound, e.g. *would should could*
- reinforcing the right spelling of the word (sensitively) by writing it above or next to their script. When learners commonly misspell words without any correction it reinforces the wrong image
- using a mnemonic like:
  - **big**
  - **elephants**
  - **can**
  - **always**

- **u**nderstand
- small
- **e**lephants
  Learners should always make up their own mnemonics once
  you have given them one example.
- using: 'look, cover, write, say, check'
- having lists of words or subject vocabulary available in the classroom
- letting them know that there are tricky words and difficult parts
  of words that are not always phonetically regular, which they can
  use these strategies for:
  e.g. ne**cess**ary – one **c**ollar and two **s**leeves.

Phonological processing

To write, learners need to be familiar with a range of words and vocabulary. They need to be able to identify sounds in a word, hold
sequences of sounds in their head, and break words up into phonemes,
onset and rime and syllables, and remember the letters that represent
these. Reading a word aloud and breaking it up into syllables is often
helpful here e.g. Mis-un-der-stand-ing.

Sound-symbol relationship

A pupil will use their knowledge of phonic patterns to be able to spell.
You may be implementing any one of the phonic programmes, or
using a specialist resource like *Toe by Toe* or *Beat Dyslexia*. When
they are learning children sometimes use a logical phonetic alternative like 'stashun' for 'station', so you should show them the correct
phonetic pattern for each word, depending on the age and ability of
the writer.

Applying rules and generalisations

Learners should become familiar with the main generalisations and
rules used, as this helps them to have a framework for spelling. There
are some simple guidelines that help with spelling, like adding *ly* to
make an adverb and when you double consonants. They should learn
simple rules like *'i* before *e* except after *c* unless it says *a*, like in neigh-
bour'. Make sure you keep a good spelling rule book with you so that
you can explain any relevant rules. Many of these are explained in
Alpha to Omega (1999).

Semantics

The use of meaning is vitally important in learning to spell, particularly for older pupils. The English language contains words influenced
by many other languages, for example, German, Latin, Greek, French,
Arabic, Italian, Indian, American, and many more. Language is now
incorporating techno-speak or Internet technology. It makes English
an interesting and varied language – but one that is difficult to spell!
Here are some words and their origins:

Arabic	khaki, lemon
Turkish	divan
Indian	bungalow, jodhpur
Germanic	ox
Viking (Scandinavian)	dash, anger
Italian	pizza
Latin	via, submarine
Greek	perimeter, analysis
French	liaison, court
American	hamburger, diner
Techno-speak	download, fax

Most learners really enjoy finding out about the derivations of words and it helps them with common spelling patterns.

Prefixes, suffixes and roots

Many words consist of a root, which carries the meaning, a prefix, which changes the meaning, and a suffix, which changes the grammatical use.

Prefix		*Root*	*Suffix*
mis	(bad, not)	behave	
re	(again)	view	ing
		colour	ful
dis	(apart, away)	appear	ance
pro	(for)	fess	ion al
		critic	al

Using prefixes and suffixes helps pupils to spell and helps with meanings too. For example, the suffix *er* often refers to someone who does something, e.g. farm*er*, football*er*: It also helps learners with curriculum vocabulary. For example, much scientific terminology comes from Greek:

photo	light
sepa	covering
endo	inner
exo	outer
syn	together with
epi	over

There are some words like 'here'/ 'hear', 'were'/ 'where', 'are' /'our', 'there' /'their', that are commonly confused because they are homonyms – they sound the same but are spelled differently. These should always be taught in groups by meaning rather than sound.

here, there, where – to do with place
hear, ear
their, his, her, our, its – to do with ownership
are, were – parts of the verb 'to be'.

Motor skills

We have already seen the importance of developing motor skills in learning handwriting. They also have a specific part to play in learning to spell because the brain can remember and reproduce the pattern of movement needed to write the letters in a particular word, given plenty of practice. It is always easier to remember if writing is joined up rather than printed, which is why it is important to use cursive (joined-up) handwriting as a strategy to improve spelling. You may find yourself using this technique with dyslexic learners as it is often particularly effective. Sometimes learners with dyspraxia really struggle with this as they have difficulty reproducing remembered patterns of movement. There are many commercially available programmes like *A Hand for Spelling*, or you may be using your school or class approach.

Using dictionaries and spellcheckers

Children should be taught to use a dictionary by using the quartile method, where they divide the dictionary into four to help them locate a letter. There are several commercially available dictionaries that sequence words by sound. Learning Development Aids produce the ACE (aurally coded) dictionary which lists words by their initial sound, e.g. sugar under *sh*. Spellcheckers are often useful in helping a learner to sequence sounds in a word, but they need sensitive use. Pupils will still need guidance in how to use computer spellcheckers, as there are so many words that look or sound almost the same but have different meaning (here, hear; from, form).

Grammar and sentence structure

To write confidently, children should be familiar with the different parts of speech like nouns, verbs, pronouns, know how to use apostrophes and speech marks and be able to construct sentences and paragraphs. Grammar is the organising system for the way we use written language. You should model grammar when you are working with pupils so make sure you are confident about it yourself. Buy a good grammar book and keep it with you.

Key Stage 2: "A child I was working with had learning difficulties and never actually spoke in sentences. As a result, his written sentence structure was non-existent. I helped him to form spoken sentences, which he gradually was able to remember long enough to write down. I used to draw a dash for each word as he said the sentence to help him. If he couldn't spell one of the words, he left it blank and I would help him break it up into phonemes to spell afterwards. This enabled him to become an independent writer, producing writing that made sense. He was much more confident about tackling written work in any subject."

Many children are highly motivated by using ICT and find it easier than traditional forms of communication. They should be encouraged to use texting and messaging as these develop communication skills, as long as they follow accepted protocols and safety guidelines. Language is always living and growing. For more information on literacy and ICT, and indeed on any aspect of literacy, go to the literacy trust website on http://www.literacytrust.org.uk/.

Writing difficulties

Every teaching assistant will be familiar with the learner who finds it difficult to get their ideas down on paper, even though they may be very confident when speaking. You may find this yourself when you have to write a report or do an assignment. As you have seen, writing is a complex process requiring many sub-skills and pupils can experience difficulty at every stage. If you are working with a learner with writing difficulties it is important to make a really accurate analysis of their problem areas so that you can discuss and implement effective strategies in conjunction with teaching staff. You may want to consider the questions below (some suggestions to resolve each problem are given in brackets).

Do they have:

- problems generating ideas for writing? (A prompt sheet or further discussion; use a different resource to stimulate ideas)
- difficulty writing because they don't understand the concepts they are explaining? (More explanation; a different method of explanation; or a different resource to explain) or is it their ability to write their explanation down that is problematical, in other words, can they explain it to you verbally but not write it?
- difficulties with structure and organisation? (Writing frame or flow chart; software program)
- problems with grammatical structure? (Reinforce grammatical conventions)
- limited vocabulary and expression? (Vocabulary support; discussion of ideas).

Does their:

- spelling ability limit their expression, i.e. do they use complex vocabulary when speaking but not writing? (Spelling programme, games, individual spelling checklists, etc.)
- work have the same persistent errors? (Individual proofreading checklist on their desk, compiled by pupil with your help, to be used after every piece of writing)

As in every other situation, make sure you ask each learner to tell you what they find difficult and what might be helpful to them.

Key reading

Key references are given in bold.

Beard, R. (2000) *Developing Writing 3–13,* London: Hodder and Stoughton

Browne, A. (1993) *Helping Children to Write,* London: Paul Chapman Publishing 1993

Calver, J., Ransen, S. and Smith, D. (1999) *Helping with Reading Difficulties,* Tamworth: NASEN *[Specialist help for pupils with reading difficulties.]*

Clipson-Boyles, S. (2001) *Supporting Language and Literacy 3–8,* London: David Fulton, *[Practical Early Years guide.]*

Edwards, S. (1999) *Speaking and Listening for All,* London: David Fulton

Edwards, S. (2004) Supporting *Writing,* London: David Fulton

Fox, G. and Halliwell, M. (2000) *Supporting Literacy and Numeracy,* London: David Fulton *[Practical guide written specifically for teaching assistants.]*

Graham, J. and Kelly, A. (2003) *Writing Under Control,* London: David Fulton *[Useful overview of writing development.]*

Guppy, P. and Hughes, M. (1999) *The Development of Independent Reading – Reading Support Explained,* Buckingham: Open University Press *[Detailed manual of reading support strategies.]*

Hodson, P. and Jones, D. (2006) *Unlocking Speaking and Listening,* London: David Fulton

Hornsby, B. et al. (1999) *Alpha to Omega, the A to Z of Teaching Reading, Writing, and Spelling,* London: Heinemann *[Comprehensive practical guide with examples of spelling rules and conventions.]*

Iley, P (2005) *Using Literacy to Develop Thinking Skills with Children Aged 5-7,* London: David Fulton

Layton, L. and Deeny, K. (2002) *Sound Practice – Phonological Awareness in the Classroom,* London: David Fulton *[A very practical manual with activities and resources.]*

Mason, M. (1998) *Grammar Dictionary,* Birmingham: Questions Publishing *[An excellent pictorial representation of all grammatical formats.]*

Riley, J. (1998) *The Teaching of Reading,* London: Paul Chapman Publishing *[Good overview of reading development.]*

Riley, J. (2006) *Learning and Literacy 3–7: Creative Approaches to Teaching,* London: Paul Chapman Publishing

Whitehead, M. (1999) *Supporting Language and Literacy Development in the Early Years,* Buckingham: Open University Press

References

Key references are given in bold.

Beard, R. (1993) (Ed.) *Teaching Literacy: Balancing Perspectives,* London: Hodder and Stoughton

Browne, A. (1996) *Developing Language and Literacy 3–8,* London: Paul Chapman *[Comprehensive discussion of successful approaches.]*

Chomsky discussed in Oates, J. (1994) *Foundations of Child Development,* Buckingham: Open University Press

Corden, R. (2000) *Literacy and Learning Through Talk,* Buckingham: Open University Press *[Interesting activities and ideas; reinforces the essential role of speaking and listening.]*

Cowley, S. (2002) *Getting the Buggers to Write,* London: Continuum *[Very practical suggestions for encouraging reluctant writers at KS 3/4.]*

DfES (2003) *Excellence and Enjoyment – A Strategy for Primary Schools,* http://www.dfes.gov.uk/primarydocument/

DfES (2004) *Every Child Matters* London: DfES

DfES (2006) *Independent Review of the Teaching of Early Reading,* London: DfES

Doherty, M (2006) 'The Development of Mentalistic Gaze and Understanding', *Infant and Child Development* 15, pp. 179-86, available at www.interscience.wiley.com

Goswami, U. and Bryant, P. (1990) *Phonological Skills and Learning to Read (Essays in Developmental Psychology)* London: Psychology Press *[Theoretical background to reading difficulties.]*

Mercer, N. (2000) *The Guided Construction of Knowledge* Clevedon: Multilingual Matters

Moseley, D. (Ed.) (1986) *The ACE Dictionary, Learning Development Aids,* Wisbech *[Aurally-coded dictionary (spelling by sound).]*

McGuinness, C. and McGuinness, G. (1998) *Reading Reflex,* New York: The Free Press *[The manual for the phonographic method to teach reading.]*

Neville, H. (2003), *Lecture on Cognition and Neuroscience,* Georgetown University, Washington DC, 23 April 2003

Pinker, S. (1989) *The Language Instinct: How the Mind Creates Language,* New York: Harper Perennial *[Complex explanation of the development of language.]*

Ramscar, M., *Department Of Psychology,* Stanford University, 15 November 2003 *[Discussion with Michael Ramscar, Assistant Professor.]*

Savage, R. and Carless, S. (2005) 'Learning Support Assistants Can Deliver Effective Reading Interventions for "At-risk" Children', *Educational Research* vol. 47, no. 1, March 2005

Semel, E. and Rosner, S.(2003) *Understanding Williams Syndrome: Behavioural Patterns and Interventions,* New Jersey: Lawrence Erlbaum Associates, Inc.

Thomas, F. (1997) *Une Question de Writing,* London: TTA*[TTA-sponsored action research implemented at Herne Infants School, Kent.]*

Voors, R. Write Dance© *[System of handwriting that involves development of coordination skills through art, music, games, etc.]*

Wedel, A (2005) available at http://dingo.sbs.arizona.edu/

11 Teaching numeracy

Just as there has been debate about the way Literacy has been taught over the years, Mathematics teaching has also been the subject of much controversy. During the 1980s and '90s, concern about falling standards of numeracy in the general population led to a re-examination of the teaching and learning methods used in schools. At this time, Maths was usually taught by individualised programmes, often commercially produced, which pupils worked through at their own pace. Research about teaching methods in other countries like Hungary and Japan, where pupils seemed to have higher achievement levels in Maths, indicated that the development of mathematical thinking and problem solving through whole class teaching might be more effective.

In 1999, the National Numeracy Strategy (NNS) was introduced at Key Stage 1/2. The emphasis of the NNS included whole class teaching and discussion to encourage mathematical thinking. The use of mental Mathematics strategies and problem solving techniques were encouraged, with less emphasis on formalised written procedures and recording. The initial success of this strategy led to its extension to Key Stage 3 in 2001 (DfES, 2000) (Tanner, Jones and Davies, 2002). In 2006 a renewed Primary Framework for Mathematics introduced a simplified structure with seven strands of learning, including a recommendation for a variety of teaching approaches and activities to support mathematical development. New technology, such as interactive whiteboards has also had a big impact on the way Mathematics is now taught in some schools.

The importance of mathematics

The renewed Framework emphasises that Mathematics is a combination of concepts, facts, properties, rules, patterns and processes (DfES, 2006). Mathematics is the study of relationships in the everyday world, which has evolved from the practice of counting, measuring, and identifying shapes. It has its own symbolic representation and language to describe, explain and manage those logical relationships. Maths should be exciting and creative, but too often the whole subject provokes considerable anxiety in both adults and children.

In 1982, the Cockroft Report highlighted the fact that many adults lacked confidence in their everyday mathematical ability (Cockroft, 1982). Some people are so lacking in confidence where Maths is concerned that a kind of 'numbing panic' comes over them when they have to attempt some mathematical task (Buxton, 1991). Others will cheerfully confess that they are hopeless at Maths, but would be ashamed to say they had difficulty in reading. They usually attribute this to some fault in themselves rather than being the result of unsuccessful teaching methods. You may yourself have this view of your own mathematical ability because of your experiences. Some teaching assistants say that they are quite happy to support Literacy but feel underconfident about Maths. The teaching techniques introduced by the National Numeracy Strategy and the daily Mathematics Lesson are often successful in giving teaching assistants confidence too.

> **Key Stage 2:** "I hated Maths at school. The Maths teacher could never understand why I found it so difficult, but I just did. I was dreading having to support numeracy but it is really different now. We encourage the children to try different strategies and record in different ways. We talk about the methods we use. We do fun activities like games and quizzes. I never thought I would say it, but I really enjoy Maths now."

Everyday Maths

Maths needs to be seen as an essential part of everyday life, rather than something that people are either good at or not. The fact is that Maths has a crucial part to play in everyone's life and it is hard to think of a single activity that does not include it. Sport, play, cooking, gardening, shopping, DIY, using computers, arranging a mortgage, sewing, travelling and programming a DVD recorder all involve some element of Maths. It is therefore vital that children understand the relevance of Maths to their everyday lives and use every opportunity to extend and develop their mathematical thinking. This does not have to be in a daily Mathematics lesson. It can be within any area of the curriculum from Art to Science, Music to a Modern Language, or indeed, in any of the extra-curricular areas, like after-school clubs, or in the playground. For example, planning a class trip or activity gives pupils lots of opportunities to use mathematical thinking and problem solving. A confident and supportive teaching assistant can give teachers a great deal of help to make the teaching of numeracy interesting and relevant to pupil's lives.

Maths should not be seen as some dry subject studied only on paper. Ian Stewart, Professor of Mathematics at Warwick University, has written extensively on the links between Maths and the natural world by linking Science, History, Art and Mathematics. He explains how mathematical relationships are a fundamental part of nature, from the stripes on a zebra to the structure of a snowflake (a perfect hexagon, but no two the same!) (Stewart, 1992, 2001).

Theories of mathematical development

The information about the nature of learning is just as relevant when we talk about the development of children's mathematical ability.

Piaget

Piaget's description of stages of learning included a discussion of the concept of conservation of number. This is how he described a child's ability to understand that a number or amount of something remained the same, even when arranged differently. Piaget thought that children developed the ability to do this during the concrete operational stage of development around the age of seven. He has been criticised for having limited expectations about children's ability to engage in sophisticated thinking and tying them to age-related expectations. In the past, this has led some teachers to wait for 'readiness' to learn, rather than allowing a child to move quickly on when they can demonstrate understanding. You may notice yourself that some learners seem able to conserve number at a much earlier age than others. Piaget's idea that children reach a cognitive plateau of development in early adolescence has also been challenged by modern neuroscientists, who have used brain imaging techniques to study thinking and processing in teenagers. Some researchers have also argued that Piaget's ideas may have contributed to an over-reliance on individualised learning programmes for Maths.

Behaviourism

The behaviourist approach to learning is still evident in the use of programmed tasks that give instant feedback to the learner. This is often the method used in visually rewarding computer software programs (*Successmaker* is a popular example). Although these programs are very valuable, learners may sometimes have trouble in transferring these skills into ordinary life.

Bruner

Bruner's identification of three modes of thinking is relevant to teaching and learning in Maths (see page 104):

- Enactive – action
- Iconic – images
- Symbolic – symbols

Although much of mathematical thinking involves the use of symbols, like adding signs or algebraic letters, it is grounded in practical e x p erience. Concentrating too much on procedures and formal methods of recording Maths can sometimes leave learners unsure of the underlying concepts and principles, so the idea that all children need concrete apparatus when they are learning is an accepted part of today's Maths and numeracy teaching.

Using resources and apparatus

You will find yourself helping pupils with all kinds of apparatus, from bead strings, number lines, place value cards, base 10 blocks (Dienes) and multilink cubes, to counting Teddy bears, weighing scales, coins, clocks, metre sticks, and 2D and 3D shapes. The National Numeracy Strategy made recommendations on the kinds of practical apparatus to be used (NNS, 1999, p.9). It is particularly important for children in the Foundation Stage or in nursery provision to have plenty of hands-on experience with everyday activities that help develop mathematical understanding. Using the sand or water tray, playing with construction toys, singing games, reading stories, lining up for lunch or making patterns in PE can all provide opportunities to explore the practical basis of mathematical thinking. However, it is important for all learners to see a concrete representation of a problem or concept when they are in the early stages of understanding. Of course, counting on their fingers is part of this too!

Software

Many schools now have sophisticated ICT equipment to enable learners to see and manipulate mathematical processes. LOGO was one of the first examples of this. It began as a computer programming language that was accessible to children because it gave them the ability to approach the very abstract concept of programming through typing in concrete instructions to move a 'turtle' – a robot or on-screen trailing arrow. It has been the longest lasting and probably most useful ICT application, with direct mathematical relevance to shape, space and problem solving. Instructions and procedures based on 'backwards' and 'forwards' and turns through different angles can produce a huge variety of shapes and patterns for all sorts of purposes.

LOGO aside, mathematical software has progressed from 'drill and practice' game-type programs to powerful interactive teaching programs (ITPs). These programs allow a teacher (or learner) to use 'virtual' representation of all sorts of mathematical processes and scenarios on a computer screen, via a projector and screen, or interactive white board for preference. The DfES has released a wide range of free ITPs for download from its website and details of these are given at the end of this chapter. These programs mimic the same range of practical equipment described above, for example, bead strings, number lines, place value cards, fraction walls, multiplication and number squares, interactive rulers, protractors, weighing scales, measuring cylinders and clocks. As a guide, if a piece of practical equipment is used in lessons, an ITP probably exists to provide additional practice in an attention grabbing form. Other publishers of mathematical

Key Stage 4: "The pupils I support in Maths are on a Link motor vehicle course at a local college. They really struggle with some of the work but it is always easier when they are in the workshop and can see the practical bit of cylinder sizes or tyre pressures. Learning the Maths afterwards is much easier."

teaching materials have developed their own suites of ITPs, some of which provide differentiated activities for individual or pairs of pupils.

Nature and nurture

Vygotsky's ideas on cultural learning are also of interest here. In some countries, mathematical skill is highly valued and this is reflected in the importance of Mathematics teaching in the curriculum and the achievement of pupils. On the other hand, neuropsychologist Brian Butterworth, who has written extensively on mathematical thinking, believes that it is seen as far more acceptable in some Western cultures to admit that you are bad at Maths! You need to be careful that you do not give negative ideas about Mathematics to children based on your own experiences. Parents can also sometimes unintentionally undermine their child's confidence by giving the impression that being bad at Maths somehow runs in their family. It is important to be aware of gender issues too; sometimes girls may think they are no good at Maths, even when that is patently untrue. According to the American mathematician John Paulos, although some people find Maths easy and a few genuinely struggle, most people are capable of a good level of achievement (Paulos, 1988). As a teaching assistant, you can do a great deal to give all learners positive learning experiences.

Butterworth also believes that babies are born with an innate sense of number, based on research showing that very young babies notice and respond to changes in numbers of objects. He calls this sense a 'start-up kit for learning about numbers'. Using this as a starting point, children can then learn to use cultural tools like language, notation (writing numbers and signs) and procedures to be numerate. He sees this as a basic survival instinct – maybe it was useful to see just how many wild animals were heading your way! (Butterworth, 1999).

Certainly, numeracy skills are just as important in modern society. Basic numeracy skills are essential in everyday life to obtain and keep a job, to feed and house a family. Because of rapid technological development, Maths is involved in everything from satellite TV, new sources of fuel and electronic washing machines, to landings on Mars.

The nature of Maths learning

Mathematics is a cumulative subject. In other words, you need a pretty secure grasp of each stage before you can progress to the next. This is why it is important to identify gaps in pupils' understanding and skill. However, it is not a wholly linear subject. It does not mean that children cannot experience different concepts and ideas before they have mastered every aspect of a topic. For example, some learners with dyslexia have difficulty remembering tables. However, if they understand the concept of tables and know how to work out the answer, it is unhelpful for them to spend months stuck on memorising their two times tables!

The mathematician Richard Skemp (1987) thought that Mathematics learning should be *relational* to be effective; in other words, pupils should understand the relationships between concepts in maths rather than just knowing how to follow a procedure or algorithm like multiplication. He likened this to finding your way round an unfamiliar city. If you have just learned one route or way to go somewhere, then you will have a problem if there is a diversion or road closure. However, if you explore and become familiar with the whole city, then you can choose another route to take because you understand the way the roads are connected. Other researchers, including Mike Askew, have also emphasised that mathematical understanding should focus on the connections between ideas (Askew *et al.*, 1997).

Learning and cognitive styles can also affect mathematical development. Gardner's original concept of multiple intelligences identified logical mathematical ability and visuo-spatial ability as helpful for mathematical competence. Much early mathematical development happens as children develop their visuo-spatial skills through play and physical activity, like climbing and running or using toys. Mathematical thinking involves several kinds of processing. Making mathematical connections is often a right-brain activity, while the kind of logical step-by-step approach needed to work out problems by following a procedure is a more left-brain activity. Different areas of Maths such as number, trigonometry or algebra require different kinds of thinking too, so learners may find some areas easier than others, depending on their individual profile. Researchers like Mark Wahl have recommended that teachers use strategies that utilise all types of intelligence. For example, Wahl encourages pupils to:

- use spatial intelligence to represent a problem in visual diagrammatic form
- use music to help with number pattern recognition
- use linguistic and interpersonal intelligence by talking through and paraphrasing problems.

However, Guy Claxton feels that the place of discussion has been over emphasised, particularly in the National Numeracy Strategy. He would like to see learners using more intuitive, imaginative and physical ways of learning rather than constant verbalisation. He considers that pupils are all capable of learning if they use the right strategies (Claxton, 1999).

Steve Chinn has identified two types of thinking styles in mathematical learners, which have some relation to the left/right brain operations: the 'grasshopper' and the 'inchworm'. Others have described these as 'lumpers or splitters'. According to Chinn, a grasshopper:

- has a more holistic approach by seeing the whole problem
- uses estimation to approximate the answer or help choose a method
- uses flexible approaches
- performs mental rather than written calculations

- rarely documents all their thinking
- uses an alternative method to check answers.

An inchworm, as the name suggests, prefers to:

- focus on details and break down a problem into parts
- follow given procedures
- use pen and paper
- work in a series of steps
- concentrate on numbers and facts
- use the same method to check the answer as was used to work it out.

(Adapted from Chinn, 2004, p.60)

In the past, because they often get the right answer without following a laid down procedure, grasshoppers may have fallen foul of teaching approaches that gave marks for showing working out. On the other hand, inchworms may lack flexibility in their approach. Many teachers and teaching assistants stick rigidly to inchworm methods if they are insecure about their own Maths and, therefore, unwittingly put the grasshoppers in their class at a disadvantage. The Primary Framework for Mathematics has opportunities for both types of mathematical thinkers because of the mixture of tasks and learning outcomes. It encourages a more grasshopper approach initially then introduces the formalised procedures and formulae that enable learners to work out problems. It is important for you to be aware of your own and your learners' thinking styles, and to remember that teaching methods will also influence these. The way you help learners will have an effect on their thinking styles.

The Primary Framework for Mathematics emphasises thinking skills and problem solving. Wallace (2001) contains a specific chapter on developing problem solving and thinking skills in numeracy.

You will find a very useful review of the theories of early mathematical development in Pound (1999).

Good practice for teaching assistants supporting Maths

Much of the following information is relevant for all learning, but it is particularly important to encourage independence in Maths, so that pupils do not feel helpless and dependent on adult help.

- Do not hold negative stereotypes about who should be good at Maths and who is not. Give learners confidence in their abilities.
- Try to find opportunities to develop mathematical concepts and thinking in everyday situations and in all subject areas, not just numeracy.
- Try to make learning relevant to pupils' everyday life.
- Encourage learners with achievable tasks and realistic praise.
- Encourage problem solving rather than just following procedures.

- Help learners to understand first, then give them drills, procedures and techniques later.
- Recommend and use appropriate apparatus and concrete materials. It is far easier to understand fractions when you can see something like a pizza divided into equal slices. You may be able to use an ITP on a class PC or laptop as an additional way to mimic the practical apparatus.
- Help learners to 'see' Maths using visualisation.
- Encourage learners to talk through their thinking and ask questions (if you don't know the answer, you can find out!). ITPs are really good at encouraging learners to make suggestions and ask questions. If you do not have access to this technology, make sure you try to work in a non-threatening and positive environment too.
- Encourage different approaches to the same problem.
- Accept different mathematical learning styles and the need for a multi-sensory approach in general.
- Check for gaps in knowledge or understanding and be prepared to go back if necessary, particularly to a more concrete stage.
- Encourage estimation when appropriate.
- Do not be tempted to say an answer is wrong too quickly. Accept divergent thinking.
- Allow uncertainty. Good problem solvers can think through several scenarios before they come up with the best one.
- Reinforce concepts in different ways, e.g. you can count objects (such as pencils) and abstract things ("name three things you like...").
- Help learners with technology, including software.
- Use games wherever available.
- Make sure workbooks and sheets are readable.
- Feedback accurately to the teacher.

Key Stage 2: "You have to know the children you are working with. I can say to some 'this is really hard' and they love it. They love problem solving. It motivates them to try and they get a great sense of achievement. With others, I have to be careful to give them confidence by breaking everything down and helping with every step."

Key Stage 1/2: "Everyday, I supervise a group of children putting out the chairs and tables in the dining hall. We count them, arrange them in size order, or by colour, or make different patterns with the tables. When we put them away, we stack them differently too."

Key Stage 2: "One of our pupils has very poor auditory memory. She was really struggling with all parts of Maths lessons where she had to listen and keep information in her head before working things out, especially mental Maths tests. Now we get her to jot down all the information, particularly numbers, as she hears or thinks it. This has made an enormous difference to her ability to 'get the right answer' and her confidence has soared."

Mathematical games

Many pupils enjoy playing mathematical games, and these have several important purposes. They can be very motivating and enjoyable for learners, and they can either provide reinforcement and practice for concepts that they already know, or introduce and represent new concepts that they need to learn. Before you use any game, you should check to make sure it has clear objectives and also that you understand the mathematical learning that will take place and how this connects with the learning outcomes for the pupils you are working with. You will also need to think about the sub-skills that are required to play it, whether it is flexible enough to be differentiated or extended, and whether it develops and extends the use of mathematical language. You may have the opportunity to make or adapt a game yourself. In that case, you can add the following to your checklist. Is it:

- suitable for independent learners or does it need adult supervision
- motivating
- well made
- robust
- age appropriate
- easy to store
- easy to use
- competitive?

Does it have:

- clear instructions
- a realistic time frame?

You can find more information on mathematical games at http://www.madras.fife.sch.uk/maths/games/.

The Primary and Key Stage 3 Strategies

The National Numeracy Strategy, launched in 1999, was intended to complement the Literacy Strategy and came about in response to statistics that showed that a high number of children were starting secondary school with poor mathematical skills, which often meant that they left school ill equipped to cope with even the simple numeracy demanded by many jobs. The Strategy aimed to give learners confidence and competence in numbers and measures and the ability to use practical information to solve problems and present solutions.

After the Numeracy Strategy became established in primary schools, its principles were then extended into secondary schools as part of the Key Stage 3 National Strategy. The aim was to continue the work started in primary schools in strengthening standards in Mathematics. In particular, pupils who had got used to the way that Mathematics was now taught in primary schools responded well when the same principles and structures were extended into Years 7, 8 and 9.

A particular feature of the Key Stage 3 strategy is the support given to those pupils who have not reached the desired level in Mathematics at the end of Key Stage 2. A catch-up programme called Springboard 7 was devised for those who had attained level 3 but not level 4. Teaching assistants are heavily involved in delivering this programme. The same goes for catch-up/booster programmes in Years 3 to 6 (Springboard 3 to Springboard 6), where the programmes have been designed so that teaching assistants can deliver some of the sessions to groups of children. In some schools where Maths sets (grouping by ability) are used, these are delivered in whole class sessions.

In 2006 the Primary Strategy was renewed and given a more flexible and simplified format. Like the Literacy Framework, the renewed Mathematics Framework is also available electronically at

http://www.standards. dfes, gov.uk/primary frameworks.

The objectives have been simplified into seven strands:

- Using and applying (including problem-solving)
- Counting and understanding number
- Knowing and using number facts
- Calculating
- Understanding shape
- Measuring
- Handling data.

Each year is structured about five blocks of work, which cover sets of learning outcomes from the strands. This helps teachers to adapt lessons for learners who need more, or less, support, or to help plan mixed-age classes. As in the original NNS, the emphasis is on mental methods of calculation and early mathematical development through the Foundation Stage and Key Stage 1. However, there is less emphasis on the rigid structure of the hourly lesson that was at the core of the old strategy, and more on lively and engaging teaching that involves a planned blend of activities and approaches. And where the old strategy had a plenary (whole-class) session at the end of the lesson, now teachers are encouraged to review learning at any time during the lesson.

Covering the objectives in the seven strands supports children in their progression towards the Early Learning Goals and National Curriculum levels at Key Stage 1 and Key Stage 2.

The strands for Key Stage 3 are similar to those for Primary:

- Using and applying Mathematics to solve problems
- Numbers and the number system
- Calculations
- Algebra
- Shape, space and measure
- Handling data.

Teachers are not necessarily expected to follow the Framework, provided that they have methods in place that will effectively deliver the desired results. Although the Framework is used in most schools, it should be adapted and refined according to schools' or teachers' own requirements. As you will be working within the Framework yourself, you may find it useful to spend a little time looking at it with the class teacher, seeing what the objectives are and how it informs planning and day-to-day lessons.

Mathematics lessons

A typical lesson may include any or all of:

- practice for mental methods of calculation
- a period of whole-class teaching
- a review of learning.

Practice for mental methods of calculation
The whole class works together on a calculation activity or calculations to reinforce and sharpen their mental and oral skills. It is important that all children actively contribute, not just those who are already good at the task chosen.

In a primary class, this might consist, say, of counting in steps of different sizes, working out new mathematical facts from those that children have already learned, playing a mathematical game or reviewing an activity done at home. Particularly with the younger age groups, the children might be encouraged to chant answers together – for example, if they are counting up or down in regular steps. In Key Stage 3, the starter might involve an algebraic calculation, visualising and describing shapes or interpreting data.

The electronic framework includes an emphasis on calculation through practical, oral and mental activities with appropriate informal and formal recording techniques. Calculators are introduced in Year 4, when learners are secure in their own mental methods, although they can be used earlier if required.

A period of whole-class teaching,
The period of whole-class teaching is followed by children applying what they have just learned in group work, in pairs or individually. The teacher may start either by introducing a new topic or by going back to an old one to consolidate or extend it. The teacher will develop the vocabulary relevant to this topic and then show how concepts and skills are used and applied. In the pupil work that follows, the teacher may work closely with one or two of the groups and should make it clear to the teaching assistant what their role in this part of the lesson is.

A review of learning

In a review of learning a teacher may clear up any misunderstandings the children may have, reinforce the key learning points and identify progress. They may also set homework.

The role of the teaching assistant during a mathematics lesson

During the calculation practice, you may well be asked to sit with a small group of children who might otherwise struggle with the lesson or who are too reticent to contribute unprompted. Your role would be to encourage them to take part in the activity and suggest answers when they have them, alerting the teacher to the child if necessary ("Mrs Patel, I think Andrew has a suggestion."). If the teacher is using a particular resource such as a display card, you may have a smaller version to show to the children you are working with, to help them concentrate.

You might need to check that the children are following what the teacher says by quietly asking them to repeat it to you, or you may have to repeat the teacher's questions to them. Some children may have difficulty paying attention. It may be necessary to help them keep focused on task by repeating the questions and prompting them to think about the answers. Above all, observe them and make notes – mental if necessary – about how they are responding to the questions, so that you can discuss their progress later with the teacher.

During whole-class teaching, you may be asked to spend some time moving around the class and supporting individual children who need help. Alternatively, you may find that you are expected to spend the majority of this part of the lesson working with a particular group or pair of pupils, helping to keep children on task, ensuring that they understand what they are supposed to do, encouraging them and giving them relevant strategies.

It is important to be able to ask children the right sorts of questions to help them unpick problems, or to extend the problems into wider contexts. It is also important to remember that children are often expected to work in groups, and they should therefore be encouraged to work collaboratively. All the information in Chapter 9 on managing small group work is essential here.

Mathematics is a communication system with its own very specific language. Learning that language is an essential part of understanding and using maths, so it is important that you use the same vocabulary as the teacher. In that way children are not confused by your giving them less precise terms. The teacher should brief you so that you do not need to interrupt either them or your group too frequently to ask questions, but you should feel free to draw the teacher's attention to any particular difficulties children may have in understanding the work.

You may not always work with the same group of children. Not all groups will receive direct attention from either the teacher or teaching assistant in every lesson but, overall, all learners should get their fair share. The teacher will probably work with each group of children over time. They may also ask you not to work with any group during one lesson, but to keep an eye on the whole class while they work with a particular group themselves or circulate.

During a review of learning, remember to support the teacher in their aim of reinforcing the important points of the lesson and clearing up any misunderstandings the children may have. It may be appropriate to sit with the same group as in the starter, and to check that they follow what is being said and put forward answers when they have them.

Games

As a way of getting children involved in the lesson, mental or practical calculation may be built around a game. This is not just for younger children; games are suitable for pupils in catch-up lessons in Key Stage 3 as well. Any game chosen will be designed to respond to a teaching objective.

A game might involve identifying sequences of numbers or learning to understand the status of each digit in a number, such as that the first digit in a three-figure number represents the number of hundreds, or the second digit after a decimal point represents tenths. The games may involve using dice and often require the children to have cards with questions printed on them.

'Loop card', 'Who am I?' or 'Follow me' card games can be used in groups or for whole classes. They hold pupils' attention well because the children all need to be ready for their 'go'. Some of the newer games are better attention grabbers because they work in lots of different permutations and combinations so that a child's card should come up more than once (see Adrian Pinel – www.loopcards.net).

Teaching methods

As you have seen, the way that Mathematics is now taught will almost certainly have changed since you were at school. This can create confusion as we used to be taught that there were set methods of doing things. For example, if you were doing long division, you would have been expected to write down the divisor and then the number to be divided with a line over it, and then perform calculations with columns of figures underneath. As discussed earlier, the problem with these set methods is that they suited some children but not others and, as a result, Maths became a complete turn-off for large numbers of children who had no problems with other subjects. They also concentrated on the means of getting to answers without instilling a sense of how numbers worked, so that the child might not have an immediate sense of whether the answer they came to was likely to be correct or not.

Now it is recognised that there are often several ways of getting to the answer, and that methods in themselves are not 'right' or 'wrong'. Different methods will suit different people. When introducing children to mathematical calculation it is important to give them methods that are not only interesting and easy to grasp, but which develop a grasp of mathematical concepts, building on the ones they already have. In addition, the way they learn should help children relate Maths to their experience of the everyday world.

This is one reason why the Primary Framework emphasises whole-class work and group work. Solving mathematical problems is not presented as some lone endeavour with individuals grappling heroically with really difficult problems, nor is teaching a matter of drilling rules and methods into pupils' heads. Instead, teaching is a two-way process, where pupils not only respond to teachers but also learn from each other and share their methods. For example, using individual whiteboards, where children can record their answers and show them to the teacher, gives instant and useful feedback on their understanding to the teacher or teaching assistant. Children can share their ideas easily and can amend their responses without the fear of 'spoiling' their book or sheet.

Teachers are expected to bring Maths to life through illustration and demonstration, and the use of interactive electronic whiteboards is one way of doing this. It can also involve the use of objects or even physical movements by the teacher to illustrate how numbers or shapes move about. Children can be involved with the delivery of the lesson by being asked to come out individually to demonstrate or check. During an interactive class session, adults and children will anticipate, speculate and hypothesise – asking questions such as 'what if ...?'. It is easy and quick to check with the computer to see what would happen as a result of the suggestions made. Learners are often happier to do this with a computer because computers 'don't get upset' if they do it wrong! In addition to the DfES ITPs, which mimic practical apparatus and equipment, some ITPs model pencil and paper activities and methods.

Mental calculation

You will already have noticed the importance of mental calculation in the Strategy. The purpose of this is not so much to foster an extraordinary ability to do complicated sums without the aid of pen, paper or calculator, as to develop familiarity with numbers. There are various 'number facts' that have to become second nature to children, for example, progression in tens, the relationship of fractions and decimals, or that multiples of even numbers are always even. Doing mental calculation helps embed these facts so that children can recall them quickly. Once a child has a good grasp of these, they are less likely to be put off Mathematics as a 'difficult' subject. They are also more likely to recognise if an answer is wrong when they make a mistake, such as by missing out or duplicating a digit when doing a calculation on a calculator. It is only when children have a good grasp of mental calculations that they are introduced to formal written methods of calculation; starting children too soon on written methods can jeopardise their ability to calculate mentally.

The way that children are asked to perform calculations should reinforce their grasp of number facts. For example, a Year 4 class might be asked to count back from 377 to 50 by counting down in tens, a Year 6 class could be asked to continue the sequence of square numbers 1, 4, 9, 16 ..., or a Year 8 class might be given a recipe for making a dish for six people, asked to adapt it for four people, and then be required to change all the measurements from pounds and ounces to metric.

Written methods

When children do calculations in writing they are often asked to set them down horizontally, for example:

$$122 - 79 = ?$$

This correlates with early work on the number system based on number lines. Using number lines develops a child's ability to 'bridge through the next 10' (or 100, 1000, etc.) and to count on or back in easier steps of 10 (or 100, 1000). This is in contrast with the old vertical method, whereby the calculation would be expressed as:

$$\begin{array}{r} 122 \\ -\ 79 \\ \hline ? \end{array}$$

The vertical way of working, relying on 'decomposition' and 'exchange' for addition, concentrates on the method and therefore children are less likely to recognise that they have got it wrong. It can also encourage children to perform calculations mechanistically, without really understanding numbers. The horizontal method, on the other hand, concentrates on the numbers, and children are more likely to recognise whether the answer is correct or not. In performing this calculation when set out horizontally, a child is quite likely to work it out by taking 100, seeing how many more than this 122 is, how many less 79 is, and then adding the two figures together. Once again, there is no one 'right' way of doing sums. The vertical method might not be recommended for approaching this particular sum, but is appropriate for adding together several large numbers, where quick mental calculations are not possible.

Once children have developed an understanding of place value and the number system, they can recognise quick ways of doing calculations. For example, when presented with:

$$46 + 63 + 74 + 8 + 17 = ?$$

a child might immediately pair 46 with 74 and 63 with 17, and then come up with the answer very quickly.

The Primary Framework for Mathematics

Listening to children

Children need to understand the language of Mathematics, because Mathematics itself is very precise, and therefore the language used needs to be accurate. Two plus 2 does not equal *about* 4, but *exactly* 4, and similarly it is '2 *plus* 2', not '2 and 2' as that would be ambiguous.

Children should be encouraged to talk about Mathematics, because in talking they reinforce their learning. When children (and adults too) explain ideas, they are clarifying their own understanding of those ideas. They come to understand mathematical terms by using them, not just by reading them. For these reasons, some group activities encourage children to discuss their mathematical reasoning together. If you are listening to such a discussion, resist the temptation to jump in and immediately correct anything that is said that is wrong. Let the conversation develop; other children may correct what has been said, or the children may correct themselves and, if not, you can make your contribution when they have finished.

When children give answers in whole-class sessions, it is a chance to listen carefully to what they say and ensure that they give full answers, using the correct terms; you may be able to prompt them if they do not. Children who have difficulties with Mathematics, those with a hearing impairment, or children for whom English is an additional language, may not initially understand what is asked of them. If you suspect that this is the case, you should ask them to repeat or rephrase the question. Remember that these learners' written understanding of Mathematics might be much greater than their aural understanding. Because mathematical symbols are universal, they may understand a calculation when it is written down but struggle with it when it is read out to them.

Types of questions

Of course, just listening to children is not enough. You need to be able to ask them the right sorts of questions. In Mathematics, this means prompting them to think in a mathematical way. You may find it useful to refer to the section on Effective Questioning in Chapter 8.

There is an important distinction between *closed questions* and *open questions*. A closed question only has one correct answer: "What is 7 add 3?", "What does 68 divided by 17 equal?". Open questions have more than one possible answer: "Give me two numbers that total 20.", "Name some factors of 72.", "The sum of four even numbers is divisible by 4 – is this statement ever true? When is it not true?"

Both types of questions are useful. Asking closed questions encourages precision – most mathematical problems have only one answer. But you need to ask open questions as well to broaden children's understanding. Mixing open and closed questions helps them to think for themselves. You often need to encourage them to think of more than one answer to open questions; don't just take the first answer given, but prompt the group to come up with other possible answers.

Prompt children to explain how they reached an answer. Whether the one they give you is right or wrong, ask them how they came to the answer. In fact, if the answer is wrong, this is a good way of getting them to see for themselves that it is wrong and to realise where they made their mistake.

You are likely to find that the questions teachers ask children are quite varied, not only mixing open and closed questions, but also inventing little scenarios that children can relate to their own experience, such as "Andy spent 54 pence on three apples, and Salim bought two apples with a 50p piece and was given 22 pence change. Whose were the cheaper? By how much?"

When a child is stuck with a problem and cannot find a way through, ask them questions that will act as prompts, tackling individual parts of the problem one by one: "What is 54 divided by 3?" "If Salim was given 22 pence change from 50p, how much did he spend?" See if the child can describe the problem in their own words. The problem will almost certainly draw on something they have learned in a previous lesson – ask them what they have recently learned that might be relevant. Over time, you should develop a range of types of question to ask. And when children have understood the calculation, go over it again to reinforce their learning.

Numeracy terms

As a teaching assistant, you will come across a variety of numeracy terms:

Number line

The way that addition, subtraction, multiplication and division are taught involves their own aids and vocabulary. An important tool in addition and subtraction is the number line. This is not a specific object but the name given to a line drawn anywhere with numbers marked on it. The numbers shown are determined by the person using it, in order to solve their problem. The way it is used is explained in the next section.

Counting stick, or count stick

Serving a similar purpose is the counting stick, which is a ruler or stick marked into 10 equal divisions. It might be used to help children recognise the relationship between numbers. Depending on the type of stick and the purpose it is being used for, numbers, including fractions, decimals and percentages, may be written or stuck on some or all of the divisions.

Partitioning

Much used in all types of calculation is a technique called partitioning

– splitting up multi-digit numbers, usually into units, tens, hundreds, etc., or into other groups.

Spider diagrams

In doing multiplication and division, teachers may ask children to draw spider diagrams, which link up related number facts.

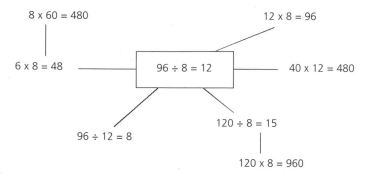

8 x 60 = 480   12 x 8 = 96

6 x 8 = 48   96 ÷ 8 = 12   40 x 12 = 480

96 ÷ 12 = 8   120 ÷ 8 = 15

120 x 8 = 960

Grid method and expanded method

When doing multiplication and division calculations that are too complicated to be done mentally, children are usually shown how to use the grid method and/or the expanded method. Both of these are explained below.

Factorising

The process of splitting a number into its factors is called factorising. For example, 24 can be factorised as 2 x 3 x 4.

Commutative, associative and distributive laws

Mathematics teachers refer to the commutative, associative and distributive laws. They will probably not use these terms with the pupils, particularly at Key Stage 1/2, but they are worth understanding because they underpin the strategies used in calculation, and are particularly relevant to algebra. They are also used widely in the Framework for teaching Mathematics.

The *commutative law* applies when someone making a calculation reorders the components. For example, a child at any early stage of learning multiplication might change 3 x 11 to 11 x 3. The commutative law works for + and x but not for – and ÷.

Children are following the *associative law* when they change the way numbers are grouped and calculated, such as changing (7 x 3) x 11 to 7 x (3 x 11). Note, however, that the order of doing the calculation is changed by the position of the brackets. Again, the associative law works for + and x but not for – and ÷.

Under the *distributive law*, numbers are moved around or re-expressed. The number and operation outside the brackets are 'distributed' over those inside the brackets. An example is if the calculation 49 x 7 were re-expressed by the person doing it as (50 − 1) x 7 = (50 x 7) − (1 x 7). In this case, the number outside the brackets can only be 'distributed' with the operations x or ÷, over the operations + or − inside the brackets, not the other way round.

The terms for these laws might seem a bit off-putting, but what they describe underlies a lot of Mathematics work because children are encouraged to see quick ways of making calculations using facts that they have already learned about numbers. For most people, the example shown for calculating 49 x 7 will get to the answer faster than "7 times 9 equals 63, and 40 times 7 equals 280, so 280 plus 63 equals 343". At secondary school level, the understanding of algebra in particular, depends on these concepts.

Inversing

Another key term you will come across is inversing. Inversing is turning an operation round, thus, the inverse of adding a number is subtracting it; the inverse of multiplying two numbers is to divide one by the other. The point of doing this is that children can quickly make a calculation using number facts that they already know; for example, they can work out 72 ÷ 12 by already knowing that 6 x 12 = 72. Using the inverse operation 'takes you back to where you started from' and is therefore a powerful method for checking calculations.

Subitising

Subitising is the ability to recognise small numbers without having to count, i.e. to see five apples and recognise that there are five of them, without counting each one. The patterns on dice, dominoes and playing cards provide useful props.

Addition and subtraction methods

The commutative law underlies one of the most common techniques taught in Mathematics, especially to young children. This is to reorder calculations into elements that they recognise or can easily work out. So, if asked to add together 8 + 4 + 5 + 2 + 6, a child might mentally reorder this into 8 + 2 (= 10) + 6 + 4 (= 10) + 5. This technique is clearly much more likely to be applied when the sum is written horizontally than when it is written vertically.

Horizontal working underlies the blank, or empty, number line. This is used as a visual means of helping children do calculations in primary schools, and also in catch–up lessons in secondary schools. The line is simply that: a line on which useful numbers for the particular problem are written, often linked by arrows, jumps, or hops. It is used to split calculations up into steps that are easy to do. Thus, the calculation

$$307 − 282 = ?$$

can be shown on a blank number line as:

This line could be further subdivided with a marker at 290, or with a mark at 277 with an arrow back from 307 and then forward to 282, encouraging children to take away 30 and then add 5. It is a device to encourage flexible thinking and show that there are different ways of arriving at an answer.

Multiplication and division methods

Although a certain amount of multiplication and division can be done in the head, complex calculations, or those involving large numbers, will be beyond most children's ability (and most adults!). The most usual written method taught now is the *grid method*, which most children will encounter in their last two years in primary school. This is built on partitioning. Partitioning involves splitting numbers up into units, tens, etc., or into other groups that the child recognises. Therefore, if you were asked to calculate 67 x 4, you could partition 67 into 6 tens and 7 units. This makes the calculation (60 x 4) + (7 x 4), which can easily be done with a knowledge of basic multiplication.

The grid method takes partitioning a step further, and involves writing the numbers down, split into units, tens, etc. Thus, the calculation 67 x 34 is first partitioned into (60 + 7) x (30 + 4). The first element goes across the top, the second down the side, and the totals put in the right-hand column:

x	60	7	
30	1800	210	2010
4	240	28	268
			2278

The method can, of course, be used for numbers in hundreds, thousands and so on. The numbers of columns or rows increase accordingly. There is a DfES ITP that can be used to support this method that will develop into a method for decimals too.

When a child has become familiar with the grid method, they may be taught the *expanded method*. This is the method familiar to most adults:

$$
\begin{array}{r}
67 \\
\times\ 4 \\
\hline
240 \quad (60 \times 4) \\
+28 \quad (7 \times 4) \\
\hline
268 \\
\end{array}
$$

Written methods for division are still a problem area for a significant number of children, especially in primary schools. Most schools build up a progression of pencil and paper methods, which will probably lead eventually to what adults used to know as 'long division' (now 'standard written method for division'). Intermediate stages in this progression depend on children knowing that division is the inverse of multiplication and understanding the effects of subtracting multiples of the divisor.

In doing division, pupils are encouraged to split numbers up into usable parts. They will 'chunk' the numbers so that they can see blocks of the same number. Very simply, if they are calculating $30 \div 5$ they will keep on subtracting the chunk 5 from 30 until they get to nought. With larger calculations, they will build on this method. For example, if calculating $147 \div 8$ a child may first recognise that $8 \times 10 = 80$, and that $8 \times 20 = 160$. The second figure being greater than 147, this indicates that the answer is between 10 and 20. They will therefore deduct 80 from 147, leaving 67 to be calculated. If they are familiar with their 8 times table, they will quickly see that 67 is 3 more than (8×8), or eight chunks of 8, so the answer is $10 + 8 = 18$ with a remainder of 3. The whole calculation might be written down as:

$$147 \div 8$$
$$10 \times 8 = 80 \qquad 20 \times 8 = 160$$

$$
\begin{array}{rl}
147 & \\
-80 & \quad 10 \times 8 \\
\hline
67 & \\
-64 & \quad 8 \times 8 \\
\hline
3 &
\end{array}
$$

Therefore $147 \div 8 = 18$ R3

The method also works when dividing by larger figures:

$$582 \div 23$$

$$10 \times 20 = 200 \qquad 20 \times 20 = 400 \qquad 20 \times 30 = 600$$
$$\qquad\qquad\qquad\quad 20 \times 23 + 460$$

$$
\begin{array}{rl}
582 & \\
-460 & \quad 20 \times 23 \\
\hline
122 &
\end{array}
$$

$$5 \times 20 = 100$$
$$5 \times 3 = 15$$

$$
\begin{array}{rl}
122 & \\
-115 & \quad 5 \times 23 \\
\hline
7 &
\end{array}
$$

Therefore $582 \div 23 = 25$ R7

Springboard programmes

As a teaching assistant you may be involved in delivering Springboard programmes. These are designed to complement the general Mathematics teaching in class by giving intensive support to learners.

Springboard 3

Springboard 3 aims to bring children's understanding to a level where they can more easily benefit from the Year 3 teaching. Springboard 3 sessions should complement the teaching units and be done at the same time as the topic in the daily Mathematics lesson. It is usually delivered in the first half of the school year.

Springboard 4

In the same way, Springboard 4 aims to bring children's understanding to a point where they can more easily benefit from the Year 4 teaching. Springboard 4 sessions should complement the teaching units and be done at the same time as the topic in the daily Mathematics lesson. It is usually delivered in the first half of the school year.

Springboard 5

Springboard 5 is for use in Year 5. It is intended for learners who, without help, could achieve level 3 by the end of Key Stage 2. The programme helps teachers plan and implement targeted support to enable children to reach level 4 by the end of the key stage.

Springboard 6

Springboard 6 is designed to provide intensive targeted support in booster classes to children in Year 6, who are considered capable of achieving level 4 in the Key Stage 2 national tests. It consists of 22 half-hour lessons for use during the spring term of Year 6, alongside the work in the daily Mathematics lessons for that term. The lessons follow the three-part model developed by the National Numeracy Strategy.

The following principles are particularly important if you are working with booster classes:

- a step-by-step approach
- built-in consolidation and summaries
- the use of direct questions and discussion about ideas and methods
- the expression of the same mathematical ideas in a variety of ways
- the use of demonstration by the teacher to model ideas and methods
- helping children to visualise the processes involved
- the reinforcement of key mathematical vocabulary
- encouragement of children to articulate their mathematical thinking.

(DfES, 2001)

These programmes can be adapted or supplemented to account for the different strengths and problems learners may have. Make sure you observe the strategies learners use and the way their mathematical thinking is developing. You should also watch for any persistent areas of difficulty they may have. Your feedback to the teacher (using the feedback sheets provided) will be absolutely essential in future planning. You can also play a very useful role in suggesting different activities and methods for individual children.

Numeracy in secondary schools

The *Framework for Teaching Mathematics: Years 7, 8 and 9* (DfES, 2001) is intended to extend the principles of numeracy teaching from primary schools into Key Stage 3. It was produced because evidence showed that there was a worrying number of pupils whose numeracy skills stood still or even declined in their first year in secondary school. It was also produced in order to help pupils who were still struggling with numeracy. The Framework therefore continues and extends the principles of Mathematics teaching established in the Primary National Strategy.

One of the aims of the Key Stage 3 Framework is that lessons should have clear objectives and be run at a pace appropriate to the pupils' abilities. The lesson format is similar to that used in the Primary Framework, with practice for mental methods of calculation, a period of whole-class teaching, and a review of learning. However, it is recognised that too rigid a structure can be inappropriate, and so in secondary schools you may find considerable variation on this scheme. Nevertheless, regular oral and mental work and a time of whole-class discussion are emphasised as important contributions to pupil progress. As with primary schools, pupils should learn to use correct mathematical terms, and links are made in lessons with other subjects in the curriculum.

Although the calculations that Key Stage 3 pupils are expected to perform are much more complicated than those in primary school, mental calculation methods still have primacy. Pupils are encouraged to think about a problem and see how much of it they can do in their heads. They may well not be able to get as far as the answer, but it is expected that they can make some estimate, based on their mathematical knowledge. They should then be able to recognise whether the answer they come to through a written method is at least likely to be right or is way off beam.

To learn basic number facts there is no substitute for working out answers for yourself. However, mathematical calculators play an important role in developing mathematical thinking and competence and, for certain calculations, they are indispensable. In Key Stage 3, pupils learn how to use calculators effectively, and should be familiar with the special function keys such as square root, cube root, memory, fraction keys and sign change keys.

Algebra plays an increasingly important part in Key Stage 3 Mathematics, building on work with numbers done in Key Stage 2. Pupils also learn to work with concepts like probability, percentages, ratios, graphs and geometrical shapes.

As in primary schools, teaching assistants may well be asked to work with specific groups of children, both during whole-class work and in group or individual work. The teacher should make it clear to you before, or at the start of the lesson what is required of you. You should also expect to report back to the teacher afterwards on how individual pupils coped with the lesson and what progress they are making. However, some teaching assistants involved in teaching Key Stage 3 Mathematics may find that their most active role is not in the ordinary class but in Springboard 7 classes.

Springboard 7

Springboard 7 is a Mathematics catch-up programme for pupils who start Year 7 (the first year in secondary school) without having reached level 4, but who are reasonably expected to reach this level with special support. If they are successful, they will then be able to progress in Mathematics at the same rate as their classmates.

Springboard 7 is designed to be delivered by teaching assistants, either working with the teacher, or on their own under the teacher's direction. It is a course of 15 units of work spread over two terms and delivered to pupils in special lessons additional to normal Mathematics lessons. This may mean lunchtime or even after school sessions. Usually, the groups will be quite small, ensuring that each pupil receives a lot of attention. Sessions usually take about three hours a week. Each pupil will not necessarily do the whole course. The objectives of each unit are quite clear so they can be matched to pupils' needs. Some pupils may just do a few units to address particular weaknesses.

The content of the units is given in some detail in *Springboard 7: A Mathematics catch-up programme for pupils entering Year 7* (DfES, 2001). If you are asked to deliver some of the units, you will find that the programme gives you the exercises and problems to set pupils. You can see from the programme that lessons are arranged in a two-term programme (autumn and spring), according to each half term. The objectives mesh with those of the Year 7 Mathematics programme, as laid out in the Key Stage 3 Framework, so that the catch-up work relates closely to what pupils will be studying in their main Mathematics lesson. This close link is important as it means that a group doing catch-up work might be given work from Springboard 7 during the group work part of the Mathematics lesson.

The units in Springboard 7 repeat the subjects covered in the Primary

Strategy: number; measures and the properties of shapes; handling data; fractions, decimals and percentages; probability; coordinates and shapes; ratio and proportion; shape and space.

The content of the Springboard 3 to Springboard 6 programmes is similarly highly structured.

Key Stage 2: "The children in our Maths 'set' of lower ability Year 5 pupils respond well to the Springboard 5 materials. They know that the work is special for them and they like the cartoons on the activity sheets. Working directly onto the sheet helps them work more quickly because they only have to jot down responses rather than all the extra writing necessary in their exercise books such as question numbers, headings, etc."

Difficulties with numeracy

Any learner can have difficulty with numeracy, but some pupils have persistent problems. For example, pupils with Moderate Learning Difficulties can struggle with conceptual understanding; learners with Cerebral Palsy may sometimes have a difficulty with spatial awareness, which affects their mathematical learning; pupils with Dyspraxia can have problems with organising and processing mathematical information or with remembering sequences. Some Dyslexic pupils also have difficulty with organisation, or have reading problems, which can make Maths inaccessible. However, not all pupils with Dyslexia struggle with Maths – it depends on the profile of their abilities. Some have an holistic approach to mathematical problem-solving, which enables them to be successful at degree level study, if they are allowed to learn in the way best for them.

Recently, a new Specific Learning Difficulty has been identified: Dyscalculia is described as a persistent problem with the acquisition of numeracy skills. In 2001, DfES issued guidance to schools on how to help learners with Dyscalculia, but there is still discussion about the exact nature of the difficulty and ways to deal with it (Chinn, 2004, p.5). The whole area of mathematical difficulties is complex and continuing research by neuroscientists will definitely tell us more about it in the future.

As a teaching assistant, you are often in a good position to watch a pupil working and talk with them about any problem areas. Some children who have trouble with learning numeracy find that their minds literally go blank when faced with a task. You have an important part to play in giving them appropriate help to boost their confidence. In addition to the good teaching assistant practice noted before, you can suggest some specific strategies to help. Just as in the teaching of literacy, it is important to use multi-sensory methods.

Language

Maths is a communication system, and just like any other subject area, it has its own vocabulary and terminology. DfES has produced detailed guidance for this in the *Mathematical Vocabulary* booklet (DfES, 2000). You should familiarise yourself with this and make sure that you understand what the terms mean. The terminology we use for Maths is a varied mix. For example, even English number names are not straightforward, especially the 'teen numbers', which is why some children use numbers like 'eleventy five'! Other terms can be confusing because they may have a different meaning in everyday life. For example, the word 'net' has very specific meanings in Maths. Sometimes, learners with language difficulties can experience problems understanding this terminology, even though they have a grasp of the meaning. Richard Branson (Chairman of Virgin), who has dyslexia, says that he used to confuse *gross* and *net* profit sometimes, although this does not seem to have affected his business success.

It is even more confusing when we use many different ways to describe the same process, e.g. *take-away, subtract, less, minus*. Some learners with language difficulties prefer to use the appropriate symbol rather than to verbalise as it is less confusing. Sometimes, when questions are presented in a complicated verbal format, it is hard to identify what needs to be solved. You will need to help learners to simplify information presented in this way, or translate it into a different format, e.g. diagrammatic. Those learners who have trouble reading will also need your help to access the information.

> **Key Stage 4:** "One of my GCSE students with language difficulties always confuses *mean*, *mode*, and *median* even though he understands the concept of each one. He just can't identify which is which, so he has made up his own rhyme to remind himself."

How to help:

- Explain mathematical terms specifically, preferably using concrete examples.
- Keep a check on a pupil's understanding of vocabulary in your questioning.
- Help learners to recognise, read and write the vocabulary.
- Relate mathematical terms to the symbols used.
- Allow learners to use a mathematical dictionary, or more effectively, to make their own.
- Help learners to use word derivation to understand meanings (e.g. *bi* = two, *dia* = across).
- Keep a check on worksheets or textbooks to make sure the language is accessible.
- Put word problems in diagrammatic or picture form, or on tape in the case of a reading difficulty. You could also read to learners.
- Re-phrase information, if necessary.

Memory

Memory difficulties can also cause problems for learners. These can affect the recall of facts, e.g. number bonds (2 + 2 is always four), or times tables, or the recall of instructions. Problems with procedural memory can also affect a learner's ability to remember how to follow a formula, or memorise a sequence.

How to help:

- Simplify instructions so that they can remember what to do. Check that they have heard and understood. Repeat and explain, if necessary.
- Explain concepts first, using apparatus and concrete examples, e.g. show the pattern of multiplication tables.
- Relate to practical experience and encourage learners to visualise.
- Identify things that can be learned through rote (i.e. unchanging information).
- Use multi-sensory methods, e.g. movement, colour and music; rap or chant times tables; coloured tables square; pacing up and down as actors do when they learn their lines.
- Learn tables in this order: 1, 2, 5, 10, number squares e.g. 3 x 3, 4 x 4. etc., then 9, 4, 3, 6, 7, 8.
- Use a calculator or multiplication square.
- Use software programs to reinforce facts.
- Break down processes, procedures or algorithms (a procedure for calculating or working something out) and teach each part of the procedure.
- Use cue cards or memory joggers that show an example of the thing that needs remembering. It is best for the learner to make these themselves, for example:
  - a slogan "Brackets say 'do us first'"
  - a diagram of the torn off corners of a triangle stuck together for "the angles of a triangle add up to 180°"
  - formulas such as:
    Area of a triangle = 1/2 base x height, or the pictorial equation "Speed equals Distance over Time" .

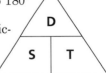

Key Stage 3: "The pupil I support had got a whole page of questions wrong. It wasn't until I looked really carefully that I saw that he had copied the sums from his textbook and accidentally added the number of each question in with the sum. No wonder they were all wrong! From then on, he used a different colour pencil for the number of the question."

Spatial awareness, direction and organisation

As we have seen, an almost instinctive spatial awareness is an important part for mathematical understanding. Some learners have difficulty with directionality in Maths, particularly if they are confused about left and right. Procedures using place value, decimals and long multiplication or division all involve several changes of direction. It is natural for younger learners to reverse numbers, but some pupils with dyslexia/dyscalculia may continue to do this. Pupils may also be disorganised and forget equipment, or have difficulty setting out their work. Spatial awareness is important in several areas of Maths, e.g. using graphs and shape and space.

Key Stage 2: "It was standard practice for all children in Years 4, 5 and 6 in our school to use exercise books printed with small squares for Maths. I noticed that some of the children I was working with had bigger writing than would easily fit in the squares or between the lines, especially when it came to drawing up tables and charts. My teacher agreed and now any child with larger writing or poor spatial awareness uses the 1cm square books. The children who take a pride in their written work are particularly pleased by this change, because their work doesn't look squashed, and the slower writers have speeded up."

How to help:

- Help learners to make a checklist for each Maths activity and make sure they use it.
- Use colour to separate different types of information on the page.
- Check textbook/worksheets are clear and easy to read.
- Encourage learners to use squared paper to keep numbers separate, with large enough squares to accommodate the size of their numbers and writing.
- Use arrows and highlighters to indicate direction.
- Help pupils to check information copied from the board.
- Use pre-set-out sheets as examples.
- For number reversals (e.g. 9 for 6) use a number line or individual checklist.

Conceptual difficulties

Learners may have persistent difficulties in retaining an understanding of concepts, or they may just have individual areas that they find difficult for one reason or another. The more abstract concepts are often a particular problem.

How to help:

- Use practical or enactive methods wherever possible (learning by doing).
- Break down activities into easy steps or parts.
- Draw attention to patterns and relationships.
- Help learners to visualise the concept (e.g. if working out distance/speed/time, give them the story of a car journey to visualise).
- Draw a picture story for the problem.
- Do a task analysis to check the skills and knowledge required. Check what learners can and cannot do. Go back over these, if necessary.

- Listen to learners thinking out loud.
- Use games to reinforce understanding.

For more information on helping learners with mathematical difficulties, see Chinn (2004).

Key reading

Key references are given in bold.

Aplin, R. (1998) *Assisting Numeracy,* **London: BEAM** *[A great deal of relevant information for TAs.]*

Clemson, D. and Clemson, W. (1994) *Mathematics in the Early Years,* **London: Routledge** *[Very readable, well-explained book, which remains useful. Contains information on cross-curricular Maths teaching.]*

Cockburn, A. (Ed.) (2001) *Teaching Children 3 to 11,* London: Paul Chapman *[Includes a useful chapter on teaching numeracy by Derek Haylock.]*

Edwards, S.(2006) *Primary Mathematics for Teaching Assistants*, London: David Fulton

Harries, T. and Spooner, M. (2000) *Mental Mathematics for the Numeracy Hour,* London: David Fulton

Hughes, M. (1986) *Children and Number,* Oxford: Basil Blackwell *[Theory related to practice.]*

Haylock, D. (2005) *Mathematics Explained for Primary Teachers*, **London: PCP** *[Comprehensive guide with sections on mathematical language and ideas]*

Lewis, A. (1996) *Discovering Mathematics with 4 to 7-Year-Olds,* **London: Hodder & Stoughton** *[Full of practical ideas on active learning.]*

Thompson, I. (1997) *Teaching and Learning Early Number,* **Buckingham: Open University Press** *[Theory and practice of early number.]*

Math in Daily Life, www.teachernet.gov.uk/teachingandlearning/library/secondarymaths/ *[Website with practical advice.]*

References

Key references are given in bold.

Askew, M., Brown, M., Rhodes, V., William, D. & Johnson, D. (1997) *Effective Teachers of Numeracy: Report of a Study Carried out for the Teacher Training Agency* London: King's College, University of London

Butterworth, B. (1999) *The Mathematical Brain,* London: Macmillan

Buxton, L. (1991) *Math Panic,* New Hampshire: Heinemann *[Neuropsychologist's view of the brain's inborn ability to process numbers. Includes a useful section on learners with mathematical difficulties.]*

Chinn, S. (2004) *The Trouble with Maths – A Practical Guide to Helping Learners with Numeracy Difficulties,* **London: RoutledgeFalmer** *[Comprehensive analysis of mathematical difficulties with practical suggestions for help.]*

Claxton, G. (1997) *Hare Brain and Tortoise Mind,* London: Fourth Estate *[How we should slow down to learn more!]*

Claxton, G. (1999) *Wise Up*, **Stafford: Network Educational Press** *[Problem*

solving and creativity.]

Cockroft, W. (1982) *Mathematics Counts, Report of the Committee of Inquiry into the Teaching of Mathematics*, London: HMSO

Devlin, K. (2000) *The Language of Mathematics: Making the Invisible Visible*, New York: W.H. Freeman *[Universal Maths.]*

DfEE NNFT (1999) *Framework for teaching Mathematics: Reception to Year 6*, London: DfEE

DfES (2001) *Framework for Teaching Mathematics: Years 7, 8 and 9* London: DfES 0020/2001

DfES (2001) *Springboard 7: A Mathematics catch-up programme for pupils entering Year 7*, London: DfES 0049/2001

DfES (2001) *Springboard 3: Catch-up programme for children in Year 3*, London: DfES 0091/2001

DfES (2001) *Springboard 4: Catch-up programme for children in Year 4*, London: DfES 0092/2001

DfES (2000) *Springboard 5: Catch-up programme for children in Year 5*, London: DfES 0151/2000

DfES (2000) *The National Numeracy Strategy Mathematical Vocabulary*, London: DfES 0313/2000 *[Identifies the words and phrases used in numeracy.]*

DfES (2001) *The National Numeracy Strategy: Guidance to Support Pupils with Dyslexia and Dyscalculia*, London: DfES 0512/2001

DfES (2001) *Springboard 6: Lessons for use in booster classes*, London: DfES 0778/2001

DfES ICT resources, http://www.standards.dfes.gov.uk/numeracy/publications/ *[Carroll diagram, Counter, Function machine, Handy graph, Sorting 2D shapes, Venn diagram, What's my angle?, Minimax, Monty, Play train, Take part, Toy shop]*

DfES Interactive Teaching Programs, http://www.standards.dfes.gov.uk/numeracy/ publications/ *[Area (version 2.0), Coordinates (version 1.0), Counting on and back (version 1.0). Data handling (version 2.8). Difference (version 1.1), Division grid (version 0.8), Fractions (version 1.0), Grouping (version 1.2), Isometric grid (version 1.5), Line graph (version 0.9), Measuring cylinder (version 1.1), Measuring scales (version 1.7), Multiplication facts (version 0.6), Multiplication grid (version 2.1), Number facts (version 1.2), Number grid (version 3.8), Number line (version 1.5), Ordering numbers (version 1.0), Place value (version 1.0), Polygon (updated version 1.4), Ruler (version 1.1), Symmetry (version 1.1), Tell the time (version 0.9), Thermometer (version 1.6), Twenty cards (version 0.9)]*

DfES (2006) *Primary Framework for literacy and mathematics*, London: DfES (DfES 02011-2006BOK-EN)

Paulos, J. (1988) *Innumeracy: Mathematical Illiteracy and Its Consequences*, New York: Hill and Wang,

Pound, L. (1999) *Supporting Mathematical Development in the Early Years*, Buckingham: Open University Press *[Comprehensive look at the theory and practice of early mathematical development.]*

Skemp, R. (1989) Mathematics in the Primary School, London: Routledge.

Stewart, I. (1992) *The Problems of Mathematics*, Oxford: Oxford University Press *[Fairly complex look at higher-level mathematical thinking.]*

Stewart, I. (2001) *What Shape is a Snowflake?* New York: W.H. Freeman *[Illustrated guide to the link between Maths and the natural world.]*

Tanner, H., Jones, S. and Davies, A. (2002) *Developing Numeracy in the Secondary School – A Practical Guide for Students and Teachers*, London: David Fulton *[Gives a very useful overview of the research which led to the implementation of the NNS at KS3.]*

Wahl, M. *Math for Humans: Teaching Math Through 8 Intelligences* www.mark-wahl.com *[Web site where the author explains the application of Gardner's theory of multiple intelligences to the teaching of Maths.]*

Wallace, B. (2002) *Teaching Thinking Skills Across the Early Years*, London:

12 Inclusive education

Inclusion is an important cornerstone of current educational and social thinking and one of the reasons why teaching assistants play such a key role in schools, colleges and early years settings today. Inclusion is all about providing relevant and successful teaching and learning opportunities for every learner, regardless of, for example, their age or ability, gender, cultural or ethnic background, learning difficulty or disability, economic or social background, or the type of school they attend. It is important that schools are welcoming and successful communities for all learners and that the curriculum is relevant and accessible for everyone.

The previous chapters have emphasised the kinds of flexible and adaptable approaches to learning that benefit all pupils. However, there are some learners who have more complex individual or additional needs. They may have a sensory impairment or physical disability. They could have emotional or behavioural difficulties, or social problems that have prevented them from attending school. They could be learning English as a second language, or have a specific learning difficulty like dyslexia. All these factors can affect their achievement in school. Being gifted or talented in some way can also influence the way in which pupils learn. It is essential to know as much as possible about pupils' individual needs so that the right kind of support and help can be given.

This chapter concentrates on the concept of *inclusion*, and the individual or additional needs of learners together with the processes and strategies for effective support. It will also look in detail at the concept of Special Educational Needs (SEN) and the processes and procedures that are used to support learners with SEN in school. More detail on each individual need will be included in the next chapter and behavioural issues will be dealt with in Chapter 14.

A whole-school approach

Inclusion is a process rather than an end result. It should provide an effective and positive climate for most pupils to learn together in their local school. It requires a real commitment and whole-school approach that looks at staffing, resources, teaching and learning strategies, the classroom environment and the curriculum, in addition to focusing on the individual needs of learners. Your own school's inclusion policy will set out its approach.

INDIVIDUAL LEARNER NEEDS

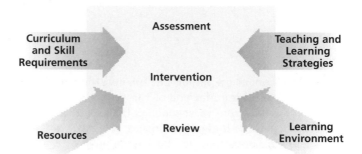

A model for successful inclusion

Disability

A child is disabled if they have a physical or mental disability that has a substantial, adverse and long-term effect on his or her ability to carry out normal day-to-day activities. The term 'disability' includes sensory impairment (e.g. hearing difficulties) long-term medical problems (e.g. epilepsy), severe and complex learning difficulties, physical disabilities (e.g. cerebral palsy), and mental health problems. Not all pupils with disabilities will have SEN. Many can learn in the same way as their peers, as long as they have the specialist resources and aids that they need, such as hearing aids or wheelchairs. However, teachers must still ensure that these learners are not disadvantaged in any way and have the same opportunities and access to the curriculum, wherever possible. For example, they may need extra time to complete work, or the use of alternative methods of assessment.

Timeline for inclusion – a summary

1978 Warnock Report – Introduced the concept that 20 per cent of children would need support for SEN at some stage in their education. Recommended that children with SEN should wherever possible be educated in mainstream schools. Used the term 'integration'.

1981 Education Act – Introduced new definition of SEN and made LEAs responsible for identifying learners and providing help.

1988 Education Reform Act – Right of all learners to have access to a broad and balanced curriculum.

1989 Children Act – Concept of children having a say in their own education.

1994 Salamanca Statement – Adopted by the UNESCO Conference on SEN. It called upon *all* governments to adopt the principle of inclusion.

1994 Code of Practice on the Identification and Assessment of Pupils with SEN – Guidance for schools on identifying and providing for learners with SEN, using a 5-stage model.

1995 Disability Discrimination Act – Schools to report on arrangements for meeting needs of disabled pupils.

1996 Education Act – Strengthened the right of children with SEN to be educated in mainstream schools.

1997 Excellence for All Children – Meeting SEN – Government Green Paper called for a coordinated response to learners with SEN, including practical strategies, multi-agency working, high expectations and increased inclusion. Followed by...

1998 Meeting SEN – A Programme of Action – Report identifying a framework for action to develop a more inclusive approach, including early identification, standards for SENCOs, inter-agency working and partnership with parents.

1998 Supporting the Target Setting Process – Guidance for effective target setting for pupils with SEN. Provided P levels or criteria for those working below Level 1 of the National Curriculum, or with Levels 1 and 2 (Revised 2001).

2000 Revised National Curriculum – Included a statement about inclusion, developing learning and participation in schools.

2000 Index for Inclusion – Guidance and training materials for schools to help them build inclusive communities. (Extended to Early Years settings in 2004.)

2001 Special Educational Needs and Disability Act – Applied 1995 Disability Act to education to prevent discrimination against children with learning difficulties or disabilities in school. It established legal rights for disabled pupils and students in pre- and post-16 education. As a result of the Act schools are no longer allowed to treat disabled pupils 'less favourably' than non-disabled pupils for reasons that relate to their disability. They must anticipate and make reasonable provision and adjustments for their needs. What is considered 'reasonable' depends on individual circumstances. Strengthened the right to mainstream education.

2001 Revised Code of Practice for Special Educational Needs – Replaced 1994 Code. Provides guidance on identifying, assessing and meeting the needs of pupils with SEN, through a 3-stage process (DfES/0581/2001), reflecting duties under SENDA

2001 Inclusive Schooling (Children with SEN – Statutory Guidance 2001) – Provides advice on practical implementation of framework for inclusion as set out in 1996 Education Act and 2001 Special Educational Needs and Disability Act (DfES/0774/2001).

2001 **SEN Toolkit** – Gives practical advice for schools on all aspects of the implementation of the Code of Practice. Designed to be used in conjunction with the Code (DfES SEN Toolkit, 2001).

2004 **Every Child Matters: Change for Children** – Government strategy for childcare and education aimed at improving the outcomes for all learners, including those who are disadvantaged or vulnerable in any way. Key features are recognition that health, happiness and safety are vital for learning, early intervention is crucial to stop problems becoming too difficult to manage, and that collaborative working, where all those involved with children share information and working practices, is central to success. It takes a child-centred approach to the needs of all learners.

2004 **Removing Barriers to Achievement** – Government strategy on SEN, which aims to make education more effective by responding to the needs of all learners, particularly those with SEN. The strategy focuses on four key areas:

- early help and intervention
- removing barriers to learning by using teaching and learning strategies that include all learners (personalised learning)
- raising expectations and achievement by giving all teachers access to targeted training about SEN
- taking a hands-on approach to working in partnership with parents.

2005 **Disability and Discrimination Act** – Schools, colleges and early years settings must promote equality for those with disabilities. They must provide equal opportunities and encourage positive attitudes to prevent discrimination and address underachievement by pupils with disabilities. Employers and institutions must keep data and records which demonstrate the progress of the institution on these issues.

2006 **Third Report of House of Commons Select Committee on Education 2005-6** – Called for SEN to be "prioritised, brought into the mainstream policy agenda and radically improved". Recommended training of workforce (teachers, TAs and Early Years professionals).

Issues of inclusion

Social model of disability

Pupils with learning difficulties and disabilities used to be categorised by a deficit model. In other words, they were identified as having a problem or difficulty (deficit) and then allocated to a school or unit for children with that problem. This is often referred to as the 'medical model' as children were categorised in medical terms, like 'maladjusted' or 'delicate' or 'mentally subnormal'. Once they had been identified and placed, there was little chance for them to move between schools.

However, the Warnock Report (1978) reflected a change of thinking about SEN. Children were categorised according to their educational needs rather than a medical condition, and it was recognised that some 20 per cent of children might have some form of SEN at various times in their school lives and would therefore need appropriate support. This is called a 'social model of disability', in that it says society should be responsible for including and meeting the needs of all these learners.

Definition of SEN

The 1996 Act provided this definition of SEN:

> "Children have Special Educational Needs if they have a learning difficulty which calls for special educational provision to be made for them."

Children have a learning difficulty if they:

a. "have a significantly greater difficulty in learning than the majority of children of the same age; or

b. have a disability which prevents or hinders them from making use of educational facilities of a kind generally provided for children of the same age in schools within the area of the Local Education Authority;

c. are under compulsory school age and fall within the definition at a. or b. above, or would do so if special educational provision was not made for them."

(2001 Code of Practice, p.6)

A child is not regarded as having SEN just because they have English as an additional language.

Special – or not?

In the past, a key issue with SEN has been the provision of specialist help. Many mainstream teachers felt that they were not equipped or knowledgeable enough to deal with pupils with SEN, and that support needed to be provided by experts in Special Schools or units. However, nowadays we recognise that inclusion is all about teamwork, communication and sharing expertise. Within their overall expertise, *all* teachers should be effective teachers of learners with SEN and will be judged on that basis by Ofsted. Of course, this means that advice, support and help need to be available to schools at all times. Many Special Schools provide expertise and advice to mainstream provision and LAs have advisers and specialist teams who provide a similar service. Schools often have high levels of expertise in certain types of SEN. If you feel that you need help or information, start by asking your SENCO or Inclusion Coordinator (see page 270). It is vitally important that your practice is effective. For inclusion to work there needs to be a continuous circle of information, communication and teamwork, as illustrated overleaf.

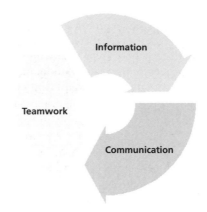

The continuous cycle of inclusion

Special v mainstream

Although inclusion is a far broader concept than this, the process has involved the gradual movement of more learners from special schools into mainstream education. Nevertheless, where children have severe and complex difficulties that require a high level of specialist support, or where they have a disruptive effect on other pupils' learning, then Special School provision can be more appropriate. Here they will receive expert targeted teaching and resources. However, in 2006 Ofsted found that the most important indicator for successful progress for learners with learning difficulties and disabilities was the quality rather than the type of provision.

The Ofsted report added that there was a misconception that the provision of extra resources was the 'key requirement' for those with learning difficulties and disabilities. Their investigation found that extra resources, including teaching assistant support, did not necessarily guarantee good progress for learners. Where effective provision was seen in both special and mainstream schools, various key factors were present:

- the involvement of a specialist teacher (with qualifications and experience across a range of learning difficulties)
- good assessment; work tailored to challenge pupils sufficiently
- commitment from school leaders to ensure good progress for all pupils.

(Ofsted, 2006)

KS2 Teacher: "I have a learner with Asperger's Syndrome in my class, supported by a TA. She has been on several courses on autism and understands his difficulties really well. She is really good at looking at ways for him to take part in all the class activities and to be happy and successful. She will give me advice if I need it. I see her as a great resource in the classroom. Although I know that I have overall responsibility, I don't feel I have to be an expert in everything."

Labelling

When you work with learners with SEN, you will become familiar with the terminology and labels used. Children are often described as 'PH' or 'dyspraxic' or 'EBD'. The way we label learners can be a problem: on the one hand, a label is useful to give you a starting point when you are providing support. If you know a learner has AD(H)D (attention deficit hyperactivity disorder – see pages 317 19), you can apply your knowledge of AD(H)D to help you find and use appropriate methods of support. It is also a way of accessing funding, as it places a child in a recognisable category of need. On the other hand, learners are individuals and it is so easy to make wrong assumptions about them when using labels. Not all dyslexic learners have problems with reading and not all learners with ADD (attention deficit disorder) are hyperactive! You can make stereotypical judgements if you are not careful so do not jump to conclusions. Treat all pupils as having an individual profile of need.

Many children with SEN have complex profiles of difficulty. This is sometimes referred to as 'co-morbidity' as they may have difficulties in many areas. They may have problems with acquiring literacy (dyslexia?), difficulties with coordination (dyspraxia?) and be inattentive (AD(H)D?). Looking for an accurate label is often unnecessary. What you should always focus on is their need and the strategies to meet that need. Labelling someone as having 'dyslexic tendencies' is unhelpful unless you can be specific about their difficulty and the means to help them.

There is also concern that we may label too many children as having a Special Need (the figure for 2005 was 18 percent of all pupils), placing the problem within the child, instead of adjusting our teaching and learning methods to deal with the diversity of pupils in school today. This may be in part because schools are encouraged to identify learners as having SEN in order to access funding. Chapters 5–9 explain how to provide flexible teaching and learning for all learners.

The whole concept of labelling and SEN has been examined in detail by Jenny Corbett of the Institute of Education (Corbett, 1996), and Baroness Warnock has recently expressed concern about the way we now identify and label learners with SEN in a single category rather than recognising the range of their needs (*Hansard*, 2005, 14 July, Co.l 1297).

Working individually with learners outside the classroom

There may be occasions when pupils need individual support and help and so work with a teaching assistant outside the confines of the classroom. This is sometimes referred to as 'withdrawal'. There is nothing wrong with learners working in this way as long as they are not excluded from the mainstream activity in the classroom too often. Research in 2004 (Dyson *et al.*) found that being flexible and responsive to the needs of pupils by using a mixture of unsupported mainstream class placement and small group teaching outside the classroom was the most effective way of educating some pupils. But while a little target- ed support can be very effective, it is not so if the pupil has always to miss PE, assembly or the Literacy Hour to do so.

Inclusion and the role of the teaching assistant

Teaching assistants are "increasingly seen as integral to successful inclusion. Theirs is no longer a peripheral, supporting role but a key teaching and learning collaboration" (Corbett, 2001, p.87). However, there has also been concern that the use of teaching assistants can exclude rather than include some learners and that working with teaching assistants can prevent pupils from developing as independ- ent learners, or from taking a full part in the class. This depends on the way a teaching assistant works. Sitting with one child all day, helping them with everything they do, can be counter-productive. You have already looked in detail at the role of the teaching assis- tant in every aspect of teaching and learning. You need to build on this everyday practice when working with learners with SEN. How can teaching assistants be effective in implementing inclusion? Many of the following examples of good practice are useful for all pupils but they are particularly valuable when working with learn- ers with SEN.

Good practice

- Maintain high expectations for all learners at all times and look for potential in every area. Always focus on what they *can* do, not just on what they cannot. Look for achievement at the learner's own level. Ensure that your practice is anti-discriminatory.
- Make sure that you encourage pupils to develop independent learning strategies. This is probably the single most skilled and rewarding part of a teaching assistant's role – helping a child to learn without making them dependent on you or your help. You have the opportunity to work closely with pupils to analyse each task, work out what they will need support in, and make sure they receive just the right amount of support, guidance, explana- tion and resource to enable them to be successful. To do this you need to become an expert in *Task Analysis*: breaking down each activity into the skills, knowledge and processes required and then matching them to the individual needs of learners. You need to be able to regulate your support and help for each individual learner and task.

Tutor TA course: "The most effective TAs are so well organised that they move effortlessly around the classroom, supporting wherever they are needed, yet always able to move back at once if their targeted pupil requires help. Often they are so skilled that you can't tell who they are actually employed to support!"

- Be sensitive in the way you support. Try to move between learn- ers, giving support where required. Unless you are employed as a communicator for a child with a sensory or physical impairment, you should not stick to them like glue. You should also be a support for other learners and the teacher. Some older learners dislike the idea of having a 'helper', and resent the presence of a teaching assistant.

- Help learners to develop an understanding of their own difficulties by talking through their problem areas; asking them about the things they find easy or hard and suggesting strategies to help them. This insight into their own learning profile will help learners to develop self-management skills.
- Help learners to use self-management skills so that they can manage their own learning effectively. Many children with SEN have become used to the idea that they need help – they are 'controlled' by a teacher or teaching assistant. They need to learn to take responsibility for themselves and their learning. This could be achieved by teaching them organisation skills; study skills; helping them to use ICT and resources effectively or just talking through the idea of responsibility for learning. This is particularly important in secondary education. There is more on organisation and study skills in Chapter 15.
- Help learners to develop self-advocacy skills. This does not just refer to speaking skills but the wider idea of communicating to make their needs and requirements clear. Many learners with SEN get their needs met without asking, or not met at all! You should encourage them to be able to speak on behalf of themselves, rather than always being their representative. However, the ability to communicate effectively requires good language and cognitive skills, so some pupils will need skilled support.
- Focus on building confidence and celebrating achievement. Learners with SEN usually have to work harder than other children without achieving as much. It is easy for them to become demotivated. Draw their attention to positive role models in society so that they can recognise achievement, e.g. dyslexia, Tom Cruise; physical disability, Tanni Grey-Thompson (Olympic athlete); and speech and language difficulty, Gareth Gates.

Key Stage 1: "Concentrating on something which appears very small and insignificant to us, but is of great importance to a child, can increase their confidence enormously. I always ask SEN children I am working one-to-one with what they would really like to be able to do. Twice (both Year 4s) the answer has been to spell their own surname. In both cases we worked on their surnames and both could spell and write their names within a week. After that they were very pleased with themselves and always wrote their names accurately on everything and derived great satisfaction from this everyday task that they had been failing at until then."

- Become a problem solver. Look for ways to make sure that learners you support can have full access to all the curriculum activities.

Key Stage 2: "I support a learner with Cerebral Palsy and find a bit of blue tack invaluable for fixing paper to the desk so that she can write without the paper moving, or stabilise the end of a compass when she is drawing circles in Maths. I tie the end of her pencil to the desk with string so that if she drops it on the floor she can pull it back up. Before I used to sit next to her and hold the paper or pick up her pencil!"

- Help learners to work with their peers, and encourage collaborative activities. Monitor how they get on with others and make it part of your role to help them play a full part in the life of the class. It is useful to educate other children in the class about a learner's difficulties too. This can be done as part of PSHE or circle time.

Key Stage 3: "We have a learner in class who has severe epilepsy and sometimes has a fit in class. I helped him prepare a talk to the rest of the class about how the epilepsy began, the medication he takes, what he feels just before a seizure and what he would like us to do. It has really helped everyone understand and accept it instead of being frightened by it."

Helping SEN learners to access the curriculum

A House of Commons Select Committee on SEN (2006) strongly recommended all staff in schools should be trained on special needs. It suggested seeing who needs what skills as a triangle:

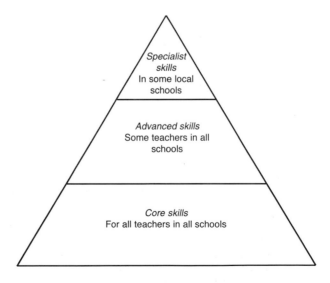

The DfES has produced detailed guidance for teachers in order to help learners with additional needs access the curriculum (DfES, 2000, 2002). You can look at these on the DfES website. You may also find the SEN Toolkit useful. This is issued to all schools as a practical resource to accompany the Code (DfES, 2001).

Although you will need to tailor your support to the individual needs of the learners you support, here are some practical suggestions, which can help you in any situation.

- **Pre-teach.** Many learners with SEN need extra explanation or reinforcement of sub-skills or language before they start an activity. This may mean going over key vocabulary, concepts or skills before they begin. In some cases, for example where learners are hearing impaired, it can be useful to reinforce subject matter before a whole class lesson so that they know the kind of language to expect. Children with reading difficulties can benefit from going over a shared text in advance to give them a 'jump start'.
- **Post-teach.** Reinforce concepts, skills or language at a later opportunity.

Key Stage 1: "I support a learner with speech and language difficulties. I monitor her during whole class or group teaching to see how much she understands and then give her a bit of extra individual support later in the day if she needs it."

- Ensure the work is at the right level for each learner. Discuss with the teacher if you have any concerns.
- Check resources are appropriate and easy to use.
- Break each task down into easily manageable, step-by-step chunks. This will help to build confidence.
- Let learners explain to you to clarify their own understanding.
- Use feedback and praise effectively and realistically.
- Use your learner's interests to motivate them.
- Support them with tasks they find difficult (e.g. scribe for them) and give them plenty of opportunity to gain confidence by practising skills that they *can* do.
- Check you are confident about using or adapting specialist resources (e.g. language programmes, sound dictionaries, pen grips).
- Become familiar with ICT and technological support for learners with SEN (communicator, word processor, video, hand-held spellchecker, digital camera, Internet, specialist software, tape recorder, pens, memory aids, etc.).
- Use multi-sensory methods wherever possible and encourage the use of visualisation to allow learners to create mind pictures.
- Have a bank of study and organisational skills ready to show to pupils (how to take notes, colour coding work, how to research, list making, taped memory joggers, cue cards, etc.).
- Ensure there is enough active learning in each task. Discuss with the teacher if you are concerned.
- Help learners to make connections with previous learning.
- Take every opportunity to reinforce language and understanding.
- Observe the strategies learners use. Listen to what they say.

> **Further Education:** "Part of my role is to help the students to understand their own difficulties, develop their own helpful strategies and talk to the lecturers direct, rather than expecting me to speak on their behalf all the time. Some of the students, who have had a TA in school, are just so passive. They expect you to do everything for them, take notes in class, explain why they can't get work done or need extra help, run around finding them resources or information. We have to work hard to make them take more responsibility for themselves. They will have to when they get a job!"

Every Child Matters: Change for Children (2004)

The government's initiative Every Child Matters focuses on better outcomes for all children by encouraging collaboration between Education, Health and Care. It has introduced lots of new arrangements, procedures and terminology which you need to be familiar with if you are working in Early Years settings or schools. Some of these are listed below:

Common Core of Skills and Knowledge for Children's Workforce
This sets out the basic skills and knowledge needed by those whose work brings them into regular contact with children, young people and families. The skills and knowledge are described under six main headings:

- effective communication and engagement with children, young people and families
- child and young person development
- safeguarding and promoting the welfare of the child
- supporting transitions
- multi-agency working
- sharing information.

Multi-agency working
Collaborative working between health, social care, education, voluntary and community services and justice.

Service directories
Online information bank for all services for children and young people.

Lead professional
Lead professionals are accountable to their own agency but provide a single point of contact for a family who will coordinate the delivery of the intervention agreed and maintain consistency across the various services.

Common Assessment Framework
To be implemented by 2008, will provide a holistic approach to the assessment of needs and can be used by all professionals. Should prevent children having to undergo lots of different assessments.

Development of Child
Health: • General health   • Physical development   • Speech, language and communications development
Emotional and social development
Behavioural development
Identity, including self-esteem, self-image and social presentation
Family and social relationships
Self-care skills and independence
Learning: • Understanding, reasoning and problem solving   • Progress and achievement in learning   • Participation in learning, education and employment   • Aspirations
Parents and Carers
Basic care, ensuring safety and protection
Emotional warmth and stability
Guidance, boundaries and stimulation
Family and Environmental
Family history, functioning and well-being
Wider family
Housing, employment and financial considerations
Social & community factors and resources, including education

Information Sharing Index

Record of all children in UK up to the age of 18 containing basic information, including:

- name and address
- gender
- date of birth
- contact details for parents, nursery or school,
- GP
- name of lead professional and agencies involved.

You need authorisation to access it.

See http://www.ecm.gov.uk for more information.

Code of Practice for the Identification, Assessment and Provision of Special Educational Needs

This Code of Practice, published by the DfES, gives detailed guidance to LAs and schools on how they can meet the needs of learners with Special Educational Needs (SEN). If you are working in school with learners with SEN you should make yourself familiar with the content. The Code includes separate guidance for Early Educational Settings, primary and secondary schools. It has several key principles:

- A child with SEN should have their needs met.
- The SEN of children will normally be met in mainstream schools or settings.
- The view of the child should be sought and taken into account.
- Parents have a vital role to play in supporting their child's education.
- Children with SEN should be offered full access to a broad, balanced and relevant education, including an appropriate curriculum for the Foundation Stage and the National Curriculum.

(DfES, 2001, p.7)

Learners are grouped into four categories of need:

- communication and interaction
- cognition and learning
- behaviour, emotional and social development
- sensory and/or physical.

In some cases, a child may have only one area of need, for example a hearing impaired pupil with a sensory need, or a pupil with Asperger's Syndrome with a communication and interaction need. However, as previously discussed, learners with SEN are unique individuals and may experience difficulties across all four areas. What is important is an adequate assessment of their needs, combined with the strategies to meet those needs.

The Code states that there should be three stages of assessment and action for pupils who have Special Educational Needs.

SEN Code of Practice – whole-school three-stage approach

School Action (Stage 1)

Trigger   Either a child is already identified as having SEN, or is making little progress in spite of targeted strategies in class, or is working below level expected of children of a similar age. The learner may have persistent difficulties in any of the four categories of need and be failing to respond to any of the strategies used in class to help.

Action   The SENCO gathers information from assessment and

observation, and discussion with parents, child, teachers, and teaching assistants. SENCO produces Individual Education Plan (IEP). Class teacher is responsible for content of IEP in Primary phase, which should be additional or different to the provision already in place. Extra resources, staffing and learning materials/specialist equipment (e.g. booster sessions, circle time, different learning and teaching strategies) are allocated. Provision is monitored and reviewed regularly (at least three times per year).

School Action Plus (Stage 2)

Trigger   The pupil is failing to make adequate progress in spite of the provision of an IEP and is failing to respond to any of the strategies used to help. Pupils may be experiencing persistent problems with literacy/maths, or have difficulties with behaviour, communication and interaction, or physical and medical problems that prevent them from learning effectively.

Action   The SENCO and subject specialists seek the help of external support services to review strategies already employed and revise IEP. Advice and help is given by external specialist to develop a new IEP. The monitoring and review process continues.

Statutory Assessment (Stage 3)

Trigger   In spite of strategies developed at School Action and School Action Plus stages, limited or no progress made by the child. The school, the parent, or an outside agency requests a statutory (legal) assessment and provides evidence of the arrangements made so far to meet the learner's needs.

Action   Written evidence is collected from all of these sources:

- School Action programme
- IEPs
- Reviews
- Medical information
- National Curriculum attainment
- Literacy and maths attainment
- Specialist assessments (e.g. by Educational Psychologist, Speech and Language therapist)
- Views of parents
- View of pupil
- Social services/EWO or other professionals.

The Statement of SEN

The LA will consider home and family circumstances and look at the school response (for example, the provision of equipment or teaching assistant support) before deciding whether a statutory assessment is necessary. There is a six-week time limit to get this done. The LA will then notify parents that a Statement of SEN is being issued, or send them a letter in lieu to explain why they will *not* be issuing a statement. The whole process should take no more than 26 weeks. A Statement is a legal document that sets out provision for a learner with SEN. It could include support by a teaching assistant, extra resources, specialist teaching, different methods of teaching, support from outside agencies (for example, a speech and language therapist), or placement in a Special School or Unit. Parents may also, where necessary, appeal to an SEN tribunal.

Review and monitoring

Statements can cease, or be amended if specialist provision is no longer required or needs to be changed. The whole process is not designed to be purely one way. Learners can move back through the stages if their needs are being met and they are making good progress. Teaching assistants will be involved with learners at all stages of the Code, or may be specifically employed to support a learner who has a Statement.

Make sure you know whether learners you work with have Statements. If they do, then you should always ask to be informed about the provision recommended in the Statement.

What does the SENCO/INCO do?

According to the Code of Practice, every mainstream school should have a Special Educational Needs Coordinator (SENCO), sometimes called an Inclusion Coordinator (INCO). who should normally be a member of the senior management team. The SENCO plays a crucial role in the whole-school approach to SEN and will:

- take day-to-day responsibility for the operation of SEN policy and coordination of provision for learners with SEN in school
- manage the teaching assistants working with learners with SEN
- contribute to in-service training to ensure all staff understand the needs of learners with SEN
- suggest and implement teaching approaches
- choose and evaluate resources.

SENCO's role during School Action and School Action Plus:

- Assessment
- Information gathering
- Liaison with class and subject teachers to set up IEP
- Meetings with parents
- Discussion of IEP with pupil
- Monitoring progress and keeping records
- Arranging the review meetings for IEP
- Suggesting materials and resources
- Liaison with school staff and outside professionals
- Monitoring IEP and targets
- Overview of all the records and paperwork required.

SENCO's role during formal Statement:

- Liaison with outside specialists
- Attending meetings
- Contact with parents
- Collecting relevant information
- Setting up review meetings.

There has been some debate about teaching assistants working as SENCOs. The Commons Select Committee on Education and Skills (2005-6) recommended that TAs should not take this on and that all SENCOs should have Qualified Teacher Status, although a teaching assistant could take the role of an assistant SENCO to deal with procedures and recording. The Select Committee also considered that extensive training for SENCOs was a priority. Liz Gerschel (2005) has identified this as a transition time for SENCOs and teaching assistants.

Implementing the SEN Code

Teaching assistants have a key role to play in implementing the Code by:

- taking part in formal and informal assessment and observation
- finding out the pupil's view of their difficulties and strengths
- contributing to setting targets for IEP
- implementing and monitoring IEP
- liaising with parents (if required)
- monitoring and giving feedback on strategies, whether successful or not
- making suggestions for strategies and resources
- monitoring access to the curriculum
- recording progress
- writing report for SENCO for annual review
- helping learners with assessment.

Assessment and observation

Although it is recognised that learners progress at different rates, one of the key features of the Code is the emphasis on early intervention to identify and meet the needs of learners with SEN. Class or subject teachers use the results of formal and informal assessment or observation to build a profile of a learner's strengths and weaknesses. This is used to measure the progress of pupils and is also used as a key indicator of need. A skilled teaching assistant can contribute to building an accurate profile of a learner by watching for and measuring progress. You have a key role because of the way you work closely with learners. You should always start with their strengths and interests:

- What are they good at?
- What motivates them?

- How easy or difficult do they find tasks or individual subjects?
- What areas do they have persistent problems with?
- Where are the gaps in their skills or knowledge?

For example, you may notice a child contributes well verbally in class but struggles to get their thoughts onto paper. This is particularly important in the case of learners who may have a specific learning difficulty like dyslexia, which affects their ability to learn to read and write.

You could be asked to implement Foundation Profiling, which is often used to identify learners with SEN in the Foundation Stage. You could be asked to match a learner's achievements against P Levels (DfES, 2002). You might administer more formal diagnostic assessments like diagnostic spelling or reading tests (e.g. Neale Reading Analysis or the Aston Index). Your SENCO may ask you to complete a checklist or tick sheet to indicate whether a learner may have AD(H)D or an autistic spectrum disorder. Whenever you are involved in any kind of assessment it is important to be as accurate and objective as possible.

Listen to the pupil's view

It is vitally important to talk to the pupil about their needs and discuss with them the strategies they find useful. This is particularly important, as children get older. As a teaching assistant, you are often able to have a close and productive working relationship with a pupil and are in a position to really understand and help them with any difficulties. Finding out about their strengths and interests will help to build a complete picture or learning profile.

The Individual Education Plan/Programme (IEP)

As a teaching assistant, you may be required to contribute to Individual Education Programme Targets, or to implement or monitor IEPs. An IEP is an Individual Education Plan or Programme of teaching that is additional to the main teaching and learning activities in class. It is a working document that should be reviewed and updated regularly. There are IEPs for individual learners and GEPs (Group Education Plans) for pupils with common needs who can share similar targets. An IEP focuses on three or four key short-term targets. We have already looked at the pros and cons of target setting in Chapter 8. IEP targets should be additional to or different from any general targets and should focus on the key areas of literacy, maths, behaviour and communication. They should be relevant to the individual learner and their curriculum and linked to the overall objectives set out in a Statement of SEN.

An IEP should include:

- The target(s)
- How it will be taught
- When it should be taught

- Success criteria – how to know when it has been achieved.

Targets should always be:

- **S**pecific
- **M**easurable
- **A**chievable
- **R**elevant
- **T**ime relevant.

For example:

- "By half term, Jane will be able to stay on task for 10 minutes" is SMART.
- "Jane will be able to improve her behaviour" is not.
- "Zak will use a personal checklist to check his spelling when drafting humanities work between now and half term" is SMART.
- "Zak will make sure his spelling is right" is not.

IEPs also include:

- the methods of teaching and learning (e.g. use of Circle Time, using multi-sensory methods)
- the resources used (e.g. structured spelling programme, Social Use of Language Programme (SULP), Attack)
- the staff to implement it (e.g. use of a teaching assistant).

Parents and the learner should be encouraged to take part in the target-setting process. When learners have complex and severe needs, an IEP will focus on certain areas rather than the whole spectrum of difficulties. IEPs are coordinated by the SENCO, but it is the class/subject teacher who has responsibility at School Action and School Action Plus level to devise and choose targets for an IEP. Most schools have their own IEP format and recording documentation.

Because they often work closely with learners and also see the general requirements of the curriculum in class, teaching assistants are often very good at suggesting manageable and achievable targets for the learners they support. In many cases, IEPs are implemented and monitored by teaching assistants under the supervision of teaching staff. It is important that you feedback relevant and accurate information, based on your experience of the teaching sessions. Targets should be updated regularly. You might be able to suggest other opportunities to reinforce them, or suggest different resources or teaching methods, too.

Although IEPs are useful to focus on individual needs, there are some experts who consider the concept of IEPs to be outdated because the learner is considered to have individual deficits. They prefer the concept of personalised learning for all (ASCD, 2001). Following this, some schools have moved away from the IEP model to a whole class approach instead. This trend seems set to continue.

Liaison with parents – parents as partners

The Code emphasises that the role of the parents is vital in supporting the education of learners with SEN. In the case of 'looked after' children, the Local Authority fulfils the parental role. Most LAs have an effective Parent Partnership service, which provides advice, support, information and guidance in relation to SEN.

You have already looked at the principles of a professional working relationship between parents and teaching assistants, but where children with SEN are concerned, there can be difficulties, particularly if you are supporting a statemented child. You will need to work sensitively with parents at all times. Always make sure that you follow school procedures for contact with them and be aware that there are complex emotional issues in the parent/child relationship, particularly with pupils with SEN. Parents may carry an enormous amount of guilt about their child's difficulties, or may be struggling to deal with a child with severe or complex needs, day in day out. You can be a wonderful source of support and help as long as you remember to follow professional guidelines. Sometimes it is easy to become too involved and overstep the mark. Always use agreed methods of communication, e.g. daily record books, home-school contact books.

Monitoring strategies

One of the key aspects of working with learners with SEN is to be flexible and adaptable and to use trial and error effectively. As an expert teaching assistant you can monitor the success of any approaches used and feed back this information to the teacher. Although it is important to allow time for strategies to succeed, it is no use persevering with something that isn't working. IEPs should always be under constant review.

Making suggestions for strategies and resources

Schools have limited budgets and so must be careful about buying resources. Teaching assistants can play a crucial role in trying out, evaluating, adapting and making resources for use with learners with SEN, so that the best possible use can be made of resources available.

Helping learners to access the curriculum

The National Curriculum Inclusion Statement emphasises that all pupils are entitled to access to learning, irrespective of their difficulties. However, children with SEN often have barriers to learning that prevent them from taking a full part. You can prompt and support them so that they can access the curriculum, always remembering to encourage independent working. Here are a few ideas:

Monitor the materials they are working from:

- Are the learning materials relevant, age-appropriate and easy to use?
- Can the learner read text or does it need simplifying? You can do this by enlarging it, explaining or replacing difficult words, highlighting key parts of the text, reading it to the learner or putting

it on tape. Poorly photocopied sheets are difficult to read.

- Can you use another way of giving them information, like a video, tape or model?
- Can you use written material that includes colourful diagrams or flow charts?

Here are some of the ways you can keep learners on task:

- Make sure they know what is required of them.
- Get them to use a checklist so that they have everything they need.
- Help them listen to instructions or take instructions down for them (or they can use a digital camera or tape).
- Repeat or re-explain instructions.
- Act as a sounding board for questions.
- Monitor distractions (e.g. noises and disruptions, bright or flashing lights).
- Explain any concepts and relate these to their previous experience.
- Use a cue card or visual checklist (e.g. how to take away fractions).
- Break the activity down into smaller steps and give them small targets to aim for.
- Help them to think of ideas.
- Teach sub-skills while they work (e.g. correct formation of letters, number bonds).
- Give them support in the area of skill they have real difficulty with (e.g. scribing for them if they need to write ideas down quickly).
- Relate the work to their interests and strengths.
- Ask them to help another pupil.
- Check their position in class (e.g. move them nearer/facing board).
- Suggest supplementary materials and resources.
- Use a word bank/curriculum list.
- Use ICT support.

Completing tasks:

- Give them a template or writing frame (e.g. a 'what why when where who why' prompt).
- Model some of the activities for them (e.g. how to wire a switch, how to use an index).
- Help them use diagrams or a flow chart to respond.
- Help them to use personalised checking systems (e.g. an individual proofreading checklist for the things they normally have trouble with, for example, specific spellings, capital letters, full stops).
- Help them develop a system for writing down any homework that needs to be done.

Recording progress

Schools are required to have record keeping systems for children with SEN, so that they can track and monitor the progress of their intervention strategies. Some are very detailed and require you to summarise every teaching session; others will take more of an overview. Although it is difficult to find the time to keep accurate records it is important that you find a way to do so. Just jotting a few things down in shorthand is far better than spending ages later writing it up in perfect prose when you may have forgotten key details. Keeping records will help you to plan your own methods of work and give the teaching staff feedback on the intervention strategies. Consistency of approach is vital when dealing with learners with SEN. You may be asked to put this information in a format where it can be used at in-school review meetings, or you could be asked to attend in person and give a verbal report.

Contribute to annual reviews

Learners with Statements have their progress reviewed annually at a formal meeting attended by outside agencies, parents and a representative of the LA. You could be asked to write a report or attend this review with the SENCO. Pupils in Year 9 have a transitional review to plan for their further education. Remember to focus on the positives and bring suggestions for how you can support in the future.

Help Learners with their curriculum assessment

Learners with SEN are often very anxious in situations where they are required to complete assessed work in tests and exam situations. You can play a very useful part in building their confidence and helping them to have fair access to assessment. You could do this by:

- helping them with revision and practice sessions to make sure they are prepared
- modelling de-stressing and calming techniques
- reassuring them
- giving them a chance to talk to you afterwards about how they did
- reporting observations and concerns to teaching staff
- writing (scribing) for them, for example in SATs or GCSEs (only when special permission has been obtained)
- reading questions to them
- supervising extra time allocated to them for checking work
- supervising rest periods
- operating specialist equipment.

Learners with SEN are given test and examination concessions to help them have the same opportunities as other learners, not to give them unfair advantages. Ensure that you know the assessment criteria (i.e. exactly what is being assessed) and what kind of help you may give for *every* different occasion. For example, you may write for a pupil with a Specific Learning Difficulty in a Science SAT or GCSE because it is the knowledge of Science that is being assessed. However, you cannot write for a pupil with SPLD in an English GCSE, as it is the ability to write English that is being assessed. You could, however, write for a child who had broken an arm! It is a very complex area so you need to ensure that you always follow the guidance of the teaching staff.

Working with outside agencies

If you are supporting a child with a Statement or at Sch level, you may have contact with outside agency staff. These p. resources, advice and support for schools. The LA must tell schools about the services available to them and either provide those services or provide funding for schools to buy them in.

LOCAL AUTHORITY EDUCATIONAL SERVICES

Educational Psychologist

Has teaching experience. Provides specialist advice to teachers and parents on learning and behavioural difficulties. Carries out formal assessments for Statementing process. Some have specialist responsibility for particular areas of SEN, e.g. dyslexia or social and communication disorders. Plans and monitors intervention programmes. Employed by LA. Some parents will get assessments from private psychologists. Can advise on whole-school issues like behaviour management.

Advisory Staff

Advisers cover all areas of the curriculum. Includes ICT, Literacy and Numeracy advisers, who can help with access to the curriculum for learners with SEN. Offers in-service training for school staff.

Hospital School Service

Provides tuition for children with long-term medical difficulties and liaison between school and hospital.

Parent Partnership Organisation (PPO)

Supports parents during statutory assessment.

Education Officer/Case Worker

Deals with administration of statutory assessment

Learning Support Service

A team of specially qualified staff who give advice to teachers on the learning and development of children with SEN. Can provide specialist resources and direct teaching by teachers/TAs. Where funds are devolved, staff may be employed directly by the school; in other areas they may be peripatetic (i.e. travel to different schools). Includes specialist teachers of pupils with:

- Sensory impairment (vision, hearing, physical disabilities).
- Emotional and behavioural difficulties.
- Speech, language and communication disorders.
- Specific learning difficulties.

Educational Welfare Officer

Deals with home and attendance difficulties (role is sometimes referred to as School Liaison Officer). Works with children who are at risk of disaffection or exclusion, or who have been excluded.

Language Support Service

Supports learners with EAL, who have learned their family language as a first language and English as their second or subsequent language because they originate from another country or culture. Provides advice, support and direct teaching.

LOCAL HEALTH AUTHORITY SERVICES

Occupational Therapist/Physiotherapist
Works with pupil's physical disabilities and provides advice for teaching staff.

School Doctor
School medicals and health information and assessments.

School Nurse
Vaccinations and advice on health education.

Speech Therapist
Provides support for learners with speech and language difficulties and provides advice for their teachers.

School Dentist
Dental care and preventative information and treatment.

Child & Adolescent Mental Health Service (CAMS)
Gives advice on pupils with mental health difficulties.

LOCAL AUTHORITY SOCIAL SERVICES

Child Protection Officers/Social Workers
Deal with children at risk or in need, and 'looked after' children, where the local authority has parental responsibility.

LOCAL OR NATIONAL VOLUNTARY AND CHARITABLE ORGANISATIONS

Focus or Advice Groups
Groups which provide advice and support for particular disabilities include:
• **Royal National Institute for the Blind** (RNIB)
• **Afasic** – speech and language difficulties
• **British Dyslexia Association**
• **Scope** – cerebral palsy
• **I Can** – speech and language difficulties
• **Down's Syndrome Association**
• **National Deaf Children's Society** (NDCS)

LOCAL OR NATIONAL INDEPENDENT ORGANISATIONS

Connexions – An independent, not-for-profit partnership, delivering training, skills and career guidance advice for young people.

Key reading

Centre for Studies on Inclusive Education, *Learning Supporters and Inclusion.* www.inclusion.org.uk *[CSIE, based in Bristol, is an independent education centre that supports inclusion. They produce helpful leaflets and run conferences to promote it.]*

Cheninais, R. (2000) *Special Educational Needs for Newly Qualified and Student Teachers*, London: David Fulton *[Basic guidelines for newly qualified teachers.]*

DfES (2001) *SEN Toolkit*, London: DfES *[Supports the Code of Practice with practical suggestions.]*

Gross, J. (2002) *Special Educational Needs in the Primary School – A Practical Guide*, Buckingham: Open University Press *[Lots of practical ideas and suggestions.]*

Lacey, P. (2001) *Support Partnerships: Collaboration in Action*, London: David Fulton

Lovey, J. (2002) *Supporting Special Educational Needs in Secondary School Classrooms*,London: David Fulton

Wall, K. (2006) *Special Needs and Early Years: A Practitioner's Guide*, 2nd edn, London: David Fulton

Westwood, P. (2002) *Commonsense Methods for Children with SEN*, London: Routledge *[Contains many practical ideas and suggestions.]*

http://inclusion.ngtl.gov.uk *[government website on inclusion]*

References

Key references are given in bold.

DfES, Revised Code of Practice for Special Educational Needs, London: DfES/0581/2001 *[Provides guidance on identifying, assessing and meeting the needs of pupils with SEN.]*

Corbett, J. (2001) Supporting Inclusive Education – A Connective Pedagogy, London: Routledge *[Practical guidance to teachers and analysis of the role of TAs in inclusive education through school case study.]*

Corbett, J. (1966) *Bad Mouthing, The Language of Special Needs*, London: Falmer Press *[An analysis of the culture of special education.]*

Department of Education and Science (1978), *Special Educational Needs (The Warnock Report)* London: HMSO *[Publication by the Warnock Committee (1978) entitled 'Special Educational Needs'. The report put an end to labels previously used in education, such as "handicap", and replaced them with the label "Special Educational Needs". The report's recommendations were included in the Education Act, 1981.]*

DfES (2000) Supporting Pupils with SEN in the Literacy Hour, London: DfES 0101/2000 *[Guidance]*

DfES (2002) Supporting Pupils Learning English as an Additional Language London: DfES 0239/2002 *[Training module]*

DfES (2002) Including All Children in the Literacy Hour and Daily Mathematics Lesson, London: DfES 0465/2002 *[Guidance]*

DfES (2002) Towards the National Curriculum for English, London: DfES 0517/2002

DfES (2004) *Removing Barriers to Achievement: The Government's Strategy for SEN*, London: DfES/0117/2004

Dyson, A, Farrell, P, Polat, P, Hutcheson, G, and Gallenaugh, F (2004) *Inclusion and Pupil Achievement*, London: DfES

Ferguson, D. *et al.* (2001) *Personalised Learning for Every Student*, Alexandria, Va.: ASCD *[Examples of what pupils with Special Educational Needs should be able to do at each P Level.]*

Gerschel, L. (2005) 'The Special Educational Needs Coordinator's Role in Managing Teaching Assistants: The Greenwich Perspective', *Support for Learning* vol. 20, no. 2

13 Individual needs and inclusion

It is important to make teaching and learning flexible and accessible to all learners. However, you will encounter learners in school with a variety of additional needs. These are learners who have more complex profiles and so the kind of intervention and support strategies required for them will vary enormously. It is no use lumping children with special or additional needs together and giving them all the same kind of support. To be effective you need to use appropriate and relevant strategies. It is outside the remit of this book to give detailed information on every kind of difficulty. However, very brief details are included of some of the more common needs, with basic ideas for school support, much of which can be implemented by a teaching assistant, together with sources of further information.

This chapter also covers some of the strategies and techniques used to support learners who have English as an additional language, gifted and talented pupils, and pupils who move frequently and therefore have interrupted learning, in addition to those who are disadvantaged in other ways. Signposts for further information are also included, but if you are working with learners with high levels of need, you should always ask for specialist advice and help from the relevant teacher/LA professional. You may also get more information from the following sources:

- Code of Practice/SEN Toolkit
- SENCO/INCO
- Colleagues at school, including teachers and teaching assistants
- In-service training or publications from your LA or support Service
- Parents (subject to school policy)
- The pupil
- NASEN (National Association of Special Educational Needs) publishes excellent small books on individual difficulties. Your school may have membership
- *Special Children* magazine, *Support for Learning* (Questions Publishing
- Books
- Voluntary organisations and charities
- TV programmes, including Teachers' TV
- Internet.

Each learning difficulty covered in this chapter contains a brief guide to relevant practice in teaching and learning and how teaching assistant practice can help. It also includes information on specialist assessment, as it is possible you will be helping to provide information for this.

Global learning difficulties

Global Learning Difficulty – Moderate

These pupils have difficulty or delay in learning across the whole curriculum (globally). They are often referred to as slow learners and experience problems with all aspects of learning. They may have poor comprehension and understanding and difficulty memorising information, all of which affect the speed and extent of their learning. This in turn can lead to problems with attention and concentration. At one time these learners were educated in schools for children with moderate learning difficulties but most are now placed in mainstream schools.

Specialist assessment

Teacher assessment or Educational Psychologist.

Methods of support and teaching assistant practice

Use:

- the small steps approach
- differentiated activities and outcomes
- active learning or learning by doing
- practical apparatus and materials
- opportunities to build confidence through success
- overlearning – going back over skills and knowledge to reinforce
- direct, structured skill teaching of skills in literacy, numeracy, communication and socialisation
- ICT and specialist software or structured spelling and reading programmes
- multi-sensory teaching.

As a teaching assistant, you can help the learner to move from the concrete to the abstract and back again.

Global Learning Difficulty – Severe

Often known as Profound and Multiple or Complex Learning Difficulty. These children have the highest level of need and are educated in Special Schools. They include learners with severe cognition and learning problems, or profound physical and sensory difficulties. As a teaching assistant, you should receive specialist training if you are working with these learners.

Where to find more information

Aird, R. (2001) *The Education and Care of Children with Severe, Profound and Multiple Learning Difficulties,* London: David Fulton

A theoretical overview of education that includes an analysis of the role of teaching assistants. David Fulton also publishes the *Access to the Curriculum* series, which gives guidance by subject areas.

Specific learning difficulties

Dyslexia

A *specific* learning difficulty is so-called because it affects a specific area of a pupil's ability to learn. In dyslexia, this is usually the acquisition of literacy skills that involve using symbols (letters). It can also affect the use and manipulation of numbers in mathematics, which is referred to as 'dyscalculia'. It sometimes affects notation in music too.

Dyslexia is a neurologically based condition. In other words, it is part of the way the brain is organised, connected and used. Every learner with dyslexia is different. Some have problems with retrieving language (finding the word or label for something), whereas others will be very articulate. Most will have persistent difficulties with spelling and may take longer to learn to read fluently. There is some evidence that it affects the ability to do several tasks at once, so some will have difficulties with organising themselves and others may have problems with coordination or laterality (knowing left and right).

Nowadays, we see dyslexia as more of a difference than a disability. After all, human beings weren't originally designed to look at small written symbols all day long! Some very talented and innovative people in society are dyslexic. They are able to use original ways of working and thinking to produce and create. However, dyslexics are severely disadvantaged in a school system that teaches the whole curriculum through literacy and so require specialist approaches to learning.

Assessment

An appropriately qualified teacher or an educational psychologist will undertake an assessment and look for a profile of strengths and weaknesses. An assessment may show difficulties with auditory memory (memory of sound) and/or visual memory. Some dyslexic pupils have difficulty with processing sound (phonological processing). There are several assessment programmes available in schools, including DEST (Dyslexia Early Screening Test) and computer-based COPS (Cognitive Profiling).

Methods of support and teaching assistant practice

The strategies used for supporting pupils with dyslexia are useful for many children who have difficulties with reading and writing.

- Build on their strengths and use their interests to motivate them.
- Use:
  - ICT. There are many relevant items of software including spelling, reading and study skills programmes, word processing with speech feedback and speech activated software (like Dragon Dictate©)
  - multi-sensory teaching for literacy
  - structured spelling, reading and language programmes (like *Beat Dyslexia* or *Toe by Toe, Spelling Made Easy*, etc.)

- hand-held spellchecker
- word processor
- sound dictionary (LDA)
- dictaphone to record instructions, or ideas to be written later
- reading material that is at the right level and age-appropriate
- board games to reinforce literacy or numeracy skills
- cursive (joined-up) handwriting to help with motor memory
- personal proofreading and checking system for written work so pupils can self-correct
- taped or video material rather than information that has to be read
- memory skills teaching
- scribing to take pressure off when writing.

- Be prepared for:
  - fatigue and frustration
  - inconsistency (one day they can spell the word, the next day they cannot).
- Don't overload the learner with too many tasks at once.
- Encourage:
  - collaborative working or 'study buddies'
  - pupils to use other methods of recording.
- Check pupils' ability to copy from the blackboard.
- Make sure that lessons are structured sequential and cumulative.
- Teach:
  - organisation skills
  - study skills.
- Help:
  - by applying for examination and assessment concessions.

Where to find more information

The Dyslexia Institute
Park House
Wick Road
Egham, Surrey
TW20 0HH

Tel: 01784 222300
Fax: 01784 222333
Email: info@dyslexia-inst-org.uk
http://www.dyslexia-inst-org.uk

The British Dyslexia Association
98 London Road
Reading
RG 1 5AU

www.bdadyslexia.org.uk

British Dyslexia Association (2006) *Dyslexia Handbook*, Reading: BDA
Ott, P. (1997) *How to Detect and Manage Dyslexia – A Reference and Resource Manual,* London: Heinemann

Henderson, A. (1998) *Maths for the Dyslexic – A Practical Guide,* London: David Fulton

Shaywitz, S. (2003) *Overcoming Dyslexia,* New York: Alfred Knopf

Tod, J. (1999) *IEPs – Dyslexia,* London: David Fulton

Dyspraxia

Dyspraxia is a neurological condition that affects the body's motor memory system. Learners with dyspraxia have difficulty in carrying out learned patterns of movement, such as the fine motor skills in handwriting, or the gross motor skills in riding a bike. It can also cause difficulty with forming and articulating speech and language and sometimes affects the organisation of thought processes.

Assessment

Although an educational psychologist may carry out an initial assessment, any formal diagnosis is usually done through a medical practitioner. An occupational therapist may also be involved.

Methods of support and teaching assistant practice

- Work to keep self-image as high as possible. These children may be rather clumsy and uncoordinated so are often unpopular with their peer group unless they are supported appropriately and given every chance to succeed. Build on their strengths.
- Give targeted help with handwriting:
  - try out different pens to find one that is comfortable and easy to use
  - teach cursive handwriting
  - provide templates or line guides to help with setting work out
  - provide a sloped desk surface and/or stick paper to the work surface
  - do not place them too near to other learners so they clash arms.
  - use alternatives to handwriting, e.g. word processors, diagrams or concept keyboard.
- Help with planning and organising activities (making lists, timetables, sequencing cue cards and organisational software such as *Inspiration©*).
- Follow any exercises recommended by an occupational therapist, speech therapist or physiotherapist, for fine motor and gross motor control.
- Model movement patterns.
- Help with personal organisation (ensure learner wears easy to get on and off clothing without buttons or laces, tie their locker key to their belt, have a wipe clean homework diary, two sets of pencil cases, etc.).
- Allow extra time for the practice of certain skills.

Where to find more information
The Dyspraxia Foundation
8 West Alley
Hitchin
Hertfordshire
SG5 1EG

Tel: 01462 455016
Fax: 01462 455052
Email: dyspraxia@dyspraxiafoundation.org.uk
http://www.dyspraxiafoundation.org.uk
Dyscovery Centre http://www.dyscovery.co.uk

Portwood, M. (1999) *Developmental Dyspraxia – Identification and Intervention: A Manual for Parents and Professionals,* 2nd edn, London: David Fulton

Autistic Spectrum Disorder

Autism is a developmental disability that affects social and communication skills. Learners with autism have three areas of impairment:

- Social interaction
- Social communication
- Imagination and flexible thinking.

Learners can have varying degrees of autism and those severely affected will be educated in specialist provision. Asperger's Syndrome is at the less severe end of the Autistic Disorder Spectrum and those diagnosed with it are usually supported in mainstream schools.

Pupils with Asperger's Syndrome have difficulty understanding and getting along with other people. They find the rules of social communication difficult to follow, which has a huge impact on learning and their experience in school. A lack of empathy or inability to 'read the minds' of other people means they sometimes use people as objects. Some may have formal or pedantic ways of using language or problems with coordination, and many have rigid ways of thinking or obsessive interests.

It is important to recognise that these difficulties are not the result of a delay in development but a difference in development. However, although they may experience difficulties with parts of the curriculum that ask them to interpret and understand people (e.g English and History), they are often very able in scientific and mathematical fields. Understanding the learner with autism is an essential part of support.

Assessment
Pupils suspected of having an autistic spectrum disorder should always be assessed by a psychologist or medical practitioner using checklists and questionnaires.

Methods of support and teaching assistant practice

- Use a proactive whole school approach – plan in advance and have contingency plans.
- Have a safe base or work area within the classroom.
- Have clear classroom routines and structure – a safe, ordered, predictable environment.
- Prepare well for any change in routine.
- Help pupils in unstructured time, such as breaks.
- Use any obsessive interests positively, as rewards or as part of teaching.
- Use simple, straightforward explicit language without irony or metaphors.
- Demonstrate visually what is required.
- Give visual clues (JIGS) and information (e.g. use of visual timetables).
- Check understanding.
- Use social skills or SULP training to explain rules of interaction.
- Use social stories and role-play to teach social behaviour.
- Break down tasks and explain the concept of finishing a task.
- Use rule-based rather than socially-based behaviour policy – "When you are listening to a story you must sit still."
- Encourage learners not to verbalise their thoughts all the time but maybe to use a diary instead.
- Help with friendship skills and prevent teasing.
- Never insist on eye contact.
- Keep calm – it is not personal when they tell you that you are old or fat!

Where to find more information

National Autistic Society
393 City Road
London
EC1V 1NG

Tel: 020 7833 2299
Fax: 020 7833 9666
Email: nas@nas.org.uk
http://www.nas.org.uk

Attwood, T. (1998) *Asperger's Syndrome – A Guide for Parents and Professionals*, London: Jessica Kingsley

Cumine, V., Leach, J. and Stevenson, G. (1998) *Asperger's Syndrome,* London: David Fulton

Jordan, R. and Powell, S. (Eds) (1997) *Autism and Learning: A Guide to Good Practice,* London: David Fulton

Wall, K. (2004) *Autism and Early Years Practice: A Guide for Early Years Professionals, Teachers and Parents,* London: Paul Chapman

Speech and language difficulties

Difficulties can affect any part of speech and language development and can impact not only on a learner's achievement in the classroom but on their ability to get on with their peers. This is because we usually manage our friendships through talk. Children with language difficulties can often become extremely frustrated and this can have an impact on their behaviour in school. Language difficulties can be part of other problems like dyspraxia or Asperger's Syndrome, or can be an area of concern on their own. You will need to work closely with specialists in speech and language development and therapy if you are dealing with learners with complex difficulties. Learners may have problems in any of these areas:

Articulation and Phonology Discriminating between sounds Lip and tongue movements to produce sound	**Semantics** Use of vocabulary, concepts, association, definitions and categories
Pragmatics Turn-taking Listening Responding appropriately Proximity to speaker Eye contact Appropriateness of subject matter Body language Empathy Use of metaphor and irony Use of deduction	**Prosody** Pitch, speed and volume of speech Breathing patterns for speaking
	Syntax Parts of speech Order of words Plurals, etc.
	Expressive Language Word-finding difficulties Maintaining a conversation
Fluency Production of fluent speech (e.g. stammering)	**Receptive Language** Understanding Following instructions

Assessment

A speech and language therapist or specialist teacher will look at the impact of the learner's language difficulties in the classroom and suggest teaching programmes and resources.

Methods of support and teaching assistant practice

Note that the methods of support and practice will depend on the area of difficulty.

- Teach phonology – sounds and patterns in speech.
- Teach and explain vocabulary and word meanings.

- Teach listening skills.
- Work with the learner to keep their self-image a positive one, in spite of their difficulties.
- Forewarn the learner if they have to contribute to spoken language, so they have time to mentally prepare.
- Help them to plan their response.
- Accept and value contributions.
- Accept other methods of communication.
- Use visual material or gestures to supplement speech.
- Make allowances for mistakes/tiredness.
- Allow time for a response.
- Simplify vocabulary and syntax.
- Slow down your rate of speech.
- Say what you mean.
- Give information in short chunks.
- Use open-ended questioning.
- Describe what the learner is doing to model language.
- Expand on what the learner says.
- Clarify and explain concepts.
- Model the right pronunciation but do not over-correct the learner.
- Explain and practise social conventions in conversation, like turn-taking, responding and body language.
- Follow structured programme set by speech and language therapist.
- Use circle time.
- Use SULP (Social Use of Language Programme).

Where to find more information

I CAN is a charity that helps children with speech and language difficulties:

I CAN
4 Dyer's Buildings
Holborn
London EC1N 2QP
Tel: 0845 225 4071
Fax: 0845 225 4072
http://www.ican.org.uk

Afasic is a UK charity, established in 1968, to help children and young people with speech and language difficulties, their families and the professionals working with them:

Afasic
2nd Floor, 50-52 Great Sutton Street
London EC1V 0DJ
Tel: 020 7490 9410 (administration)
Fax: 020 7251 2834
Helpline: 0845 3 555577
Email: info@afasic.org.uk
http://www.afasic.org.uk

Martin, D. (2000) *Teaching Children with Speech and Language Difficulties,* London: David Fulton

Ripley, K., Barrett, J. and Fleming, P. (2001) *Inclusion for Children with Speech and Language Impairments,* London: David Fulton

Thompson, G. (2003) *Supporting Communication Disorders,* London: David Fulton,

Down's Syndrome

Down's Syndrome is the result of a chromosomal abnormality. These learners have a specific profile for the development of cognitive and social skills. They also have speech and language differences and may have motor and associated medical problems. However, they are also individuals and their overall abilities vary considerably. Although traditionally educated in Special Schools, these children are now successfully included in mainstream schools, with support. If you are working with a learner with Down's Syndrome, you should have some specialist training as their needs are quite specific. They need a small steps approach which builds on success, and where the teaching assistant models, prompts and scaffolds learning.

Where to find more information
The Down's Syndrome Educational Trust
The Sarah Duffen Centre
Belmont Street
Southsea
Hampshire
PO5 1NA

Tel: 02392 855330
http://www.downsed.org

The Down's Syndrome Association
Langdon Down Centre
2A Langdon Park
Teddington
TW11 9PS

Tel: 0845 230 0372
Fax: 0845 230 0373
Email: info@downs-syndrome.org.uk
http://www.downs-syndrome.org.uk

http://www.altonweb.com/cs/downsyndrome/

Lorenz, S. (1998) *Children with Down's Syndrome: A Guide for Teachers & Learning Support Assistants in Mainstream Schools,* London: David Fulton

Physical, medical and sensory difficulties

These include developmental problems like cerebral palsy or spina bifida, and medical difficulties such as epilepsy, diabetes and other illnesses that may have either short- or long-term implications. It also includes sensory disabilities like hearing and visual impairment. Illness or disability does not necessarily mean that a pupil will have Special Educational Needs, but a school will still need to be flexible to make provision for them.

Assessment

Assessment will be by a medical practitioner or other health professional, as a result of parent referral.

You should always have appropriate training before helping with personal care, medication or health procedures. Respect the dignity of the child in these situations by ensuring privacy at all times.

Methods of support and teaching assistant practice

- Help with personal care.
- Monitor medication.
- Liaise with health care professionals.
- Do not focus on the learner's disability but concentrate on what they can do.
- Help them to be independent. Do not take over or anticipate needs.
- Help with issues of access (e.g. to buildings, ways to answer questions without raising their hand).
- Encourage interaction with other children.
- Help to adapt tasks and use aids like wheelchairs, communicators, word processors.
- Deliver specialised programmes (e.g. physiotherapy).
- Help with school trips, assemblies, etc.
- Adapt resources, e.g. use gapped sheets to reduce the amount of writing required.

Where to find more information

Brooke, A. and Welton, S. (2003) *The A–Z of School Health,* London: David Fulton

Cornwall, J. and Robertson, C. (1999) *IEPs, Physical Disabilities and Medical Conditions,* London: David Fulton

DfES (2001) *Access to Education for Children and Young People with Medical Needs,* London: DfES

Kenward, H. (1996) *Spotlight on Special Educational Needs: Physical Disabilities,* Tamworth: NASEN

Muscular Dystrophy Campaign (2004) *Inclusive Education for Children with Muscular Dystrophy and Other Neuromuscular Conditions. Guidance for Primary and Secondary Schools*, Available from:

http://www.muscular-dystrophy.org/information_resources/publications/index.html

Hearing Impairment (HI)

Learners with hearing impairment may have a conductive loss such as glue ear, where a problem in the outer or middle ear blocks the sound, making it harder to hear, and/or a more permanent sensory-neural loss. This can vary from a mild hearing loss, perhaps affecting a certain range of sounds, to a profound loss where pupils are dependent upon hearing aids or sign language.

If you are working with learners with complex hearing impairment, you will be working under the supervision of a teacher of the hearing-impaired. Such pupils also have specific requirements in their support of speech and language and will have technological aids that they may need help to manage.

Assessment

A teacher of hearing impairment and/or a medical practitioner will carry out assessment.

Methods of support and teaching assistant practice

- Make sure that you understand the type of hearing loss a learner has.
- Check for background noise.
- Ensure that you can be seen by the learner and make eye contact for lip reading.
- Check on seating position of pupil in each lesson.
- Encourage interaction with peer group.
- Keep your language clear and simple.
- Repeat what they say to check if you have understood.
- Don't shout, but don't speak too quietly.
- Be natural in the way you communicate.
- Encourage learners to ask if they don't understand.
- Pre-teach key language and subject matter.
- Use visual material rather than talking.
- Be patient – do not interrupt.
- Model language.
- Re-explain instructions and concepts.

Where to find more information

National Deaf Children's Society
15 Dufferin Street
London
EC1Y 8UR

Tel: 020 7490 8656
Fax: 020 7251 5020
Email: ndcs@ndcs.org.uk
http://www.ndcs.org.uk

RNID (2004) *Inclusion Strategies; Supporting Effective Inclusion and Attainment*, Available through: http://www.rnid.org.uk

Watson, L. *et al.* (1999) *Deaf and Hearing Impaired Pupils in Mainstream Schools,* London: David Fulton

Visual Impairment (VI)

Learners can have many types of visual impairment, ranging from total loss of vision to low vision or partial sight. With low vision, learners may need extra lighting or magnification, and with partial sight they could require adapted teaching and learning resources to help them access the curriculum. If you are working with these learners, you must discuss their support programme with a teacher of visual impairment.

Assessment

An ophthalmologist/teacher of VI will carry out assessment.

Methods of support and teaching assistant practice

- Make sure that you are told the exact nature of visual loss.
- Help learners to interact with their peers.
- Check lighting in the classroom.
- Practise movement around school.
- Check the environment for hazards.
- Use white tape to mark the edges of desks and furniture.
- Be predictable in the classroom and keep things in their place.
- Use spoken or taped material.
- Help to plan in advance for each assessment – pupils might need a bigger photocopy or a different colour paper.
- Help with technological aids like magnifiers or talking software.
- Adapt resources, e.g. tactile number lines and games.

Where to find more information

Royal National Institute of the Blind (RNIB)
105 Judd Street
London
WC1H 9NE

Tel: 020 7388 1266
Fax: 020 7388 2034
Email: helpline@rnib.org.uk
http://www.rnib.org.uk

Arter, C. *et al.* (1999) *Children with Visual Impairment in Mainstream Settings,* London: David Fulton

RNID (2004) *Inclusion Strategies: Supporting Effective Inclusion and Attainment*, available through http://www.rnid.org.uk

Children with Mental Health Problems

Child mental health is a growing area of concern, with 10 percent of children now thought to suffer from mental health difficulties. These include conditions such as anxiety, depression, and eating disorders, which are often associated with educational failure, or conduct disorders, which are associated with anti-social behaviour. The DfES has issued guidance on promoting children's mental health which emphasises the importance of recognising children at risk and providing appropriate support. You can access this at:

http://www.teachernet.gov.uk/wholeschool/sen/ypmentalhealth/cyp-publications

You can also find more information at:

http://www.nmha.org/children/children_mh_matters/promoting.pdf

and http://www.youngminds.org.uk

or through Child and Adolescent Mental Health Services (CAMHS).

Remember, a child may also be struggling to cope with a parent with mental health difficulties.

Inclusive provision

The following groups of learners do not necessarily fall within the SEN category but have specific learning needs that need to be considered within inclusion:

Pupils with high mobility or interrupted schooling (Children missing education)

Some pupils underachieve because they move schools regularly or they miss long periods of schooling because of illness, pregnancy or caring responsibilities at home. Although they may not have SEN they still experience barriers to learning and achievement. Some schools employ learning mentors to support those pupils who underachieve because of difficult home circumstances or social problems.

Schools should use a whole school approach to managing the education of pupils who move regularly between schools. You may be employed by a specific service like Traveller Support, or your school may have a population of children who come and go. Travelling families have customs and conventions that need to be understood when you work closely with them (Naylor and Wild-Smith, 1997). Refugee children have often experienced considerable instability, upheaval and loss, so need a stable, secure and ordered environment. Children from Service families (Armed Forces) frequently move every two years and the disruptive effect of this on their learning and friendships can often be misdiagnosed as a learning or behavioural difficulty.

You can play an important part in settling all these learners into school, making them welcome and helping them to have happy and productive relationships with teachers and peers. Hospital schools and specialist units who deal with learners with persistent medical or psychological problems often employ teaching assistants to give sensitive individual support and help liaise with mainstream schools.

Methods of support and teaching assistant pra
- Have an induction process for new pupils, with
  named staff member.
- Use activities to help pupils get used to the sch
  and find out where everything is.
- Have out-of-school activities and clubs for frien
  run by teaching assistants).
- Communicate with pupil's previous/next school.
- Find out how much they know and use every opportunity to fill in
  gaps.
- Teach explicitly the rules and conventions of the new school.
- Understand and respect home values, social customs and rules.
- Use culturally relevant materials for learning.
- Liaise closely with families.
- Work with home tutor or home–school liaison worker.
- Use collaborative groups and peer tutoring.

Where to find more information
Birmingham Advisory and Support Service (2001) *Demonstrating Progress and Managing Performance in Schools with High Pupil Turnover,* Birmingham: BASS

Naylor, S. and Wild-Smith, K. (1997) *Broadening Horizons – Education and Travelling Children*, Essex: Essex Traveller Education Service

www.dfes.gov.uk

Learners with English as an Additional Language (EAL)

This refers to learners who already speak at least one home language when they arrive at school and who learn English as an additional language. In many cases, this gives them a sound basis for learning another language and they will already have developed their conceptual understanding through the use of their own language. Most LAs have language support services that offer support and advice, but there are some basic principles that may help.

Methods of support and teaching assistant practice
- Be aware of how many learners with EAL there are in your
  school.
- Understand and respect their first language, home values and
  social customs.
- Use culturally relevant materials for learning.
- Model English – and give them the opportunity to talk to you.
- Let them use you to practise and rehearse responses.
- Accept non-verbal responses (gestures, etc.).
- Let them use their first language to draft.
- Check they understand the context of the learning and re-explain
  teaching points, if necessary.
- Use lots of visual material.

- Use books, stories and tapes.
- Help them integrate with peer group.
- Use dual-language textbooks and dictionaries.
- Check for comprehension by asking questions.
- Be available to help them at break times.

Where to find more information
DfES, (2002) *Supporting Pupils Learning English as an Additional Language*, London: DfES 0239/2002

Mukherji, P. and O'Dea, T. (2000) *Understanding Children's Language and Literacy*, Cheltenham: Stanley Thorne's
Includes a chapter on bilingualism in the early years.

Gifted and talented

Gifted refers to learners with high academic ability and potential, and *talented* describes learners with outstanding ability in creative arts. Sometimes it is easy to feel a little uncomfortable with these learners if you think that a teaching assistant should know everything. Such learners can be a little bit threatening, but remember that you are a facilitator of their learning, not the fount of all knowledge!

Assessment
Usually through teacher assessment or cognitive (reasoning) testing like Cognitive Abilities Test (CAT) administered in Year 7, or NFER verbal and non-verbal reasoning. May also be identified through parents.

Methods of support and teaching assistant practice
It is important to discuss your methods of support and practice with teaching staff.

- Use a broader, more varied curriculum.
- Give them open-ended or extended tasks and problem solving activities.
- Let them move at a faster pace.
- Look for extension materials and resources from other Key Stages.
- Let them design their own tasks.
- Make links with other parts of the curriculum.
- Allow them to work alone or with groups as required.
- Learn with them.
- Encourage them to reflect on their own learning.

Where to find more information
Eyre, D. (1997) *Able Children in Ordinary Schools,* London: David Fulton

Distin, K. (Ed.) (2006) *Gifted Children – A Guide for Parents and Professionals,* London: Jessica Kingsley

www.standards.dcsf.gov.uk/giftedandtalented

www.qca.org.uk/8774.html

Key reading

Buttriss, J. and Callander, A. (2003) *A–Z of Special Needs (for Every Teacher)* PFP Publishing

Cheninais, R. (2000) *Special Educational Needs for Newly Qualified and Student Teachers*, London: David Fulton

DfES (2001) *SEN Toolkit*, London: DfES

DfES (2001) *Revised Code of Practice for Special Educational Needs*, London: DfES/0581/2001 *[Provides guidance on identifying, assessing and meeting the needs of pupils with SEN.]*

Soan, S. (Ed.) (2004) *Additional Educational Needs*, London: David Fulton

Spooner, W. (2006) *The SEN Handbook for Trainee Teachers, NQTs and Teaching Assistants*, London: David Fulton

14 Behaviour for learning – Emotional and social development

In an effective and welcoming school all the staff and pupils share common values and a sense of belonging, and show each other mutual respect. This chapter deals with both the management of ordered learning and discipline in school and the kinds of challenging behaviour that can be found in learners of all ages. It also looks at the new curriculum areas of Personal Social Health Education (PSHE) and Citizenship.

Behaviour is a form of communication and the way we communicate with others is a reflection of many different things – our emotional development; learned behaviour; social conventions; personal issues; and the stresses and strains of everyday life. However, behaviour is not an isolated issue. It is linked with every aspect of teaching and learning. All the flexible approaches described in this book so far affect pupil behaviour, as does a focus on inclusion.

Emotional and social development

From birth, children form a bond with a parent or primary caregiver, and this develops into their first avenue of social development. Young children are influenced and shaped by their parents and their culture, which makes the involvement of parents in all aspects of their education a real necessity. Later, peers and friends become a major influence in their social development. During adolescence, there are hormonally-influenced changes in feelings and emotions that make it particularly important for pupils to be accepted by their peer group and a biologically-driven urge to become independent of parental and sometimes adult control. Teenage years are a time when pupils are trying to establish a sense of self, and this can sometimes lead to difficulties with authority or attempts to find the boundaries of acceptable behaviour.

Moral development

As children develop and mature, they become socialised within their culture. Part of this is gaining an understanding of morality, or what is right and wrong. Piaget used observations of children being told stories to look at moral development and link it to stages in their cognitive development (1932) As a result he identified:

- Pre-morality (up to approximately age four), when children have little understanding of rules or the basis for right and wrong.
- Moral realism (up to approximately age nine), when they understand that adults decide what is right and wrong and that this is fixed and unchanging.
- Moral subjectivism, when they understand that what is right and wrong can be the subject of debate and discussion.

The pace at which they move through these stages depends on their social experience and cognitive development.

Kohlberg (1981) expanded and developed Piaget's theory. He identified three levels and six stages in moral development

Stage	Level 1 Pre-conventional Morality		Level 2 Conventional Morality		Level 3 Post-conventional Morality	
1	Obedience	Following adult rules to avoid punishment				
2	Acting for own interest	Following rules to get a reward				
3			Conformity	Being good to maintain approval of peers or adult		
4			Social conscience	Being good because it is socially right		
5					Social contracts	Socially and democratically agreed norms of behaviour can be challenged according to individual opinions
6					Universal ethics	Acting through principles or conscience in conflict with law

He thought that young children follow rules because they want to avoid punishment or get a reward. As they move through Key Stage 2, they become more reliant on doing the right thing to maintain the approval of adults or their peer group. As they enter adolescence, they become more concerned with the whole idea of socially and democratically agreed norms of behaviour.

But it is not just a question of the development of children's ability to think or reason morally. There are many other influences on their moral development and thinking, including family background and culture, society and the media. The whole concept of what is acceptable or desirable where behaviour is concerned changes over time. For example, swearing on TV is now commonplace. At one time, it was seen as an outrage! Issues such as these can be dealt with using debate and discussion in the PSHE curriculum. Schools are communities that agree and enforce their own accepted standards of behaviour, within the parameters of society and culture.

Individual needs

Individual learners may well have issues with behaviour that are a result of personal concerns or difficulties. They may have social or relationship difficulties, have been traumatised in some way by events in their lives, or have a medical condition that has an impact on the way they behave. All this makes the management of behaviour a complex area that differs from age group to age group. There are several theories that help to give us an understanding of some of the perspectives involved.

Understanding behaviour

Eco Systemic Perspective

The 'Eco Systemic Perspective' theory is based on original research by Bronfenbrenner (1979). According to this theory, behaviour is the result of interactions in the systems between learners and their environment. This can be within:

- The micro system of the child, their family, peers and neighbourhood (including school).
- The meso system of society and the media.
- The macro system of globally influenced worldwide issues (like refugees or fear of terrorism).

We can apply this to school by viewing behaviour as part of the interaction between the pupil, teachers, teaching assistants and parents in the system of school, home and the classroom environment, rather than viewing the behaviour of children in isolation. There are many examples when negative interactions can be set up and carried on:

- A teacher always arrives at school on Monday morning stressed from commuting. He views the class he teaches first lesson on Mondays as being a difficult class. The class then play up to his expectations.
- A child who is experiencing family breakdown at home may vent her feelings of frustration and hurt at school. The school report this to parents, who then become angry with the child, or blame the school for failing to meet their family's needs.
- A child who has had difficulties with behaviour has become 'a name in the staff room'. He is then always perceived negatively by

all staff, even when he tries to change.

- A teaching assistant takes over the support of a child with complex problems from an experienced teaching assistant, who insists that "he was fine with her and she never had any problem with him". The teaching assistant feels helpless and de-skilled when she experiences the inevitable difficulties of working with a new pupil.
- A pupil finds an effective way to 'wind up' a teacher and enjoys doing this at every opportunity.

The Eco Systemic view encourages teaching staff to look at relationships and the environment as a whole, before labelling individual learners as having difficulties. To assess interacting problems a teaching assistant can be asked to:

- Observe the classroom/school environment for triggers or difficult situations.
- Observe pupils interacting together.
- Fill in a questionnaire on their own perceptions of pupils/teaching situations.
- Help a child to fill in a questionnaire to find out their view of their relationships.

A teacher should also work directly with families because parental involvement plays a crucial part. Once information has been gathered, then everyone can work together to problem solve and set up positive interactions, rather than continue with negative ones.

Cultural issues

There are many ways in which society and media culture affect the whole issue of behavioural expectations. These particular examples of society values, as promoted through the media, may influence behaviour.

- The breakdown in hierarchical authority, including a more laissez faire approach to parenting.
- Instant gratification (for example, if you want something, you don't have to save – you can buy it now on credit).
- Blame culture. It's always somebody else's fault!
- Changes in censorship and Internet access that allow disturbing images to be more readily available to children.

Sometimes people have low expectations of achievement and behaviour from certain groups of learners (such as Afro-Caribbean boys), based on negative stereotypes. Gender issues are important too. Some teachers, teaching assistants and parents find themselves giving far more attention to boys than girls, or allowing boys to get away with behaviour that would be unacceptable for girls ("boys will be boys", "it's a man thing"). On the other hand, they may let girls show their feelings more than boys. Although you can take gender differences into account, it is important not to have different gender-based standards. Social class can also be a factor when low standards are accepted from children from working class families but not from middle class children.

The environment

Anyone who works in school knows that a windy day can send a whole playground of children into hyperactive mode! A calm, ordered and safe classroom environment with regular routines gives learners a sense of security. They do not have to keep testing the boundaries all the time. It is important to have clearly stated rules for the classroom, so that everyone knows the expectations. Seating and grouping can be arranged to check that children are able to work productively together without personality clashes. You can also check to make sure that learners are not distracted by other children or are so cramped that they cannot avoid knocking into each other. Often, a simple rearrangement of furniture can do wonders! Pupils should tidy away equipment and make sure work is stored safely. Teachers also look at trigger points that frequently result in behavioural problems, for example, lining up in the dining hall or having an unstructured start to lessons. They may use introductory music, a verbal introduction, or switching the lights on to signal that it is time to settle down and start work.

Behaviourist approach

You have looked at behaviourism in detail in Chapter 6. According to this approach, behaviour is learned from experience and can therefore be unlearned. Rewards, reinforcement, incentives and negative reinforcement or sanctions are used to shape and change behaviour. This can relate to whole-school behaviour management, for example using Golden Time, or individual behaviour management programmes for learners with specific behaviour difficulties. Many of the behaviour policies in schools use behaviourist principles.

The key in operating the behaviourist approach is to find the right kind of rewards to motivate children. This will vary from child to child. For some, getting individual attention or being singled out for praise is a real reward. For others it is not. Some children love the attention and respect they receive from their peer group when they are 'told off', while being kept in at playtime is a reward, not a punishment, for anyone being bullied.

It is vitally important that you find the key motivating factor for individual children. A teaching assistant is often in an excellent position to really get to know pupils. Do this by observing and asking them or offering alternatives to see what they prefer. Here are some examples of rewards and incentives that you may find in school:

- Golden Time. There are several variations on this. Pupils earn golden time by meeting acceptable standards and then bank the time so that they can have free choice activities on Fridays. They lose time through unacceptable behaviour. (It is more successful if they can then earn this time back).

- Stickers, badges, or symbols.
- House points.
- 'Proud cloud', where children's names are displayed on a picture of a cloud when they achieve.
- Photos of workers and tryers displayed in hallway.
- Marble jar – learners can earn a reward for the whole class by behaving or achieving well and adding a marble to the jar (encouraging collective responsibility).
- 'Catch me being good' cards.
- Raffle tickets.
- Vouchers for CD shops or fast food restaurants.
- Special privileges like choosing a video for the class or helping the caretaker(!).

Remember that rewards seem to be more effective in encouraging desired behaviour than punishment is in getting rid of unacceptable behaviour. Praising a pupil for doing something right is better than commenting when they do something wrong. You can use tactical ignoring when a child is behaving in an unacceptable way, so that you do not reinforce the behaviour by giving them attention, as long as their behaviour is not dangerous in any way.

Sanctions

Sanctions are actions and penalties that deal with improper or unacceptable behaviour. They can include:

- verbal warning
- withdrawal of teaching assistant/teacher attention
- time out
- removal of rewards already earned
- loss of privileges
- detention
- missed playtime/sports club
- letter home
- suspension/exclusion.

By using checklists observations and frequency scales, TAs can make an accurate observation of children's behaviour and then see how it is being reinforced. To operate this system, you can use an ABC approach. Look at instances of behaviour and record and analyse:

A   Antecedents   - what happens before?

B   Behaviour   - an exact description of the behaviour.

C   Consequences   - what happened as a result of the behaviour?

You may be asked to fill in an ABC observation for any child or group of children. You can then attempt to change the behaviour by altering the antecedents or the consequences. Remember that you can use it for analysing positive examples of desired behaviour, not just negative ones!

Behaviourism is successful, easy-to-manage and popular because it focuses on the behaviour rather than the child. However, it is heavily reliant on a consistent approach from all staff, which can be difficult to achieve. Critics also argue that it only focuses on the behaviour that you can see and does not address the causes. It also encourages children to become dependent on extrinsic rewards (rewards from external sources) rather than intrinsic rewards.

Psychological perspective

The basis for this perspective is that "unconscious processes influence conscious behaviour" (Ayers, Clarke, Murray, 1995, p.9). This perspective originated with the ideas of Freud. In simple terms, learners have early experiences that make up their psychological profile. For example, they may have suffered separation or the loss of a parent in infancy, which leaves them with unconscious feelings of anxiety (Bowlby, 1984). They may find it hard to build secure and meaningful relationships in the future, or become chronically anxious if they move schools or classes. Some children find these situations so stressful that they become school refusers. In other cases, learners may use defence mechanisms to protect themselves from the unpleasant feelings that surface. For example, they might:

- block out the feelings from their own awareness, e.g. they could hit someone and then really believe that they didn't do it
- deny their feelings, e.g. they say a task is boring so they can't be bothered to do it, when it is really too hard for them
- project their feelings onto others. So, if a child experiences anger from a teacher or parent, they might be angry and unable to show it, so they become hostile to other children
- rationalise what they have done, for example, saying it is okay to cheat in an exam because the whole system isn't fair.

An understanding of this perspective may help you to relate better to certain learners, and give you a basic understanding of some of the ways children deal with difficult feelings. However, you should resist the urge to psychoanalyse everyone, as it is such a complex area. A specially trained teacher or medical professional will be involved with any learners with severe difficulties.

Cognitive behavioural approach

It is not just the perceptions of teaching staff and parents that are important. We have already seen the value of encouraging learners to talk about their own learning and to assess their own achievement. The cognitive behavioural approach focuses on pupils' thoughts, feelings and perceptions about themselves. It is based on original research by Aaron Beck, who believed that mistaken or unrealistic thinking was responsible for many problems with behaviour (Beck, 1995). The perceptions that a pupil may have of themselves and others will influence how they react in certain situations. For example, a pupil may see himself as being 'thick', 'stupid', or 'a pain in the neck'. Classrooms are very public places, where it is hard to hide, so pupils may withdraw and try to avoid all attention, or become the class clown and 'act up' for peer group approval. They may even try to meet the negative expectations of the staff because it feels familiar to them.

This type of behaviour is related to the whole concept of self-esteem, which plays such an important part in how we relate to others. Sometimes pupils blame other people for everything and seem unable to accept responsibility. They may see external factors as responsible for everything that happens to them, or, at the other extreme, think everything is their own fault. They could also be impulsive and quick to use aggression rather than talk or negotiation. Bandura (see pages 105–6) has extended his work on social learning to study the role of personal effectiveness in people's lives: how we use motivation, thought and a belief in ourselves to be effective and how we can develop self-regulation to adapt and change our behaviour. He says we have "underestimated people's capacity to cultivate positive tendencies" (Bandura, 2003).

A pupil's perception of you may also influence how they respond to you. They may see you as a 'Special Needs Person', and therefore feel it labels them as SEN if they work with you. Alternatively, if they know that they can gain sympathy from you easily, they may tell you things that have happened to them in great detail to distract you from making them work. Pupils have different perceptions of all teachers, and this will influence how they react to them. Inconsistent teachers, who accept anything one day but jump on every instance of misbehaviour the next, are often disliked by pupils because they do not know where they are with them.

A key element of the cognitive behavioural perspective is to encourage learners to think about why they do things and to help them change their thinking and, therefore, their behaviour. It involves training pupils to observe, analyse and regulate their behaviour through a problem solving approach. As a teaching assistant, you can help them to do so by talking through their own perceptions of their behaviour, and how other people respond to them. There are some useful pupil questionnaires to help you do this in Clarke and Ayers (1995).

There are also structured schemes for Junior and Secondary schools that your teacher may ask you to use to look at perceptions of behaviour (Interactive Conduct File www.behaviouruk.com). Goleman's self-science curriculum is also an excellent program to follow (Goleman, 1996). This is a useful approach but you should be aware that it is hard to think yourself out of a strong emotional response. The emotion

> **Key Stage 4:** "I was working with a pupil who was always late for lessons (ours is a big site). Whenever the teachers commented on it when he arrived in class, he would get very aggressive and rude. He was excluded from lessons for his rudeness many times. I spent a long time talking it through with him. He had a reading difficulty which meant he was worried about being asked to read in class, so he was always late and used the teacher being angry with him to get himself chucked out. The lateness, not the aggression, was the real problem but how he reacted always made it worse. We all agreed the teacher would not ask him to read unless he gave a private signal. In return, he would turn up on time and count to ten before he responded. It was hard to change but he did!"

usually comes first and the thought second! Regulating how you respond is the key.

Bandura recommends that people (pupils) can achieve self-efficacy (self-effectiveness) if you help them to:

- have performance successes
- overcome obstacles
- manage and learn from their failures
- see competent models of success, especially pupils similar to them who are succeeding
- judge success by self-improvement, rather than comparison with others
- correct wrong perceptions about themselves and tell them they have what it takes to succeed!

(Bandura, 2003)

Whole-school behaviour policies

All schools must have a behaviour policy that sets out the principles and practice for managing behaviour. Some school policies combine behaviour, attendance and bullying, whereas others have separate policies for each. The most effective policies are commonly agreed, and it is important that pupils, staff, governors and parents are clear about what is acceptable in school. It is also vital to have a whole-school policy so that everyone knows what is expected and so responds in the same way. Midday supervisors should always be familiar with their school policy as they have a key role to play in the whole-school approach to behaviour. A standardised approach set out in a policy helps everyone to maintain a calm, ordered and predictable environment.

Each policy should include:

- Principles of behaviour management, reflecting the ethos of the school. Your school may base their policy on one of the structured systems of behaviour management, like assertive discipline (Canter and Canter, 2001) or Bill Roger's 'You know the fair rule' approach (Rogers, 2002).

- Procedures and practices to be followed, including how rewards and sanctions are used, and how detentions, suspensions and exclusions are implemented.

The policy should also provide a framework of support for staff so that they do not feel they are working in isolation, and a way of reviewing any issues that might arise at any time. You need to be very familiar with your school policy so that you can feel confident that you are following the correct procedures and taking the right approach. You may have an opportunity to have some input into your school policy, so treat it as a working document and think about what works and what doesn't work.

Basic principles

- Teachers will have individual ways of working within the framework of a whole-school policy, depending on their experience and personalities. Perceptions of behaviour will be different too. Some teachers can tolerate high levels of noise in the classroom, while others like it quieter. Some see a child who fidgets as a nuisance, others don't even notice. You will need to adapt your own style of working accordingly to maintain a consistent approach. Learn from the experienced teachers who have good management skills. Watch what they do and try it yourself. Remember, like anything else, it takes time and practise to learn.
- Be proactive and organised. Use your knowledge of teaching and learning to make sure the task is at the right level, the learner has the information and resources they need, and the learning environment is as user-friendly as possible. Many behaviour problems are started by learners who get up to find something, or who shout across to another pupil to ask something.
- Work to raise the self-esteem of pupils by enabling them to experience success. Help them to develop self-respect and respect for others.
- Focus on positives rather than negatives. It is easier to improve behaviour by rewards than to get rid of unwanted behaviour through sanctions or punishment. Use realistic praise as often as you can.
- Work with all staff to make your school a tolerant, accepting place.
- Managing behaviour is a bit like riding a horse! Children can often tell when you are nervous or unsure and seem to like to make life even more difficult for you. Often, this is because your own hesitancy and lack of confidence makes them feel insecure. So, act confident and be assertive!
- Take time to build trusting relationships with pupils. It is important that you have a positive rapport, so make sure you know their names, are aware of their thinking, and are familiar with their interests.
- Give and expect respect when you are dealing with learners. 'Do as you would be done by' is the rule here!

- Make sure you are really clear on the rules for every situation.
- Never accept unacceptable behaviour!
- Don't personalise behaviour by making it an issue between yourself and a pupil. Never say things like "Can you be good for me?" Always remind pupils about commonly accepted rules and standards.
- Label the behaviour not the child – "It was rude of you to say that to Mrs...", not "You are a very rude girl". Avoid calling children lazy, stupid or silly, or you could start a self-fulfilling prophecy.
- Resist the impulse to blame parents, teachers or other teaching assistants when there is a problem with a child. You do not know the full story and blame is unhelpful. Involve them rather than blame them.
- Be a good role model and demonstrate polite, cooperative behaviour. Do not have double standards for adults and children, e.g. "An adult is talking, do not interrupt". Instead, teach conversation skills: "If anyone is talking, wait until they pause before you interrupt."
- Remember that authority and knowledge are two different things. You do not have authority in a school because you know everything, but because of your role as a teaching assistant.
- Anticipate and prevent inappropriate behaviour whenever possible.
- Try to keep a calm and consistent approach when talking to children. Aggression on your part can make them feel defiant, and sarcasm may make them feel humiliated. Be friendly, flexible but firm. Recognise your own flashpoints and sensitivities.
- Accept that children have feelings and often cannot help showing them. Looking disappointed, sulky or defiant is okay, but being defiant is something quite different. Children should learn to regulate and control impulses, not to hide their emotions for fear of punishment. Use the language of emotions to help them understand and deal with them: "I was really disappointed when I couldn't watch my favourite TV programme. I cheered myself up by...". Work with them to regulate their emotions rather than express them in an impulsive or destructive way.
- Help children to understand the concept of secondary behaviour as illustrated in the Key Stage 4 case study example on page 307. Often, pupils use secondary behaviour to make themselves feel better. Try to focus on the primary behaviour rather than reacting in frustration to the secondary.

Handling behaviour in the classroom

Classroom rules/Code of conduct
Children learn best when they are in a safe and ordered environment. Rowdy and disorganised classes are frightening for other learners, not just the teacher. Most classrooms have class rules and procedures. Rules are most effective when they are agreed by pupils and teachers

and displayed prominently so that everyone is reminded of them. They should always be phrased in positives, although you can explain the negative:

- "Listen to people" or "We listen". ("Don't interrupt.")
- "Share" or "We share". ("Don't be selfish.")

Class rules make it easy for you to remind pupils about desired behaviour, as you can just draw attention to them. However, having rules is only half the solution. They must be implemented consistently to be effective.

Communicate and model behaviour

- Make sure the pupil is absolutely sure about the expectations for good behaviour by making your language clear and unambiguous.
- Show them what is required by modelling it ("This is what I mean by lining up quietly"). You can be a useful double act with teachers to do this.
- Apologise for your mistakes.
- Don't confuse with questions ("You should be facing the board" not "Are you supposed to be twisting round on your chair?").

Focus on positives

- Catch pupils being good and tell them! Keep your language positive.

Focus on organisation – prevention is better than cure!

- Remind them of timings or activities ("You've 10 minutes to finish").
- Help those that look puzzled.
- Plan for transition times between activities.
- Keep them occupied but not under too much pressure.

Rights and responsibilities

Make sure pupils understand the difference between their rights and responsibilities. They have the right to not be a victim of bullying behaviour. They have a responsibility not to bully others.

Incentives, rewards and sanctions

Make sure that you are aware of the rewards and sanctions available on each occasion in school by checking with the teacher. These should be relevant and age-appropriate for each learner. Always carry them through or follow them up. It is important to be consistent. Remember that rewards can be items, options to choose activities, or opportunities to have time with peers or staff. If you promise a reward, make sure there is the time and opportunity to carry it out. If you need to use a sanction, make sure it is one that you are able to follow through.

Special School: "We have a learner with Asperger's Syndrome who loves to tidy our stationery cupboard as a reward!"

Use choice and consequences

Pupils need to learn the concept of responsibility for their actions and that they have a choice in how they behave. They also need to understand the idea of what happens as a result of that choice (consequence). If they throw paint on the floor, then they will have to clear it up; if they distract other learners, then they will have to work on their own. The consequence is their choice. Make them aware of the consequence of their actions. It is helpful to use the language of choice and consequence with them ("Well done, your choice to finish your work means you can go out to play"). You may find it helpful to give limited choices yourself, so that pupils can comply easily. Do not give a choice where there is none ("Which would you like to start first?", not "Would you like to start?").

Use non-verbal signals or visual cues

Non-verbal signals can be very effective. A smile or thumbs up can really lift the spirit of a learner. A stern look or a shake of the head is a useful, low-key signal too. You can also move nearer to a pupil to reinforce a point or make them feel more secure, or if necessary, move away from them to take away your attention until they comply. Some teachers use green or red cards and traffic lights, flags to place on the desk to signal a pupil needs help, correction cards to remind the child what they should be doing ("tidy away the equipment"), or home-made noise meters to indicate when the classroom is too noisy.

Using pre-arranged signals

You may want to set up a pre-arranged private signal with a particular learner so that the communication is just between the two of you. A word, phrase or non-verbal signal will do.

Praise and criticism

It is better if praise is public and criticism or correction is given privately. There will be exceptions to this when pupils prefer private praise because of teasing from their peer group. Make sure you try to use descriptive praise by telling them what they did well. ("Well done, you sat really quietly and listened to that story"). You may need to use a quick response so give a catch phrase like "good working". Similarly, try to be descriptive in your use of corrective feedback – "You are making so much noise that no one can hear what Arun is saying", rather than "Don't be so noisy".

Self-evaluation

Give pupils opportunities to talk about behaviour. Encourage them to think through why things happen and how they can be changed.

How to deal with minor behaviour problems

Teachers and teaching assistants often find these types of behaviour problems very wearing on a day-to-day basis. Such behaviours may include talking over the teacher or other children, shouting out, throwing things, distracting others, not getting on with work, or making cheeky comments. There are several ways you can deal with this:

Praise those that do...

- You can use positive praise by ignoring the behaviour and drawing attention to a pupil that is showing the right way to do it ("I'm going to ask Alex because he has his hand up", or "Well done Alex, you have your hand up").

Or, re-state the requirement:

- Use the pupil's name.
- Describe the behaviour and the desired behaviour.
- Quietly and firmly state any rule ("Marina, you are shouting out. Remember our class rule is you must put your hand up first. Show me how you can do that. Well done").

Confrontation

It is always better to avoid conflict but, if this is inevitable, it is better that confrontation takes place in private rather than in front of a class. You should:

- Respond in a firm but non-aggressive way.
- Use distraction or humour to defuse the situation.
- Ask the child to move to one side or step out of the classroom (if there are other staff available), or arrange to speak to them later.

Rebuild positive relationships

Deal with the issue quickly and move forward, or provide a chance to re-build positive relationships by giving the pupil another chance to do it right or the chance to rewind the situation and play it back differently. Build bridges to give pupils a way back ("Let's try that again shall we?" "I don't think you really meant to do that").

Conflict management

A teaching assistant or midday supervisor often has to step in between children who have disagreements. There are some basic principles for managing conflict. If pupils are fighting you need to remember you are *in loco parentis*, so you have a duty to protect any pupil who is getting hurt. However, be very careful that you do not put yourself at risk when intervening. Use your voice instead and get help. These are the sorts of situations that you should talk through in advance with your line manager so that you can follow the correct approach. Schools will follow government guidelines on physical restraint and positive handling. These are summarised on Teachernet (www.teachernet.gov.uk).

- Get those involved to tell you about it in turn, and make sure they listen to the other person too.
- Listen to both sides.
- Use a problem-solving approach – how can we solve this?
- Agree which suggestions to follow.
- Avoid long drawn out 'Court Cases'.

Tell those involved that conflict isn't solved by force, or by ignoring it, but by negotiation and compromise.

PSHE and Citizenship

The PSHE and Citizenship curricula provide opportunities for all pupils to learn social and collaborative skills, to enable them to manage relationships and become mature and independent members of society. Through this, schools promote good behaviour, healthy living, collaboration, tolerance and understanding. This is particularly important for children who arrive at school with limited social skills that may cause friendship and behavioural problems.

Pupils are also given opportunities to learn about practical health issues like drug taking or skin cancer from excessive sunbathing. They can discuss some of the cultural, moral, environmental and spiritual issues relevant today, e.g. equal opportunities or sustainable development.

The National Curriculum provides non-statutory guidelines for Key Stages 1–4 for PSHE and citizenship to encourage learners in:

- Developing confidence and responsibility and making the most of their abilities.
- Preparing to play an active role as citizens.
- Developing a healthy, safer lifestyle.
- Developing good relationships and respecting the differences between people.

At Key Stage 3 and 4, the citizenship curriculum focuses on a deeper exploration of the moral concerns and public policy that are part of today's world. It includes an understanding of the way government works and how society is structured. These are both taught through other curriculum areas, for example, health, safety and hygiene in PE and DT, or social, ethnic and cultural diversity in History or Geography, or arguments for and against genetic engineering in English or Biology.

Your role in PSHE and Citizenship

By encouraging learners to understand themselves, listen to others, and manage their relationships on a daily basis, you are already helping them to develop the necessary skills and knowledge. However, you should also be aware of the PSHE and Citizenship curricula for the age group you work with, so that you are prepared for the learning opportunities that will arise during any part of the school day. Keep yourself updated on current issues so you can contribute to discussion. Here are some other ways that you may be involved in the delivery of these curriculum areas:

- Circle Time (Moseley, 1999). This is a whole-school approach to behaviour and emotional and social development, which focuses on a positive approach, sharing, openness and social skills, using golden rules and discussion. Pupils are encouraged to take part in formalised discussions where they learn to listen to and empathise with each other.

- Social skills training.
- Friendship coaching ("what is friendship?") and talking through common scenarios like: 'What do you do if your friend steals something/ you don't get invited to a class party/ someone says you can't play?'
- Role-play activities.
- Assemblies or collective worship.
- Stories, myths and fables.
- School council – this is an elected body made up of pupil representatives and sometimes staff. It helps pupils to make a formal contribution to the running of their school.
- After school/lunchtime activities (sport, culture, hobbies, music). Many teaching assistants run clubs and activities of all kinds.
- School trips and holidays. These often give teaching assistants the opportunity to spend time with pupils outside formalised learning.
- Playground discussion and activities. These are often occasions when pupils will talk in confidence with teaching assistants.
- Volunteer in the local community.
- Mediation or mentoring.

The PSHE curriculum also offers opportunities to deal with bullying issues.

Bullying

Many schools include guidance on preventing bullying and harassment within their behaviour policy, although some have separate guidelines. As a teaching assistant you have a key position. You will often be working with children who are vulnerable to bullying and you will frequently be in a position where you can see things that other staff might miss. Pupils are also more likely to confide in you. You need to be particularly aware of the repeated nature of some bullying – particularly the kind of low-level harassment that can make a child's life a misery.

Recently concern has been expressed about cyber-bullying, or using e-mail, mobile phones and texting to frighten, harass, intimidate or humiliate others. Girls are more likely to be the target of this than boys, and it can be the most pervasive form of bullying because it targets children in their home life. Government guidance on cyber-bullying recommends that:

- All schools should have policies.
- All ICT is monitored.
- Parents must ensure children understand how to use ICT safely.
- Young people should never give out personal details electronically.
- They should report offensive material to teachers or adults then delete it.

(http://www.dfes.gov.uk/bullying/)

You can play a part in monitoring this form of bullying and in listening to children's concerns and worries. Children are frightened to speak out, so it is important to try to break the culture of silence.

Teachers and teaching assistants can also be the target of this type of unpleasantness, and it can affect their health and even destroy their careers. There is more information on this topic at www.anti-bullyingalliance.org.

Good practice in combating bullying involves:

- Zero tolerance for bullying of any kind.
- Following school bullying policy procedures and making sure pupils know and use the support available to them.
- Promoting a safe and tolerant environment.
- Helping children to socialise and make friends.
- Discussing issues of bullying with children.
- Monitoring friendship groups and children's social behaviour in class.
- Monitoring playground behaviour and break time activity.

As children grow and develop they need to learn to socialise, often by trial and error. All friendships have their ups and downs and children do have hard lessons to learn in life. However, you must use your judgement and intervene if a child really needs support. Also, remember that on very rare occasions teaching staff or midday supervisors can use bullying behaviour. There should be zero tolerance of this too. Further information on bullying can be found on the Kidscape website at www.kidscape.org.uk. There is an interesting discussion about the destructive nature of bullying by girls in Simmons (2002).

Serious behaviour problems

Bullying, fighting, making racist comments, swearing at teaching staff, destroying equipment and leaving class without permission are always serious behaviour problems. You should be working with a teacher to deal with these. Pupils who are violent towards other pupils and staff, engage in drug-taking, or who show persistent disruptive behaviour can be permanently excluded from school. Always record and report all incidents to the relevant member of staff. There is extensive and detailed guidance for teaching assistants on all aspects of managing behaviour in both Fox (2001) and Webster Stratton (1999).

Supporting learners with individual emotional and behavioural difficulties

Some learners have more severe and long-term behavioural difficulties. Such learners may include those who:

- have experienced considerable disruption in their personal lives, or have been subject to chronic stress because of family break-down or illness, social difficulties or disorganised parenting. These pupils may have difficulties with managing feelings and have no set boundaries for acceptable behaviour. They may find it hard to cope when boundaries are set for them. They need help to de-escalate their feelings and responses by a firm, non-confrontational approach and consistent handling. They need to build trust and security.

- have a medical or neurological condition which affects behaviour, such as AD(H)D, Autism or Fragile X Syndrome. Even diabetes can have an impact on behaviour if blood sugar levels are not regulated successfully.

Sometimes behavioural difficulties are the result of unrecognised learning difficulties, like dyslexia, a motor difficulty like dyspraxia, or the frustration caused by an inability to communicate effectively when a pupil has a speech and language difficulty. It is always vital to look at a pupil profile as a whole and to meet their learning needs, before labelling them as a behaviour problem.

You may be involved in implementing a behaviour support plan for individual learners. A consistent team approach with accurate feedback and record keeping is vital here.

Specific behaviour problems

Autism and Asperger's Syndrome

These have very specific effects on behaviour. You have already looked at Asperger's Syndrome in the previous chapter. If you are working with a learner with autism you should consult a member of staff or specialist book. If you are working with learners with Asperger's Syndrome, you must use a very precise approach. This needs to be planned in advance, using proactive rather than reactive management. It is easier to avoid a difficult situation than deal with it when the learner has become upset, distressed or unwilling to cooperate. Here are some points to remember when dealing with learners with autism or Asperger's Syndrome.

1. Inflexible thinking means that learners find it difficult if routines and arrangements change. They often create a rigid picture in their mind of what will happen. They may get distressed or angry if something different happens. Try to keep routines as predictable as possible and prepare well in advance for any changes so they have an alternate mind picture. Use obsessions or interests as comforters in this situation.
2. They may appear cheeky because they answer a rhetorical question as a fact. ("How many times have I told you to put your hand up?" Answer: "27"). Check that communication is clear and unequivocal and everyone understands the way they should

respond. Discourage too much verbalising of thoughts as it can be disruptive in the classroom. Teach what to say, what not to say, and when.

3. Use a rule-based approach as opposed to talking through motivation or feelings: "This is the rule here", not "You mustn't do this because you are upsetting the other children". You can talk through feelings as part of social skills training.
4. Use obsessions as rewards and incentives.
5. Use social stories (talking through procedures and activities in advance) using a story format to help (Gray, 1999; Rowe, 1999).

Attention problems

You may encounter children in school who find it hard to concentrate and are restless and fidgety. Richard Restak, an American neuropsychiatrist, feels that this may be a by-product of modern society, where children have to sit still and learn formally for long periods of time instead of learning actively through play, or because they are use to seeing fast-moving images on TV (Restak, 2003). It can sometimes be a result of abuse, upset or trauma, when children have become used to high levels of emotional arousal. Inability to concentrate is also a side effect of anaemia or of depression, which is becoming more common among young children.

Attention problems can also be part of other conditions such as Tourette's Syndrome, or autism, or accompany Specific Learning Difficulties. There has been some research into the effects of certain foods on concentration and behaviour too, although no definitive conclusions have been reached.

Attention Deficit (Hyperactivity) Disorder (AD(H)D)

For some children attention problems are more long-term. They have great difficulty concentrating for any length of time, are easily distracted, constantly on the go and very impulsive. This is referred to as Attention Deficit (Hyperactivity) Disorder (AD(H)D). Pupils with AD(H)D can be demanding and disruptive in the classroom, so it is important that you have a good understanding of their difficulties and the methods used to support them.

Issues in support

The whole subject of the identification of AD(H)D is a controversial one. Sometimes learners who have a more active or kinaesthetic style of learning are at risk of being labelled with AD(H)D, because they are constantly fidgety and on the go. Providing them with more opportunity for learning by doing, physical activity breaks, and various 'keep you occupied' objects like worry beads or squeegy balls can be effective. Boys are also more likely to be diagnosed with AD(H)D – according to a contemporary American newspaper "Girls get extra school help while Boys get Ritalin".

Richard Restak, the neuroscientist, believes that AD(H)D may be the normal response of the brain to the demands of the modern fast-moving world (Reslak, 2003). There are two kinds of Attention Deficit Disorder: hyperactive or AD(H)D, and passive or ADD. Learners with ADD are not hyperactive, but still have the same difficulties with concentration and attention. In practice, the term AD(H)D is generally used to cover both types. It is easier to diagnose the hyperactive variety because it is more obvious. However, both involve the neurochemistry of the brain and mean that information isn't processed or communicated to other parts of the brain effectively.

Until recently, learners with AD(H)D were prescribed a stimulant like Ritalin to correct the neuro-chemical imbalance. Now other types of medication are used. The whole issue of medication is a sensitive one. Some experts think that AD(H)D is learned behaviour and we should not be medicating young people unnecessarily. One of these, Sami Timini, a child psychiatrist, thinks that AD(H)D is a cultural construct, a 'dumping ground' that allows all of us to "avoid the messy business of understanding human relationships and institutions and their difficulties, and our common responsibility for nurturing and raising well-behaved children" (Timimi, 2005). However, for many children medication is essential so that they can process and learn new behaviour efficiently.

Assessment
AD(H)D cannot be identified by any single scientific test but is recognised through behavioural observation and a developmental history. Although schools can supply information from observations, AD(H)D should always be diagnosed by a psychologist or medical practitioner because it is a recognised disability.

Effects on learning and behaviour
Learners with AD(H)D tend to:

- not pay attention or listen
- distract others
- rush into tasks without thinking
- talk over others
- exhibit out-of-seat behaviour
- be disorganised
- not finish tasks
- not follow details
- be restless
- be unpopular with staff and peers because they are disruptive.

Strategies for support
Learners with AD(H)D can be extremely challenging in the classroom. The kind of support they need is very specific. As a teaching assistant you may be involved in any of the following approaches:

- Involve the learner in managing their behaviour so that they have a vested interest.

- Teach organisational skills.
- Teach self-awareness through the Cognitive Behavioural approach, to try to develop an internal sense of control.
- Use their interests positively.
- Use distraction and time out activities like the computer.
- Use stop, wait – think, and have a quiet area in the classroom to withdraw to.
- Give them praise in front of their peers.
- Recognise that they need a stimulating environment and provide stimulating activities.
- Use worry beads, squeegy balls, etc.
- Teach one skill at a time, or break things down into steps and build in a chance to succeed.
- Use prompting and one-to-one teaching assistant support to keep on task.
- Have a well-structured class environment with minimal rules, consistently enforced.
- Label the behaviour, not the learner.
- Give immediate and instant feedback with a relevant reward – not a future promise.
- Set up positive interactions (Eco Systemic). Try to wipe the slate clean and start each day afresh.
- Use a team approach to keep staff stress levels to a minimum.
- Monitor any medication.

Special Schools and Special Units (Pupil Referral Units)

Some learners with persistent and severe emotional and behavioural difficulties will be educated in a Special School where they can be given appropriate high-level support. Others are placed temporarily in a unit run by the LA Behaviour Support Service, or sometimes a private support service. Teaching assistants are used very successfully in these units, to provide tailored support and curriculum access for these learners. They are also involved in implementing structured re-integration programmes when pupils go back to their mainstream schools.

Learners with emotional and behavioural difficulties are often the most difficult to include, because compared to learners with, for example, a physical disability, people tend to think they are doing it deliberately. They need sensitive and appropriate handling and a sense of stability and consistency in their lives. Staff who work with these learners have to recognise it is a demanding and stressful job and they need plenty of opportunity to share their concerns and to de-stress. Dealing with these learners should always be collaborative.

As a teaching assistant, you should not be child-minding a learner with behavioural difficulties, but be part of a skilled team managing responses and solutions. You may be asked to undertake an observation of a child's behaviour. There is an excellent section on observation in Fox (2001).

Key reading

Key titles are given in bold.

Bailey, R. (Ed.) (2000) *Teaching Values and Citizenship Across the Curriculum*, London: Kogan Page

Clough, N. and Holden, C. (2002) *Education for Citizenship, Ideas into Action: A Practical Guide,* London: Routledge

Goldthorpe, M, Buchanan-Barrow, P, Phillips, M (2006) *Sharing Books for Social and Emotional Understanding*, Learning Disabilities Association

McNamara, S. and Morton, G. (2001) *Changing Behaviour. Teaching Children with Emotional and Behavioural Difficulties in Primary and Secondary Classrooms,* London: David Fulton *[Full of ideas and practical suggestions.]*

Rief, S. (2002) *The ADD/ADHD Checklist,* New Jersey: Jossey Bass Wiley *[Very practical manual packed with relevant information.]*

Swale, J. (2006) *Setting the Scene for Positive Behaviour in the Early Years*, London: David Fulton

References

Key references are given in bold.

Ayers, H., Clarke, D. and Murray, A. (1995) *Perspectives on Behaviour: A Practical Guide to Effective Interventions for Teachers,* London: Taylor & Francis *[Overview of theories relating to behaviour.]*

Bandura, A. (1997) *Self-efficacy: The Exercise of Control,* New York: W.H. Freeman

Beck, J. and Beck, A. (1995) *Cognitive Therapy: Basics and Beyond,* Guildford: Guildford Publications *[Description of therapy.]*

Bowlby, J. (1988) *A Secure Base: Parent-Child Attachment and Healthy Human Development,* New York: Basic Books *[Updated review of the theory.]*

Bronfenbrenner, U. (1979) *The Ecology of Human Development: Experiments by Nature and Design,* Cambridge, MA: Harvard University Press

Canter, L. and Canter, M. (2001) *Assertive Discipline: Positive Behaviour Management for Today's Classroom,* 3rd Edition, Los Angeles: Canter & Associates

DfES *Guidance on the use of Restrictive Physical Interventions for Pupils with Severe Behavioural Difficulties* London: DfES LEA/0264/2003

Fox, G. (2001) *Supporting Children with Behaviour Difficulties – A Guide for Assistants in Schools,* London: David Fulton *[Comprehensive manual providing clear description of behavioural difficulties with practical suggestions and strategies.]*

'Girls get extra school help while Boys get Ritalin', *USA Today,* 29 August 2003.

Goleman, D. (1996) *Emotional Intelligence,* London: Bloomsbury

Gray, C. (1999), http://www.thegraycenter.org *[Carol Gray's website – originator of social stories.]*

Kohlberg, L. (1981) *The Philosophy of Moral Development, Moral Stages and the Idea of Justice,* London: Harper and Row

Moseley, J. and Tew, M. (1999) *Quality Circle Time in the Secondary School,* London: David Fulton

Restak, R. (2003) *The New Brain: How the Modern Age is Rewiring Your Mind,* Philadelphia: Rodale Books *[Looks at the effects of fast-moving images on concentration and attention.]*

Rogers, B. (2002) *Classroom Behaviour: A Practical Guide to Effective Teaching, Behaviour Management and Colleague Support,* London: Paul Chapman *[Comprehensive review of Bill Rogers' approach.]*

Rowe, C. (1999) 'Do Social Stories Benefit Children with Autism in Mainstream Primary Schools?', *British Journal of Special Education,* March 1999, vol. 26, no. 1

Schaffer, H. (2002) *Social Development,* Oxford: BlackwellSimmons, R. (2003) *Odd Girl Out – The Hidden Culture of Aggression in Girls,* New York: Harcourt *[Examines social interaction among groups of girls.]*

Timimi, S. (2005) *ADHD: The Medicalisation of Naughty Boys, Human Givens Journal,*vol. 12, no. 2, and discussion available at: http://www.psychminded.co.uk/news/news2005/oct05/ADHD%20is%20biobabble.htm

Webster-Stratton, C. (1999) *How to Promote Childrens' Social and Emotional Competence,* London: PCP *[Very practical hands-on manual for teachers and teaching assistants, which looks at strategies for helping children develop their social and emotional competence. Includes lots of suggestions for positive behaviour management. Includes a useful chapter on the importance of parents in a child's education.]*

http://www.behaviour4learning.ac.uk/

www.Team-teach.co.uk

15 Professional development and training

You have already looked at a professional code of practice for those working as teaching assistants. This chapter focuses on some of the core skills you will need to use when you work in this field.

Improving your skills

Reflective practice

Teachers continually monitor and analyse their practice to find ways to improve and develop teaching and learning in the classroom. They are always looking for ways to teach more effectively. One of the best and worst aspects of teaching is to be in constant search of improvement!

As a teaching assistant, you may be working within a strict format or you could have the freedom to choose or adapt the way you work with learners and the materials you can use. Whichever is the case, you need to become a 'reflective practitioner' yourself, so that you can vary, adapt and extend the way you work to make it relevant and success-ful for every learner. This is particularly important when you work with learners with additional needs.

Here are some guideline questions that may help you to reflect on your practice and can form the basis of discussions with a teacher after the activity:

- Did everyone learn?
- If not, why?
- What did they learn?
- Did we all achieve what we wanted to?
- Was the activity at the right level for all?
- Could I have explained it better?
- Could I have used different resources?
- Could I have adapted the learning environment?
- Was the grouping right?
- Was the teaching method effective?
- Did I cater for individual needs?
- Could I have used help from anyone?
- What did I learn?
- Did I manage behaviour adequately?

As you become more experienced you will learn to do this automati-cally, but you can start by thinking about some of the above questions each time you work with pupils. Self-evaluation is important for everyone,and is the basis of the current Ofsted inspection process.

Reflective journal

You may be asked to keep a reflective log or to reflect on work-based tasks as part of a teaching assistant qualification. Jennifer Moon describes this process as "personalising or deepening the quality of learning" as it enables you to record and think about what you have learned (Moon 1999). You can find more information about reflective writing in Cottrell (1999) or online at:

http://www.ucd.ie/teaching/good/lea2.htm.

Appraisal and performance management

You should also reflect in a broader way on your working practice to ensure that you are happy and successful in your role. When you have completed a certain amount of time in school you should be offered a review of your job, known as appraisal or performance management. This is when you meet with your manager and discuss your views on how the job is going. It is an opportunity for you both to bring up any successes or concerns from your practice. It is easier if you can complete a self-review or reflection first to take to the meeting. This may focus on:

- What you do well
- Successes you have had
- Problem areas
- Organisation of your time
- Resources available
- Training issues
- Career development
- Comments from other colleagues
- Teamwork issues
- Personal targets or objectives.

At the review meeting you will have a chance to discuss these issues, look at your job description again, and set new targets for achievement by the next appraisal session. You may also have an observation of your practice as part of the performance management cycle (this should always be agreed by you in advance). Reviews are usually a yearly procedure but if you have not had one in that time you could ask your line manager to set one up.

Constructive feedback

Just as you will reflect on your own practice, you need to develop the ability to take constructive feedback on your performance from a manager, colleague, college tutor or pupil. After all, children have to take it from you every day! When you have an emotional stake in your work it can be hard to receive feedback on your practice, particularly if it is not all positive. However, it is always useful to use someone else's perspective to help you think about your own practice. Listen to what is said and explain your own point of view

Observation and active research in the classroom

Observing in the classroom is a very useful part of your professional practice, and is an absolutely key task when working in an Early Years setting. You may do this informally by watching how other staff teach and support, or by noticing the strategies pupils use to learn. You could be asked to undertake more formal observations to see how a particular part of the curriculum is delivered, for example a numeracy/literacy lesson or a science investigation. The best way to do this is to use a form to note down all the activities during the lesson from warm-up to end. You might need to monitor how effective certain teaching and learning methods are with individual learners by tracking one particular child, or may be asked to check on a pupil's progress by using a checklist or tick sheet. It is important to be professional and objective when undertaking any observation and to make sure you are clear about the reasons for observing.

Active research is a development of this concept when you use observation and reflection of your own practice to investigate a subject in more detail. You might want to focus on an aspect of teaching, learning or behaviour, the use of a resource or the layout of the classroom environment during activities. You can try out different approaches to see what is effective and then analyse the results.

Using ICT

ICT has now become an integral part of the whole curriculum, rather than being taught in isolation. You will see pupils using ICT in every subject area. If you work in school you need to become familiar with and confident about using ICT because you could be working with any type of technology from tape recorders, OHPs and digital cameras to communicators or computer software. Some schools make a great deal of use of e-learning and put homework, class and subject pages on an intranet. Most have their own Web page. In others you may be required to do your record keeping on a computer.

Although many teaching assistants are experts in the use of ICT, sometimes the whole idea of technology can be daunting, particularly if you are above a certain age! Like anything else, the best way to learn is by doing. Try to find time to just try out and practise using the equipment and ask when you need help. Most schools have used New Opportunities Funding (NOF) to ensure staff are trained in using basic ICT. This can be delivered in school or by an outside course. You could also try your local Adult Education Centre for details of introductory courses.

As you become more confident about ICT you should be familiar with:

- Safety issues, including the use of the Internet.
- Use of word processing.
- Saving and managing files.
- Loading and using software relevant for the learners you support.

- Accessing the school web pages, if appropriate.
- Using:
  - e-mail
  - administrative software for record keeping
  - packages like *SuccessMaker* to support literacy or numeracy
  - a good search engine on the Internet
  - a digital camera
  - roamers
  - interactive whiteboards.

Your job may also require you to learn to use specialist equipment for learners with individual difficulties, e.g. brailling machines or communicators.

> "I support a learner with AD(H)D who is really good on the computer. I have learned a lot by working with him and he has benefited from having to explain and show me (slowly!)."

Study and organisation skills

When you use effective study and organisational skills it is not only of benefit to you yourself but helpful to pupils that you work with. All these suggestions are designed to be used with learners. If you are delivering Literacy Progress Units, you can develop your own skills in information retrieval and writing organisation by understanding and practising these skills while you are teaching the units.

Finding and using information

There are so many sources of information nowadays, because of the Internet and the increase in paper-published material, that it is essential to be able to access and use information efficiently and effectively. As a professional you have a responsibility to try to keep yourself updated. Here are some of the sources of information you may find, with some tips on how to use them. Remember that with any information source you need to consider possible bias; in other words, how accurate and subjective is this information? Who has produced it and why?

Other educational professionals
Your first source of information should be your colleagues. Sometimes we are so busy looking for printed information that we overlook the people we work with, who may have a wealth of experience or expertise. Look beyond your school too.

Staff development or Inset training
Staff development and training can range from informal sessions held at school to courses that lead to qualifications held at colleges or by training providers. One of the best reasons for attending an outside course is that you will meet other teaching assistants there who have

different experiences from your own. You will also find it easier to think outside of your own school environment.

Learners' observations and discussions

Pupils can often give you very valuable insights into the way they learn and the teaching methods that suit them best.

DCSF publications

The government produces vast amounts of information for schools, some of it statutory and some of it for guidance only. It is a common complaint from teachers that they cannot keep up with paperwork *and* have time to teach, so you shouldn't even attempt to read it all. There is some really useful and easy to access information on Teachernet and the Standards website. Check what is essential with colleagues.

LA material

From pamphlets to training programmes, many LAs produce excellent materials on all aspects of education. These may be found in local professional development centres, via the support services or on their Internet sites.

Schools

School websites may also include useful material to share on delivering certain parts of the curriculum or some expertise they have in supporting groups of learners

Books, journals and newspapers

Your school, college or local library will contain books on almost every aspect of teaching and learning and every type of additional need. Some are practical 'how to' manuals, while others are theoretical works aimed at educational researchers. Starting with a practical book and working to the theoretical is usually easier. Get into the habit of jotting down your thoughts or examples from your practice as you read. Make sure you note the author, title and page numbers if you want to take detailed notes.

There are some excellent articles in newspapers and magazines that often summarise some new research finding or approach. Most daily newspapers are also available on line. Journals like *Child Education* or *Special Children* have an educational focus. When you read these you need to cultivate the art of critical reading, which means asking questions like "Do I agree with this, based on what I see in the classroom? What is the author trying to achieve? What evidence is given?", rather than accepting everything at face value. Remember that your own classroom observations based on your practice are just as valuable.

The *Times Educational Supplement* (TES) includes useful reviews and articles and includes promotional advertisements for publishers and other organisations. TES online has a useful chat room that enables you to share practice with other professionals. When you are supporting in a curriculum area that you are not familiar with, for example science or technology, it is often easier to look at books aimed at younger children that include diagrams and pictures, just to give you a grounding in the subject. Used sensitively, they can be helpful for older pupils too.

Also the *Guardian* publishes an educational supplement on Tuesdays.

TV, radio and video

Some extremely valuable programmes are broadcast on all channels, including *The Learning Zone* (which includes Open University programmes) and *The Learning Curve* on Radio 4. The BBC website enables you to listen again to many of its programmes. Other channels have some excellent programmes that focus on contemporary issues, like early learning or autism. Teachers' TV is an innovative television channel and website for teachers and schools where you can pick up information and new ideas.

Freebies from businesses and organisations

Many organisations have produced free material to support the national curriculum, e.g. Tesco and I CAN for Language Development, the Army for Maths and Barclays Bank for PSHE and Citizenship.

Charities and disability organisations

These often produce pamphlets and training packs.

Internet

You can find just about anything on the Internet. However, you need to be discriminating when you use 'the Net'. Because anyone is free to put information on it, you could find information there that is totally misleading or unsupported. Check any website to make sure it is a reputable organisation, is dated and the author is listed. Pupils can also be tempted to download information and pass it off as their own. Explain to them about plagiarism (see next page) and copyright.

Statistics and data

You might be required to look at test or assessment results for evaluation purposes, e.g. to see whether English SAT results have improved as a result of ALS sessions, or to record scores from testing.

Study skills

You may find the following information useful for both you and the learners you support.

Recording information

The skill of note taking is one which takes time to develop. It is always tempting to write too much down, whether you are listening to a speaker or reading something. The important thing is to understand first and record the minimum to help you remember. You could use:

- keywords

- different coloured pens, e.g. purple for dates or green for quotes
- mind maps which use a multi-sensory right-brained approach to learning
- abbreviations for common words (e.g. 'bc' for 'because')
- visual pictures (e.g. a quick sketch of a car exhaust for environmental pollution)
- your own anecdotes to illustrate a point.

Structuring information
You can use:

- brain storming, where you write down everything that you can think of about a subject. This is often done as part of a whole class activity
- concept maps that explore, plan, connect and understand several concepts (Caviglioni, 2000)
- mind maps that take a central idea and record all the different ideas associated with it (Buzan, 1993)
- linear planning, where you list things in order.

Personal organisation
You may find it useful to colour code work files for each subject or class. Some people find personal organisers or electronic organisers helpful. Learners who have difficulty with short-term memory may like to use a pocket Dictaphone, whilst some pupils find it easier to record information in diagrammatic form, e.g. as a flow chart. Encourage pupils to use colour-coded timetables and help them to develop a concrete concept of time so that they are aware of how long they have to complete work. You can help pupils to prioritise tasks and to develop regular work routines. Make sure pupils understand the importance of organising themselves so that they are working in the way best suited to their own learning preferences.

A useful website for information on study skills and learning is:

www.support4learning.co.uk/education/index.htm.

There is more information on specific study skills for Teaching Assistants in Ritchie and Thomas (2004).

Academic study
Here are some terms you may meet in your professional development:

- Critical analysis: Examining theories or ideas or the work of others by "presenting a case through providing reasons, using relevant evidence, comparing and evaluating alternative arguments, weighing up conflicting evidence and forming judgements on the basis of evidence" (Cottrell 2005)
- Theory: a collection of ideas to explain how or why something happens or might happen, based on evidence and reasoning
- Writing descriptively: describing what happens without any discussion or explanation
- Plagiarism: presenting the work or ideas of another person as if

they were your own without referencing them. It has become particularly easy to do this now that you can download and cut and paste documents from the internet. Colleges, universities and examining boards now have software that can recognise cases of plagiarism.

- Harvard referencing: referring accurately and appropriately to your sources will help you to avoid plagiarism. There are many different ways to reference depending on the subject area, but most university education departments use the Harvard System as a standard. It just makes it easier to find sources. It is the system used for the references in this book.

There is more useful information on concepts in academic study available from the Sussex language Institute at:

http://www.sussex.ac.uk/languages.

Learning styles and preferences

The study of how adults learn is known as andragogy. You have already looked at children's learning styles in Chapter 7, but you may also find it helpful to develop an understanding of your own learning style and preferences to help you to study more effectively.

The whole concept of learning styles has been the subject of considerable controversy and contention. Many of the published checklists used to identify learning styles are based on little research evidence and their effectiveness is unproven (LSDA, 2002). However, thinking about your own learning can be interesting and motivating, as long as you keep an open mind! You may also find David Kolb's explanation of how adults go through different stages as they learn helpful:

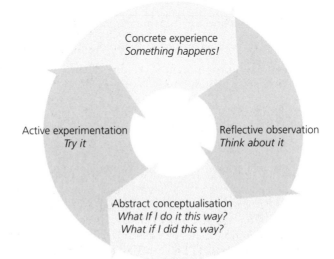

Concrete experience
Something happens!

Active experimentation
Try it

Reflective observation
Think about it

Abstract conceptualisation
What If I do it this way?
What if I did this way?

The Experiential Learning Cycle (Kolb, 1984)

But remember, as Oscar Wilde said, "Experience is the name everyone gives to their mistakes."

Key skills

The QCA has identified six main areas or key skills important for the workplace:

- communication
- working with others
- application of number
- Information Technology
- improving your own learning and performance
- problem solving.

You may find that you have to provide evidence of your ability or progression in these areas as part of a course through action planning and review. You will find help with this in Ritchie and Thomas (2004).

Teaching assistant qualifications – finding your way through the maze

Confused? You will be!

As a professional working in education, you should take advantage of all the opportunities available for training and further professional development. These can range from being mentored by an experienced professional to induction training, inset courses or degree and postgraduate work. Teaching assistants are usually very popular students at any educational or training organisation. They have a reputation for hard work, enthusiasm and very high standards!

The framework of teaching assistant qualifications can be confusing. In the past, individual local authorities often failed to recognise qualifications earned in other parts of the country. Some qualifications, like NNEB and STA, were seen to be unhelpful for teaching assistants supporting at Key Stage 3/4. In 2002, in an effort to standardise, the government introduced an NVQ for Teaching Assistants at Level 2 and Level 3, based on the National Occupational Standards introduced in 2001 (LGNTO 2001). They were under revision in 2006. Level 2 is intended for teaching assistants who are working under supervision, or who may be new to the role. Level 3 is for more experienced teaching assistants who have a considerable degree of autonomy, or who are working with learners with SEN. Both are offered by most of the relevant awarding bodies. Other courses still have different names and are set at different standards. It is therefore no surprise that headteachers are often as confused as anyone else about what course would be suitable for individual teaching assistants!

Choosing a qualification

There are several factors to take into account when you are deciding on what qualification to go in for.

Awarding Body

National awarding bodies include:

- OCR (Oxford, Cambridge & Royal Society of the Arts)
- CACHE (Council for Awards in Children's Care and Education
- Ed Excel
- OCN (Open College Network)
- City and Guilds
- NEC (National Extension College).

Individual universities are their own awarding bodies. Sometimes the name of the awarding body is confused with the title of the qualification.

Level

- First check to see if the qualification is a Further or Higher Education qualification. In general, Further Education (FE) qualifications are offered by awarding bodies like OCR or CACHE, whereas Higher Education (HE) ones are offered by universities and other Higher Education institutes.
- Find out what level it is within FE or HE. Confusingly, both have 1–3 levels.
- The level of the qualification is shown by its title (i.e. certificate or diploma) and its awarding body. A Cert HE from South Bank University will therefore be HE; a Cert from City & Guilds will probably be FE.
- At present, NVQs relevant for teaching assistants are only at FE level, although there are plans to have a Level 4 NVQ (equivalent to Level 1 HE), which would be at the same level as the first year of a degree.

Content

- Find out what the content (subject matter) is. Does it include information on learners with SEN, for example?
- Ask about the knowledge and skills provided by the course. Some vocational qualifications have been the subject of criticism, because candidates may not receive much input or underpinning knowledge to add to their own.

Age relevance

- Check which key stage the qualification is relevant to.

Practicalities

- Find out the time commitment involved in studying for the qualification. Are classes held during the day or evening? How much of it takes place within school and how much is outside?

Cost

- Find out the cost of the qualification and who is expected to pay.

You can investigate the kind of funding that is available through your school, LA, or training organisation.

- Some FE qualifications are free to those on income support.

Course admission requirements

- Most vocational qualifications are open access (open to everyone) if they are in a relevant workplace. Some institutions will screen candidates for other FE qualifications to make sure they have the necessary literacy and numeracy skills to succeed.
- Universities have their own admissions procedures and will set their own requirements, often on an individual basis.

Assessment

- Find out how the qualification is assessed: by exam or assignment or through a portfolio of evidence. Vocational qualifications, like NVQs, are nearly always assessed through evidence that occurs naturally in the workplace, rather than by exams, because they are *competency* based. In other words, you have to show you can do something, which is why they are ideally suited for people who are working at the job already. So if you are doing a vocationally assessed qualification, make sure you can provide the evidence needed from the work you do in school – such qualifications have VQ in the title.
- If you are taking an HE qualification you will need to develop the skill of essay writing.

Courses that have no assessment tasks are usually for training purposes only, and have no transferable credit. They are ideal if you want to improve your knowledge or skills but do not have time to complete assessment tasks. Many inset courses come under this category.

Transferable credit

All courses that are assessed (i.e. those that require you to complete and submit work) have a value that you can take away and 'bank'. This will be at FE or HE level. At HE level this is called 'Credit Accumulation Transfer' (CAT). CAT points can give you exemption from courses *at the same level*, but you may not get exemption from any new course unless the content of both courses is similar. For example, 120 CAT points in a civil engineering course will not get you exemption from the first year of a Foundation Degree in Learning, because the content will be different. HE CAT points are as follows:

- Level 1 (First year of a degree or Cert HE) = 120 CAT.
- Level 2 (Second year of a degree or Diploma or Foundation degree) = 120 (+ Level 1 = 240 CAT).
- Level 3 (Third year of a degree or Diploma) = 120 (+ 240 from Levels 1 and 2 = 360) = degree.

Points at FE level may be given in the form of UCAS points. In other words, they contribute towards the qualifications needed to apply to university.

Qualified Teacher Status (QTS)

You usually need three or four years of HE education to achieve Qualified Teacher Status. FE qualifications will only give you access to HE, not provide you with any HE credit. There are several ways you can get to qualify, either full-time or part-time. Many HE institutions offer work-based routes into QTS for teaching assistants. These usually involve at least one day in college and the remainder of the week working in school as a teaching assistant. The following are available routes, if the candidates also have English and Maths GCSE or equivalent.

- BA (Ed) (3 years)
- Foundation degree + Registered Teaching Programme (RTP) (4 years)
- A foundation degree + Yr 3 + Post-Graduate Certificate in Education (PGCE)
- A degree + PGCE
- A degree and Graduate Training Programme (GTP).

A list of courses and providers was published by the Teacher Training Agency in 2000, although there are many more options available now (TTA, 2000).

To be able to teach in a secondary school you need a degree level qualification in a curriculum subject, such as English, History or Science.

Higher Level Teaching Assistants

As a result of workforce remodelling, the government introduced the status of Higher Level Teaching Assistant (HLTA) to provide a level of teaching assistant with advanced skills. Like other TAs, HLTAs work under the supervision of teaching staff but they have a greater degree of autonomy and have more responsibility to implement and adapt teaching and learning activities. In September 2003, the DfES and the TTA (now the TDA) published Professional Standards for Higher Level Teaching Assistants. These standards set out exactly what a teaching assistant should know and be able to do to be awarded HLTA status. They cover:

- professional values and practice – the attitudes and commitment required
- knowledge and understanding – of the curriculum and the skills required to help pupils learn
- teaching and learning activities – the planning, assessment and monitoring of teaching and learning activities.

The Standards apply to all key stages and all teaching assistant work roles and are designed to support progression of teaching assistants to QTS.

The HLTA assessment process is carried out by regional assessors, funded through the TDA. There are two different pathways:

- a three-day preparation followed by a three-day assessment-only route, for those candidates who already have the knowledge and skills required

- a full training and assessment route, often linked to a foundation degree.

All candidates for HLTA must have achieved a Level 2 English and Numeracy qualification, e.g. Certificate in Adult Numeracy or GCSE. Candidates are visited in school by an assessor who will provide evidence of competence through observation, questioning teachers and prompting the candidate.

Detailed information on the whole HLTA assessment process is given on www.tda.gov.uk or in Rose (2005).

Career development for teaching assistants

In the past it has been very difficult for teaching assistants to follow any sort of progressive career path that rewards them for their skill, expertise and experience, without following the path to QTS. However, there are many teaching assistants who enjoy their job and do not necessarily want to teach, but have become dispirited by the lack of opportunity and financial reward in return for their commitment and expertise.

Now LAs are grading posts under the new Single Status arrangements, and with the advent of the HLTA, there should be far more opportunities for a career path. For example, some schools have appointed at the top grade:

- a lead teaching assistant to supervise the work practice of other teaching assistants
- a teaching assistant as Assistant SENCO to implement and monitor support for learners with SEN
- a teaching assistant to lead on implementing differentiation for learners in curriculum areas
- a teaching assistant who leads on ICT support for learners with SEN
- a lead teaching assistant for each curriculum area to coordinate and monitor practice.

"I've been a TA for nearly 10 years and I really enjoy my job. I work with learners who need extra support and help to succeed. I really like working one-to-one and I find it really rewarding to be able to make a difference, even if it's just a small one. I don't want to go into teaching – not yet anyway. I see how hard the teachers work and I have a young family so I want time for them too! I have done lots of courses on literacy and SEN and I find it really interesting to specialise in that area. I would just like the opportunity to have some career progression without having to get QTS."

Other teaching assistants find that their work in the classroom has given them a real interest in education and they find themselves drawn to a career as a qualified teacher. Such teaching assistants often make excellent teachers as they bring experience from outside the school environment and the perspective of a teaching assistant to their new role.

> **Headteacher:** "One of my teachers is an ex-TA who used to work with learners with SEN before she became a class TA. At the last Ofsted, the inspectors were really impressed by the way she moved all the children in the class on. I know it is because of her background. She has the ability to think about the learning of every child in an individual way, without losing her focus on the class as a whole."

National qualifications framework

HE	Level 4	Adv Cert (MA credits)	PGCE/ GTP				PGCE/ GTP
	Level 3 (6)		Year 3	RTP	2+2		Year 3
	Level 2 (5)	BA Ed Full time		Foundation Degree part time		Dip HE	BA/BSc
	Level 1(4)					Cert HE	
FE	Level 3	NVQ 3	*OCR Cert level 3*	*Ed Excel B Tec N Dip*	*CACHE Early Years Dip (NNEB)*	*City & Guilds Cert*	*A+ A/AS Level*
	Level 2	NVQ 2	*OCR Cert level 2*	Support Work in Schools Cert	*CACHE Cert*	*City & Guilds Cert*	GCSE
	Level 1	NVQ 1		Foundation Certificate e.g. *CACHE* or *OCN* or *WEA*			

These qualifications include QTS.

Examples of some past and present TA qualifications

Constructing a professional portfolio

It is always useful to keep a professional portfolio that reflects your work, in the same way that an artist keeps a record of their paintings. More recently, a professional development portfolio has become an essential part of graduate skills requirement. You can add to it over time and take it with you when you move to a new post. It will provide the basis for your CV. Your portfolio could eventually include:

- evidence of qualifications you've completed/are undertaking, with certificates
- courses and inset training you have attended
- your present job description
- past job descriptions
- any reflective or review notes you have made
- records of any observation made of your work
- books, articles and TV programmes consulted
- your ICT competence
- any individual areas of expertise (e.g. delivered LPU, supported learners with hearing impairment)
- any information on the progress of pupils you support that might be relevant
- the ways you have updated yourself on the curriculum areas you support.

Collecting evidence for a competency-based award

In simple terms, undertaking a competency-based award, such as an NVQ, means that you have to show evidence that you can do something in different ways and know how and why you are doing it. The competences are laid down in the qualification documents and you need to match these against what you are doing every day in your workplace. You can then gather evidence to show that you can meet these competences and annotate it to show that you have the necessary underpinning knowledge without involving yourself in lots of additional work. For example, NVQ Level 3 for Teaching Assistants, Units 3–7, Support the Use of ICT in the Classroom, requires you to:

- show that you can give support as needed to help pupils develop skill in the use of ICT
- know and understand the range of ICT skills needed by pupils and what can be expected from the age group with which you work.

All the awarding bodies include detailed guidance on the kind of evidence that you need to collect and how you should do this.

Key reading

Key titles are given in bold.

Alfrey, C. (Ed.) (2003) *Understanding Children's Learning – A Text for Teaching Assistants,* **London: David Fulton**

Burnham, L. and Jones, H. (2002) *The TA Handbook,* **Oxford: Heinemann,** *[Based on NVQ in Childcare in Early Years.]*

Cottrell, S. (1999) *The Study Skills Handbook,* **Basingstoke: Palgrave**

Caviglioni, O. and Harris, I. (2000) *Mapwise: Accelerated Learning through Visible Learning,* Stafford: Network Educational Press

Farmer, M. and Farmer, G. (2000) *Supporting Information and Communications Technology* London: David Fulton *[Written specifically for teaching assistants at Key Stage 1.]*

Fox. G. *A (1998)* *Handbook for Learning Support Assistants,* **London: David Fulton** *[A particular focus on supporting learners with Special Educational Needs.]*

Handy, C (1999), *Inside Organisations,* London: Penguin Books

Kay, J. (2002) *Teaching Assistants Handbook,* **London and New York: Continuum**

Rose, R. (2005) *Becoming a Primary Higher Level Teaching Assistant: Meeting the HLTA Standards,* **Exeter: Learning Matters**

Watkinson, A. (2003) *The Essential Guide for Expert Teaching Assistants: Meeting the National Occupational Standards at Level 3,* **London: David Fulton**

References

Key references are given in bold.

Buzan, T. (1993) *The Mind Map Book,* London: BBC Books

Cottrell, C (2005) *Critical Thinking Skills: Developing Effective Analysis and Argument,* **Basingstoke: Palgrave**

DfES/TTA (2003) *Professional Standards for Higher Level Teaching Assistants,* London: DfES

Local Government National Training Organisation (2001) *National Occupational Standards for Teaching Assistants,* London: LGNTO

Ritchie, C. & Thomas, P. (2004) *Successful Study: Skills for Teaching Assistants* **London: David Fulton**

http://www.teachers.tv/home.do
http://www.bbc.co.uk/

16 Practicalities

Working practice

You may be working in the same class every day, in which case it will be a fairly straightforward task to find out all the relevant information that you need. However, you could be moving between classes in the same age group, working across Key Stages supporting children with additional needs or working in one curriculum area only with several different teachers. Whatever your work pattern, it is essential for you to establish the ground rules and review the timetable with each teacher involved. In the inclusive school, your work practice must form an integral part of the holistic approach to the needs of all learners. As you become more experienced and your working relationship develops, you will take a larger part in the decision-making process in the classroom.

Although you will get some of your information from pupils, they will often enjoy telling you wrong information for fun! Make sure you know the start and finish times for lessons and how the teacher will be introducing you to the class. Check on entry and exit protocol for each class.

To begin with, it is getting the small things right that often make for a good relationship. All of these issues are dealt with in more detail throughout the book but the following should provide a useful reminder.

Summary – classroom ground rules

Arranging a review

Discuss with your teacher when it will be possible to review your working partnership and how you will do this. Set up a provisional timetable.

Location of resources

Give yourself time to make sure you have all the resources that you need. Check on the location of equipment so that you can bring anything that is not available in class, and make sure everything is in working order. Make sure you know where everything is stored and the procedure for putting it away. In most classes children are encouraged to tidy up as part of their experience, so don't do it for them!

> **Tip:** Take a resources box or 'goody bag' around with you. It can contain pens, pencils, dictionary, coloured overlays, glue stick, scissors, spell-checker, sharpener, Post-its, stickers, coloured paper, ruler, calculator, fill-in activity, books, highlighter and anything else you think that you might need.

Class timetables

Check on the daily, weekly and yearly timetable so that you know what is happening and when. Make sure you know of any class outings and trips, as these things often get overlooked and it is very frustrating to get to the classroom and find everyone is out for the day! There may be special events like book week when you need to dress up, so give yourself time to prepare your costume. Some teaching assistants produce a class diary to display on the wall to make sure that information is readily accessible for anyone coming into the classroom.

Location of activities

It is also important to ensure you know where all the class activities take place, including, Art, Music, Drama, and PE, as well as any individual work with support staff. Check on the changing arrangements for PE too. If you are supporting at Key Stage 3 and 4, you need to know the room number for every class that you support in.

Curriculum

Always check with the teacher to make sure you know which part of the curriculum is being taught, and how it fits into the overall scheme of work. Find out if they are hoping to cover any cross-curricular themes too, or if they are focusing on more than one area of the curriculum (like teaching literacy through science).

Assessment

Ask for the assessment timetable for the class and each subject area. You need to know when children have tests or exams and what format they take. Make sure you check on the individual assessment concessions that some learners may have. It is important to know in advance so that you can support them effectively.

Learning outcomes

Make sure you are absolutely clear on the learning outcomes for each individual activity, i.e. what the children are expected to have learnt or be able to do by the end of the session.

Record keeping

Find out what records the teacher would like you to keep. Ask the teacher what format these should be in.

Learners with additional needs

You will need detailed information and guidance on any learners you are working with who have Special Educational Needs and the techniques used to support them. This is dealt with in Chapters 12 and 13.

However, even if you are not working directly with such learners, make sure you are at least aware of all learners with additional needs in the classroom. It is important to have a consistency of approach at all times, particularly with children with behavioural difficulties. Be proactive and check with the teacher to make sure you follow the current approach to meeting their needs. You don't need a tremendous amount of detail; just ask if there are any particular strategies or approaches being used that you should know about.

Learners with additional needs may include children with:

- sensory loss – hearing or visual impairment
- behavioural/emotional difficulties
- specific learning difficulties like dyslexia or dyspraxia
- English as an additional language (EAL)
- high ability or special talents
- medical difficulties and physical disabilities
- social and communication disorders
- language difficulties.

Behaviour management

It is vital that you follow the school behaviour policy and that you are in tune with the behaviour management system used successfully by each teacher. Make sure you know the class rules, how the system was set up, and the sanctions and rewards used. Agree jointly how you deal with situations. Once again, consistency is very important in behaviour management issues. This is dealt with in detail in Chapter 14.

Breaks

You may need to share break time cover with your teachers, so make sure you know all the procedures for the playground and what happens if there is wet play.

Drinks and snacks

Find out if children have a regular snack time or are allowed to drink water during class. Some schools only allow fruit as snacks.

Coats and bags

Check on the facilities for hanging up coats and storing bags. This is particularly important at Key Stage 3/4, when children may have lockers in different areas of the school and may need help in organising their belongings.

Extra adults

Check that you know who else is in the classroom and why they are there. They may be working with children, carrying out observations, or monitoring teaching and learning. Other adults in the class could be parents, volunteers, support staff, other teaching assistants, students, members of the school management team or people from outside agencies.

Procedure for using stationery and calculators

Some children have elevated pencil sharpening to an art form as a distraction from work; some teachers may be concerned that children keep rubbing out unnecessarily. Teachers often have a classroom policy on the use of these items so make sure you discover what it is. There may also be policies on using ink pens or other types of pens. Some classes or teachers have informal policies on the use of calculators and laptop computers in class. Check on these too.

Marking completed work

Ask if you are allowed to mark completed work and, if so, how it should be done. Make sure you find out where completed work is kept. Assessment and feedback on work are a crucial part of teaching and learning. A good teacher will give a great deal of thought as to how they assess and feedback for each individual learner, so make sure you understand their thinking and follow their procedures.

Special programmes or teaching approaches

Find out if the teacher is following any particular teaching programme, like Plan/do/review or a thinking skills programme.

Leaving the classroom

You need to check on the procedure that children use to leave the classroom and make sure you follow it. Sometimes teachers use a card system so that they know where everyone is; if so, you will need it explained to you. Make sure you are clear whether you can give children permission to leave the classroom.

Homework

Find out about homework. You need to know what is expected, when it is given out, and when it is required to be in.

Contact with parents

Although you will be following the school policy on contact with parents, make sure you ask each teacher to discuss how they would like you to work with parents, particularly if you are supporting children with Additional Needs. Find out what goes home from each class, e.g. reading books, home–school contact books, newsletters, etc., and what your role will be in this. In some classes the teaching assistant fills in the home–school contact book and manages any reading book changeover. You need to know if this is part of your role and how you should do it.

Using your initiative

Don't be frightened to say if you need more explanation for something or if you know that you do not have the right skills to complete a task. It is far better to speak up, even though it may make you feel uncomfortable, than to struggle through and do it wrong. Remember, in school everyone learns!

As you develop a close working relationship with teachers, you should become more confident about using your own initiative. However, this will take time and will depend on the working relationship that you have with individual teachers. As they become more confident in your ability, and you increase your expertise, mutual trust will develop and you will become an even more valuable part of teaching and learning in the classroom.

A passport to work

The following pages are intended as useful checklist guides to help you gather relevant classroom and whole-school information. Photocopy them and fill them in or tick them as appropriate.

Passport to work

Classroom information

Health & safety • Fire drill rendezvous point • Medical information for children • Safety equipment
Classroom layout • For individual activities • Any special requirements for individual learners • Coats/bags
Resources • Location • Organisation • Tidying up procedure
Class timetable • Daily • Weekly • Activities outside classroom • Arrangements for PE • Special events • Off-site activities
Procedures • Permission to leave classroom • Toilet • Use of erasers, pens, sharpeners, calculators • Marking work • Completed work
Break time • Drinks/snacks • Wet play resources
Other adults • Collaborative procedures
Special programme/Teaching approaches • e.g. Highscope/Thinking Skills/Accelerated Learning
Planning meetings • Schedule

Equal opportunities • Classroom focus or issues
Curriculum policies
Use of ICT
SEN information
Homework • Procedures
Class targets
Behaviour management • System • Class rules • Sanctions and Rewards
Record keeping requirements
Assessment • Schedule • Individual concessions
Ideals, philosophies & goals
Liaison with home • Policy on contact with parents • Resources that go home • Home–school contact method
Procedure at beginning of day/lesson

Whole-school information

Prospectus/Staff handbook
Special designation
Governing body
School focus/targets
School Development/Improvement Plan
School family tree • Organisational structure • Location of each person
Communication system • Staff meetings • Newsletters/memos • Website • Staff notice boards
Health & safety • Fire drills • Accident procedures • Site security • Visitors procedure • Giving medication • Child Protection designated person • First Aiders • Hygiene requirements
School timetable • Dates of school year • Staff development days • Times of school day • Weather closure procedure • Timetable for school trips • Assemblies • Special events • Exact lesson times
Recording • Data protection requirements • Location of all records • Whole-school requirements

School policies: procedures
- Uniform, jewellery
- Behaviour (sanctions and rewards)
- Anti-discrimination issues
- Homework
- Use of resources/Internet
- Use of photographs of pupils

School policies: curriculum

Outline assessment timetable

Location and timetabling of resources
- ICT and booking schedule
- Photocopiers
- Books
- Library
- Other equipment
- Technician support
- Procedure for broken equipment

Personal work protocol
- Line Manager
- Reporting sick or staff absence
- Use of photocopier/telephone/Internet
- Continuing Professional Development Programme
- Appraisal procedure
- Dress code
- Times of work
- Social events
- Requirements for evening/outside work
- Staff room protocol (coffee money/birthdays)

Map of school
- Room locations
- Specialist areas (gym, hall, lunch)

Pupil transport to/from school: procedures

Break-time procedures
- Arrangements for lunchtime

Parent Teacher Association
- Programme
- Communication with parents

School clubs

Outside agency involvement

Whole-school meetings and assemblies

Learning activity prompt sheet

Before the activity starts	
Do you know:	All learning objectives?
	Subject knowledge required?
	Needs of individual learners?
	Any individual/group targets?
Do you check with learners that they have:	All the resources they require?
	Space to work?
	Suitable environment?
Do you know:	Assessment methods?
	Time-frame (share with learners: "we have 15 mins")?
At the start of the activity	
Do you:	Share learning objectives (visually if possible)?
	Provide clear directions and procedures?
	Give ground rules?
	Use learners' names?
	Provide an assessment of previous learning ("where we are at")?
	Help pupils to 'open' mental files by putting learning in context?
	• Relate new learning to old
	• Give purpose and relevance of the activity
	• Check understanding so far.
During the activity	
Do you:	Use active memory techniques?
	Monitor your body language?
	Use individual learning preferences if you can (use VAK, see pages 133–4)?
	Encourage language development?
	Teach curriculum language concepts explicitly?
	Use questioning techniques?
	Encourage self-directed learning?
	Promote independence?
	Maintain momentum?
	Include all learners?
	Keep the task at the right level and not over-teach the obvious?
	Adjust teaching? Extend some; reinforce others?
	Help pupils to construct new thinking?
	Give measured praise and encouragement?
	Maintain behaviour through a positive approach?
	Actively involve learner(s)?
	Let pupils self-evaluate?
At the end of the activity	
Do you:	Review, repeat and reinforce?
	Have a structured finish?
	Look forward to the next activity?
	Feedback to the teacher/record for later feedback?
	Evaluate?

Invigilation and school trips checklist

School trips

- Make sure that you know the relevance of the trip to each curriculum area.
- Check that you know the purpose and learning outcomes for the trip.
- Make sure that you exchange mobile phone numbers with other supervisory staff, if necessary.
- Check exact timings and exact places to meet transport.
- Check how the children are being divided up and supervised.
- If you have a group of your own, you should know any problems that your children might have, e.g. medical needs, behavioural difficulties or emotional needs.
- Make sure that you know and reinforce any expectations of behaviour.
- Ensure you know what work has to be completed during the trip.

Exam invigilation

Find out:
- The exact format and timing of exam.
- Which staff you will be invigilating with.
- Any special concessions for individual students.
- The regulations for each particular exam.
- What happens if candidates want to leave early?
- What happens if candidates arrive late?
- What happens if there is a crisis (e.g. a candidate taken ill or you taken ill)?
- Are toilet breaks allowed and how are they managed?
- Is food or drink allowed?
- Are calculators or other resources allowed?

During the exam

- Check that all mobile phones are switched off.
- Make sure that there is a visible clock.
- Give out candidate numbers if necessary.
- Make sure that every candidate has a question paper.
- Make sure that candidates are given the exact instructions for the exam.
- Make sure that paper booklets and extra paper are available.
- Produce an attendance register and a seating plan.
- Maintain silence.
- Walk around, quietly. No squeaky shoes.
- Keep an eye on candidates without obviously looking over their shoulder.
- Keep a record of any incident during the exam.

At the end of the exam

- Collect all papers and ensure that they are returned safely to the correct place.
- Make sure you know what candidates are allowed to take away with them.

Glossary

A

Academies	Publicly funded independent schools set up and run by sponsors, who provide £2 million of the capital costs for each, with the government providing the balance and funding the recurrent costs. They are designed to replace schools in challenging circumstances, or are set up as part of wider school reorganisation or where there is unmet demand for school places. Academies provide free education to secondary age pupils of all abilities, including provision for children with special educational needs, and have state of the art facilities, through which they offer a broad and balanced curriculum including a specialism.
AD(H)D	Attention Deficit (Hyperactivity) Disorder – a condition whereby a child has a short concentration span and is unable to stay on task.
Additional Needs	Learning needs that require extra planning and support.
ALS	Additional Literacy Support
Andragogy	The art of teaching adults
ASD	Autistic Spectrum Disorder – autism occurs in differing degrees of severity and in a variety of forms, including Asperger's Syndrome, which describes people at the higher functioning end of the autistic spectrum. Further information at www.nas.org.uk.
Asperger's Syndrome	At the higher end of the Autistic Spectrum Disorders (ASD) – individuals are of average or higher than average intelligence. People who are autistic have a disability that affects the way they communicate and relate to people around them. Further information at www.nas.org.uk.
Attainment Target (AT)	Sets out expected standards of pupils' performance at end of each key stage; pupils are assessed at ages 7, 11, 14 and 16.
Autism	Autism (Autistic Spectrum Disorders (ASD)) affects over 500,000 people. People who are autistic have a disability that affects the way they communicate and relate to people around them. The three main characteristics of autism are problems with social interaction, social communication and imagination. There is an autistic spectrum – from those who never learn to speak, to those with Asperger's Syndrome. Further information at: www.nas.org.uk

B

Behaviour Support Plan	A statement that sets out local arrangements for schools and other service providers for the education of children with behavioural difficulties.
Benchmarking	Finding a comparative standard
Boff	Boffin, derogatory term used by children to describe clever pupils

C

CAT	Computer Axial Tomography – method of brain scanning
CAT	Credit Accumulation Transfer
catheterisation	Medical procedure to release urine
Circle Time	Whole-school approach to behaviour and emotional development using formalised discussion
CLANSA	Certificate for Literacy and Numeracy Support Assistants. OCR qualification for teaching assistants.
Connexions	Service that provides a single point of access for all 13–19-year-olds to help them prepare for the transition to work and adult life.
CP	Child Protection
CRE	Commission for Racial Equality
CTC	City Technology College

D

DCSF	Department for Children, Schools and Families.
Designated Teachers	Advocates who liaise with other services on behalf of young people in care.
DfEE, DfES	Department for Education and Employment, Department for Education and Skills, predecessors of the DCSF.
Disapplied Pupils	The National Curriculum assessments have been designed to make sure that as many children as possible can be assessed. There may, however, be a small number of pupils who are not able to take part in some or all of the assessments, even allowing for the full range of arrangements that can be made. Usually this only happens if all or part of the National Curriculum is not suitable for a pupil because he or she has certain special educational needs. The assessments are designed to cater for most pupils with special educational needs.
Dyslexia	A learning difficulty of which the chief manifestation is a particular difficulty with reading and spelling. For more information go to: http://www.bda-dyslexia.org.
Dyspraxia	Generally recognised as an impairment or immaturity of the organisation of movement. Associated with this may be problems of language, perception and thought – further information from the Dyspraxia Foundation.

E

EAL	English as an Additional Language.
Early Years Profile	An assessment of a child's skills and abilities, usually made by a teacher within the first seven weeks of starting primary school. It shows teachers what a child can do when starting school and helps them to plan lessons and measure progress. Areas covered include Language and Literacy, Maths and Personal and Social Development.
EAZ	Education Action Zone – groups of 15–25 schools that aim to create new partnerships, raise standards and generate innovation within education. These groups of schools receive £1million a year for three to five years. An EAZ based on a single secondary school and its associated primaries will receive £350,000 a year.

	These smaller EAZs are only being set up in Excellence in Cities areas.
EBD	Emotional and Behavioural Difficulties – children who display these problems may be placed on the Special Needs Register and given extra support.
EFA	Essential fatty acids
ELG	Early Learning Goals
ELS	Early Literacy Support
epipen™	Used for emergency administration of epinefren for severe allergic shock, caused by, for example, a bee sting or peanut allergy.
ethos	Belief structure
EWO	Education Welfare Officer – person employed by an LA to help parents and LAs meet their statutory obligations in relation to school attendance.
Exposition	Teaching through explaining
EYP	Early Years Professional

F

Fair Funding	The term that describes the system of funding for schools introduced in April 1999, which sets the framework for the financial relationship between schools and LAs.
Family Literacy and Family Numeracy Courses	Offered by most Local Education Authorities, these courses let you and your child learn skills together, and separately, in small courses run in co-operation with local schools.
Federation of Children's Book Groups	A national, voluntary organisation that aims to promote enjoymentand interest in children's books and reading.
Feeder schools	Primary schools whose pupils are given priority entry to the secondary school in question on grounds of proximity
FLS	Further Literacy Support
Foundation schools	Type of state school introduced on 1 September 1999 by the School Standards and Framework Act 1998. These schools have more freedom than community schools to manage their school and decide on their own admissions. At foundation schools the governing body is the employer and the admissions authority. The school's land and buildings are either owned by the governing body or by a charitable foundation. Funding comes from the local authority (LA) which also pays for any building work.
Foundation Stage	Covers education provided from 3-years-old to the end of the Reception Year.
Fragile X	Hereditary condition that causes a wide range of impairment, from mild to severe learning difficulties.
Fresh Start	A school is given a 'Fresh Start' when it is closed and reopened on the same site under the normal school reorganisation procedures. Schools eligible for Fresh Start must be in Special Measures, have serious weaknesses, be subject to a formal local authority warning, or (for secondary schools) achieving less than a 15 per cent rate of pupils gaining at least 5 A*–C GCSEs over three years from a given date.

G

GCSE	General Certificate in Secondary Education
GTP	Graduate Teacher Programme – an employment-based training programme where schools can benefit from grant payments to help cover the salary costs of their trainees. Schools keen to become more involved in initial teacher training (ITT) can take on additional unqualified teachers and train them on the job. Entry to the GTP is competitive, with places allocated to the best schools and best graduate trainees in priority recruitment areas like London and shortage subjects. The Training and Development Agency (TDA) pays an additional grant to cover their training costs, and also pays for their final assessment for QTS.

H

HE	Higher Education
Hierarchical	Vertically structured layers of authority
HLTA	Higher Level Teaching Assistant
HMI	Her Majesty's Inspectorate, the core of Ofsted
Home–School Agreements	All state schools are required to have written home–school agreements, drawn up in consultation with parents. They are non-binding statements explaining the school's aims and values, the responsibilities of both school and parents, and what the school expects of its pupils. New parents are invited to sign a parental declaration, indicating that they understand and accept the contents of the agreement.

I

ibid	Latin term meaning 'in the same place'. Used in bibliographic references to mean that publication details are the same as for the previous reference.
ICT	Information and Communication Technology
IEP	Individual Education Plan or Programme
IiP	Investors in People – a national standard that can be used by any organisation to enhance the development of its people. The standard provides a coherent framework for whole-school staff development that links and supports other developments within the school.
in loco parentis	Latin term meaning 'in the place of a parent'. Usually used to refer to the role of a school or teachers.
Independent School Approved for SEN Pupils	A Special School equivalent of an Independent School, catering wholly or mainly for children with statutory statements of special educational needs. Has been approved by the DfES for SEN provision.
IQ	Intelligence Quotient

J

K

Kinaesthetic	Using movement
KS	Key Stage
KS 1, 2 etc	Key Stage 1, 2, etc.

L

laissez faire	French term, which in this context means overly permissive.
LA	Local Authority
Learning Card	A card issued to all children over the age of 16 to remind them of their continued access to careers guidance and information
LGNTO	Local Government National Training Organisation
Line manager	The person who has direct responsibility for the management of your job role
Link governor	The terms 'Link', 'Curricular' or 'Specific Subject Governor' are often used for governors who are given responsibility for specific subjects, e.g. ICT, Numeracy, Literacy, RE, SEN, etc. It is not a statutory requirement for subjects to have governors assigned to them, but it is considered good practice. 'Link governors' can also be the term used for governors who are the link between the LA and the school.
Literacy Hour	Daily hour-long lesson in primary schools given to the teaching of literacy
LMS	Local Management of Schools
LPU	Literacy Progress Units
LSC	Learning and Skills Council

M

Mathematics Lesson	Daily, normally hour-long lesson in primary schools given to the teaching of numeracy
MLD	Moderate Learning Difficulty
MRI	Magnetic Resonance Imaging – method of scanning the brain while it is working

N

NASEN	National Association of Special Educational Needs
National Curriculum Levels	All pupils in England undergo national tests and teacher assessments at ages 7, 11 and 14. The school will then send a report to parents telling them what National Curriculum Levels their child has reached in both tests and assessments.
National Literacy Strategy	A government initiative that aimed to raise standards of literacy for all children in infant, primary and junior schools. It tried to involve parents as much as possible. Now part of the Primary National Strategy
National Numeracy Strategy	A similar initiative to the National Literacy Strategy, aimed at raising standards of numeracy. Also now part of the Primary National Strategy
NFER	National Foundation for Educational Research
NGfL	National Grid for Learning – government-funded project to connect schools to the Internet and to provide learning materials for them via the World Wide Web. Responsible for Information and Communications Technology (ICT) in schools.
NIACE	National Institute of Adult Continuing Education
NLS	National Literacy Strategy

NNEB	National Nursery Examination Board
NNS	National Numeracy Strategy
NOF	New Opportunities Fund. A lottery distributor created to award grants to education, health and environment projects throughout the UK.
Non-Maintained Special for Schools	Independent Special Schools approved by the Secretary of State Education and Skills. They are run on a not-for-profit basis by - charitable trusts and normally cater for children with severe and/or low incidence special educational needs.
Notice to Improve	A school judged by Ofsted inspectors to be in difficulties, but not so severe as to be put in special measures, is given a Notice to Improve. The school is expected to address how to remove the causes of weakness and will be reinspected after a year.
Nursery Classes in State Primary Schools	These take children from the age of three or four and are open during school term time. They usually offer five half-day sessions a week. There must be one adult for every 13 children and staff are qualified teachers and assistants.
Nursery Phase of Education	Nursery schools provide education for children under the age of 5 and over the age of 2.
NVQ	National Vocational Qualification
O	
OCR	Oxford Cambridge and RSA awarding body.
Ofsted	Originally Office for Standards in Education; from April 2007 Office for Standards in Education, Children's Services and Skills
On roll	Number of pupils who attend a school
P	
PANDA	School performance and assessment data
para-educators	American name for teaching assistant
PAT	Phonological Awareness Training
PAT software	Pupil Achievement Tracker – uses national test results to graphically present a school's pupil achievement figures compared to national trends and schools of similar social make-up. The assessment software can also assist schools with setting pupil targets and was developed to take in data from the QCA's Diagnostic Software. This facility provides further analysis of National Curriculum Tests and optional tests against national trends.
PE	Physical Education
Pedagogy	The art of teaching children
Personal Education Plan (PEP)	PEPs are schemes developed for young individuals in public care, designed to support their education.
Personalisation	Concentrating on the needs of each pupil as an individual
PGCE	Post-Graduate Certificate of Education
PH	Physical Handicap – note: this term is no longer used.
Phonics	The relationship between basic sounds in language and the way they are represented in writing
physiological	To do with the workings of the human body

Playing for Success	Through 'Playing for Success', the DfES is establishing out-of-school hours study support centres within top football clubs and at other sports grounds and venues. The centres use the environment and medium of football to help motivate pupils who have been identified by their schools as being in need of a boost to help them get back up to speed in literacy and ICT.
Primary National Strategy	Government initiative and programme to raise standards of literacy and numeracy in primary schools
PRU	Pupil Referral Unit – any educational establishment set up and maintained by a local authority, which is specially organised to provide education for children who are excluded, sick or otherwise unable to attend mainstream school, and is not a Special School. PRUs are normally much smaller than schools
PSHE	Personal, Social and Health Education
PTA	Parent Teacher Association
Pupils with Statements of Special Educational Needs (SEN)	These Statements describe any learning difficulties that pupils have, and specify the extra help or equipment they need. Around 3 per cent of school pupils nationally have Statements. Some pupils with special educational needs are academically able, but schools face challenges in achieving Level 4 at Key Stage 2 for many pupils with SEN. The information on the numbers of pupils with SEN in each school helps you take this into account when looking at the school's results.
Pupils without Statements	These are other pupils registered as having special educational needs but their school meets their needs without Statements.

Q

QCA	Qualifications and Curriculum Authority
QTS	Qualified Teacher Status
QUIET	Quality in Education and Training Associates

R

RAISEonline	Single document issued on-line annually to schools combining the data in the PANDA and the Pupil Achievement Tracker
Reading Recovery	Structured reading intervention programme originating in New Zealand (with Marie Clay)
Registered Teacher Programme (RTP)	Employment-based training leading to qualified teacher status.
roamers	Computer hardware that can be programmed to move around.

S

Sanctions	Actions and penalties used to deal with improper or unacceptable behaviour.
SATs	Standard Assessment Tests. The official designation is 'National Curriculum Tests', but 'SATs' is the commonly used term.
SDP	School Development Plan
SEN	Special Educational Needs
SEN Code of Practice	This provides practical advice to LAs, Maintained schools, Early Years settings and others on their statutory duties to identify and make provision for children's special educational needs.

SENCO	Special Educational Needs Coordinator
SENDA	Special Educational Needs and Disability Act
Single Status Arrangements	Agreement affecting Local Government manual and non-manual jobs to evaluate and harmonise roles and standardise pay and conditions.
SIP	School Improvement Plan *or* School Improvement Partner
SLD	Severe Learning Difficulties
SMT	Senior Management Team
Socratic	Extending thinking through philosophical discussion.
Special Measures	When a school is judged by Ofsted to be failing, or likely to fail, to provide an acceptable standard of education, it is put in special measures and closely monitored by Ofsted for evidence of improvement.
Specialist Schools	Schools offering particular expertise in one of Technology, Language, Sports, Arts, Business & Enterprise, Engineering, Science, Maths & Computing, Humanities and Music. Further information: http://www.standards.dfes.gov.uk/specialistschools/
Springboard	Maths catch-up programme
STA	Specialist Teacher Assistant
STAC	Specialist Teacher Assistant Certificate
Stanford-Binet test	Test of intelligence
Statement	Pupils who are issued with a Statement have a serious SEN requirement and will receive extra assistance with their learning.
Statutory EAZ	A partnership of schools, private businesses and other local organisations established by the Secretary of State under the Schools Standards and Framework Act 1998. It aims to overcome local barriers to achievement and improve standards of education at each of the participating schools.
Study Support	Voluntary learning activity outside normal lessons that aims to improve children's motivation, build their self-esteem and help them to become more effective learners.
SULP	Social Use of Language Programme

T

TA	Teaching Assistant
TDA	The Training and Development Agency for Schools. It was known as the Teacher Training Agency (TTA) until 2005 when it was renamed to reflect the extension of its remit to cover training for school support staff.
Teacher Assessment	A formal assessment made by a teacher when a child is aged 7, 11 and 14. Used in England alongside the national tests to judge a child's educational progress.
TES	Times Educational Supplement
TTA	Teacher Training Agency – see TDA

U

V

VAK	Visual, Auditory and Kinaesthetic preferences – whether a child

	learns best through looking, hearing or moving and being physically involved.
Voluntary Aided Schools	Schools in England and Wales maintained in part by a charitable organisation – in nearly all cases the Church of England or Catholic Church – in partnership with the LA. The governing body is the employer and the admissions authority. The school's land and buildings (apart from playing fields, which are normally vested in the LA) will usually be owned by the charitable foundation.
Voluntary Controlled Schools	Schools in England and Wales that are maintained by the Local Education Authority, with a foundation (generally religious) that appoints some – but not all – of the governing body. Very similar to former controlled schools. The LA is the employer and the admissions authority. The school's land and buildings (apart from the playing fields, which are normally vested in the LA) will usually be owned by a charitable foundation.
Voluntary Grammar Schools	Grant-maintained, integrated schools in Northern Ireland that take both Protestant and Roman Catholic pupils.
Voluntary Maintained Schools	Schools in Northern Ireland that are mainly managed by the Catholic Church
W	
WISC	Weschler Intelligence Scale
X	
Y	
Z	
ZPD	Zone of Proximal Development

Note: Some of these entries have been taken from: 'Jargon Buster' at http://www.governornet.co.uk.

Index

A

A levels 141, 155, 196
ability 171
academic study 329–30
academies 79
accelerated learning 186
accident reporting 45
accommodation 100
active learning 169
AD(H)D see attention deficit disorder
addition 243–4
Additional Literacy Support 13, 88, 148, 149, 195
Advanced Skills Teachers 53
advisory staff 277
Afasic 278, 289
after school clubs 50
alcohol 38
algebra 248
All Our Futures 87
alphabet 211
ALS *see* Additional Literacy Support
analytic phonics 191
anxiety 293–4
appraisal 324
ARTS Alive! 87
AS levels 141
Asperger's Syndrome 296, 310, 316–17
assessment 62, 139–62, 192; of children with SEN 271–5; assessment of needs 256
assessment timetable 340
assimilation 100
associative law 242
Aston Index 146
Attention Deficit (Hyperactivity) Disorder (AD(H)D) 146, 152, 261, 316, 317–19
attention problems 317
attribution theory 127
auditory learners 133–4
autism 316–17
Autistic Spectrum disorder 128, 286–7, 316–17

B

Bandura, A. 105–6, 397
Beckham, David 114
behaviour 299–321
behaviour management 341
behaviour policy 307–8
Behaviour Support Service 76
behavioural difficulties 341
behaviourism 97, 197, 227
behaviourism and behaviour 303–5
Binet, Alfred 112–13

biological development 108-12
blending 207
Bloom's taxonomy 154–5
Bobo doll 105
books 327
brain damage 112
brain gym 186
break duty 44
breakfast clubs 124
breaks 341
British Dyslexia Association 278, 284
Broffenbrenner, U. 301
Bruner, J. 103–5, 140, 227
bullying 38, 67, 314–15
bursar 54
Butterworth, B. 229

C

CACHE 332, 336
calendar 57
career development 335–7
careers education 84
careers staff 53
caretaker 54
case worker 277
catch-up programmes 87–8, 89
centration 102
cerebral palsy 249, 264, 290–91
child & adolescent mental health service 278
child protection 43
child protection officer 278
Children Act 41
Children's Centres 80
Children's Trusts 74
Chinn, Steve 230
choice and consequences 310
chunking 245, 265
Circle Time 126, 128, 196, 313
Citizenship 91, 313
City and Guilds 13, 332, 336
City Technology Colleges 79
CLANSA 12
classroom 118–19
classroom ground rules 339–43
classroom rules/code of conduct 309–10
Claxton, Guy 230
closed questions 240
code of practice 39
cognition 198–9
cognitive acceleration 182–3
cognitive behavioural approach 305–7
cognitive development 96–7, 99–106

cognitive learning 129–33
cognitive preferences 133–5
cognitive styles 135
collaborative working 27–31
combined assessment 143
Common Assessment Framework (CAF) 140, 266
common core of skills 266
communications 55–6
community schools 79
commutative law 242
Complex Learning Difficulty 282
comprehension 212
conceptual difficulties in maths 252–3
confidentiality 37–8
conflict management 312
confrontation 312
Connexions 77, 278
conservation 102
consonants 209
context 212
contracts 36–7
count stick 241
counting stick 241
CRB see Criminal Records Bureau
creativity 184–5
Credit Accumulation Transfer 333
Criminal Records Bureau 42
criterion-referenced assessment 142
criticism 311
curriculum 62, 340
curriculum coordinators 52

D
data protection 61
De Bono, Edward 182
decomposition 239
Department for Children, Schools and Families (DCSF) 72, 73, 327
department heads 52
depression 293–4
DfES see Department for Children, Schools and Families
diabetes 291
diagnostic assessment 146
dictionaries 221
diet 112
differentiation 95–6, 164–7
digraphs 209
disability 256, 341
Disability and Discrimination Act (1995) 258
Disability Discrimination Act (2005) 257
discovery 169–70
discrimination 41,64
discussion with colleagues 159
display 121–2
distributive law 242
division 244–5
Down's Syndrome 290
Down's Syndrome Association 278, 290
drink 341
drugs 38, 112

dyscalculia 249
dyslexia 19, 249, 255, 263, 283–5, 341
dyspraxia 249, 285–6, 341

E
EAL see English as an Additional Language
Early Learning Goals 90, 143, 147, 191, 234
Early Learning Support (ELS) 13, 24, 88, 148, 149, 195
Early Years 12
eating disorders 293–4
Eco Systemic Perspective 301–2
education officer 277
Educational Psychologist 76–7, 269, 277, 282
educational visits 46
educational visits coordinator 53
Educational Welfare Officer 76, 269, 277
ELS see Early Learning Support
emotion 131
emotional and social learning 122–9
emotional development 96–7, 299
emotional difficulties 341
emotional intelligence 115, 127–9
emotional literacy 128
emotional safety 124–5
employed staff 54
English as an additional language (EAL) 19, 20, 31, 176, 203–4, 295–6, 341
environment 303
epilepsy 291
equal opportunities 62
equality 62–7
ethical issues 37–8
ethos 49
evaluation 156
Every Child Matters 15, 20, 33, 42, 54, 122, 140, 190, 258, 266–7
five outcomes of 33-4
exam invigilation 27
Excellence and Enjoyment 49, 87, 190
Excellence for All 13
Excellence in Cities 78
Excellent Teachers 53
exchange 239
expanded method 242, 244
experiential learning 169–70
extended schools 54–5, 80
extrinsic motivation 127

F
facilities manager 54
factorising 242
faculty managers 52
faith schools 79–80
federations 80
feedback to pupils 156–7
feedback to TAs 324
feedback to teachers 159–60
feeder schools 77–8
Feuerstein 181–2
fighting 315
finance officer 54

fire drill 45
first aid 45
Fischer, Robert 182
FLS *see* Further Literacy Support
formative assessment 145–6
foundation schools 79
Foundation Stage 143, 147, 185, 191, 234
Foundation Stage Profile 140, 142
14-19 curriculum 90
Fragile X Syndrome 316
Framework for Teaching Mathematics: Years 7, 8 and 9 247
freedom of information 61
friendship groups 172
full service schools 80
full-service extended schools 55
furniture 120
further education 332, 333, 336
Further Literacy Support (FLS) 88, 148, 149, 195

G
games 233, 237
Gardner, Howard 113–14, 230
gays 65
GCSEs 85, 141,196
gender 19, 135–6, 200, 302
gifted and talented children 125, 296, 341
Global Learning Difficulties 282–3
Golden Time 303–4
Goleman, Daniel 115, 127–9, 173, 306
good practice for TAs in supporting maths 231–3
Good Practice Guide *see Working with Teaching Assistants*
governing body 71
grammar 221
grammar schools 79
grammatical knowledge 211
graphic knowledge 210
graphophonic knowledge 208
grasshopper 230–31
grid method 242, 244
group work 125, 1716

H
handwriting 217
health and safety 41–2, 61
Health and Safety Act 41
health authority 77
Healthy Schools Initiative 124
hearing impairment 292–3, 341
hemispheres of the brain 110–11
hidden curriculum 50
hierarchy of needs 123
high scope 186
Higher Education 12, 332, 333, 336
Higher Level Teaching Assistant (HLTA) 15, 24, 26, 139, 334–5
home–school agreement 59
home–school liaison worker 53

homework 341
horizontal method of calculation 239, 243
Hospital School Service 77, 277
hospital schools 294

I
I Can 278
ICT 62, 325–6, 335; and thinking skills 183; and bullying, 314; and dyslexia 283; and SEN 263, 265, 275
IEP *see* Individual Education Plan
'in the flow' 184
inchworm 230–31
inclusion 19, 62, 255–97
Inclusion Coordinator (INCO) 259, 270, 281
Individual Education Plan (IEP) 269, 272–5
induction 37
information and communications technology *see* ICT
information sharing index 267
information, finding and using 326–7
Inset 326–7
instrumental enrichment 181–2
interactive teaching programs 228–9
interest groups 173
Internet 328
interrupted schooling 294–5
intrinsic motivation 127
intuition 110-11
inversing 243
investigational learning 169–70, 173
invigilation 349
ipsative assessment 143
IQ 113
ITP 232, 238

J
job description 36
journals 327

K
Key Skills 91, 331
Key Stage 1 234
Key Stage 3 National Strategy 88–9, 151, 155
Key Stage 3 National Strategy for mathematics 233–5
Key Stages 84
kinaesthetic intelligence 113
kinaesthetic learners 134
knowledge 168
Kohlberg 300

L
language acquisition 197
language acquisition device 198
language difficulties 341
language experience 206
language of Mathematics 240, 250
Language Support Service 76, 277
lead professional 266
Leading Edge schools 80

learning 117–38
learning activity prompt sheet 348
learning managers 53
learning mentor 53
learning outcomes 340
learning styles 133–5, 330–31
Learning Support Assistants 13
Learning Support Service 76, 277
learning, nature of 95–116
lesbians 65
librarian 54
Library Service 77
light 119
literacy 189–224
literacy hour/lesson 86, 147, 193
literacy intervention programmes 194–6
Literacy Progress Units (LPU) 13, 89, 195–6
local authorities 73, 277
local health authority 278
logic 110-11
LOGO 228
long-term plans 147
Look and Say 190
lunchtime clubs 50
lunchtime supervisor 54

M
management of teaching assistants 35–7
management team 52–3
Maslow, Abraham 123
mathematical development 227–9
Mathematics 225–54
Mathematics learning 229–31
Mathematics lesson 153, 226, 235–7
Mears Irlen Syndrome 213
medical information 45
medication 45–6
medicinal drugs 112
medium-term plans 147–8
memory 129–33
memory difficulties in Mathematics 251
mental calculation 225, 235, 238–9, 247
mental health problems 293–4
metacognition 129,183–6
Moderate Learning Difficulties 249
moral development 299–301
Morris, Estelle 13–14
motivation 125–6, 215
motor skills 221
multi-age grouping 172
multi-agency working 266
multiplication 244–5
multi-sensory learning 134

N
narrative 211
National Curriculum 12, 83–94, 151; and assessment 139; and creativity 185; and differentiation 96; and literacy 190, 191; and Mathematics 234
National Curriculum Inclusion Statement 274

National Curriculum Tests (SATs) 85, 141, 142
National Deaf Children's Society 278
National Extension College 332
National Literacy Strategy 13, 86–7, 190
National Numeracy Strategy 86–7, 225, 228, 233–5
National Occupational Standards 13, 331
National Vocational Qualifications (NVQs) 13, 15, 331, 332, 333, 337
National Workforce Agreement 14, 23, 36
Networked Learning Communities 80
New Opportunities Funding 325–6
newspapers 327–8
NNEB 331
noise 119
norm-referenced assessment 142
number line 241, 243
numeracy 225-54
nursery nurses 12, 53
nutrients 111
NVQs *see* National Vocational Qualifications

O
Object permanence 102
observation 158, 194, 325; of children with SEN 271–5
occupational physiotherapist 278
occupational therapist 278, 285
OCR 332, 336
Office for Standards in Education, Children's Services and Skills (Ofsted) 72, 75–6, 259, 260
one-to-one working 176–7
onset 207
Open College Network 332
open questions 240
outcomes 167, 340
oxygen 112

P
paired work 125
PANDA 141
parent partnership organisation 277
parents 59–60, 91, 159, 274, 341
partitioning 241–2, 244
passport to work 343–9
pastoral staff 53
Paulos, John 229
Pavlov, I. 97–8
pedagogy 193
performance management 324
personal development 96–7
personal information 38
personal safety 46
Personal, Social and Health Education 84, 126, 313; and Citizenship 43
personalised learning 92, 95–6, 273
philosophy 182
phonemes 207
phonics 190, 207–10
phonological processing 219

phonology 200
photocopying 38
physical education 91
physical environment 118–22
Physical/Sensory Service 77
Piaget, Jean 100–102, 140, 227, 299–300
planning 26, 30, 147–9, 192
Planning, Preparation and Assessment (PPA) 14, 24, 26, 168
play 106–8
playground duty 44
policies 60
policy coordinators 53
positives 310
PPA see Planning, Preparation and Assessment
pragmatics 201
praise 311
prefixes 220
prejudice 64
Primary Framework for Literacy 191–4
Primary Framework for Mathematics 225, 231, 238
Primary National Strategy 86–8, 147, 149, 151
Primary National Strategy for Mathematics 233–5
Primary National Strategy for Literacy 155, 190–94
problem solving 170
procedures, school 60
professional development 323–38
professional portfolio 337
profile of the school 56–62
Profound and Multiple Learning Difficulty 282
Programme of Study 147
project work 170
PSHE see Personal, Social and Health Education
psychological learning 129–33
psychological perspective 305
pupil behaviour 61
Pupil Referral Units (PRUs) 79, 319–20

Q
QCA see Qualifications and Curriculum Authority
qualifications 331–3
Qualifications and Curriculum Authority 72, 74
Qualified Teacher Status 15, 334, 335
questioning as part of assessment 153
questioning in teaching literacy 202
questioning in teaching Mathematics 236, 240-41

R
racism 315
radio 328
RAISEonline 151
'Raising Standards and Tackling Workload' see National Workforce Agreement

random grouping 173
reading 205–14
reading difficulties 213
reading genres 212–13
record keeping 340
recording assessments 146–7, 160–61
reflective practice 323–4
religious education 84
Removing Barriers to Achievement 20
reporting assessments 160–61
resources 57, 120–21, 339
Restak, Richard 112, 318–19
review 339
reviewing assessment 146–7
rime 207
risk assessment 45
roots 220
Rose Report 190
rote learning 178
Royal National Institute for the Blind 278

S
safeguarding children 42
safety 44
sanctions 304–5
SATs (Standard Assessment Tests) see National Curriculum Tests
scaffolding 104, 173–5
schemas 100
schemes of work 147
School Action 268–9, 270, 273
School Action Plus 269, 270, 273
school councils 72
school dentist 278
School Development Plan 57–8, 151
school doctor 278
School Improvement Plan see School Development Plan
school nurse 278
school trips 46, 349
school uniform 50
Science Booster Kit 89
scientific thinking 179–80
Scope 278
scribing 276
secondary behaviour 307, 309
segmentation 207
selective attention 130
self-esteem 125–6
self-evaluation 311
self-regulation 185
semantics 200–201, 219–20
SEN see Special Educational Needs
SENCO see Special Educational Needs Coordinator
sensitive problems 38
sentence structure 221–2
service directories 266
sex education 84
short-term plans 148
Single Status arrangements 335

site manager 54
site security 44
Skemp, Richard 230
skills 168
Skinner, B.F. 98–9
SMART 273
snacks 341
social class 302–3
social development 96–7, 299
social disorders 341
social model of disability 258
social services 269, 278
social workers 77, 278
Somerset Thinking Skills 182
sound symbol relationship 219
spatial awareness 251–2
speaking and listening 192,196–7, 203
Speaking, Listening and Learning 191
Special Educational Needs (SEN) 11, 19, 20, 62, 255-97, 335, 341; definition of 259; and diagnostic assessment 146; and differentiation 164; and governing body 71; and one-to-one working 176
Special Educational Needs and Disability Act 257
Special Educational Needs Code of Practice 268–71, 281
Special Educational Needs Coordinator (SENCO) 52, 259, 268–9, 270, 273, 276, 281, 335
Special Educational Needs Toolkit 258, 281
special schools 11, 19, 79, 205, 260, 319–20
Special Units see Pupil Referral Units
specialist schools 80
Specialist Teaching Assistants (STAs) 12, 331
Specialist Teaching Certificate 12
specific language impairment 200
Specific Learning Difficulties 276, 283–94
speech and language difficulties 288–90
speech and language therapist 269
speech therapist 278
spellcheckers 221
spelling 217–21
spider diagrams 242
spina bifida 290–91
spiral curriculum 104–5
Springboard 148; Springboards 3 to 6 88, 234, 264; Springboard 7 89, 234, 248–9
staff development 326–7
staff development officer 53
staff noticeboard 55
staff structure 52–4
Standard English 203
statement of SEN 269–70, 271, 276
statutory assessment 269
study skills 326, 328-31
subitising 243
subject coordinators 52
subtraction 243–4
suffixes 220
summative assessment 143–5

supervision 42
supply cover/staff 26, 27
supported reading 214
Sure Start 77
syllables 207
syntax 200, 211
synthetic phonics 191

T
target setting 151–2
TDA see Training and Development Agency for Schools
teachers, working with 25
teaching 117–38, 163–87
teaching and learning 62, 193
teaching methods 167–79
teaching/learning assessment cycle 140
teamworking 27–31
temperature 120
thinking skills 181–3
Thorndike, E.L. 97
TTA see Training and Development Agency for Schools
timetables 340
training 36, 323–38
Training and Development Agency for Schools (TDA; previously TTA) 72, 74, 334
training schools 80
Traveller Support 294
trust schools 80
TV 328

U
UCAS 333
understanding 168

V
vertical grouping 172
vertical method of calculation 239
visual impairment 293, 341
visual learners 134
visual, auditory and kinaesthetic preferences 133–4
visual/spatial intelligence 113
voluntary aided schools 79
voluntary controlled schools 79
Vygotsky L.S. 102–3, 140, 198–9, 229

W
Wahl, Mark 230
WALT 150
Warnock Report 11, 256, 258
water 112
welfare assistants 11
Weschler Intelligence Scale 113
whole-class learning 193–4
whole-class teaching 168–9
Whole Language approach to literacy 189
whole-class work 168, 235, 248
word recognition 210
working practice 339

Working with Teaching Assistants: a good practice guide 22, 35
writing 215
writing difficulties 222
writing genres 215–16
writing processes 216
written methods of calculation 239

Y
Year 6 booster units 195

Z
zero tolerance 315